THE SEVENTY WONDERS OF CHINA

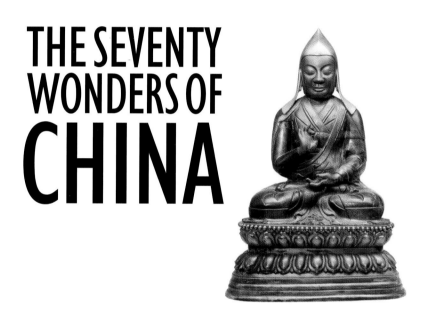

THE SEVENTY WONDERS OF CHINA

Edited by Jonathan Fenby

with 370 illustrations, 313 in color

Thames & Hudson

Contents

First published in 2007 in hardcover in the United States of America by Thames & Hudson Inc., 500 Fifth Avenue, New York, New York 10110

thamesandhudsonusa.com

Library of Congress Catalog Card Number 2006940572

ISBN 978-0-500-25137-9

Printed and bound in Singapore by C S Graphics Pte Ltd

Half-title *Partial-gilt silver statue of the Zhangjia National Preceptor. Height 75 cm (30 in.).*

Title page *The Temple of Heaven in the Forbidden City, Beijing.*

Woman washing vegetables in a stream, Guilin

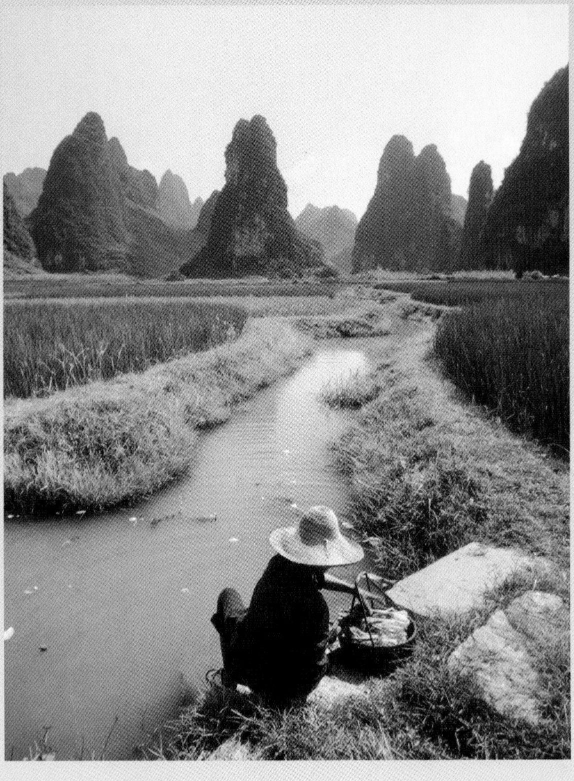

Natural Wonders

People & Life

Marble boat, Kunming Lake, the Summer Palace

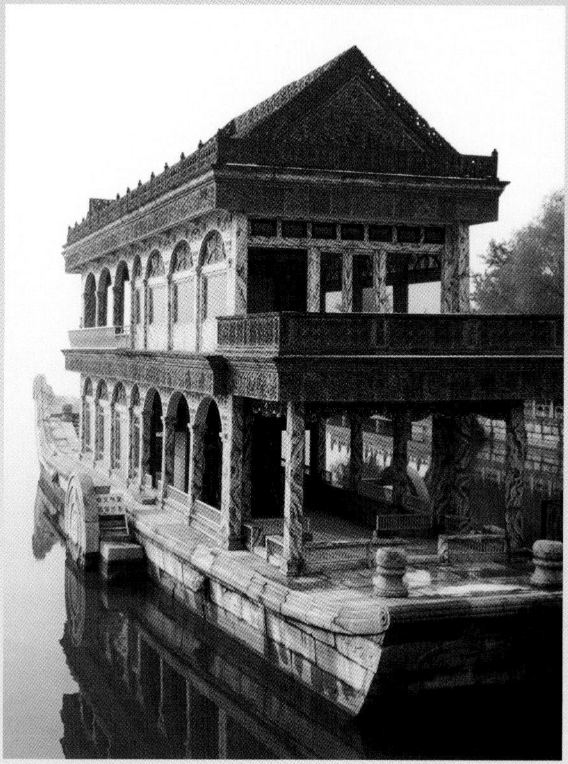

Chinese acrobats competing in Hebei province

Cities & Towns

Monuments & Buildings

Traditional Beijing Opera performance

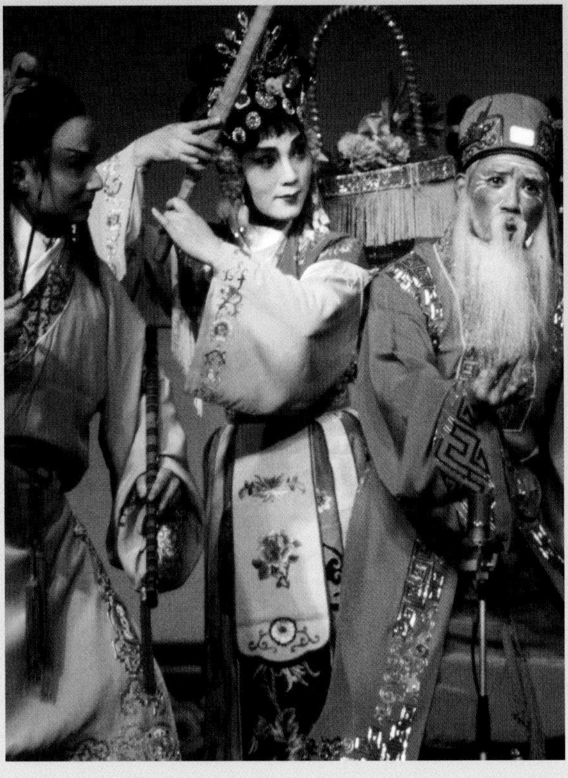

The Qianxun Pagoda in Dali, Yunnan province

The Arts

Inventions & Achievements

Old meets new: Taiwan at night

Bridge at Huang Shan, Shaanxi province

Greater China

Contributors

JONATHAN FENBY is a historian of Modern China, author of a biography of Chiang Kai-shek and of a forthcoming history of the country since 1850. Former Editor of *The Observer*, *The South China Morning Post* and *Reuters World Service*, he has also held senior positions at *The Economist*, *The Independent* and *The Guardian*, and has written ten books. **7, 12, 26, 27, 28, 32, 43, 68, 69, 70**

JOSEPH A. ADLER is Professor of Religious Studies at Kenyon College in Ohio. His area of research is Neo-Confucian religious thought in China. He is the author of *Chinese Religious Traditions* (2002); translator of *Introduction to the Study of the Classic of Change*, by Chu Hsi (2002); co-author of *Sung Dynasty Uses of the I Ching* (1990); and contributor to *Confucianism and Ecology* (1998), *Sources of Chinese Tradition*, 2nd. ed. (1999), *Confucian Spirituality* (2004), and *New Qing Imperial History* (2004). **14**

ROBERT ASH is Professor of Economics with reference to China and Taiwan at the School of Oriental and African Studies (SOAS), University of London. Since 1999 he has been Director of the SOAS Taiwan Studies Programme. From 1986 to 1995 he was Head of the Contemporary China Institute at SOAS; and in 1997–2001 he was Director of the EU-China Academic Network. His most recent books are *China, Hong Kong and the World Economy, China Watching: Perspectives from Europe, Japan and the United States* and *Taiwan in the Twenty-First Century*, all co-authored or co-edited (2006). **20**

NICHOLAS BUNNIN is Director of the Philosophy Project at the Institute for Chinese Studies, University of Oxford and Chairman of the British Committee of the Philosophy Summer School in China. Among his publications are *Contemporary Chinese Philosophy* (co-edited with Chung-ying Cheng, 2002), *The Blackwell Dictionary of Western Philosophy* (with Jiyuan Yu, 2003), *The Blackwell Companion to Philosophy* (2nd ed., co-edited with E. P. Tsui-James, 2004) and several papers on Chinese philosophy. He is currently editing *Topics in Comparative Ancient Philosophy: Greek and Chinese*. **13**

PHILIP DENWOOD is Emeritus Reader in Tibetan Studies at the School of Oriental and African Studies, University of London. His interests include the Tibetan language and the art history of the Himalayas, particularly architecture and textiles. Among his publications are *Tibetan Art: Towards a Definition of Style* (with Jane Casey Singer, 1997) and *Tibetan* (1999). **39, 40**

MICHAEL DILLON is Senior Lecturer in the Department of East Asian Studies at the University of Durham, and was founding Director of its Centre for Contemporary Chinese Studies. His publications include *China's Muslims* (1997), *China's Muslim Hui Community: Migration, Settlement and Sects* (1999), *Religious Minorities and China* (2001) and *Xinjiang: China's Muslim Far Northwest* (2003). He has carried out fieldwork and travelled extensively in China, particularly in the Muslim regions of northwestern China. Current projects include a history of modern China and an in-depth study of 20th-century Xinjiang. **17**

FUCHSIA DUNLOP trained as a chef at the Sichuan Institute of Higher Cuisine in Chengdu, Sichuan province, and is now a writer, journalist and broadcaster specializing in Chinese cuisine. She is the author of two cookery books: *Sichuan Cookery* (2001) and *The Revolutionary Chinese Cookbook* (2006), and is a regular contributor to publications including *Gourmet*, *Saveur* and the *Financial Times*. **21**

RICHARD LOUIS EDMONDS is Visiting Professor in the Geographical Studies Program and Associate Member, Center for East Asian Studies, University of Chicago. His interests focus around historical geography and environmental studies. He was editor of *The China Quarterly* (1996–2002) and has written extensively on China, Japan, Taiwan, Macau and Hong Kong. He is the author of *Macau* (1989) and *Patterns of China's Lost Harmony: A Survey of the Country's Environmental Degradation and Protection* (1994), and has (co-)edited *Managing The Chinese Environment* (2000), *The People's Republic of China After 50 Years* (2000) and *Taiwan in the Twentieth Century: A Retrospective View* (2001). **1, 2, 3, 4, 8**

MAREILE FLITSCH, sinologist and anthropologist (of technology), has led the Volkswagen Foundation-funded research project 'History and anthropology of Chinese everyday technologies' (2002–2005) and is currently heading the study group Philosophy and History of Chinese Science and Technology at Berlin Technical University. Among her publications are *The Ginseng Complex in Han-Chinese Folk Literature of Jilin Changbai Mountain Area* (in German, 1994), *Papercut stories of the Manchu woman artist Hou Yumei* (1999), and *The Kang. A Study of Rural Everyday Material Culture in Manchuria* (in German, 2004). **66**

NICHOLAS GRINDLEY has been dealing in and researching Chinese art for 25 years, with particular interest in furniture and works of art. During most of this time he has conducted his business as a private dealer although, since 1998, he has held two exhibitions a year, in London and in New York. He contributed to the catalogue of the *Mimi and Raymond Hung Collection of Chinese Furniture* (1996), co-wrote, with Robert Jacobsen, the catalogue of *Classical Chinese Furniture* from the Minneapolis Institute of Arts (1999), and more recently wrote *Pure Form, Classical Chinese Furniture, Vok Collection* (2004). **55**

ALISON HARDIE is a lecturer in Chinese Studies at the University of Leeds. Her main research interest is in the social and cultural history of early modern China. She translated Ji Cheng's 17th-century garden manual, *The Craft of Gardens* (1988), and revised the 3rd edition of Maggie Keswick's *The Chinese Garden: History, Art and Architecture* (2003). She has published many translations and articles on Chinese garden history for both academic and general readers. **56**

ERLING HOH is a freelance writer based in Sweden and specializing in Chinese culture, history and current affairs. The magazines he has contributed to include *Natural History*, *Archaeology*, *Spektrum der Wissenschaft*, *Pour la Science* and the *Far Eastern Economic Review*. He is currently co-writing a History of Tea (with Professor Victor H. Mair) for Thames & Hudson. **67**

RONALD G. KNAPP is SUNY Distinguished Professor Emeritus, State University of New York at New Paltz. His interests include Chinese frontier settlement as well as China's cultural and historical geography. Among his many publications are *China's Living Houses: Folk Beliefs, Symbols, and Household Ornamentation* (1999), *China's Old Dwellings* (2000), *China's Walled Cities* (2000), *Asia's Old Dwellings: Tradition, Resilience, and Change* (2003), *House Home Family: Living and Being Chinese* (co-edited with Kai-Yin Lo, 2005), *Chinese Houses: The Architectural Heritage of a Nation* (2005) and *Chinese Bridges: Architecture Over Water* (2006). **63**

QU LEI LEI began studying taiji as a child. He now teaches taiji both in the UK and abroad and has won the Millennium Adult Tutor Award. He is also an award-winning Chinese calligrapher and internationally recognized contemporary artist. His books on martial arts include *The Simple Art of T'ai Chi: Step-by-Step Fitness & Harmony for Body & Mind* (2004). **15, 16**

VIVIENNE LO specializes in the history of Chinese medical practice. She translates and analyzes excavated and recovered manuscripts from the early imperial and medieval periods concerned with the development of acupuncture, moxibustion and therapeutic exercise. Among her many publications are *Mediaeval Chinese Medicine* (2005, edited with Christopher Cullen) and 'Cooking up fine remedies: On the culinary esthetic in a 16th century Chinese materia medica', *Medical History* (2005). She is also founder editor of *Asian Medicine: Tradition and Modernity*, a new journal published by Brill. **60**

VICTOR H. MAIR is Professor of Chinese Language and Literature at the University of Pennsylvania. His research spans a wide range of subjects from the earliest vernacular writing in Chinese, to Sino-Indian and Sino-Iranian cultural relations, the Bronze Age and Early Iron Age civilizations of Eastern Central Asia, and the history of tea. His publications include *Painting and Performance* (1988), *Wandering on the Way* (1994), *The Tarim Mummies* (with J. P. Mallory, 2000) and *Contact and Exchange in the Ancient World* (2006). **18, 48**

SHANE McCAUSLAND is Curator of the East Asian Collections at the Chester Beatty Library, Dublin. His interests include the history of Chinese calligraphy and painting, and artistic relations between China and Japan. He is the author of books and articles including *The Admonitions Scroll: First Masterpiece of Chinese Painting* (2003), *Gu Kaizhi and the Admonitions Scroll* (ed. 2003), and 'Nihonga meets Gu Kaizhi: a Japanese copy of a Chinese painting in the British Museum', *The Art Bulletin* (Dec 2005). He was previously lecturer in Chinese art at the School of Oriental and African Studies, University of London. **46, 47, 50**

CAROL MICHAELSON is Assistant Keeper in the Department of Asia, the British Museum. Her research interests include jade of all periods, snuff bottles and early Chinese material up to about AD 1000. Amongst her publications are *The British Museum Book of Chinese Art* (with co-authors, 1992), *Chinese Jades from the Neolithic to the Qing* (co-author, 1995, 2002), *Gilded Dragons: Buried Treasures from China's Golden Ages* (1999) and *Chinese Art in Detail* (co-author, 2006). **45**

IAIN ORR worked for many years as a diplomat, delighted that his name translated smoothly into Chinese – Ou Yi'en. His last posting in China was as UK Consul-General in Shanghai (1987–1990). Under the banner of BioDiplomacy, his environmental and diplomatic interests now focus on China, biodiversity and small islands. He writes for the bilingual China Dialogue website, is the China consultant for the Convention on Migratory Species, and is currently compiling a *Dictionary of Environmental Quotations*. **9, 10**

ANN PALUDAN was educated at Oxford. One of the first women to enter the Foreign Service, she has also worked for the BBC and the Treasury. She lived in Beijing from 1972 to 1976, and has returned regularly for long study trips in the field, making the first 20th-century comprehensive and factual record of Chinese sculpture. Her books include *The Imperial Ming Tombs* (1981), *The Chinese Spirit Road* (1991), *Chinese Tomb Figurines* (1994), *Chronicle of the Chinese Emperors* (1998) and *Chinese Sculpture: A Great Tradition* (2006). **37, 42, 53**

STACEY PIERSON is Curator of the Percival David Foundation of Chinese Art, and lecturer in Chinese ceramics at the School of Oriental and African Studies, both at the University of London. Her areas of specialization include Chinese ceramics and ceramic technology, as well as the history of collecting and museology. Her recent publications include *Qingbai Ware: Chinese Porcelain of the Song and Yuan Dynasties* (2002), *Song Ceramics: Art History, Archaeology and Technology* (2004), *Blue and White for China* (2004) and *The Art of the Book in China* (ed. 2006). **51**

ROSEMARY SCOTT is International Academic Director to the Asian Art Departments of Christie's. Her interests include Chinese ceramics, Chinese lacquer and Chinese textiles. Among her many publications are *The Chinese Imperial Collections* (2000), *Chinese Porcelain of the Yuan Dynasty* (2001), *Qingbai Porcelain and its place in Chinese Ceramic History* (2002), *A Remarkable Tang Dynasty Cargo* (2003), *Song dynasty wares in the Percival David Foundation in the light of the Laohudong excavations* (2004), *A Newly Discovered Yuan Blue and White Narrative Jar* (2005), and *Some Areas of Transcultural Exchange* (2006). **52**

MICHAEL SHERINGHAM was editor of *Asian Affairs*, the journal of the Royal Society for Asian Affairs (2001–2005). He is now involved in running a family bookshop, Arthur Probsthain Oriental Bookshop, in Bloomsbury, London, which has just passed its centenary year. **11**

NATHAN SIVIN is Professor of Chinese Culture and of the History of Science Emeritus at the University of Pennsylvania. He writes on every field and period of Chinese science and medicine. His most recent books are *Science in Ancient China: Researches and Reflections* (1995), *Medicine, Philosophy, and Religion in Ancient China: Researches and Reflections* (1995), *The Way and the Word: Science and Medicine in Early China and Greece* (with Sir Geoffrey Lloyd, 2002) and *Granting the Seasons: The High Point of Chinese Astronomy* (in press). **57, 58, 61**

NANCY STEINHARDT is Professor of East Asian Art and Curator of Chinese Art at the University of Pennsylvania. Her research focuses on East Asian architecture, but her broader research interests include problems that result from the interaction between Chinese art and the art of peoples at China's borders. She is author of *Chinese Traditional Architecture* (1984), *Chinese Imperial City Planning* (1990) and *Liao Architecture* (1997); editor of *Chinese Architecture* (2002), and has written more than 60 scholarly articles. **33, 36**

NANCY NORTON TOMASKO earned a PhD in Chinese literature at Princeton University and is editor of the *East Asian Library Journal* at Princeton. Her research on the traditional arts of the Chinese book (paper, printing techniques and binding styles) takes her frequently to China. Over the past 10 years, she has taught many workshops on Chinese book binding. A recent article was entitled 'Chinese Handmade Paper – A Richly Varied Thing', *Hand Papermaking* (2004). **59**

MATHIEU TORCK is currently Assistant Professor at the Department of Languages and Cultures of South and East Asia at Ghent University, Belgium. His main interests include scurvy, Asian seafaring history, the logistics of premodern Chinese armies and navies, nomadic cultures, migration and the history of food and foodways. Among his publications are 'Maritime travel and the question of provision and scurvy in a Chinese context', *East Asian Science, Technology, and Medicine* (2005), and 'Xu-duo-da, Island of Blood's Desiccate and Dragon's Spittle: Socotra in early Chinese sources', *Socotra: A Natural History of the Islands and their People* (2006). **62**

SHELAGH VAINKER is Curator of Chinese Art at the Ashmolean Museum and University Lecturer in Chinese Art at Oxford. Recent publications include *Chinese Silk: A Cultural History* (2004), *Pu Quan (1913–1991) and his Generation: Imperial Painters in Twentieth-Century China* (2004) and several articles on modern Chinese painting. **54**

FRANCES WOOD is Curator of the Chinese collections at the British Library. Her publications include *Did Marco Polo Go To China?* (1995), *No Dogs and Not Many Chinese: Treaty Port Life in China 1843–1943* (1998), *Hand Grenade Practice in Peking: My Part in the Cultural Revolution* (2000), *The Blue Guide to China* (2002), *The Silk Road* (2002) and *The Forbidden City* (2005). **5, 6, 22, 23, 24, 25, 29, 30, 34, 38, 41**

ROBIN D. S. YATES is James McGill Professor of History and East Asian Studies, McGill University, Montreal, Quebec, Canada, and Chair of the Society for the Study of Early China and Editor of its journal, *Early China*. He teaches pre-modern Chinese history, the history of Chinese science and technology, and the history of women in China. His books include *Washing Silk: The Life and Selected Poetry of Wei Chuang (834–910)* (1988), 'Military Technology: Missiles and Sieges', *Science and Civilisation in China* vol. 5, part 6 (with Dr J. Needham, 1994), *Five Lost Classics: Tao, Huang-Lao and Yin-Yang in Han China* (1997, published in Chinese in 2002), and more than 40 articles on diverse topics in pre-modern Chinese history. **64, 65**

NI YIBIN was born in Shanghai and is now an independent scholar, after teaching Chinese art and culture at the National University of Singapore. He obtained MA and PhD degrees at University College London. In recent years, he has made breakthroughs in deciphering lost story scenes in Chinese art, which is being prepared to form a reference book. He wrote 'The Fine and Decorative Arts' and 'The Performing Arts' in *China: the Land of the Heavenly Dragon* (2000) and has published in several exhibition catalogues and art history journals. **19, 49**

ZHANG YINGLAN is Associate Professor of Archaeology, Assistant Director at the Terracotta Army Museum outside Xi'an, China, and is a PhD student at Northwest University, also in Xi'an, China. His many publications include *An Archaeological Report of Emperor Qin Shihuang's Mausoleum* (1999), *The Burial System of Emperor Qin Shihuang's Mausoleum* (2003), and *The Application and Prospects of GIS in Archaeology* (2006). **31, 35, 44**

Great Wall of China
International boundary
Province boundary
Grand Canal
RUSSIA
KAZAKHSTAN
MONGOLIA
UZBEKISTAN
KYRGYSTAN
TAJIKISTAN
AFGHANISTAN
PAKISTAN
ALTAY MOUNTAINS
TIANSHAN (MOUNTAINS)
Urumqi
Korla
Kashgar
TARIM BASIN
XINJIANG UYGHUR AUTONOMOUS REGION
Loulan
PAMIR PLATEAU
Lop Nor
GANSU
TAKLAMAKAN DESERT
KUNLUN MOUNTAINS
Dunhuang
Jiayugang
Khotan
QINGHAI
Xining
TIBETAN PLATEAU
QINLING
DANGLA MOUNTAINS
Mount Kailash
TIBET AUTONOMOUS REGION
Amdo
Chengdu
HIMALAYAN MOUNTAINS
NEPAL
Shigatse
Lhasa
SICHUAN
Gyantse
Mount Everest
BHUTAN
Leshan
Lijiang
Dali
Kunming
INDIA
BANGLADESH
N
YUNNAN
0
500 km
0
200 miles
BURMA (Myanmar)
Bay of Bengal
THAILAND
LAO

HEILONGJIANG
Harbin
GREAT HINGGAN MOUNTAINS
MANCHURIA
JILIN
Changchun
CHANGBAI MOUNTAINS
INNER MONGOLIA
AUTONOMOUS
REGION
Shenyang
LIAONING
NORTH
KOREA
GOBI DESERT
Yellow River
Hohhot
Shanhaiguan
BEIJING
Datong
TIANJIN
ORDOS DESERT
Yellow Sea
SOUTH
KOREA
JAPAN
Yinchuan
Yungang
HEBEI
Shijiazhuang
TAIHANG MOUNTAINS
Taiyuan
Jinan
Qingdao
NINGXIA
HUI
A. R.
SHANXI
SHANDONG
Luoyang
Gongxian
Kaifeng
Lintong
Zhengzhou
JIANGSU
Xianyang
Xi'an
Longmen
Dengfeng
Purple
Mountain
Yangzhou
SHAANXI
HENAN
ANHUI
Nanjing
Suzhou
SHANGHAI
Hefei
HUBEI
Ningbo
Yangtze River
Wuhan
JIANGNAN AREA
Hangzhou
East China Sea
THREE
GORGES DAM
Mt Huangshan
Binhai
Dazu
ZHEJIANG
CHONGQING
Jingdezhen
Nanchang
Changsha
HUNAN
JIANGXI
NANLING MOUNTAINS
Fuzhou
GUIZHOU
FUJIAN
Taipei
Guiyang
TAIWAN
Guilin
GUANGXI
ZHUANG
AUTONOMOUS
REGION
GUANGDONG
Pearl River
Guangzhou
(Canton)
HONG KONG
Nanning
MACAU
South China Sea
Haikou
HAINAN

Chronology

DYNASTIES OF CHINA

Xia **c. 2070–c. 1600 BC**
First known rulers of China, located on the Yellow River; agrarian people using bronze and pottery

Shang **c. 1600–c. 1046 BC**
Civilization also located on the Yellow River using earthenware and bronze

Zhou **1046–221 BC**
Western Zhou 1046–771 BC
Confucius (551–479 BC) and the development of iron ploughshares
Spring & Autumn 770–476 BC
Warring States 476–221 BC
Political disunion; spread of Confucian culture

Qin **221–206 BC**
Qin Shihuangdi, known as the First August Emperor, who ruled from 221 to 210 BC, unified China, created a centralized administration, began the Great Wall and left the terracotta army in his tomb

Han **206 BC – AD 220**
Western Han 202 BC – AD 8
Eastern Han AD 9 – 220
The rulers enlisted the scholar class to hold the country together, and adapted Confucianism for state purposes; the era saw the invention of paper and the Silk Road opened China to foreign influences, including Buddhism

The Three Kingdoms **220**–280
(Wei, Shu, Wu) and the
Period of Disunion 220–**581**
Division of China into Northern and Southern kingdoms; spread of Daoism

Sui **581–618**
Revival of imperial glory, including the building of the Grand Canal

Tang **618–907**
Military expansion and pacification; flowering of the arts, notably sculpture, porcelain, poetry, architecture and tomb figurines

Five Dynasties **907–960**
Fifty years of strife

Song **960–1279**
Invention of gunpowder and printing, bringing paper money; construction of the most advanced ships on earth

Yuan **1279–1368**
Kubilai Khan, grandson of Genghis Khan, conquered China

Ming **1368–1644**
Restored the Chinese imperial tradition, built the Forbidden City and the Ming tombs; development of porcelain, rise of eunuch power and admission of the first European into the Forbidden City – a Jesuit

Qing **1644–1911**
Apogee under the Three Emperors of the 17th and 18th centuries, then decline leading to abdication of last emperor in 1912

Republic **1912–1949**
An unsettled period marked initially by warlord rule, then by the primacy of the Kuomintang (Nationalist Party) under Chiang Kai-shek, which was weakened by the Japanese invasion and eight years of warfare before being defeated by the Communists

People's Republic **1949–present**
Mao Zedong dominated China for a quarter-century that saw the Great Leap Forward and the Cultural Revolution; in the mid-1980s, China changed economic course to adopt market methods and became the fastest-growing big economy on earth

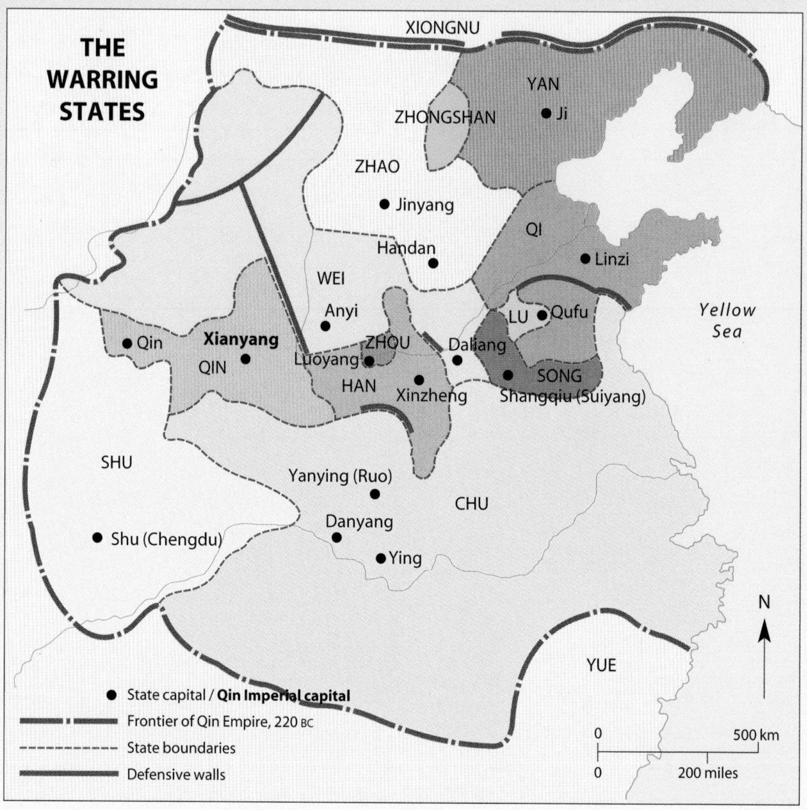

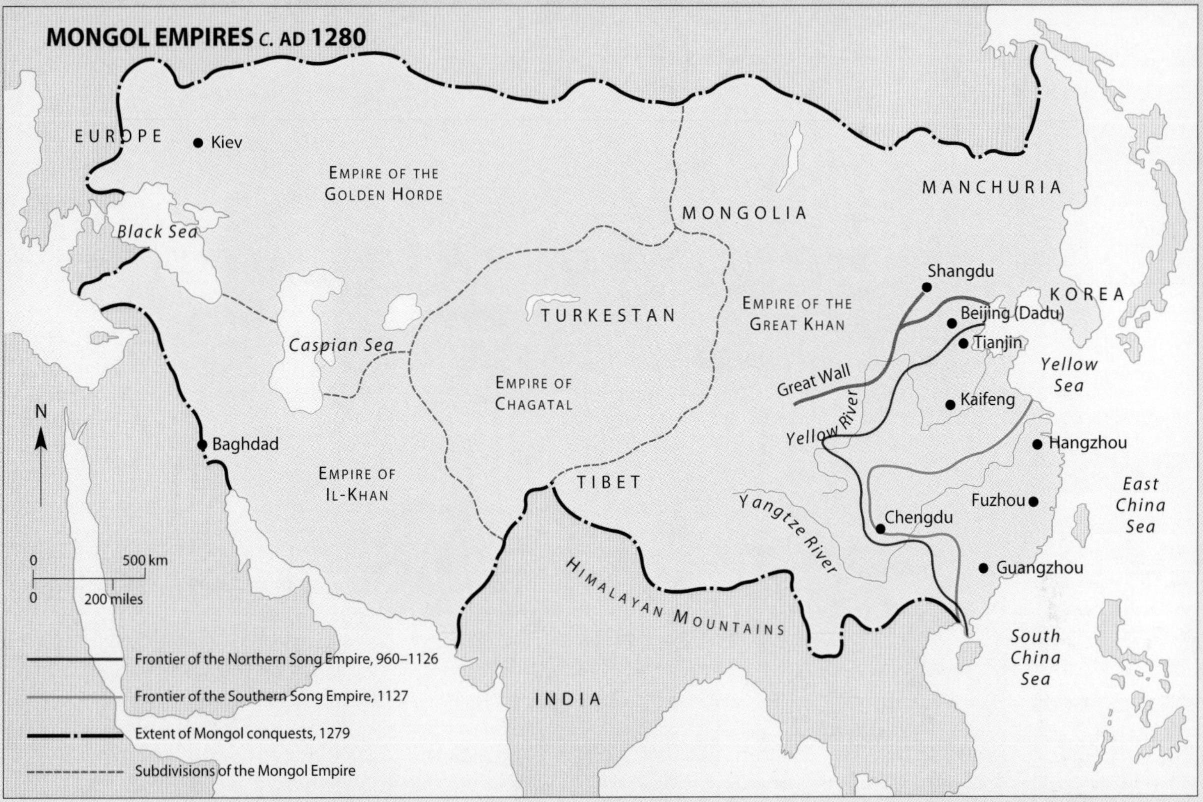
EUROPE
Kiev
Empire of the Golden Horde
Black Sea
Caspian Sea
Baghdad
Empire of Il-Khan
Turkestan
Empire of Chagatal
Mongolia
Tibet
Empire of the Great Khan
Manchuria
Korea
Shangdu
Beijing (Dadu)
Tianjin
Kaifeng
Hangzhou
Fuzhou
Chengdu
Guangzhou
Great Wall
Yellow River
Yangtze River
Yellow Sea
East China Sea
South China Sea
Himalayan Mountains
India
N
0 500 km
0 200 miles
Frontier of the Northern Song Empire, 960–1126
Frontier of the Southern Song Empire, 1127
Extent of Mongol conquests, 1279
Subdivisions of the Mongol Empire

MONGOL EMPIRES c. AD 1280

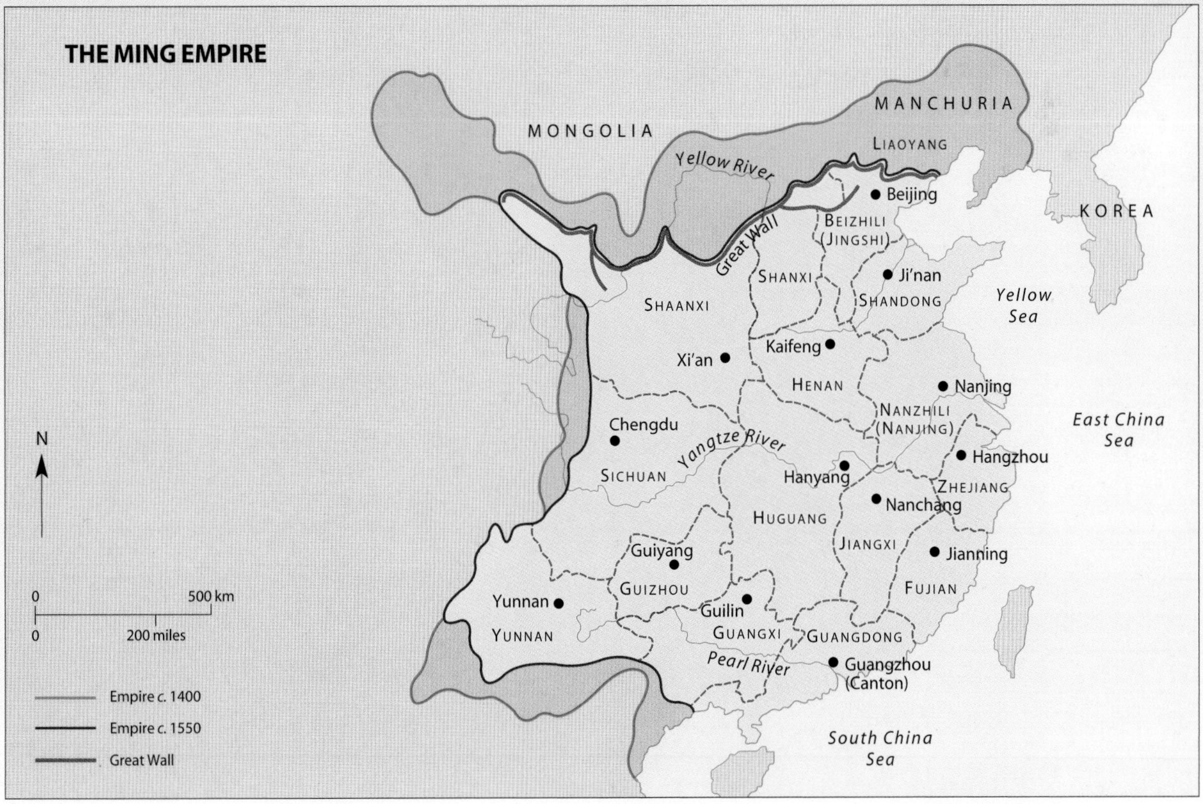
Mongolia
Manchuria
Liaoyang
Yellow River
Beijing
Korea
Great Wall
Beizhili (Jingshi)
Shanxi
Ji'nan
Shandong
Shaanxi
Yellow Sea
Xi'an
Kaifeng
Henan
Nanjing
Nanzhili (Nanjing)
Chengdu
Yangtze River
Hangzhou
East China Sea
Sichuan
Hanyang
Zhejiang
Nanchang
Huguang
Jiangxi
Jianning
Guiyang
Guizhou
Fujian
Yunnan
Yunnan
Guilin
Guangxi
Guangdong
Pearl River
Guangzhou (Canton)
South China Sea
N
0 500 km
0 200 miles
Empire c. 1400
Empire c. 1550
Great Wall

THE MING EMPIRE

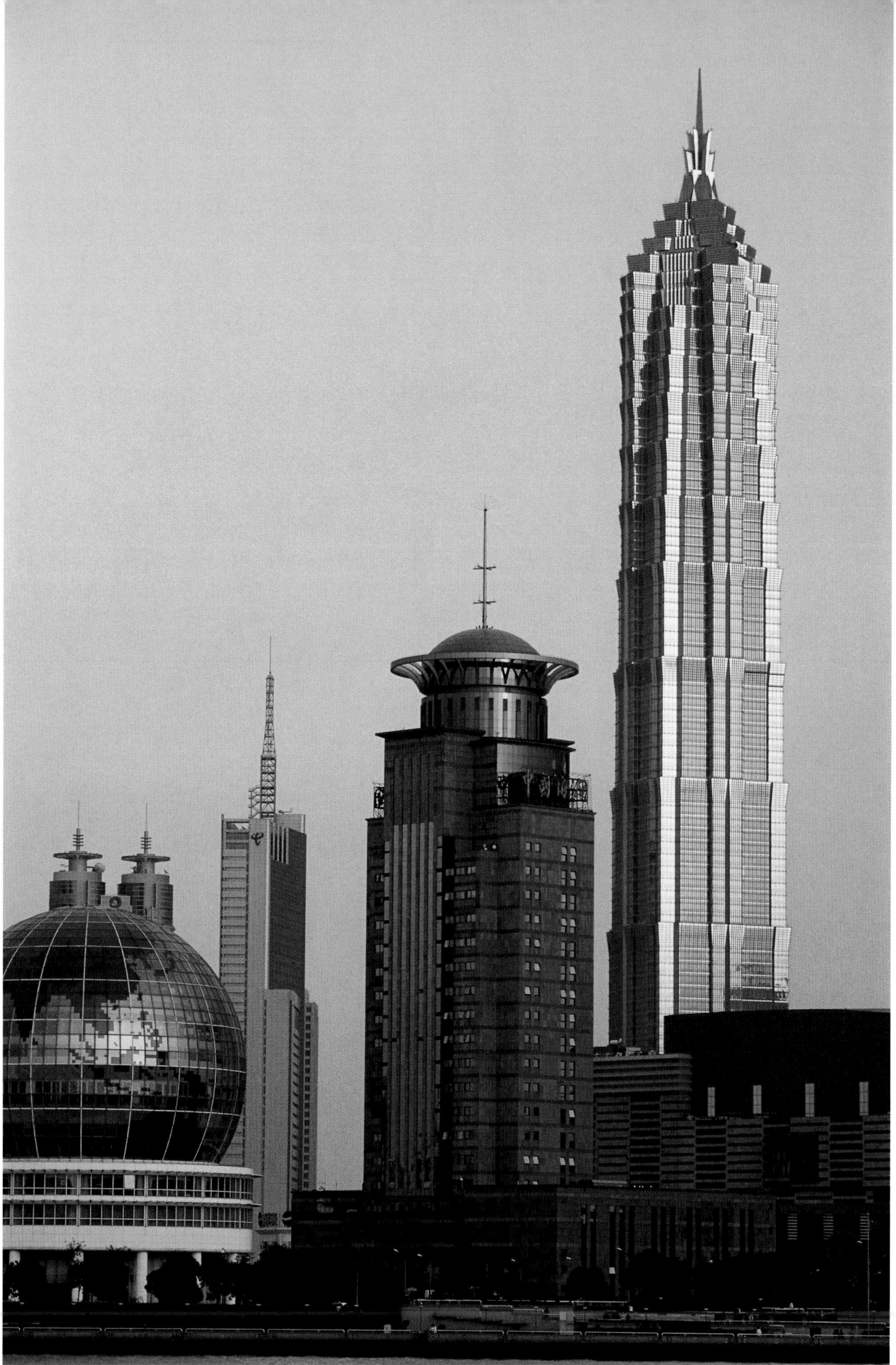

Introduction

With the oldest continuous civilization on earth, China holds a special place among nations. For millennia, it saw itself as the Middle Kingdom, constituting all that lay under Heaven. Its people, predominantly Han Chinese (p. 61), considered themselves the 'children of the Yellow Emperor' uniquely placed on earth, self-sufficient, not necessarily hostile to the rest of the world, but confident that they did not need anybody else.

Thus, China imported Buddhism (p. 71) from India, but then forgot about the other huge Asian land, and regarded the religion as its own. It sent fleets to distant seas, but did not nurture relations with foreign countries – the view it took of neighbours like Korea and Vietnam was shown in the description of them as 'tribute states'. The Silk Road (p. 43) from the old imperial capital of Xi'an to the Mediterranean was one of the great historic commercial routes, and some Byzantine influences travelled eastwards, but there was little or no interchange of ideas with Europe. As for trade in goods, until the middle of the 19th century, foreign ships were restricted to Canton, in the south, emigration was forbidden, and foreigners were officially banned from learning Chinese. When, at the end of the 18th century, Britain sought to forge a relationship akin to that between European powers, an imperial decree said there was no way in which Chinese and Westerners could work together. Foreigners were, by definition, 'barbarians'. China had no need of the manufactured presents the British brought, the decree added, since 'we possess all things'.

Whereas Europe experienced the – sometimes violent – interchange between nations, China remained a universe to itself, convinced it was at the centre of the world. Now that it has engaged so deeply with other countries, one of the major issues for our time is how this land of 1.3 billion people, which stood apart for so long, will integrate with the rest of the globe.

The economically expansive China of the early 21st century is the heir to a civilization whose achievements stretch back as far as 8,000 years, in the case of silk production. Jade was being worked 6,000 years ago. In the cradle of the nation, the Yellow River valley (p. 36), in north-central China, rune-like inscriptions on oracle bones have been found dating from 4,000 years ago. From that sprang calligraphy (p. 198) which has traditionally been considered as the greatest of art forms. Early literature (p. 204), in the shape of classical works including the Analects of the national philosopher, Confucius, began to emerge in the middle of the 1st millennium BC.

Lacquer work (p. 222) has been found in a Neolithic site in eastern China dated from 5000–3000 BC. Bronzes (p. 189) can be traced to 4000 BC, subsequently reaching their heights under the Shang (*c.* 1600–1046 BC). Porcelain (p. 217) came much later – in the Sui period (AD 581–618), expanding significantly under the next dynasty, the Tang (618–907), to reach such perfection that it became a major Chinese export, rivalled only by silk and tea. Such achievements, often mixing art and practical use, were central to national culture through the millennia. They were not put in museum cases as artifacts of the past, but used – or admired – in everyday life, at least by the elite.

Geography

China is more a continent than a country. Its regions range from the deep freeze of the winter in Manchuria to the semi-tropical lushness of Yunnan (p. 48) in the southwest. Thriving cities of the eastern coast stand in stark contrast to vast expanses of desert. Though the national language, Putonghua, is used everywhere in writing,

The Jin Mao Tower (on the right) in Shanghai, 420 m (1,380 ft) high, with a hotel at the top.

The Great Wall of China was never really one single structure, and survives in parts. Designed to keep out invading forces from the north of China, its defensive capacity was constructed during successive dynasties starting with the First Emperor.

local dialects can make communication difficult. Cuisine varies enormously, from the light seafood dishes of the Pearl River delta to the fiery recipes of Sichuan, with a basic dividing line between the rice-growing southern half of the country and the wheat lands of the north.

Physical types differ from north to south, east to west. While the Han people constitute an overwhelming majority of the population, there are more than 50 minority groups (p. 80), mainly in the southwest, Tibet and among Muslim Uyghurs in the far west. Since 1997, the last major country ruled by a Communist party has included a bastion of international capitalism in the former British colony of Hong Kong (p. 281) under the 'one country, two systems' principle worked out by the patriarch, Deng Xiaoping. The Portuguese colony of Macau followed suit at the end of 1999.

One hundred and forty-five km (90 miles) off the east coast, the island of Taiwan (p. 285), to which the Nationalist government fled in 1949 as it finally acknowledged defeat in the civil war with the Communists, is regarded by China as an integral province of the nation, and has become a major investor in the mainland, though its presidential elections have twice returned a candidate who bases much of his appeal on the assertion of a separate 'Taiwanese identity'. In the mountainous west, Tibet is seen by Beijing as a rightful part of its domain, and Han Chinese are moving in, but the Dalai Lama and autonomists proclaim the vast region's separate being. Further afield, in Southeast Asia, North America and Europe, 34 million Overseas Chinese (p. 288) form another element in China's global presence, fuelling the inward investment boom in the mainland.

Power and politics

Politically and territorially, the basic Chinese system was established between 221 and 210 BC by the first Qin emperor, who gave the country its name for foreigners. A model for autocrats, he came to the throne as a minor when China was divided among warring states, and imposed unity by ruthless warfare and unrelenting control – non-utilitarian books were burned to stamp out

dissidence. Using hundreds of thousands of forced labourers, he began to build part of the Great Wall (p. 160) and constructed a vast mausoleum outside his capital of Xi'an in northern China (p. 137), with serried ranks of terracotta warriors (p. 155). His harsh rule did not long outlive him; a revolt soon overthrew his successor, establishing another model – dynastic decline and fall under the canopy of enduring empire.

The succeeding Han rulers (206 BC–AD 220) ushered in prosperity and a lively intellectual life while China's sway spread across Central Asia, Korea and Vietnam. To this day, most Chinese see themselves as 'the people of the Han' (p. 61). In the following centuries, the throne's power ebbed and flowed. Under the Tang dynasty it reached a new 'golden age' in which Chinese influence stretched from Japan to the Caspian Sea, the bureaucratic system was perfected, art flourished and the Silk Road reached its apogee.

The last great dynasty of Chinese origin, the Ming (1368–1644), replaced the Mongol descendants of Genghis Khan, who had swept down from the northern steppes to rule from 1279 to 1368, their military skills not matched by the requisite political arts. The Ming brought economic advance, technical innovations like movable type, and the dispatch of armadas to explore the oceans – they also left a unique collection of tombs (p. 165) outside Beijing. As this dynasty weakened, the Manchus rode in from the northeast to establish the Qing dynasty (1644–1911) which skilfully adopted Chinese traditions. Under their great emperors up to the end of the 18th century, China became even larger and more multicultural with the invasion of the vast Muslim territory of Xinjiang in the far west. Then, in 1912, the growing weakness of the Qing ended China's imperial system after more than 2,100 years, with the abdication of Puyi, the last emperor, at the age of six, and the declaration of a Republic.

Till the end of the 19th century, the Chinese took for granted that they had the most perfect political and social system (p. 64), operating on

Bronze mirror back from the Shang dynasty (c. 1600–1046 BC).

time-honoured precepts of Confucianism (p. 68) to achieve social harmony. The emperors were the Sons of Heaven: wise, benevolent rulers who were owed the filial devotion of their subjects, just as fathers from their sons – daughters were not taken into account. Below them, bureaucratic armies of scholars and officials were greatly venerated for their ability to perpetuate traditional ways, proving themselves through imperial examinations based on classical texts. The imperial residence in the Forbidden City (p. 105), with its mandarins and eunuchs, was a place of intricate ceremonies and graduations of rank designed to buttress the central mystery of an empire given to man by the gods through the person of the ruler.

If, as happened repeatedly over the centuries, harmony was lacking and disasters swept the country, this was attributed to the rulers falling short of their duties. If administration proved ineffective, corruption rose to unacceptable levels and internal opposition mounted, the reason must be that the occupant of the throne no longer merited the Mandate of Heaven. So it was time for a new claimant – a general or the leader of a revolt – to seek the throne, and the blessing of the gods. Thus, dynasties came and went; but the regime and the Mandate of Heaven lived on.

Foreign invasion

The inbred self-confidence of the imperial centuries would prove to be the worm in the bud of old China. The prime aim of the court and the scholarly elite was to preserve the political and social system handed down through the ages. Having reached a steady state of being able to feed a growing population, agriculture was regarded as being in no need of technological innovation. The great inventions (p. 244 ff.) of Chinese history were largely confined to separate boxes, not connected to provide a broadly based corpus of knowledge and spur fresh thinking. Learning was highly venerated, but inquiry and the exercise of reason were not – they might prove subversive.

Thus, during the centuries when the West grew economically and politically and expanded across the world, China remained as it always had been. Confucianism took a dim view of commerce. Industry was confined largely to handicrafts. There was no banking system. The middle class, which played such an innovative role in the West, was co-opted into the system through the examinations and the privileged status it was accorded in the social hierarchy so long as it perpetuated tradition. As a result, a country which may have accounted for one third of the world's wealth in the 18th century, slipped behind. Even when the empire was overthrown, the revolution was the work of military men and provincial gentry seeking greater authority for themselves, perpetuating conservatism into the 20th century, before the invasion by Japan from 1937 to 1945 opened the way for the Communists' victory against the severely weakened Nationalist Republic in 1949.

For the Chinese, the rejection of foreign connections had appeared perfectly logical. When the British went to war to press the right of the East India Company to ship opium to China in the 1830s, the ruler was advised by an official that they belonged to 'the class of dogs and horses' and need not be taken seriously. The result was a series of national humiliations. In 1860, the emperor was forced to flee from Beijing as an Anglo-French expedition descended on the capital to impose treaties on China, burning the Summer Palace and looting ancient temples. Another 30 years on came a disastrous military defeat at the hands of the Japanese. In 1900, the Boxer Rising, intended to drive out foreigners and protect the dynasty, ended in another occupation of Beijing. Foreign powers spoke of splitting up the Chinese 'melon' and Karl Marx wrote of the country as a mummy that would crumble if exposed to daylight.

What made the foreign incursions all the more damaging was that they coincided with severe internal weaknesses as the empire proved unable to modernize itself and faced a series of enormous challenges. Between 1850 and 1877, rebellions across the country killed many tens of millions, and caused enormous devastation. To preserve itself, the court ceded authority to the gentry class in the provinces, and then stumbled through a set of switchback policies under

Porcelain lamp produced in the Han dynasty (206 BC–AD 220), a time when the arts were flourishing.

Chinese cities, like Beijing (pictured here) have undergone breakneck modernization.

the formidable Dowager Empress, Cixi, who dominated the court for four decades, but could not re-assert the glory of the past.

The end of the Qing era was one of the violent upsets of China's long civilization. There had been similar periods in the past. During the Tang era an empress, Wu Zhao, had grabbed power and a general, An Lushan, had led a revolt that may have killed 35 million people. The Mongols and Manchus had both penetrated the Great Wall to supplant enfeebled dynasties. The great Ming dynasty had ended in weakness later attributed, in part, to the power of eunuchs at court. But, in 1912, there was no dynasty-in-waiting, and the nation descended into the chaos of the warlord era from 1916 to 1928,

Consumerism is a major force in today's China.

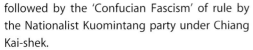

followed by the 'Confucian Fascism' of rule by the Nationalist Kuomintang party under Chiang Kai-shek.

Despite its troughs, there were more peaks across China's history, under emperors who sat gloriously atop the system, ran an effectively organized state, knew how to use the power and majesty conferred on them, encouraged learning and the arts, and consolidated and expanded Chinese territory. They set the underlying rhythm by which the nation ran. The achievements presented in this book come mainly from the peaks. But, as other entries show, the traditions offered a form of national solidity and cohesion, even in the worst eras.

Hugely different in scale, each of the 70 wonders stands on its own; together, they span an enormous range. Some are natural, others man-made. Taken together, they represent a guide to the nature of the nation. The iconoclasm of the 20th century, the overthrow of the empire and nearly 60 years of Communist rule – including the Cultural Revolution – have not erased the past, into which the rulers of modern China have often reached for inspiration.

Chiang Kai-shek re-iterated classical nostrums and took many of the finest art treasures with him when he fled to Taiwan. Mao Zedong referred to imperial history and lived behind the Forbidden City in Beijing. Today, China has launched a worldwide programme of 'Confucius Institutes' to promote the country's culture, language and arts – and the teachings of the sage, which are reflected in President Hu Jintao's promotion of a 'harmonious society' to overcome uneven economic growth. Despite regime changes and recurrent upheavals, China's past is always present, not far below the surface and kept alive by all the wonders shown in this book.

Natural Wonders

The natural wonders of China are both vast and focused. They range from huge mountains and great rivers to corners of beauty, a bamboo grove, a highland valley with a cascading waterfall, a lake surrounded by willows. There are extraordinary geological formations, such as the karst outcrops at Guilin (p. 29), and one of the widest variety of trees and flowers (p. 55) to be found anywhere on earth, many of which have been exported over the years to the West. The national flower, the Chinese peony, is known as 'the colour of the nation and the scent of heaven'. With 10 per cent of the world's vertebrates, wildlife (p. 52) is equally varied – from pandas and tigers to dolphins and tall crane birds that represent longevity.

The terrain of this land of 9.6 million sq. km (3.7 million sq. miles) falls into three stair-like sections – low-lying coastal areas, a higher north–south plateau and then towering mountains topped by Everest. At the other extreme, the Turfan Depression on the Silk Road (p. 43) is the second lowest place on earth. Each geographical and topographical region has influenced the constituent elements making up China. With their diverse populations, economies and social systems, they have long presented a challenge to central governments seeking to ensure national unity.

Great grasslands (p. 50), like the steppes leading to Mongolia, have bred a nomadic culture which was long seen as a menace by the rulers in the capital as hardy, fast-riding tribal groups threatened northern China – and, in the case of the Mongols, took over the empire from 1279 to 1368. The Gobi and Taklamakan deserts (p. 39)

Sheep grazing by Muztagh Ata, a mountain in the Kunlun range that provides much-needed runoff water to the Xinjiang region.

stretch over vast expanses of northern and western China, crossed for centuries by camel trains but now more often flown over by travellers, except for those intrepid enough to drive through their usually stony wastes, stopping at isolated oases like Lop Nor, which was used as an atomic test site but also produces a pleasant light red wine. Beyond the Taklamakan and the Silk Road which crossed it lie the towering Pamir Mountains where the great conqueror from what is now Uzbekistan, Tamir the Lame (better known as Tamburlaine), died on his last campaign to invade China.

In the north are great plains, in the south fertile rice lands. The lush, semi-tropical province of Yunnan (p. 48) in the southwest has always been a place to itself, sheltered from the rest of the country amid the jungles leading to Vietnam and Burma, and the beginning of the Tibetan plateau where, to attract tourists, a town claims to be the site of the fictional paradise of Shangri-La – invented, in fact, by a British novelist drawing on accounts written by an Austrian botanist for the *National Geographic* magazine who lived in Yunnan for two decades.

The two natural waterways of China, the Yangtze (p. 32) and the Yellow (p. 36) rivers, hold an important place in the national memory and culture. The Yellow River was the cradle of the country's civilization and the Three Gorges Dam on the Yangtze (p. 183) is today the symbol of massive infrastructure projects being launched to modernize China. Both have been major communications routes for many centuries, along with other waterways such as the Xiang, the Han and the network of rivers in the Pearl River delta round Guangzhou in the south.

But, while rivers provided the main transport arteries up to the 20th century and remain important economically, they were also sources of danger. Floods repeatedly destroyed villages and crops, and the heavily silted Yellow River became known as 'China's Sorrow' for the devastation caused by water spilling over its dykes, making millions homeless.

Economic development, intensive farming and tourism pose a threat to the wonders of China's natural world, from wildlife and plants to rivers affected by the logging of trees securing their banks. Along with severe pollution and acid rain, desertification is spreading in the north, with Beijing subject to growing sandstorms. China's natural wonders are so extensive and varied that they will continue to be a deep source of national richness, but the need to protect them can only grow as the country powers ahead economically.

The Linjiaxia Dam blocks the Yellow River as it flows through the Linjiaxia Gorge near Lanzhou.

RICHARD LOUIS EDMONDS

Mountains

1

You ask for what reason I stay on the green mountain,
I smile, but do not answer, my heart is at leisure.
Peach blossom is carried far off by flowing water,
Apart, I have heaven and earth in the human world.
LI BO, *QUESTION AND ANSWER ON THE MOUNTAIN*, AD 753

China has often been described as a land composed of three stairs. There is a low coastal stair and an intermediary level of basins and plateaux stretching from south to north and northwest. Finally there is the high Qinghai-Tibetan plateau in the west. There are many important mountain ranges starting with the Himalayas, the highest mountains in the world, which form the border between Tibet on the one side, and Nepal and India on the other.

Mount Qomolangma

Mount Qomolangma, better known to the English-speaking world as Mount Everest, is the most famous mountain in the People's Republic of China. However, located as it is in the Himalaya

The Himalayan Mountain range seen from Nepal showing Mount Qomolangma, or Mount Everest as Westerners have named it.

Mountains, it is only partially in the People's Republic, as the peak forms part of the boundary with Nepal. Qomolangma is named after a Tibetan mother earth goddess, but Everest comes from Sir George Everest, a British surveyor general who had led a surveying team into the Himalayas in the early 1840s.

Mount Qomolangma is regarded as the world's highest peak; in 2005, the Chinese claimed the exact height as 8,844.43 m (29,017.07 ft). It is considered to be the ultimate mountain challenge. The first known successful ascent to the peak was undertaken from the Nepali side by Tenzing Norgay and Sir Edmund Hillary on 29 May 1953. Since then many people have climbed the peak starting from base camps in Nepal or Tibet. Several of these people were Chinese. The Chinese plan to take the Olympic torch to the top of Mount Qomolangma for the start of the 2008 Beijing Olympic games.

The Himalayas have risen from the water over the last 65 million years. The mountains and the adjacent Qinghai-Tibetan plateau have a tremendous effect on climate by blocking air flow below 4,000 m (13,120 ft) in altitude. The plateau blocks the southward movement of cold air and also the northward flow of the Indian or southwest summer monsoon into China.

Other mountain ranges

As noted with the Himalayas, east–west ranges often form political frontiers and climatic region boundaries. The Kunlun Mountains stretch from the Pamirs in the west to the Sichuan Basin in the east, marking the northern end of the Qinghai-Tibetan plateau and are generally above 5,000 m (16,400 ft) in elevation. The location of this range is very important for the oases in Xinjiang to their north as runoff supplies water to these towns. The Tianshan range runs across Xinjiang, dividing it into two large basins. These mountains are between 3,000 and 5,000 m (9,840 and 16,400 ft) in elevation and are dotted with a large number of basins that are watered by the Tianshan's glaciers. It is in these basins that the political core of Xinjiang is found. In the far north, the Altay Mountains are part of the boundary with Kazakhstan and Mongolia and provide some timber from the south slopes.

A view of the Tibetan plateau facing south. The Taklamakan desert is in the foreground, separated from the plateau by the Kunlun Mountains.

In central China, the Qinling Mountains at 2,000 to 3,600 m (6,560 to 11,810 ft) are an important natural divide of China into north and south. In climatic terms the Qinling keeps the cold out of the south and the precipitation out of the north. In a similar fashion, the Nanling further south helps keep the frost out of Guangdong. The lower elevation of the Nanling (1,000–1,500 m / 3,280–4,920 ft) and their broken nature means that frost does on occasion penetrate to the south.

Mountain ranges that stretch in a northeast–southwest pattern are largely found in north China. The Great Hinggan Mountains (1,000–1,400 m / 3,280–4,590 ft) run through eastern Inner Mongolia with gentle slopes on the west side and much steeper slopes on the east. This range does, however, have an impact, rendering the climate to the northwest generally drier and colder. Parallel to the Great Hinggan but along the Korean border is the somewhat higher (2,000–2,750 m / 6,560–9,020 ft) Changbai range with its beautiful crater lakes formed around dormant volcanoes. Moving southwest into China proper we find the Taihang Mountains (1,500–2,000 m / 4,920–6,560 ft). The Taihang divide lowland China from the mid-level Loess plateau on its west, and like the Great Hinggan, they appear much smaller from the plateau than they do from the east.

Opposite *Hua Shan at sunrise, also known as the Western Sacred Mountain, Shaanxi province.*

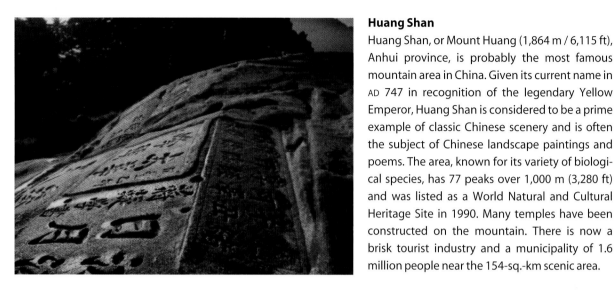

Words left by famous people on Huang Shan, a centre of Daoist activities and a place to which scholars of many dynasties have journeyed on pilgrimage.

Huang Shan

Huang Shan, or Mount Huang (1,864 m / 6,115 ft), Anhui province, is probably the most famous mountain area in China. Given its current name in AD 747 in recognition of the legendary Yellow Emperor, Huang Shan is considered to be a prime example of classic Chinese scenery and is often the subject of Chinese landscape paintings and poems. The area, known for its variety of biological species, has 77 peaks over 1,000 m (3,280 ft) and was listed as a World Natural and Cultural Heritage Site in 1990. Many temples have been constructed on the mountain. There is now a brisk tourist industry and a municipality of 1.6 million people near the 154-sq.-km scenic area.

Sacred mountains

Mountains were probably first felt to be sacred because they were seen to function as pillars holding up the heavens. In shamanistic and Daoist traditions, many sages lived in remote mountain locations supposedly for centuries. Mountains which allowed for such longevity and which connected to the heavens naturally became regarded as sacred. Indeed one can speculate that remoteness was seen as a quality making a mountain more sacred. In some cases whole ranges became designated as such and were seen as the home of spirits.

There are many mountains in China that were considered sacred. There are references to the Five Peaks (Hua Shan, Tai Shan, Heng Shan, Heng Shan Nan, Song Shan) as being Daoist and the Four Famous Mountains (Putuo Shan, Wutai Shan, Emei Shan, Jiuhua Shan) as being sacred to certain 'bodhisattvas'. The Five Peaks had taken on a special status in China before Daoists started to claim them as their sacred mountains in the late 6th century. Other mountains besides these played key roles in Daoist and Buddhist history. Perhaps one of the more famous of these is Mount Kailash in Tibet that has attracted Buddhist, Hindu, Jain and Bön pilgrims. All these mountains today function as tourist sites, although Mount Kailash is seen as politically sensitive with only a limited number of pilgrims allowed.

A 17th-century ink drawing showing Hua Shan, one of the sacred Five Peaks.

RICHARD LOUIS EDMONDS

Guilin

2

I often sent pictures of the hills of Guilin which I painted to friends back home, but few believed what they saw.
FAN CHENGDA, SONG-DYNASTY POET

Guilin (in Guangxi Autonomous Region), one of China's most picturesque cities, is famed for its karst topography which has made it one of the most spectacular and famous sites in China. With surrounding mountains that often rise abruptly from the ground, numerous caverns and subterranean rivers, Guilin's landscape is often depicted in traditional Chinese paintings and poetry.

The predominantly warm and moist climate, combined with significant deposits of calcium carbonate, makes the area one of the largest regions in the world for karst, a topography formed by the dissolution of limestone into calcium hydrogen carbonate, producing special and unusually shaped landforms.

While there are many historical sites in the area such as the Jingjiang Princes City, the most famous attraction is the scenery created by the karst and the Li River, especially the 83-km (52-mile) stretch of the river from Guilin south to Yangzhou. A case in point would be the 1.5-km (1-mile) long Seven Stars Cave with its spectacular stalactites and stalagmites, now part of Seven Stars Park in the eastern part of the city, named after seven peaks that replicate the pattern of the Ursa Major constellation. Another attraction is Elephant Trunk Hill in the south, a cliff resembling an elephant drinking from the water. The rivers also provide ample fishing opportunities, and Guilin is famed for the cormorant fishing practised in the region.

Cultural heritage

In 1981, the State Council listed Guilin as one of the first four cities where historical-cultural heritage as well as natural scenery protection should be given priority. In recent years, Guilin has invested a considerable amount in tourist-related facilities, especially transport. Along with the larger cities of Beijing, Shanghai and Xi'an, Guilin was first recommended as a tourist destination by the World Tourism Organization in 2003.

Today, tourism revenue makes up about 10 per cent of the economy. Other major industries include machinery, textiles, chemistry, cement and pharmaceuticals. There are several higher education institutions in the city including Guangxi Normal University. In recent years Guilin was rated as one of China's ten quietest cities, with the least traffic noise. It is thus considered a good place in which to live as well as to visit.

Seven Stars Cave, Guilin.

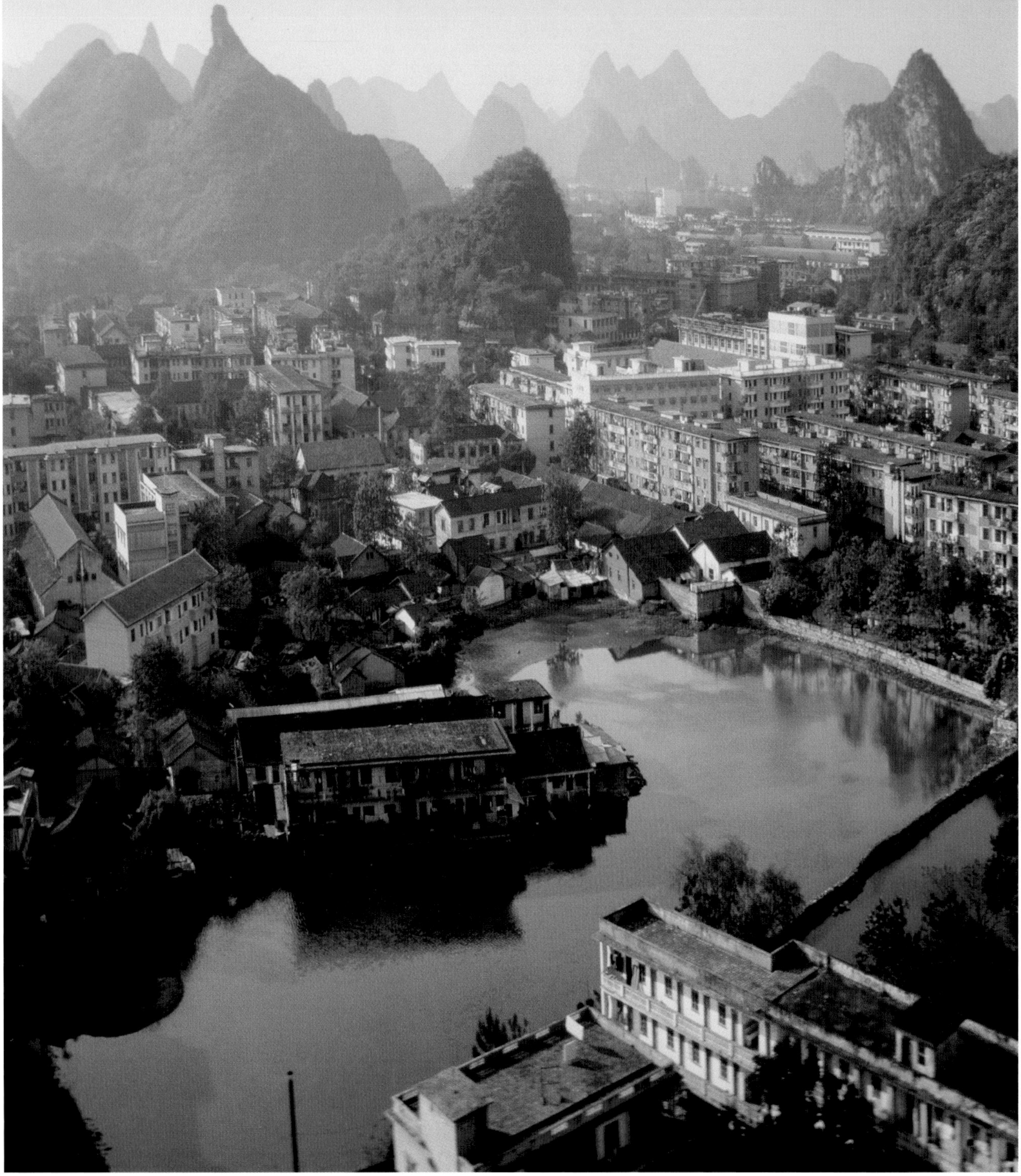

View of Guilin showing the city nestled amongst the unusually shaped karst rock formations.

Guilin was originally founded on the west bank of the Li River in southern China, and four other small rivers flow through the city. Guilin is also the name of the surrounding district in the northeast of the Guangxi Autonomous Region. The name Guilin was used first for a neighbouring area during the Qin dynasty (221–206 BC). In 1914, a county of the same name was established, but the city only acquired its current name in 1940. Today, Guilin (which can be translated as 'osmanthus forest') is a major domestic and international tourist destination, industrial and cultural centre for northeast Guangxi, and home to thousands of stone carvings undertaken over the centuries.

Although there are earlier archaeological remains from about 8000 BC, cave dwellings from 5000 BC have been discovered that contain pottery. A settlement was founded on the Guilin site as early as the 4th century BC.

Centre for Guangxi

Though a county was established here in 111 BC, the town really began to prosper during the Tang and Song dynasties (AD 618–1279). In the subsequent Ming dynasty, what was to be named Guilin became the Guangxi provincial capital, although it lost that title to the more centrally located city of Nanning in 1914. Thus Guilin was the political, economic and cultural centre for the Guangxi area from the Song dynasty to the Qing dynasty (1644–1911).

Guilin is a city of hills and contains five urban wards totalling 565 sq. km (218 sq. miles), which could be considered the actual city proper with a population of around 620,000. This urban area is surrounded by 12 counties which became part of an enlarged Guilin Municipality in 1998, making for a total population in the municipality of 4.76 million.

There is a considerable amount of ethnic diversity in Guilin. Although Han Chinese and Zhuang are the largest groups, Yao, Hui, Hmong and Dong can also be found in considerable numbers. The Zhuang are China's most populous minority group and are concentrated in Guangxi. The Yao live at specific elevations in mountainous areas and are famous for having the knowledge to make herbal-medicine baths. The Hui are Chinese who have converted to Islam or intermarried with Muslim traders and were largely resettled here from the northwest after several rebellions in the 19th century. The Hmong are known in Chinese as the Miao and are celebrated for handicrafts including musical instruments. The Dong have a unique style of housing architecture.

Guilin has a subtropical climate with considerable rainfall. Its yearly average temperature is close to 19°C (66°F). The hottest month, August, has an average temperature of 28°C (82°F), while the coldest months, which are January and February, average 8°C (46°F).

Rice terraces in Longsheng, Guilin district. Terraces of this sort have been in use for hundreds of years by the Yao ethnic people of this region.

RICHARD LOUIS EDMONDS

3 The Yangtze River

The rivers are blue satin ribbons,
The hills ornaments of green jade,
Secluded are the caves deep and dewy,
Everywhere a glorious gorgeous sight.
MARSHAL CHEN YI, EARLY 20TH CENTURY

The Chang River (*Changjiang*), better known abroad as the Yangzi or Yangtze River, is the longest in China (6,300 km / 3,915 miles) with the largest drainage area and the greatest water discharge. *Changjiang* literally means 'Long River' – only the Amazon and the Nile are said to be longer. The common English name, Yangtze, has designated the lower reaches of the river since the 6th century. The name Yangtze became common in English to refer to the whole of the river as this was the portion that the Europeans first encountered.

A major world waterway, the Yangtze is the fifth largest in terms of water discharge and has the fourth largest sediment load of any river in the world. The river's basin makes up close to 19 per cent of China's total area. As such, it is the single most important river system in the country.

The Tibetan plateau is not only home to part of the Qinghai-Tibet Railway, but is also the source of the mighty Yangtze River.

The scenery along its course, said to be some of the most beautiful in China, is celebrated in poetry and literature.

While the Huang (Yellow) River valley to the north is usually seen as the cradle of Chinese civilization, recent archaeological discoveries demonstrate that the Chang (Yangtze) valley was home to several early civilizations, such as the Ba and the state of Chu. In the last thousand years much of the growth in the Chinese state took place in the Chang valley, which is now considered to be the economic core of the country. Economic plans speak of the river as a corridor for development of the interior, with Shanghai and Chongqing functioning as key cities linking with others along the river's course.

Origin in Qinghai

The Yangtze originates from glaciers in the Dangla Mountains in southwestern Qinghai province at the heart of the Qinghai-Tibetan plateau. There has been considerable debate as to which tributary is the source of the river, although this now seems settled on one little creek in Qinghai. As the river begins its journey, it comes under the control of fault zones found along the border between Tibet and Sichuan province, and flows in essentially a north–south direction through steep narrow gorges and over rapids. The upper reaches contribute 50 per cent of the water flow and a large amount of the total sediment load because tributaries

Above *Map showing the course of the Yangtze River out to the sea, and the location of the Three Gorges Dam.*

Below *Ships passing through the Qutang Gorge, one of the famous Three Gorges along the Yangtze.*

The upper reaches of the Yangtze bearing north, having just emerged from the world's deepest gorge, Tiger Leaping Gorge (Yunnan province).

here have steep slopes and relatively poor vegetation cover.

The Three Gorges

Next, the river crosses the Sichuan Basin and cuts through the eastern edge of the basin forming the famous Sanxia (or Three Gorges). The name comes from the three gorges carved into the limestone mountains that are interrupted by broad valleys and gentle hills with rocks. Steamers can make it up the river for 1,600 km (995 miles) to the city of Yichang, Hubei province. After the Three Gorges Dam (p. 183) is operational, probably not until 2009, such vessels should be able to reach as far as the municipality of Chongqing.

This highly controversial dam is the second major dam to span the Yangtze after the Gezhouba Dam immediately downstream. Critics warn of flooding by sedimentation, pollution problems, wildlife destruction, navigation difficulties due to the lock system, landslides, earthquakes, loss of scenery, and security issues. Since construction began in 1993, more than one million people have been relocated.

Middle and lower reaches

In its middle reaches, the Yangtze River flows through a wide alluvial plain with a few headlands of red sandstone projecting into the river. Along the border between Hubei and Hunan provinces it is composed of a series of significant meanders – here the river is actually 240 km (150 miles) long, but only covers a direct distance of 80 km (50 miles).

In the roughly 800 km (500 miles) of the lower reaches, the river broadens out with many shoals found in the middle of the channel. At the mouth the river widens to 90 km (55 miles) before and flowing into the East China Sea. The silt deposited at the outlets of the river along the east coast have made this area into the 'land of rice and

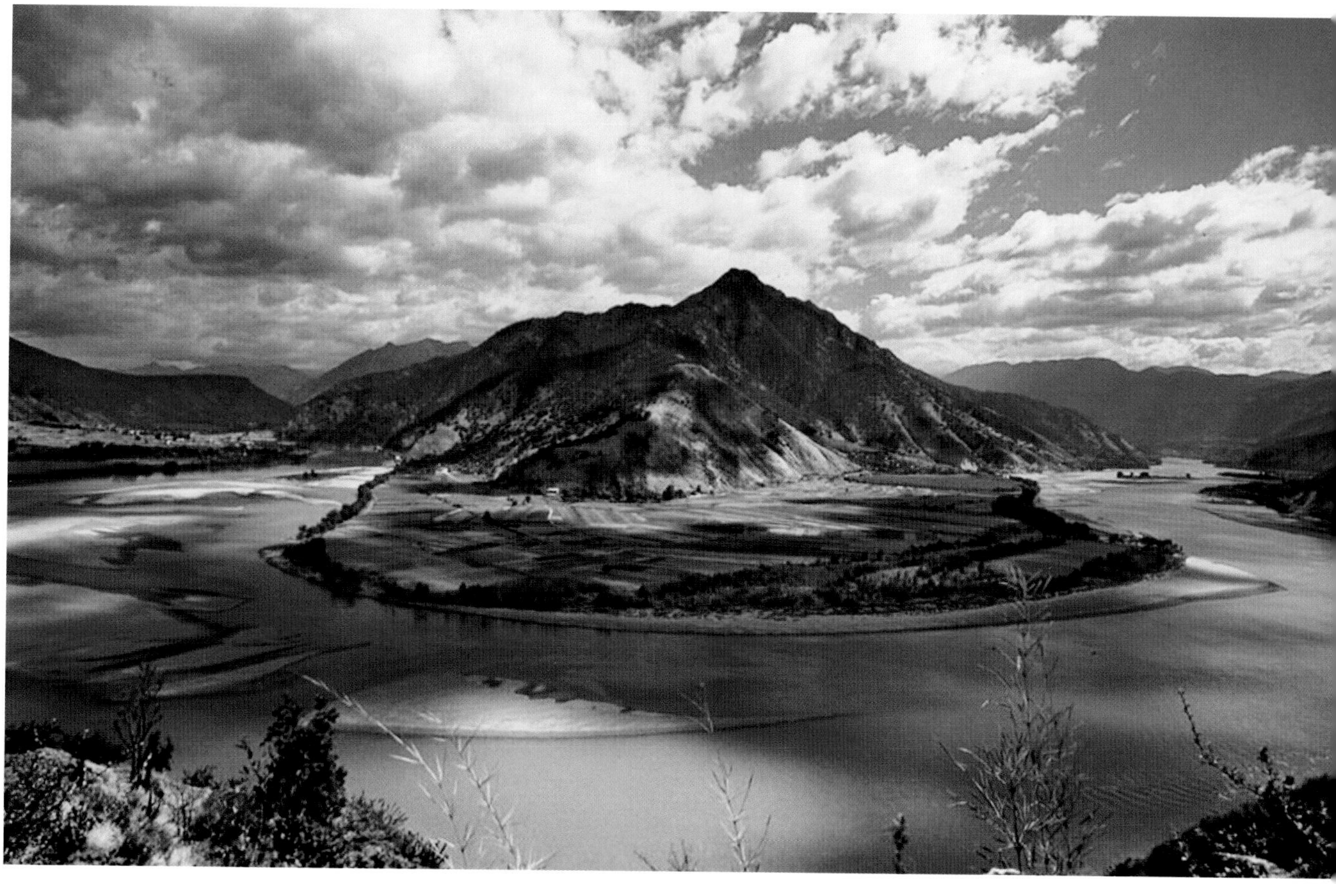

fishes' – one of China's most agriculturally productive and rich areas.

Compared to the Huang or Yellow River to the north (p. 36) with its low water flow and high sediment load, and to the Zhu or Pearl River to the south with its high water flow and low sediment load, the Yangtze can be said to have both a large water discharge and a high sediment load. But the sediment discharge is nowhere near as high per cubic metre as in the Yellow River. The main part of the Yangtze Basin has a relatively high annual precipitation level of over 1,000 mm per year.

With a large number of tributaries north and south of the main river course, the flow of the Yangtze remains more evenly distributed throughout the year than the Yellow River, as rain in one part of the basin is offset by drier weather in other areas due to the monsoonal nature of the climate. Moreover, there are a relatively large number of lakes along the middle reaches that help to regulate the Yangtze's flow as floodwaters can be taken into the lakes and, during low water, the lake waters can move out into the river, thereby balancing the overall flow downstream.

Developments in the Yangtze River valley these days pose serious problems. Rapid economic development has led to high levels of pollution and soil erosion along with deforestation. Today there are massive projects underway to try and alleviate these issues.

Above *Bend in the Yangtze River flowing into Shangri-la, the fictional enchanting, mythical wonderland in James Hilton's novel* Lost Horizon. *(Diqing county, Yunnan).*

Left *A 60-km (37-mile) stretch of the Yangtze as seen from space, including the Xiling Gorge. In the left part of the image is the construction site of the Three Gorges Dam.*

RICHARD LOUIS EDMONDS

4

The Yellow River

See the waters of the Huang River leap down from Heaven,
Roll away to the deep sea and never turn again!
See at the mirror in the High Hall Aged men bewailing white locks –
In the morning, threads of silk,
In the evening flakes of snow.
Snatch the joys of life as they come and use them to the full;
Do not leave the silver cup idly glinting at the moon. ...

LI BO, EXTRACT FROM *JIANG JIN JIU* ('SONG BEFORE DRINKING'), TANG DYNASTY

Far right *The Yellow River starts in the Qinghai-Tibetan plateau before taking a course through numerous gorges. At the Loess plateau it picks up the 'yellow' silt.*

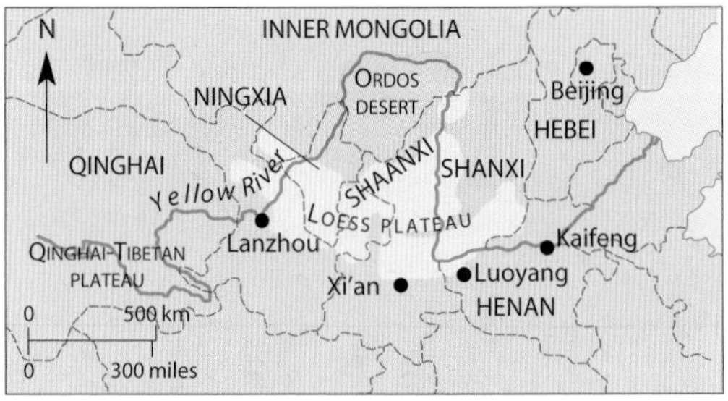

The Huang River (*Huanghe*), also known as the Yellow River, is widely considered to be the cradle of Chinese civilization. On its plain are found many of the older capitals of the country such as Chang'an (now Xi'an), Luoyang and Kaifeng. It is the second longest river in China. The term *huang* has been translated as 'yellow' but *huang* actually spans the yellow-brown spectrum and arguably a better translation might have been Brown River since it is the heavy level of yellow-brown silt that gives the river its name. In ancient texts it was often just referred to as 'The River'. Despite its historical significance, the Huang River Basin accounts for less that 8 per cent of modern China's total area and only a little more than 2 per cent of national total water flows.

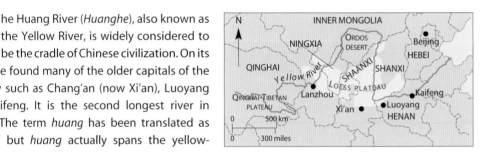

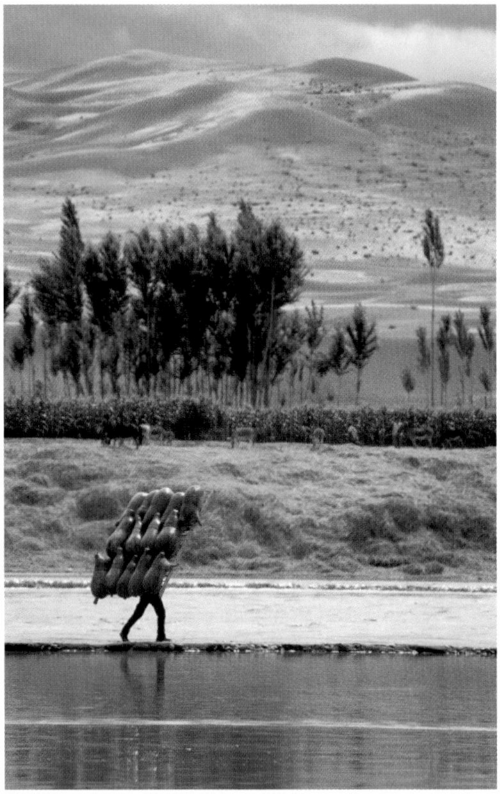

Right *A man carries a raft made of sheep-hide by the arid upper reaches of the Yellow River in Ningxia province.*

Opposite *The dark, silt-laden waters of a tributary that feeds the Yellow River.*

Source

Like many of China's major rivers, the Yellow River's source is found on the Qinghai-Tibetan plateau. After flowing across an extensive swampy area in eastern Qinghai dotted with small lakes, the Yellow River drops 140 m (460 ft) to the relatively fertile Hetao Plain. Here the river flows through about 20 gorges, but no significant tributaries join the river as it travels through these arid portions of Ningxia and Inner Mongolia. A lot of river water is lost through evaporation, seepage and, increasingly in recent decades, irrigation. As such, the river water decreases by about 25 per cent between the city of Lanzhou and the Inner Mongolian-Shaanxi border. Still at this point the water does not have a tremendous amount of silt.

The river becomes 'yellow'

From the border area the Yellow River enters the Loess plateau for the next 1,240 km (770 miles). At first it is confined by a 723-km (450-mile) long gorge along the Shaanxi-Shanxi provincial border. Crossing the Loess plateau, the Yellow River and tributaries that join the river at this point (the Wei, Jing and Fen rivers) become extremely muddy so that when the river leaves the Loess plateau it has eight times the amount of silt it had when it entered. The additional silt represents 80 per cent of the river's total sediment load.

As the river flows eastward it crosses the North China Plain for another 780 km (485 miles) before reaching the sea. In this relatively flat and slow-flowing stretch, one quarter of the river's total sediment is deposited, raising the bed an average of 10 cm (4 in.) per year. In parts of this giant floodplain, the river is now called a 'hanging river' (*xuán hé*), which can rise to 11 m (35 ft) above the surrounding plain due to the building of dykes.

Many times in history the lower river has changed course dramatically. In 1938 the Chinese blew up the dykes and changed the course in an unsuccessful attempt to slow the Japanese invasion. There are virtually no tributaries in these lower reaches and the river loses more water to the plain through seepage than it picks up. In recent years, with considerable water shortages in China, the river often does not even reach the sea for a good part of the year.

Floods and dams

The Yellow River is unique amongst rivers of the world because of its small discharge and heavy sediment load. Due to the special nature of the Loess plateau, the river can produce flood water with a very high sediment content. Flooding has been disastrous along the lower river, although in recent decades the levees have held while the river bed continues to rise. There are even hydrologists

A 19th-century 'China trade' print of the type that were so popular in Europe at this time, showing barges on the Yellow River.

Below *Ice has formed an arch over the Yellow River at the Hukou Falls.*

who say that technically the river is better classified as a 'mud flow' than a 'river'. For comparison, the Yellow River has an average level of discharge at its mouth of 0.7 per cent of that of the Amazon but carries 118 per cent of the Amazon's silt load. It also has a great variability in its flow discharge and in its sediment load during the year and from year to year. This has made river management extremely difficult, and the threat of both flooding and drought from this irregular flow leads to the river's other name: 'China's sorrow'.

In an attempt to manage the flow and to harness power, the Yellow River has been dammed. The most infamous barrage is the Sanmenxia Dam, completed in 1960. The storage capacity of Sanmenxia was threatened within a couple of years and had to have its sluice gates modified drastically, reducing its hydro-electric-generating capacity. Today the dam has lost the ability to control floods, accounts for only a small amount of generation, and another dam was constructed upstream at Xiaolangdi to help relieve sedimentation pressure on the Sanmenxia structure.

While flooding is currently under control, the river is failing to supply enough water to support agricultural irrigation, and has proved ineffective as a generator of hydro-electricity. In a new way the river remains China's sorrow.

FRANCES WOOD

Deserts

5

The desert is reported to be so long that it would take a year to go from end to end, and at the narrowest point it would take a month to cross. It consists entirely of mountains and sand and valleys. There is nothing to eat ....

ATTRIBUTED TO MARCO POLO, *THE TRAVELS*, 13TH CENTURY

China's relationship with the deserts of Central Asia – the Taklamakan and the Gobi – have varied over the centuries, depending upon the strength of central power and the needs of foreign relations. During the Han dynasty (206 BC–AD 220), there was considerable interest in the far west, in trade in horses (needed for the army) with the Ferghana valley and, by intermediaries, silk with Rome. The Chinese government maintained the Great Wall as far as Jiayuguan, and a series of watchtowers out beyond, into the Gobi desert. The watchtowers were intended as beacons, to alert the authorities to trouble out on the fringes of the Chinese polity – many documents on woodslips survive to tell us of the daily life of the garrison troops on this distant frontier.

Again, during the Tang dynasty (AD 618–907) this frontier area was of significance, as monks travelled the Silk Road (p. 43) to India, and Chinese

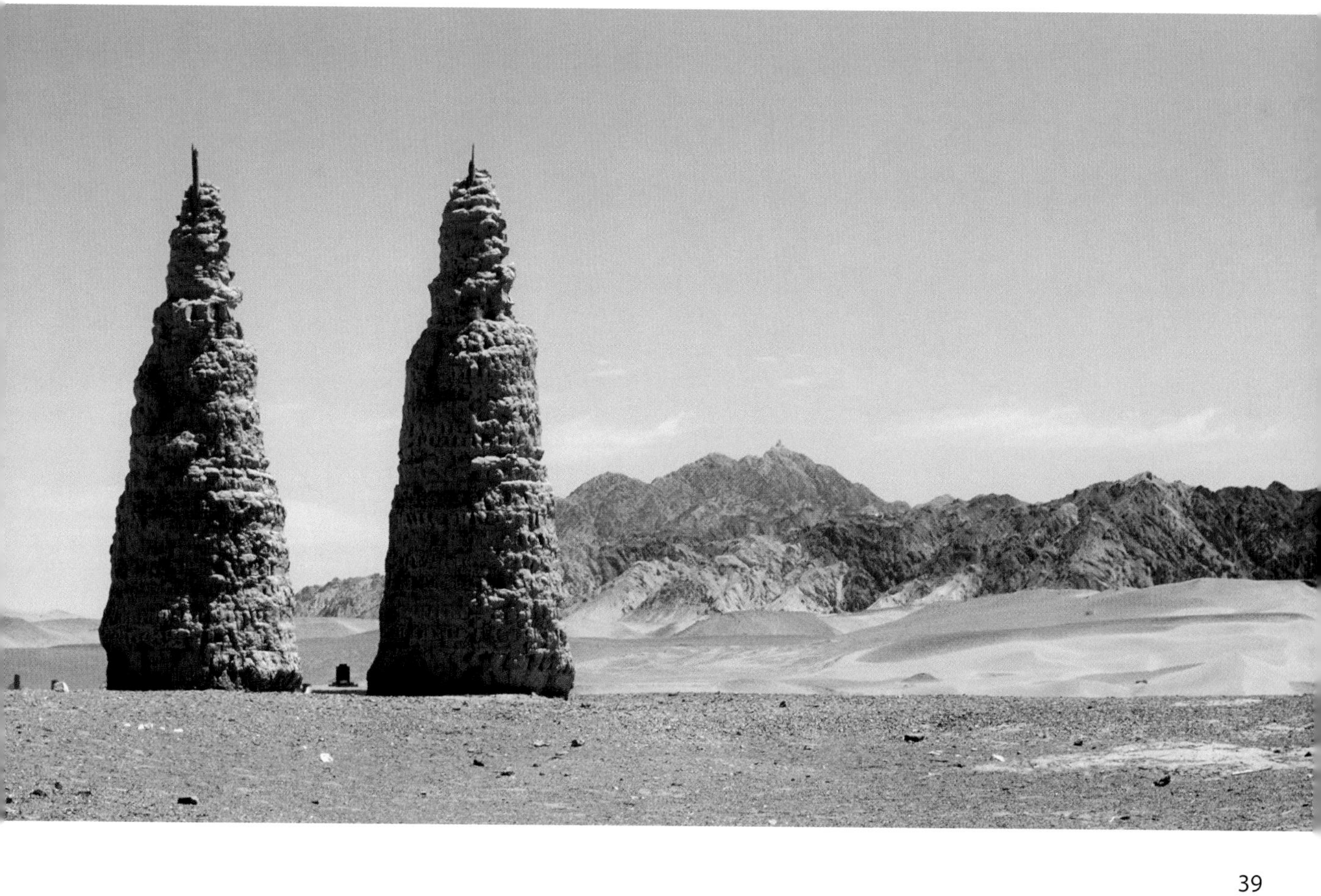

Ruins of ancient towers in the desert, Dunhuang.

settlement increased. But it was not until the Qing, during the 18th century, that the Chinese really extended their control over the further desert, that of the Taklamakan, taking the city of Kashgar in 1759 and enforcing Chinese rule over both the major deserts of Central Asia until the fall of the dynasty in 1911.

Central Asia consists of a massive desert area surrounded to the north and south by mountains. To the north is the Tianshan Mountain range, frequently snow-capped but, because of the reddish brown colour of the lower slopes, often described as the 'Flaming Mountains'. To the east is the Gobi desert with, at the north, the Turfan Depression, some 300 m (1,000 ft) below sea level, one of the world's deepest depressions. South of this area is Lop Nor, a salt lake, sometimes fed by the Tarim River. The Tarim, which has changed direction many times over the centuries, marks the divide between the Gobi and the more eastern part of the Taklamakan desert which stretches towards the Pamir Mountains.

Temperature

In the Turfan Depression, the oasis settlements have adapted to conditions. Houses built with substantial underground (cooler) rooms, have vine-covered terraces, and agriculture is maintained through the 'karez' system, thought to have originated in Persia. Underground channels dug from the foothills of the Flaming Mountains take meltwater from the snowy slopes in cool tunnels to the grapevine and melon fields. If the water went over ground, the great heat of summer, well over 38°C (100°F), would mean a loss through evaporation, but, thanks to the karez, the raisins and grapes of Turfan are famous throughout China.

A man hanging grapes to dry in the Turfan Depression.

The oasis towns of Turfan and Dunhuang in the Gobi, as well as towns on the southern and northern Silk Roads, are filled with poplar trees whose leaves turn a wonderful yellow in autumn. Contrary to popular belief about deserts, both are exceptionally cold in winter, the bare branches of the poplars are witness to occasional snowfalls and temperatures that sink to minus 12°C (54°F).

The fascination of these desert areas lies in the changes that have occurred over the centuries. Even as late as 1937, the explorer Sven Hedin was photographed drifting in a boat along the Karim

Above *Fields near Jiaohe City, Turfan, showing the lush green fields in the midst of desert.*

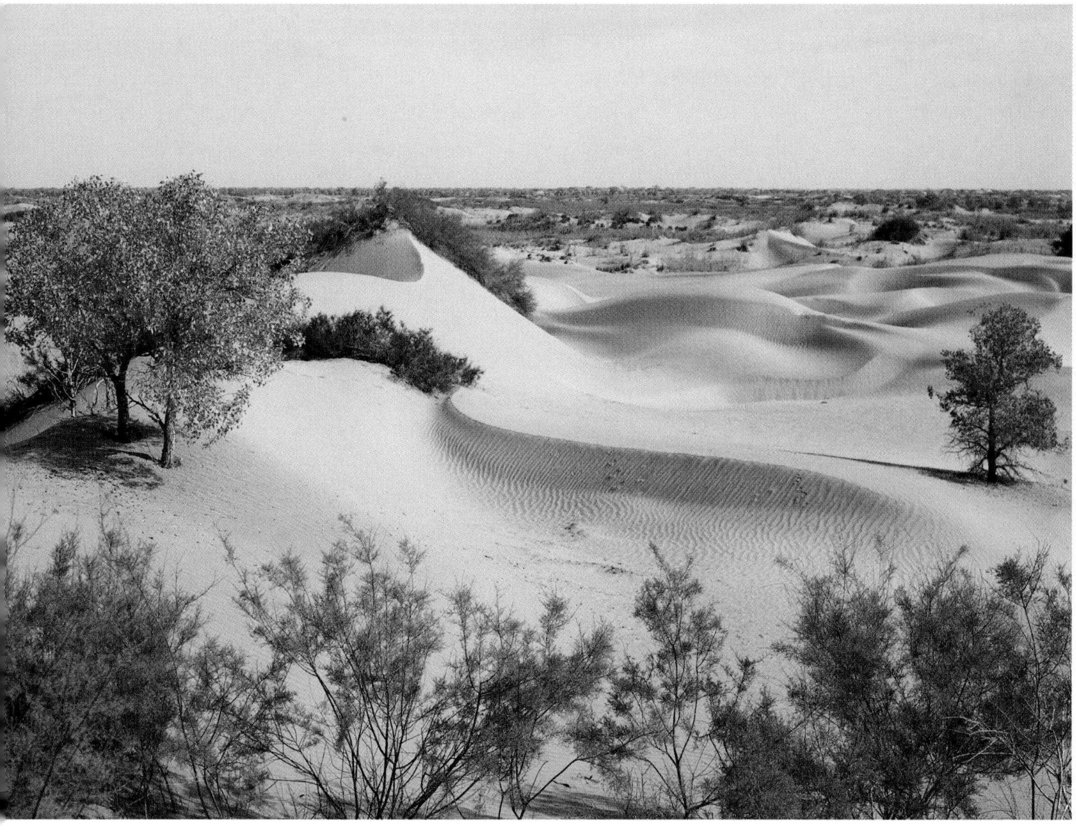

Left *Poplar trees in the sand dunes, Korla.*

River as he navigated the outer reaches of the salt lake of Lop Nor. Explorers photographed dried-up groves of poplars buried in sand, all revealing the problems of the area which included the natural effects of drifting sand dunes and the man-made problems of water shortage.

Lop Nor in particular has seen an extraordinary shift. Once a thriving settlement, it is now a desiccated salt lake, used for nuclear tests. Thousands of years ago, it had a very varied population as can be seen from the discovery of numerous well-preserved Caucasoid mummies (p. 84). At that time, the local town of Loulan was an important caravan stop with water and food in abundance; thus it is clear that, before recent human activity reduced the flow of the rivers that have historically crossed the Central Asia deserts, there was far greater contact between West and East than might have been thought.

The area of the Gobi and Taklamakan deserts has, over the centuries, seen considerable changes in its inhabitants and the main merchants, and it was regarded in the past as much less of an obstacle to travel. From the 2nd to the 10th centuries AD, trade along the Silk Roads was dominated by the Sogdians, whose homeland was in the Chinese capital of Samarkand. They had temples and homes there, and the Chinese claimed that they were taught to trade from the age of five. They dealt in horses, Lucerne grass (to feed the horses) and grapes, and imported luxury items in silver and glass from Persia to China. They brought the Zoroastrian religion to China and were probably responsible for the transfer of paper-making technology from China to the West.

A donkey race during a grape festival, Turfan.

Just as different groups of merchants controlled much of the trade along the Silk Road at different times, so different towns along the Silk Roads held positions of importance at different times. In the early 20th century, the explorer Aurel Stein (p. 44 ff) visited many abandoned sites along the dried-up Keriya River, and Niya, a major settlement on the southern Silk Road, which had been overcome by sand, preserving even the desiccated poplars of the vanished oasis.

The oasis town of Hetian (Khotan), which survives today, was once the capital of the independent kingdom of Khotan, a Buddhist stronghold for most of the 1st millennium AD. The great significance of Hetian for the Chinese was that, until the 17th century when alternative sources of a different kind of jade were found in Burma, it was the sole source of jade (p. 194). Vast quantities of jade boulders were transported along the southern Silk Road on camel-back to be transformed into precious ornaments and vessels in China.

After 1911 the Central Asian deserts were fought over by local and international warlords but when the Communist Party took control of China in 1949, attempts were made to bring Xinjiang (the region that includes the great Central Asian deserts) back under Chinese control by relocating Chinese in great agricultural farms, particularly in the Urumqi area. The increasing desiccation of the Central Asian deserts through agricultural needs, the use of the Lop Nor salt lake for overground nuclear testing, and the desire to exploit its natural reserves which include oil and gold, have led to increasing conflicts with the local Uyghur peoples, some of whom feel a greater loyalty to other Muslim countries than to the Chinese state.

FRANCES WOOD

The Silk Road

6

When those long caravans that cross the plain,
With dauntless feet and sound of silver bells,
Put forth no more for glory or for gain,
Take no more solace from the palm-girt wells,
We travel not for trafficking alone,
By hotter winds our fiery hearts are fanned,
For lust of knowing what should not be known,
We make the Golden Journey to Samarkand.
JAMES ELROY FLECKER, 1913

The 'Silk Road' is a European name given to the centuries-old series of trade routes that led from China across Central Asia and, eventually, to Europe. The name was coined in 1877 by the German geographer Baron Ferdinand von Richthofen and is somewhat misleading for it conveys the sense of a single road crossing the Central Asian deserts. In fact, the movement of goods across the area had taken place since the Neolithic era, before the discovery of silk, when Khotanese jade was moved to China, and was usually effected through a series of merchants making short trips, rather than the long haul that the name suggests.

There were traditionally two Silk Roads, northern and southern, running along the perimeter of the massive and impassable deserts of Central Asia. Silk was transported along them, reaching Rome in the 2nd century BC. The Roman poet Virgil, in the 1st century BC, supposed that silk might have been combed from leaves, and the geographer Strabo thought it was dried from

A Chinese camel caravan, c. 1925. The camel, cold- and drought-resistant, was the most practical beast of burden on the Silk Road.

Right *A Sunday market in modern Kashgar.*

bark. The flimsiness of the material provoked criticism, Seneca the Elder complaining that silk-clad women were 'naked hardly less obviously than if you had taken off your clothes'. It was, however, a two-way trade since European food like coriander, peas and cucumbers travelled to China.

Exploration of the Silk Roads by Europeans began in the late 19th century with classically educated scholars like von Richthofen well aware of the movement of silk to Rome. One of the preeminent explorers of the Silk Road was Aurel Stein (1862–1943), a Hungarian trained in surveying during his period of military service, who had subsequently studied Sanskrit and gone to work as an educationalist for the British Government in India. In Kashmir, he had become excited by the possibility of discovering ancient texts in Central Asia and led three major expeditions into Chinese Central Asia (1900–1901, 1906–1908 and 1913–1916), financed by the Government there and the British Museum. The fact that he was based in India and partly financed by the Government of India influenced his approach to Chinese Central Asia. He invariably started from and returned to Kashgar, at the Chinese western end of the Silk Roads, where the northern and southern routes converged, before proceeding westwards, either via Ferghana or Bactria.

Below *The series of routes known as the Silk Road. Merchants not only traded goods between east and west, but also facilitated the transfer of highly influential Buddhist ideas from India to China.*

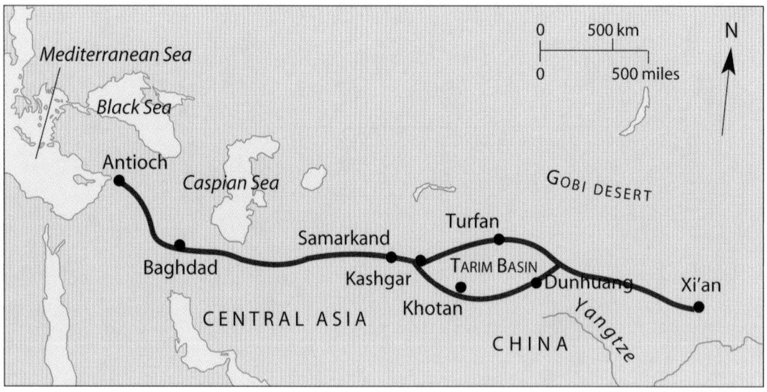

Kashgar

When Chinese imperial power reached its greatest extent, during the Qing dynasty, Kashgar had been incorporated into the Qing domains in 1759. By the late 19th century, it had become a focus of interest in the 'Great Game', with both a Russian and a British Consul stationed there. Stein stayed many times with the British Consul, Lord Macartney, and his wife in 'all the comforts of a British home' and invariably returned to India via Kashgar, entrusting the packaging and forwarding of his precious finds to the Consul.

When Stein visited Kashgar in the first years of the 20th century it was, as it is today, effectively two towns: a Chinese town and a Uyghur town. The Chinese part was – and is – the centre of administration, whilst the Uyghur town contains the market and the mosques, and is still famous for its Sunday market where horses, camels, donkeys, goats, raisins, melons, hats and knives are noisily traded. In Stein's time, British-Russian relations were hostile, but when the writer-explorers, Peter Fleming and Ella Maillart, arrived in 1935 after crossing the desert, they found 'Kashgar-les-bains' very much dominated by the

to collect scriptures for translation into Chinese. In about AD 366, Buddhist monks started to carve out the first caves near Dunhuang, beginning to create what would become the last – and first – major Buddhist site in China for pilgrims on their way to India and back. The 500 or so caves were plastered and painted with Buddha images, scenes from the life of the historic Buddha and usually had a stucco Buddhist figure or group of figures in the centre. As the cave-temple complex was abandoned in about AD 1000 and the dry desert air preserved the contents perfectly, the Caves of the Thousand Buddhas at Dunhuang are one of the greatest centres of Chinese Buddhist art, revealing early landscape painting and the depiction of Tang-dynasty buildings in frescoes, as well as the development of Buddhist art in China during a period of some 700 years.

When Stein first visited Dunhuang he was made aware of a further treasure preserved there, which fitted even better with his search for early manuscripts. Shortly before the whole complex was abandoned to the desert sands in about AD 1000, a huge collection of Buddhist manuscripts had been walled up in Cave 17. Dating from *c.* AD 406 to 1000, these thousands of manuscripts, printed documents and paintings had been perhaps walled away in a form of 'burial'; being

British, playing football with the Embassy guards and enjoying English armchairs, beers and baths.

Through Kashgar Stein shipped, first to India then London, his extraordinary finds from the Buddhist caves at Dunhuang, at the far end of the Silk Road, at an almost parallel point to Kashgar, for it was near Dunhuang that the northern and southern Silk Roads diverged at the eastern end of the great trade route.

Dunhuang – the Mogao Caves

The cave-temple complex at Dunhuang is of huge significance to the history of Buddhism in China. The religion probably first entered China around the turn of the 1st millennium. But, since the homeland of the faith was India, from about the 2nd century AD, brave monks began to make the long trip along the southern Silk Road to India

Below *Exterior of the caves at Dunhuang.*

A camel caravan heading along part of the Silk Road that crosses the Pamir plateau.

no longer useful, they were accorded a religious burial, though we also know that paper was often re-used to repair sutras. It also seems that locals deposited precious family documents such as contracts and notices of loan with local temples for safe-keeping – so there is a considerable body of material that tells us much about daily life in traditional China through original documents.

Stein removed around 25,000 documents and paintings, some in a very fragmentary form, and sent them to London via Kashgar. His visit was soon followed by that of Paul Pelliot who collected on behalf of the Bibliothèque Nationale de France and the Musée Guimet. Subsequently, most of the remaining contents of Cave 17 were taken by the Chinese Government to Beijing but this did not prevent the Russian archaeologist, Nikolai Petrovsky, from removing yet more documents, and a further raid by the Japanese Count Otani. Ancient sites in the

Right *Xuanzang, the first Chinese monk to travel to India, is pictured here on his horse with his companions in the fictionalized account of his travels on the Silk Road.*

Left *The Diamond Sutra, printed in AD 868, is the world's earliest dated printed 'book'.*

Turfan Depression were similarly raided by the German explorer-archaeologists Albert Grunwedel and Albert von Le Coq.

The Dunhuang corpus of manuscripts is now divided between London, Paris, Beijing, St Petersburg and Japan. Its significance as the world's earliest paper archive, the world's earliest corpus of Buddhist manuscripts and the source of the world's earliest dated printed 'book', a copy of the Diamond Sutra dated AD 868, ensure that the cache created on the Silk Road remains a major authority for scholars.

Below *One of the Silk Road routes today.*

JONATHAN FENBY

7 Yunnan

In a cloudless sky before me rose the peerless pyramid of the finest mountain my eyes ever beheld ... the apexes suddenly turned a golden yellow as the sunrise kissed them.

YUNNAN RESIDENT JOSEPH ROCK, C. 1930

Lijiang. The Jade Dragon Snow Mountain, as seen from Black Dragon Pool.

Covering 440,000 sq. km (170,000 sq. miles) in the far southwest of China, Yunnan province is one of the most unusual parts of the country, set apart through the centuries by its geographical isolation, its semi-tropical climate, its minorities, its substantial Muslim population and its links with Burma, Vietnam and Laos. Though air travel has brought its capital of Kunming into the reach of the rest of China, the province is still a very different place.

Stunning scenery includes the great first bend of the Yangtze River at what are known as the Golden Sands, and one of the world's deepest valleys at Leaping Tiger Gorge. Tropical plants

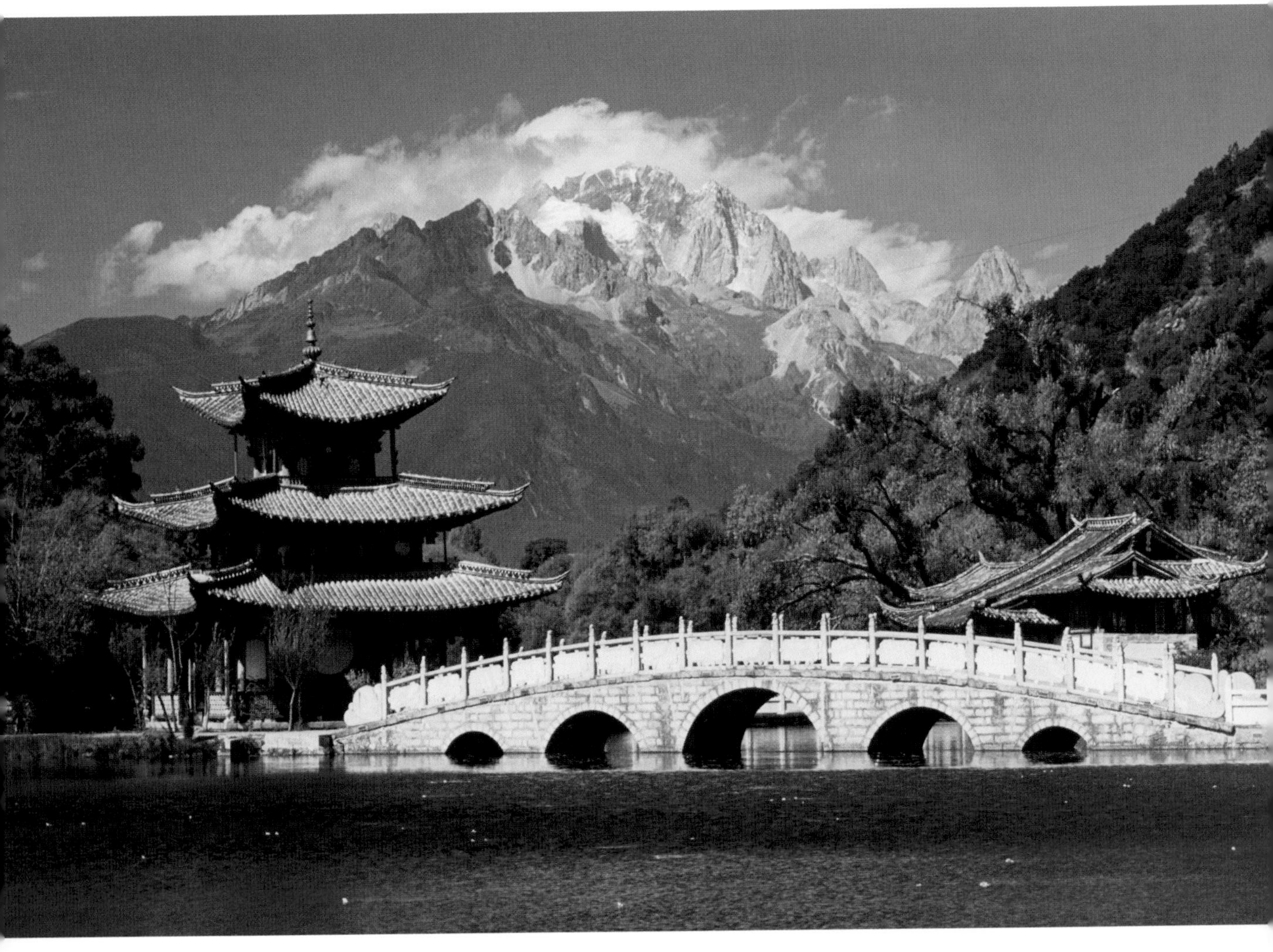

bloom. Views from mountain ridges stretch out to Tibet. Rivers tumble from snowy heights. Outside Kunming, the 17th-century Golden Temple, actually made of copper, unites Daoism, Buddhism and Confucianism in spacious gardens. Down the hill, celebrated flower shows make the most of the climate. Two hours' drive away, the Stone Forest is a geological marvel, a fantastic jumble of huge rocks thrown from the ocean bed 70 million years ago.

Though the province has been subject to modern building and development, the fine old trading town of Lijiang has been preserved, the curved grey roofs of its wooden-walled houses forming a giant mosaic along water channels. Its Black Dragon Pool has a perfect arched marble bridge, and the Moon Embracing Pavilion stands against the backdrop of the Jade Dragon Snow Mountain. Local music is played on ancient lutes, drums, cymbals and horns. The famed Yunnan ham is coated in fiery chillies.

The novelist, James Hilton, based his description of Shangri-La in the novel *Lost Horizon* on reports from an Austrian botanist, Joseph Rock, who lived in a northern Yunnan village. The botanist's home can still be visited in the town claiming to be the original site of that idyll.

The province's ethnic minorities retain colourful clothing, customs and stories of gods creating the human race by laying eggs and showing their displeasure at ecological degradation by unleashing earthquakes. A local language is written in stick-like pictograms. Among some minorities, women are regarded as superior to men, though this means that they do most of the work. In one area, they sleep with whoever they wish, and the fathers have no claim on the offspring. Women of the Naxi group wear quilted capes divided into halves representing day and night, separated by a row of seven circles standing for the stars to signal that women are at the centre of the universe.

History

Until 1253, Yunnan was independent, ruled by kings whose authority reached into Burma, Laos and Thailand. The kings' capital was in the lakeside town of Dali, where their cream-coloured pagodas still stand, flanked by 19 peaks. Then Kubilai Khan's Mongol army conquered the region for the Chinese empire, and moved the capital to Kunming. But imperial control was limited to the plains and river valleys. Though the succeeding dynasties sent expeditions to try to subdue the mountains and forest regions that cover much of the province, they found the going hard. In the mid-19th century, Muslims staged a 17-year rebellion. Then the French established their influence in the province from their colonies in Indochina, and the British did the same from Burma.

After the fall of the Qing empire in 1911, Yunnan became virtually autonomous under a warlord who did all he could to keep the central government at bay, prospering from the opium trade which still presents a local problem. During the Second World War, Yunnan served as the main route for supplies brought into China along the 'Burma Road', and Kunming became a centre for critics of Chiang Kai-shek's Nationalist regime. Its wily warlord survived to join the Communist administration after 1949. Today, apart from being a major tourist attraction, the province, with a population close to 40 million, provides China with tin and tungsten, and there are plans to develop its transport links with Vietnam and Burma.

Group of Hani people eating at table, Yuanyang, Yunnan province.

RICHARD LOUIS EDMONDS

8 Northern Grasslands & Pastures

All the grasslands are yellow
and all the days we march
and all the men are conscripts
sent off in four directions.
All the grasslands are black
and all the men like widowers.
So much grief!
Are soldiers not men like other men?
We aren't bison!
We aren't tigers crossing the wilderness,
but our sorrows roam from dawn till dusk.
Hairy-tailed foxes slink through the dark grass
as we ride tall chariots along the wide rutted roads.
Shi Jing ('The Book of Songs'), *c.* 600 BC

Arid and semi-arid lands, China's largest ecosystem type, make up approximately one third of China's territory. By definition, these territories get less than 500 mm of precipitation a year. Sub-humid areas are defined as having between 500 and 700 mm per annum. China's grasslands straddle all these climatic divisions but tend to be concentrated in the north, the northwest and on the Qinghai-Tibetan plateau. Approximately 4 million sq. km of this area is what the Chinese designate as grassland; only Australia has a larger area of grassland. Within China's total, over 3.1 million sq. km are what the Chinese term as 'usable grasslands'. Another 0.3 million sq. km are 'fenced grasslands' and 0.6 million sq. km are 'undergoing degradation'. The areas are also home to about 340 million sheep, goats, cattle, horses and camels – a three-fold increase since the early 1950s. Inner Mongolia alone has about one third of the total grassland area of China.

Population growth & grassland degradation

Prior to the 1950s much of the Inner Mongolian grasslands and grasslands in northern Qinghai province were exclusively occupied by Mongols, Tibetans and other herding minority peoples. The building of railway lines in these areas led to the

in-migration of large numbers of mainstream or Han Chinese so that by 1982 minority peoples were outnumbered in most of eastern Inner Mongolia and northern Qinghai despite rapid population growth amongst the local minorities. Subsequently over 6.5 million hectares were put under the plough and new roads were constructed. Roads alone may account for 10–20 per cent of the degradation. Town and herd populations have grown tremendously, putting additional pressure on the lands. In some places the herd overload is estimated to be as high as 300 per cent. In addition, warmer temperatures and deforestation in neighbouring areas may be impacting upon the grasslands. The results are that land classified as having desertified in China since the 1980s includes a large proportion of former grassland, with central Inner Mongolian amongst the hardest hit.

In the first five years of the 21st century, Inner Mongolia, Ningxia, Xinjiang, Qinghai and Gansu have had the most serious levels of grassland degradation. Today over 90 per cent of China's grasslands are degraded to some degree or another and grassland productivity in China is only about 10 per cent of that in Australia. As classic cases in point, Genghis Khan's birthplace became a desert, and the capital of the former Xixia kingdom in Ningxia is also now a stone 'gobi' area.

Are *kuluns* the answer?

To combat the grassland degradation problem, the government during the 1980s began to promote the development of the *kulun*. *Kulun* are enclosed areas constructed to control grazing, block wind, improve soil quality, control sand, provide fodder / limited cultivation or fodder / hay, and to produce grazing grass. *Kulun* are most successful when introduced with restrictions on herd size, rationalization of well water use and construction of permanent roadways.

Today, *kulun* in Inner Mongolia have expanded to cover a considerable area. Most experts agree, however, that the area covered by this system is not enough to stop the trend towards grassland degradation. In other cases, trees are being planted, but these often use too much water or die because of lack of water. To date, the uneducated and poor of these regions continue to experience little of the prosperity felt in eastern China. In 2006 China announced plans to greatly expand its enclosed grasslands over the next 15 years. However, it remains to be seen whether the country has the resources and the political will to undertake these measures.

Kazakh yurt village. A group of Kazakh yurts are set up in the countryside, Inner Mongolia.

Opposite *A Mongolian horseman herding horses on the Hulun Buir grassland of the Inner Mongolian Autonomous Region.*

IAIN ORR

9 Wildlife

The Master fished with a line but not with a net; when fowling he did not aim at a roosting bird.
CONFUCIUS, *ANALECTS* 7.26

The diversity of China's wildlife is truly a wonder. Despite a population of over 1.2 billion, China still has some 394 mammal species, and over 1,100 breeding birds. For other vertebrates and invertebrates the estimates are less reliable. Many are now on the Red Data List of endangered species – 84 mammals, 88 birds, 34 reptiles, 91 amphibians and 59 fish in the latest report (2006). Both natural diversity and the threats to it are part of the *yin* and *yang* of Chinese culture.

Long before the term biodiversity was coined, the concept was familiar. The poet Ouyang Xiu (1007–1072) wrote in *The Cicada*:

Long since have I marvelled
How of ten thousand creatures there is not one
But has its tune; how, as each season takes its turn,
A hundred new birds sing, each weather wakes
A hundred insects from their sleep.

The poet watched without interfering; and Buddhist and Daoist values are some of the best mankind has ever evolved for sharing the earth with other species. But the Legalist perspective of Xunzi (3rd century BC) is closer in spirit to the Western big game hunters who bagged tigers in their thousands from India and China:

'You glorify Nature and meditate on her; why not domesticate and regulate her? You follow nature and sing her praise; why not control her course and use it?'

Domesticating nature works for some species – yaks, water buffaloes ploughing rice paddies, the flocks of pigeons that used to fly over Beijing with light gourds carved into whistles attached to them, the fighting crickets kept in delicately carved boxes. But sharing the scarce resources of land and rivers is not easy for many species. The title of a fine environmental history of China by Mark Elvin – *The Retreat of the Elephants* – sees the development of Chinese agriculture as a battle between farmers and wildlife, especially large animals like elephants (which pulled war chariots in ancient China). The farmers won.

Yet China is so large, with huge areas so unsuited to intensive agriculture, that it still has

The Bengal tiger is now virtually extinct in China, where poachers use its body parts in the making of various traditional medicines.

wild species as an integral part of distinctive habitats. The snow leopard is the natural top predator of the arid alpine ecosystem in Central Asia, including northwest China. The musk deer is typical of the forested mountains from northeast to southwest China, though it has been in decline through over-exploitation for traditional Chinese medicine – also responsible for the virtual extinction of the tiger in China.

The grasslands of northern China are still home for the Mongolian gazelle. Finally, the non-human primate whose call is so evocative for Chinese writers and artists – the gibbon – can still be found brachiating and calling in the tropical forests of Yunnan and Hainan.

The diversity and beauty of China's avifauna is outstanding, from the stately courtship dances of the cranes (Black-necked, Red-crowned, White-naped), the striking lappet displays of Cabot's Tragopan (a horned pheasant) to the melodious

Above *Early 17th-century textile showing a crane in a Chinese landscape.*

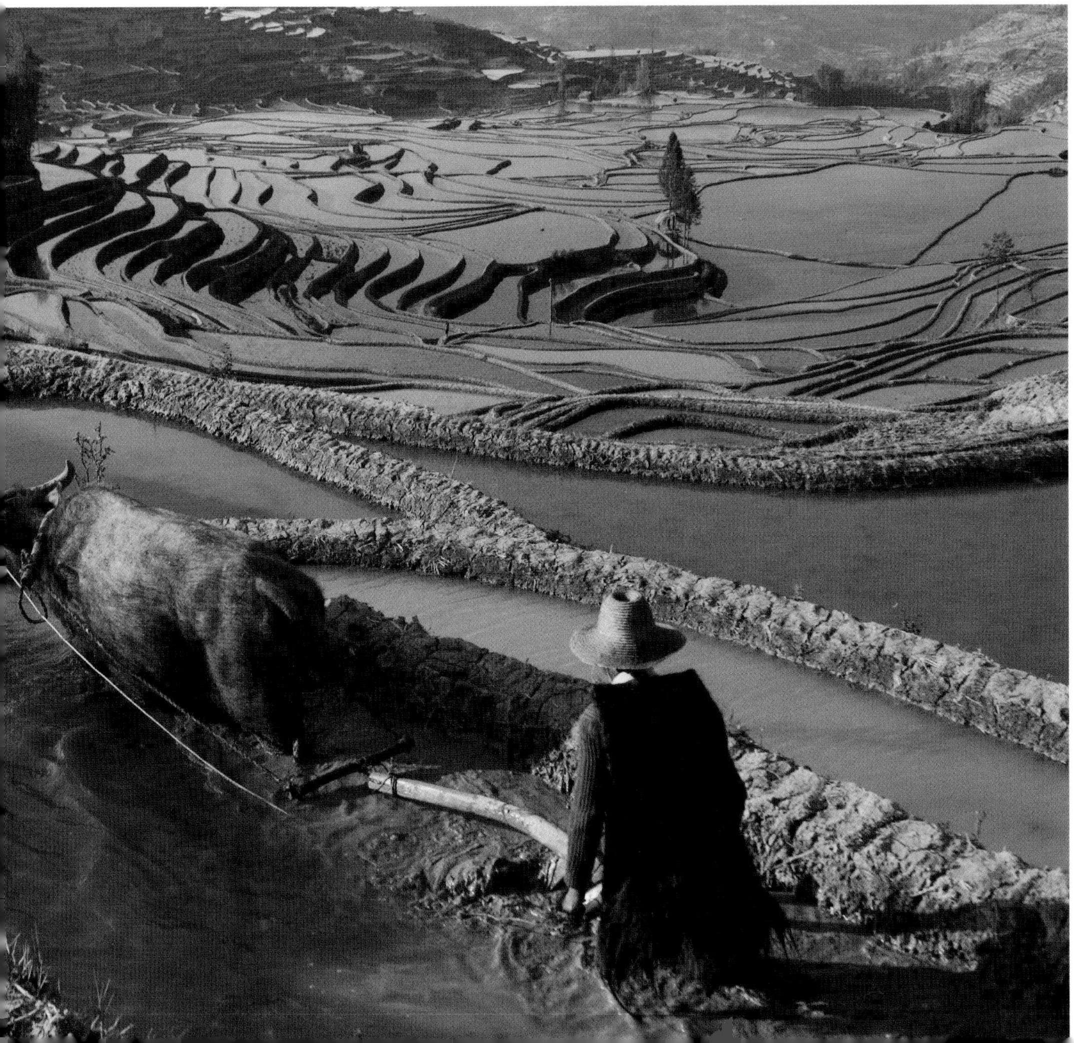

Left *A farmer ploughing a water-filled rice terrace with water buffalo.*

song of the Hwamei ('Beautiful eyebrow') and the raucous White-speckled Laughing Thrush.

Birds are a reminder that China's wildlife is shared with others. Most of the sharing is done by the birds themselves – migratory species such as the Spoon-billed Sandpiper. Other colourful and dramatic species (Golden Pheasant, the Eared Pheasants) have been introduced outside China, especially in Europe and North America. The Mandarin Duck – symbol of conjugal fidelity – has so often escaped from aviaries that the wild population in Britain now probably outnumbers that in China. But the wildlife which has spread most widely from China over several centuries has been one species of carp – the goldfish – cultivated in many exotic forms in the Imperial Palace in Beijing and now the staple of ponds and aquaria throughout the world. (A less welcome export – via bilgewater – is the Chinese Mitten crab, now a threat to indigenous species in the Thames and Elbe.)

Right *A pair of Mandarin Ducks in a 19th-century scroll painting.*

Left *Three Giant Panda cubs climbing a dead tree in Wolong, Sichuan province.*

That leads to the final wildlife wonder, spread by a strange evolution of the gift exchanges found in so many different cultures: the diplomatic Giant Panda. For some zoologists its survival is seen as being of little ecological significance. It contributes minimally to China's vertebrate biomass. But the panda's symbolism has been immense, in China and internationally. It was one of the first animal trophies to be sought alive rather than dead; it was chosen by Sir Peter Scott as the logo for WWF – the first conservation NGO to have a truly global footprint; and it has helped nurture the growth of conservation in China. Its diet leads to another natural wonder of China – bamboo – which is explored in the next essay.

IAIN ORR

Trees & Flowers

10

In China, where every available bit of land is devoted to agriculture, quite a number of trees must long ago have become extinct but for the timely intervention of Buddhist and Daoist priests.
ERNEST WILSON, *CHINA: MOTHER OF GARDENS*, 1929

China's diverse flora has offspring all over the world. Many trees and flowers in the parks and gardens of Europe and America come from remote mountain valleys of Yunnan and Sichuan. Brought back to the 19th-century Treaty Ports of Shanghai, Ningbo and Canton, plants, seeds and seedlings were shipped on to taxonomists and horticulturalists in Paris, London, Berlin and New York, eager for exotic additions to their catalogues.

In a few cases, it may be fair to talk of the collectors as having 'discovered' these plants. But for the most part, China's botanical riches were already known and catalogued, usually in two distinctive ways: the traditional Chinese *Materia Medica,* of which the most famous was the *Bencao Gangmu* of Li Shizhen (1518–1593); and in scrolls and watercolours. Chinese peasants, doctors, gardeners and artists have celebrated and used this rich flora for thousands of years.

China's botanical diversity is due to her size and the range of climate zones and ecological systems: mountains, alpine meadows, tropical and temperate rainforests, lakes, coastal wetlands, grasslands and islands. Many northern plants during the last Ice Age found secure refuges in southern China and were able to re-colonize as the glaciers retreated.

There are dramatic and sensuous qualities to much of China's natural beauty: twisted pines

A pine tree on Huang Shan.

Above *An 18th-century Chinese watercolour of pink peonies.*

Below *Detail from 'One Hundred Flowers' by Chen Jiayan.*

clustering around precipitous karst limestone crags, or willows and cassia trees gently swaying beside a lake. China's trees are notable both for their antiquity as species – the Dawn Redwood with its handsome profile, the Ginkgo with its distinctive leaves – and for the age of individual trees. Cities and villages in every province still have trees that have shaded poets and administrators of successive dynasties.

Symbolism, natural beauty and usefulness are also how flowers have infused Chinese culture. The national flower, the Mudan or Tree Peony, was probably first cultivated for the medicinal properties of its roots. But in the city of Luoyang under the empress Wu Zetian there was a mania for peonies similar to the tulipomania of 17th-century Amsterdam. Ouyang Xiu (1007–1072) in a famous treatise on the *Mudan* celebrates it thus:

My desire is, throughout the four seasons, to bring wine along
And to let not a single day pass without some flower opening.

The sheer variety China has given to the world – azaleas, rhododendrons, roses, lilies, primulas, clematis, forsythias, chrysanthemums, magnolias, camellias – leaves every lover of trees and flowers and gardens deeply in debt to her. Favourites will always be a matter of individual choice. Here is what Ernest Wilson said after his search for the vibrant yellow poppywort (*Mecanopsis integrifolia*) was rewarded on 18 July 1903:

I am not going to attempt to record the feelings which possessed me on my first beholding the object of my quest to these wild regions. Messrs Veitch despatched me on this second and very costly journey to the Tibetan border for the sole purpose of discovering and introducing this the most gorgeous alpine plant extant.

However, the greatest wonder amongst China's plants is neither tree nor flower but a type of grass – bamboo. Not even Japan can rival China in the variety of species and of bamboo products – from acupuncture needles and pipelines for transporting natural gas to T-shirts of bamboo fibre and the roof of the new Madrid international airport. Appropriately, the first international organization to have its headquarters in Beijing is the International Network of Bamboo and Rattan (INBAR).

Bamboo, with pine and plum tree, is one of the 'three auspicious things' in China whose properties symbolize eternity. At a more prosaic level, it provides essential nourishment for one of China's other natural wonders – the Giant Panda – and its shoots are a distinctive ingredient in Chinese cuisine. The poet Su Shi (1037–1101) best captures the centrality of bamboo to a Chinese vision of the good life:

I would rather eat a meal without meat
Than live in a place with no bamboos.
Without meat one may become thin:
Without bamboos one becomes vulgar.

The wind sways a bamboo forest in the Qinling Mountains.

People & Life

Alongside the great monuments, natural wonders, artistic triumphs and inventions covered in this book, the Chinese have evolved a way of life over the millennia which largely defied changes of regime to provide a wonder all of its own. This section explores facets of that Chinese achievement which shows itself in everything from religion to food, from agriculture to the martial arts. Together, they help to explain the nature of the Chinese people, and their existence.

The vast majority belong to the Han (p. 61), those living south of the Great Wall considering themselves 'Children of the Yellow Emperor', their identity greatly strengthened by opposition in the later 19th and very early 20th centuries to the last dynasty, whose rulers came from Manchuria. The Tarim mummies (p. 84) provide a tantalizing glimpse of a much earlier group of inhabitants of China in the Bronze and Early Iron Ages (2nd and 1st millennia BC). Recent writers have drawn attention to the differences among the Han – not surprising in as varied a country as China. There are many dialects, northerners are taller than southerners, and attitudes to life and work vary. There are also wide differences in what is probably the most familiar aspect of China round the world – food. Apart from the basic division between the wheat-growing north and the rice-cultivating south, there is a myriad local dishes and tastes, from the spicy fare of Hunan and Sichuan to the fine seafood of Guangdong, from juicy Shanghai dumplings to the grilled meats of Xinjiang – all accompanied by appropriate local drinks.

Martial arts students practise synchronized kung fu *at the Ta Gou academy in Henan province.*

Alongside the Han, China always contained strong ethnic minorities (p. 80) with their distinctive cultures. Fifty-five minorities are officially recognized today, numbering more than 100 million people. While the Han fill the heavily populated parts of the country, the minorities live mainly in more open lands, notably in the huge expanse of the far west, and thus occupy 60 per cent of the national territory.

For millennia, most Chinese shared a set of beliefs and behaviour patterns inherited from the sage Confucius (p. 68) and his successor Mencius. Its emphasis on filial piety and well-ordered behaviour has been seen as having held China back by its conservatism, but it undoubtedly provided glue for a vast empire. A religious mixture of Buddhism, Daoism, local gods and ancestor worship accompanied it (p. 71), though heterodox sects proliferated, showing great tenacity despite being outlawed.

Qing-dynasty handscroll on silk showing the Yongzheng emperor offering sacrifices at the altar of the god of agriculture. (Anonymous court artist.)

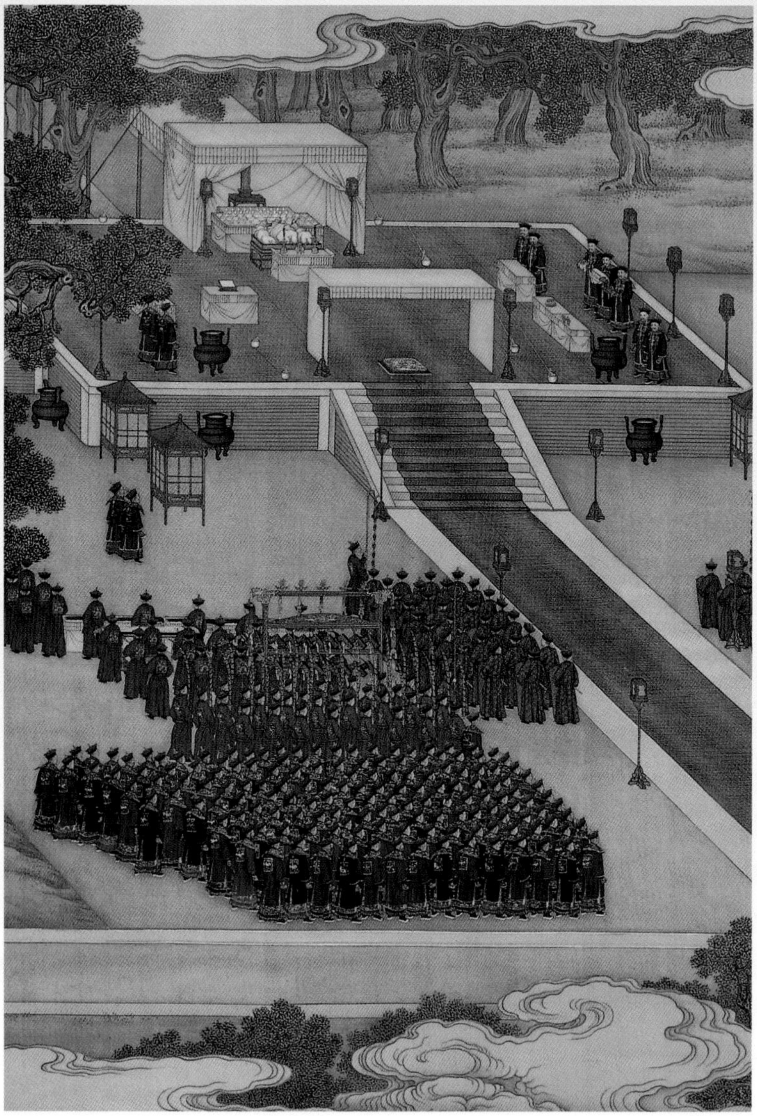

This mixed religious tradition has lasted to the present day, as can be seen from people making offerings and praying at altars to their ancestors and to local gods. The traditions of *taiji* (p. 76) and the martial arts culture (p. 78), most notably from the Shaolin Buddhist Monastery built in AD 495 in Henan province, also run through the centuries. Alongside were the diversions of circus and acrobats (p. 87), in performances at market-town fairs and in grander shows in cities, which continue to amaze watchers at home and abroad.

The great majority of Chinese have always lived and worked on the land – despite the recent breakneck industrialization, a majority of the population is still in rural areas. The people whose corpses have been preserved in the Tarim Basin were pastoralists. Early inhabitants of the Yellow River valley, the cradle of Chinese civilization, made the most of the fertile loess soil that marks the region. Confucius extolled agriculture. Wise emperors knew the importance of caring for the farmers who constituted most of their subjects. Peasant revolts were always to be feared, in protest at taxation, natural disasters or official policies.

Despite population increases, China achieved general self-sufficiency in food, though there could still be terrible sufferings from disasters. Terracing, irrigation, land clearance and the introduction of faster-growing rice, potatoes and maize increased output. There was no motivation to bring in new and more efficient techniques in the 19th century. As in other respects mentioned in this book, China felt no need to innovate at a time when the West was pressing ahead, and the way of life of most of its people remained relatively unchanged until the advent of Communism in 1949. Even then many ways inherited from the past have survived to the present day.

MICHAEL SHERINGHAM

The Han

11

The Han Chinese are the descendants of the Yan and Yellow Emperors 4,000 to 5,000 years ago. The Yellow Emperor defeated all the ghosts and monsters and finally conquered and assimilated the tribe of the Yan Emperor, establishing the Huaxia, the Han Chinese.

ANCIENT CHINESE LEGEND

The Han people can be equated with the Chinese and their unique civilization, which has endured continuously through 3,000 years of recorded history and further back into prehistoric and Neolithic times. The Han Chinese can be distinguished from their neighbours and border peoples – Koreans, Mongols, Manchus, Tibetans, Uyghurs and Southeast Asian peoples – by their physique, language, culture and traditions, but within China itself the concept of Han identity becomes more blurred and hard to define.

Origins and geographical distribution

The heartland of the Han people is the Yellow River Basin, where sedentary, village communities based on agricultural livelihoods sprang up around 2500 BC. The well-watered alluvial plains of loess or loess-derived soil were ideal for farming, while the higher afforested outcrops provided wood and water for the growing population.

Historically, the Han, who now make up 92 per cent of the population of China, have moved southwards and eastwards through the centuries.

Han Shan Temple, Suzhou, China.

A man plays the suona, *a Chinese trumpet, at the Hua'er Festival in Huzhu county, Xining, Qinghai. Some 200,000 ethnic Han, Hui, Dongxiang, Salar, Tu, Baoan and Tibetan peoples gather on 6 June of the lunar calender singing folk songs characterized by sweet and soul-stirring tunes rich with varied motifs.*

As they pressed into new territory, they tended to settle in the valleys and lowland, agricultural areas. Ethnic minorities have been pushed up into the highlands and mountains, like in Yunnan in the southwest of China. In fact, the history of the Han Chinese has been the gradual colonialist expansion of their culture and sedentary style of life based on agriculture up to natural boundaries such as steppes, deserts, mountains and jungles. Their settlement has been characterized by the felling of forests for agricultural (including horticultural) farming and the domestication of animals.

Water control, in the form of transportation and irrigation canals and ditches, has been a mark of Chinese development and centralized administration since the Qin, even before they unified China in the 3rd century BC. The Chinese established their villages, towns and cities by rivers and coasts, developing commercial centres and trade to the frontiers of their territory.

Overall, the land occupied by the Han Chinese is more concentrated, particularly in the Yellow and Yangtze river basins, in contrast to the minorities who are scattered throughout two-thirds of the Chinese land. Of course, there has also been an overlapping and intermingling of Han and minority habitats, agricultural occupations and cultures, especially in recent decades.

The language

The Chinese language is also called Hanyu, literally 'language of the Han', and belongs to the Sino-Tibetan language family. The Chinese characters are one of the world's oldest forms of writing, dating back more than 4,000 years and based originally on pictographs, then later combined with ideographs. When Emperor Qin Shihuang unified China in 221 BC and built the Great Wall of China, he also instituted a unified system of writing Chinese characters, which were revised and simplified. The Chinese script is also the uniform factor in the tapestry of different spoken languages or dialects.

Although the same written language is used throughout the country, spoken Chinese varies widely, with different regions having their own dialects and pronunciation. There are seven main language groups in China. They are the northern dialect and the six primary southern dialects – Wu, Xian (Hunanese), Gan (Jiangxi dialect), Hakka, Cantonese and Min (Fujianese).

Hanyu is spoken by the Han, Hui, Manchu and other ethnic groups that make up the majority of the population. The northern or Mandarin dialect covers three quarters of China's territory and includes two thirds of its population. In 1955, the Chinese government officially established Mandarin Chinese, based on the northern dialect centred in Beijing, as the basis for the standard spoken language – Putonghua (literally 'common speech').

Han culture and identity

Apart from their distinctive language system, the Han people established culture and administration with which it became identified and which became the predominant national system. This culture is often associated with Confucianism (p. 68) and the mandarin administration which selected officials (mandarins) from outstanding scholars who proved themselves through passing a series of examinations based on the Confucian texts (p. 64).

The identity of the Chinese is particularly complicated and much debated and analysed. The Han people have established themselves as the dominant culture in China over centuries, regarding themselves as a civilizing force in relation to outsiders or even 'barbarians'. They have resisted, sometimes withdrawn before and significantly succumbed to foreign invasion and conquest by northern tribes and marauding armies, particularly by the Mongols (1271–1368) and Manchus (1644–1911).

During some periods, such as the 3rd to the 6th centuries AD, the Han retreated southwards under pressure from the northern 'barbarians'. Sometimes the north of China was occupied by small kingdoms set up by the nomadic invaders, such as the Wei, Toba, Jin, Xiongnu (Huns) and Jurchen, while the Han regrouped in the south under fragmented dynasties. The Han Chinese survived by assimilating these invaders into their own culture and political system to a great extent. They often regained supremacy over expanded areas of dominance, extending towards the Silk Road in the northwest and into Nam Viet and Annam (present-day Vietnam) to the south.

The imperial power and its trappings from palaces to porcelain has been associated with the prominence of the Han, but in fact, this Chinese culture is a 'hotch-potch' of cultures, amalgamating the traditions of all the peoples of the Chinese nation, including the minority people (such as Tibetans, Uyghur Muslims, Southeast Asian-related Dais and Zhuang, etc.). The Han might epitomize the Chinese cultural heritage, but it has absorbed foreign impact and influence through the centuries. Foreign invaders have, in turn, adapted their (often nomadic) styles of life and culture to the all-embracing and highly developed Han civilization. The monuments of Chinese tradition, such as the Forbidden City in Beijing (p. 105), are thus symbols of a multi-ethnic culture (p. 80).

Han Chinese dancers at the Spring Festival in Qinghai province.

JONATHAN FENBY

12 The Imperial System & its Downfall

Generation after generation has upheld Confucian teachings, stressing proper human relationships, between ruler and minister, father and son, superiors and subordinates, the high and the low. All in the proper place, just as hats and shoes are not interchangeable.

ZENG GUOFANG, GENERAL AND GENTRY LEADER OF THE MID-19TH CENTURY

Below *The badge of rank of an imperial civil servant, the peacock showing that it is of 'grade three' rank. There were nine grades, number one being the most senior.*

Below right *A figurine of an official of the Ming dynasty.*

The Chinese empire was regarded by its rulers and people as the centre of the world. It constituted the divinely anointed Middle Kingdom; its rulers were the Sons of Heaven, presiding over what appeared as a perfectly organized system to run the planet's most populous nation. For centuries, this provided one of the world's great administrations, until internal weakness and the challenge of modernity brought it down.

At the summit was the emperor, isolated in the Forbidden City in Beijing (p. 105) from the 15th century onwards, surrounded by elaborate rituals, his edicts lowered from a platform over the great Tiananmen Gate to be dispatched to the outer edges of the empire. The essential glue was supplied by Confucian teaching of the need for harmony and filial loyalty – the emperor was the father; so everybody owed him allegiance, just as he showed fealty to his ancestors.

Intricate graduations of rank ran through the court and society; each man had somebody to look up to and somebody to look down on. Nine grades of mandarins were distinguished by buttons of rank on their caps and birds embroidered on their robes. There was a strict hierarchy of banquets, and failure to observe court etiquette could bring banishment.

Below the emperor sat the Grand Council, the Grand Secretariat, six boards and nine ministries, plus Censors whose job was to keep the ruler informed. There were also court eunuchs, whose influence reached its zenith in the 17th century under the late Ming dynasty (1368–1644), but whose numbers fell from 3,100 in 1750 to 1,600 at the end of the 19th century. Governors of 18 provinces and magistrates of 1,300 districts completed the system, while villages were organized for self-policing.

The scholar gentry

The bureaucracy was recruited by imperial examinations, in which young men were tested on their knowledge of the classical texts of Confucius and other teachers. Three levels of tests started in the districts and reached their summit in front of the emperor. From this emerged a scholar-gentry class which, by the 19th century, numbered around 1.4 million men, or 7 million people with their families. Apart from brain power, success was achieved by absorbing the traditional values embodied in the classical texts. By offering material advancement and status to graduates, the system ensured that the best and brightest of the nation bought in to those values and would not, as in the West, form an intellectual and middle class to challenge the traditional holders of power. In contrast to the adversarial, democratic pattern

Above left *Ming woodcut of King Liang Wudi in a temple. Worshippers offer obeisance to the emperor rather than to the Buddha behind the altar.*

Above *Ceramic box lid from the reign of the Ming emperor Wanli depicts a case being tried before a district magistrate, who is seated at his desk.*

Left *Boys learning their rote lessons for imperial examinations.*

Imperial civil servants, having graduated from the Literary Examination, or jinshi, *parade before Emperor Guangxu (1875–1908) at his wedding.*

that evolved in Europe and America, the Chinese system seamlessly melded culture, society and politics, though a decision in the 19th century to start selling lower rank degrees somewhat tarnished it.

Below the gentry were hundreds of millions of peasants, living precarious lives, buffeted by recurrent natural disasters, inhabiting primitive dwellings on rudimentary diets, with no health care and often cut off from the rest of the nation by poor transport links. In theory, a bright young man – they were all men – could rise from such roots to the top by passing the three examinations; in practice, those whose family wealth and status gave them time to study emerged as the winners; for peasant youths, eking out a living was a full-time job.

This structure, which traced its origins to the Han dynasty (206 BC–AD 220), operated effectively when the empire was strong, notably at the height of the Qing dynasty in the later 17th and 18th centuries. But, when central power declined in the 19th century, its fault lines became apparent. There were not enough officials to run such a vast, heavily populated country. The court was split into factions. The emperors were weak, or infants. Corruption was endemic. Natural disasters became more frequent, and were seen as a sign of divine disapproval of the rulers. Banditry and rebellions spread.

The dynasty's status was hit by defeats in the 1840s and 1860 at the hands of Europeans, who imposed 'unequal treaties' that forced China to make territorial concessions and put foreigners outside national law. As child emperors sat on the throne, real power was wielded by the formidable Dowager Empress, Cixi, a concubine who rose through a palace coup in 1861 and dominated the court till her death in 1908. The dynasty suffered a further debacle in a catastrophic war with Japan in 1894–95, which was followed by the conservative reversal of an ambitious bid for reform. Cixi's disastrous alliance with the anti-foreign populist Boxer Rising of 1900 led to the court fleeing Beijing as a Western and Japanese force took the capital and imposed humiliating terms.

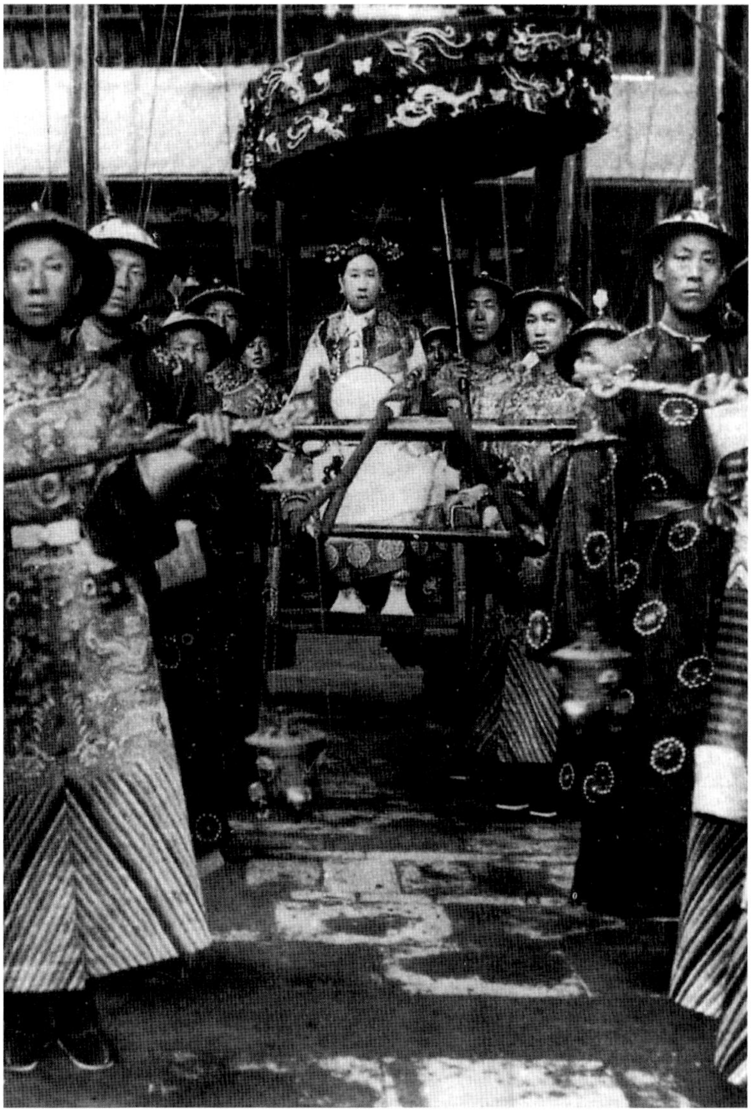

Dowager Empress Cixi surrounded by her eunuchs after the Boxer Rising.

Modernization

Other factors were at work to undermine the traditional ways. To deal with huge mid-19th century revolts, the Qing fell back on the provincial gentry, epitomized by Zeng Guofang from Hunan province who is quoted at the start of this entry. Scholar-generals saved the dynasty at enormous cost in lives, but they exacted a price. The rulers had to relinquish their monopoly on maintaining armies, allowing gentry figures to raise their own forces. To pay for these, they were permitted to levy local taxes.

As China embarked on its first attempt at modernization in the 1870s, using Western methods to develop industries, the leading figures came from the scholar-gentry. Loyal to the empire, they used official funds for finance, and their reliance on court favour restricted them to a dependent, conservative context. Still, the rise in provincial gentry power altered the balance of authority, along with the growth of modern armies staffed by officers seeking change. While they were not revolutionaries, the allegiance of such figures became strained as the dynasty showed it could not meet the high aspirations inherent in the system.

Another weakness sprang from the origin of the Qing in Manchuria, outside the Great Wall (p. 160). After conquering China in 1644, they maintained their roots in the northern plains, intermarrying with Mongol princes as well as fellow Manchus and, in the 18th century, extended their rule to the great western territory of Xinjiang. At their zenith, they headed a multi-ethnic domain that included the majority Han Chinese (p. 61), Manchus, Mongols and Muslims. Their emperors adopted the Chinese system along with its customs and beliefs, but they remained racially separate. Intermarriage of Manchus and Han was prohibited; unlike the Han, Manchu women did not have bound feet; Han men had to shave the front of their skulls and wear pigtails as a sign of submission. When the dynasty was at its height, this all gave the Qing strength, based on China's self-sufficient economy. When the throne's power and status declined, rising anti-Manchu feeling fuelled the revolutionary movement as it became ever clearer how the dynasty had let China fall behind other great powers. The resulting combination of internal fault lines and external pressure came together in 1911 to bring about the implosion of the system that had endured for more than 2,000 years but had been unable to adapt to the modern world.

NICHOLAS BUNNIN

13 Philosophy

When the Dao *prevails in your own state, to be poor and obscure is a disgrace; but when the* Dao *does not prevail in your own state, to be rich and honoured is a disgrace.*
CONFUCIUS, *ANALECTS* 8.13

The 17th-century philosopher and mathematician Leibniz considered that Chinese Confucian philosophy, ethics and government produced technology and literature that were prime exemplars of human creativity. But as interpreted by Neo-Confucian commentators such as Zhu Xi (1130–1200) and Wang Yangming (1472–1529), Confucianism had become a settled orthodoxy, rather than the contested doctrine that had emerged nearly 2,000 years earlier.

Ancient Chinese philosophy

Instead of articulating his thoughts in isolation, Confucius (551–479 BC) was only one of many figures seeking an intellectual and practical response to the decline of prosperous and stable Western Zhou society (*c.* 1046–771 BC) into the chaotic strife of the Warring States period (476–221 BC). Confucius and his rivals tried to persuade the rulers of different Chinese states to return China to unity, harmony and prosperity. They offered differing accounts of a *Dao*, a normative pattern modelled on nature or invented by men, to guide individual moral transformation and to shape social life. Their doctrines were preserved in later written texts, often in the form of collected exchanges between the sage and his followers, and by commentaries on these principal texts. Although in time these figures were seen as initiators of independent schools, recently discovered early versions of ancient texts indicate a richer interaction and mutual influence among these seminal figures than previously understood.

Underlying their individual perspectives were the doctrines of the *Yi Jing* (Book of Changes), which pictured the world in terms of creativity, flux, transformation and change. When in the dialogue *Cratylus*, Socrates argued that Greek metaphysical and ethical terms had been invented by the ancients for a world of flux and should be replaced by terms suitable for a real world of stable substance, he initiated central differences between the mainstreams of Western and Chinese philosophy. Similarly, in contrast to Greek and later Western philosophy, Chinese philosophy has been marked from early times by a conception of the self as a mind-heart that is both physical and mental, by a conception of reason that is not sharply distinguished from emotion, by a unity of the natural and the ethical which allows easy commerce between fact and value and by a conception of fundamental reality that is

A Qing-dynasty print based on a Tang-dynasty style, giving an idealized portrait of Confucius.

immanent rather than transcendent. In general, dichotomies in Chinese thought, unlike those in the West, are inclusive, each term embracing rather than excluding its opposite.

Although these broad differences are important, detailed study shows that many features legitimately ascribed as a major theme to one tradition also appear, at least as a minor motif, in the other. With this warning in mind, we can now look at some of the main figures in ancient Chinese philosophy.

Confucius and his followers

Confucius argued for a return to the important cultural rules embodied by the Zhou rites and for the cultivation of virtue, especially the virtue of *ren* (humanity). The rites distinguished the different roles in a structure of key human relationships. Self-transformation from an ordinary life pursuing individual advantage to the morally guided life of the gentleman and then to the morally perfected life of a sage is open through moral education to all, but only a few can expect to complete this difficult lifelong task. Rites and virtue are both necessary: without the guidance of proper rites, self-cultivation could not succeed; without the inward realization of virtue, the rites would be no more than empty forms.

For society, the most important self-transformation is that of the ruler. An actual ruler must, according to the doctrine of the 'rectification of names', satisfy the requirements of kingliness for society to be well ordered. A true king will communicate order and virtue throughout his domain without gesture or command. His ministers will be true ministers and his subjects true subjects. Thus, in a system of reciprocity and order shaped from the top, Zhou harmony and success will be restored.

Mencius (second half of the 4th century BC) and Xunzi (*c*. 298–235 BC) were the greatest early interpreters of Confucian thought. Mencius argued that goodness has its origin within us, both as an explanation and guide for our actions. The *Dao* is found in our nature and can be discovered by inward reflection. The seeds of goodness, however, need protection and cultivation to flourish and grow to maturity. Xunzi argued that goodness and our moral personality are products of human artifice rather than objects of inward study. The true *Dao* was invented or constructed by the ancient sages, but can be tested by its efficacy in promoting harmonious individual and social life. If the *Dao* were naturally within us, there would be no need for the central Confucian commitment to the structuring of our ethical life by rites.

Sages study and meditate upon the yin and yang symbol. Manchu-period silk painting.

Daoists

The Daoists Laozi (traditionally 6th century BC) and Zhuangzi (*c.* 370–300 BC) argued against Confucian moral education, cultivation of virtue and reliance on the meaning of ethical and social terms. All of these blocked or perverted the flow of natural human activity. Instead of the *Dao* being available to human rational discovery, invention or construction, Laozi held that the *Dao* that can be stated is not the true *Dao*: it is both ineffable and commonplace. Life is too complex for any set of rules to guide us. We are best left to free natural wandering with the accumulated burden of civilization stripped away. Instead of being, things and talk, we should seek nothingness, emptiness and silence. Non-action, not as immobility but as the expression of the *Dao*, is the best policy for both the Daoist ruler and his subjects.

Above *Song-dynasty statue of Laozi riding a water buffalo.*

Above right *Performers in traditional Chinese costume commemorate the 2,555th anniversary of the birthday of Chinese philosopher Confucius.*

Mohists and Legalists

From a different perspective, Mozi (*c.* 480–390 BC) and his followers (Mohists) challenged Confucian policy through the development of a scientific, or proto-scientific, attitude towards nature, language and society. Benevolent government should be based on universal love, according to which the well-being of each member of society should have significant weight. Institutions must be devised to obtain the good of all members of society, rather than according to the complex hierarchical determination of Confucian graded love that models political relations on those of the family. This intriguing view, which foreshadowed the development of modern utilitarian thought, ceased to have influence in China and was revived only in recent centuries.

The doctrines that provided intellectual guidance to Qin Shihuangdi, who returned China to unified rule in 221 BC, were those of Han Feizi

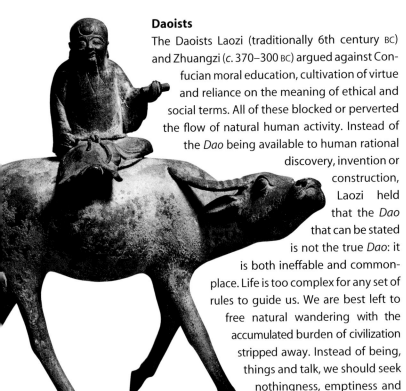

(*c.* 280–234 BC) and his Legalist followers. Social order is guaranteed by law rather than by virtue. The set of legal commands issued by the ruler should be publicly known, uniform throughout society and rigorously enforced. Even the enemies of the ruler should be rewarded for following the law, and even the friends of the ruler should be punished for breaking it. Because human beings are motivated by benefit and harm rather than by virtue, this policy would produce peaceful rule.

Later developments

If we add the later influence of technically sophisticated Buddhist doctrines from India in China's first great intellectual encounter with the West, we have the complex of resources that has shaped Chinese philosophy throughout its long and distinguished history. The great Neo-Confucians of the Song and Ming dynasties provided creative syntheses of Confucian, Daoist and Buddhist philosophies that can be compared with the synthesis of Greek and Christian thought in Aquinas. Over the last century, the most important Chinese philosophers have brought together Chinese and modern European thought, from Kant, Hegel and Marx to Wittgenstein and Heidegger, in similarly creative ways. Through their work, Chinese philosophy has a future as well as a past.

JOSEPH A. ADLER

Religion

14

The Perfect Man is godlike. Though the great swamps blaze, they cannot burn him; though the great rivers freeze, they cannot chill him; though swift lightning splits the hills and howling gales shake the sea, they cannot frighten him. A man like this rides the clouds and mist, straddles the sun and moon, and wanders beyond the four seas. Even life and death have no effect on him, much less the rules of profit and loss!

ZHUANGZI, 4TH CENTURY BC

One of the most remarkable things about Chinese religion is that certain patterns of thought and practice evident in the earliest known form – the divination and sacrificial rituals of the kings of the Shang dynasty (*c.* 1600– *c.* 1046 BC) – are still present today. These kings made offerings to their ancestors in the hope that the ancestors would bestow blessings on the royal family and the state, and they practised divination (by interpreting the cracks on heated animal bones) to determine the wishes of the ancestors and their satisfaction with the offerings. Many Chinese people today make ritual offerings at home altars to their ancestors and in temples to a wide variety of gods. And in the temples they practise newer forms of divination for basically the same reasons as the Shang kings.

This ritual dyad of divination and sacrifice forms the core of what today is called 'popular religion' or 'folk religion'. In popular religion gods, ghosts and ancestors have been worshipped in a great variety of ways for three millennia. Although the natural life of popular religion was interrupted in the early decades of the People's Republic of China (PRC, 1949–now), it has thrived continuously in other Chinese communities such as Taiwan and Singapore, and in the PRC today it is undergoing an astonishing revival.

Chinese popular religion can be considered the fertile soil from which the text-based religions of Confucianism and Daoism have sprung. Buddhism, which was brought from India in the first century, joined those two as the 'Three Religions' of traditional China. But these three always co-existed with popular religion, and all four were constantly influencing one another.

Confucianism

As we have read in the previous entry, Confucius, or Master Kong (551–479 BC), began a scholarly

Above *Seals from Confucius's* Analects. *Top: 'If you know a thing, say so; if not, admit it. That is true knowledge.' Bottom: 'If you desire haste, you will not make real progress and achieve success.'*

Left *This rubbing from a Han tomb depicts some of Confucius's disciples including Zilu (second from right) and Tseng-tzu to whom is attributed 'The Great Learning'. The youngest is probably Yan Hui, Confucius's best and favourite pupil, who died at thirty-two.*

An 18th-century painting of Mencius.

tradition with clear religious dimensions. Central to it is the concept and symbol of Heaven (*tian*), which is the ultimate reality and the source of moral values. Ancestor worship was incorporated into the Confucian tradition, as well as the worship of sages, such as Confucius and his later follower Mencius (Mengzi). Central to Confucian thought is the claim that moral inclinations are essential to human nature, and that only through the nourishment of family life, education and benevolent government can those inclinations fully develop. Confucianism has therefore always been closely associated with the family, with education (Confucius is the 'patron saint' of teachers) and with public service.

In the 2nd century BC Confucianism was adopted by the Han dynasty as the official ideology of government; but this eventually led to an increasingly conservative, politicized application of its essentially religious humanism. After the 19th century, when China was brought to its knees by European colonial domination (the Opium Wars of the 1840s) and a devastating rebellion led by a convert to Christianity (the Taiping Rebellion), Confucianism became the whipping boy for all that was wrong with the imperial system. This reached its peak in the Communist PRC during the Cultural Revolution of 1966–76.

But since 1980 there has been a nearly complete reversal of the negative evaluation of Confucianism among Chinese intellectuals and government officials. The virtual death of Marxist-

A Sui-dynasty painting of Daoist masters presenting the emperor with a new edition of the Dao De Jing, *the classic Daoist text attributed to Laozi.*

Maoist thought in the PRC and the enormous growth in the economic sphere have resulted in a perceived moral vacuum, which Confucian values are beginning to fill. Meanwhile, Confucianism has continued to define the worldviews of many Chinese intellectuals outside the PRC, and has also appealed to many Westerners, assuring it a future both within and outside of China.

Daoism

Daoism in some respects can be considered the *yin* (dark, receptive, yielding) to Confucianism's *yang* (light, creative, active) in Chinese culture. The earliest form of Daoism was not a full-fledged religion but merely an intellectual current, stemming largely from two classic texts: the *Laozi* or *Dao De Jing* (traditionally attributed to a mythical 6th-century BC figure named Laozi, or 'Old Master'), and the *Zhuangzi* (by a 4th-century BC philosopher called Zhuangzi, or 'Master Zhuang').

The *Dao De Jing* ('Classic of the Way and Virtue'), one of the most frequently translated pieces in world religions, is a short text addressed primarily to the ruler of a state. In fact it was compiled from anonymous sources in the 3rd century BC, near the end of a 500-year period of political disunity and warfare, and proposes a philosophy of statecraft and personal cultivation based on 'non-action' (*wu-wei*). This means avoidance of deliberate, goal-directed action in favour of spontaneous action that is in accord with natural patterns of change. The foundation of these patterns is the *Dao* ('path'), which in the *Dao De Jing* is the origin of all phenomena and the path to be followed to find harmony with the natural world.

The *Zhuangzi* stresses that all ordinary knowledge is limited by our particular perspectives, preventing us from understanding the *Dao* because the *Dao* is the universal process of change and transformation. But by practising certain forms of meditation we can transcend our perspectival limitations and attune ourselves to the *Dao*.

In the 2nd century AD a new form of Daoism emerged, based on a series of revelations from Laozi to a man named Zhang Daoling (Laozi by this time was conceived as a god). This was the beginning of Daoism as a full-fledged religion, with a community of believers, a large pantheon of deities, a priesthood, and several complex systems of rituals and meditation. Today there are two major sects of Daoism in China, one with a largely hereditary priesthood and another with a monastic system for training priests.

According to Buddhist and Daoist conceptions of the afterlife, the dead live as ghosts for a while, and are taken to purgatory to atone for their sins on earth. This Tang-dynasty illustration to a Buddhist text shows sinners being punished before an underworld official.

Buddhism

Buddhism, which originated in India in the 5th century BC, entered China in the 1st century AD and over the course of several hundred years was transformed from a foreign religion to a distinctly Chinese tradition. Although the monastic element of Buddhism at first struck many Chinese as disrespectful to one's parents and anti-social, the teachings of Buddhism were new and profound, so it eventually attracted many followers – especially women, who could become nuns. (Women's options in traditional Chinese society were primarily limited to the roles of wives and mothers.) Several new schools of Buddhism emerged in China, including Chan (or Zen in Japanese), reflecting influences of both Confucianism and Daoism.

Buddhism brought with it certain beliefs that were common assumptions in India but new to China. One is the eternal cycle of rebirth, or *samsara*. Another is the idea of *karma*, or 'moral causality', which means that every intentional

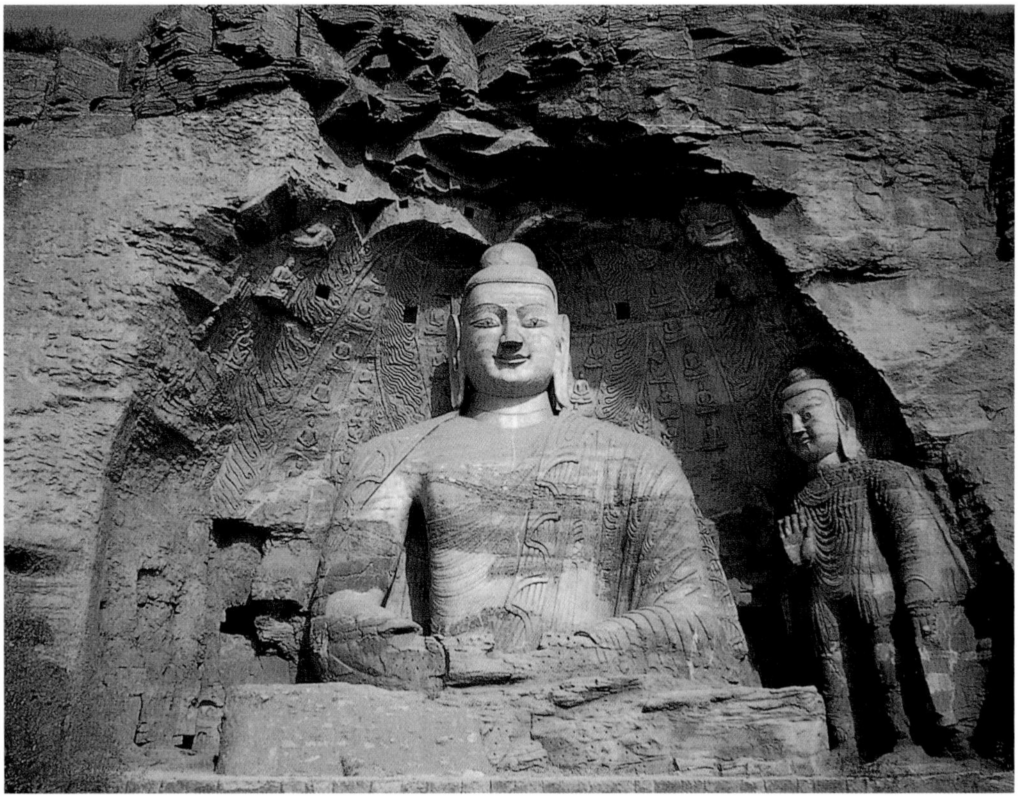

A colossal Buddha sits at 13.7 m (45 ft), carved into the cliffs of Cave 20 at Datong, Shanxi, in the Northern Wei dynasty. A smaller 'attending' Buddha stands to his left.

deed has an effect that will occur later, either in this life or the next. This is the force, so to speak, that keeps us trapped in the cycle of rebirth. In addition to these, Buddhist thought is based on the premise that everything that exists is impermanent, and that nothing is what it is independently of multiple causal factors.

Human beings naturally assume that we each have an independent, autonomous 'self' or 'soul', which remains constant as our outward attributes change. But the Buddha ('enlightened one') said that this is a mistake, and that we are complex, ever-changing, psycho-physical systems. Moreover, he said, the habit of thinking in terms of an independent, permanent 'self' leads us to crave things, and all desires are ultimately frustrated because nothing is permanent.

Therefore, by eliminating the false notion of 'self' – or by understanding that concept to be merely a conventional designation for the impermanent, dynamic 'system' that we really are – we can eliminate all craving and the frustration or dissatisfactoriness (*duhkha*, or 'suffering') that

Right *Seated Bodhisattva made of gilt bronze, in the more feminine southern artistic style of the Song dynasty.*

A Qing-dynasty painting showing a farmer and his family giving thanks for a successful harvest. 'Popular', or 'folk', religion lived alongside the three great Chinese religions of Confucianism, Daoism and Buddhism.

results from it. This is the key to a satisfying life and the way to break the karmic cycle of rebirth.

Chinese Buddhism retained this core of Buddhist thought. But while Indian Buddhism had understood the ultimate goal of human life as *nirvana*, or 'extinguishing' the karmic cycle, Chinese Buddhists tended to speak more in terms of 'enlightenment' as a transformed state of wisdom and compassion that would, in turn, positively transform society. Thus the social emphasis of Confucianism and the Daoist affirmation of the natural world were incorporated into Chinese Buddhist thought.

The religions of China have rarely been at odds with each other. The Chinese people have always been free to mix and match their beliefs and practices, although some, of course, have identified more or less exclusively with one or another. The relative harmony of Confucianism, Daoism, Buddhism and Chinese popular religion throughout history reflects the ideal of harmony between the natural, social and spiritual worlds that each tradition, in its own way, strives to realize.

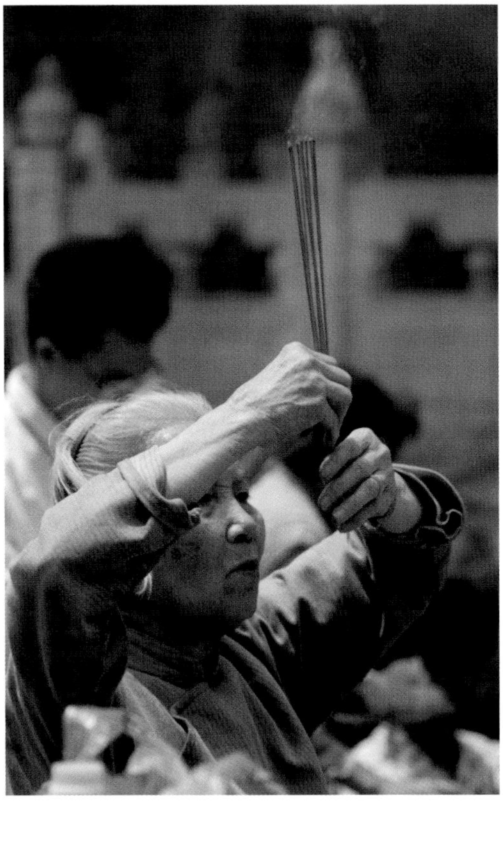

Daoist worshipper with incense sticks in modern Hong Kong.

QU LEI LEI

15 Taiji & the Dao

At first, form is needed.
Then doubt and inhibition must be dispelled.
Eventually, form is celebrated with joy
And expression becomes formless.
DENG MINGDAO, 20TH-CENTURY DAOIST AUTHOR

The symbol of taiji, *a philosophical concept that literally means 'supreme ultimate'. The* yin *(black, receptive) and* yang *(white, active) of this symbol represent all opposing elements in the universe.*

Taiji, also known as *tai chi*, means both the absolute and the infinite, a state that we cannot imagine, nor ever reach. This expression comes from the great Chinese classic, the *Yi Jing*, and is the central concept of Daoist philosophy. *Taiji quan* ('supreme ultimate fist') evolved in China by the 16th century as a soft martial art inspired by the *taiji* principles of *yin* and *yang*: resisting incoming force using the opposing force of a relaxed body.

The four layers of meaning of *taiji*

1 Everything in the universe is made from two separate elements that are in direct opposition to each other. These are called the *yin* and the *yang*, and are represented by the black and white parts of the *taiji* symbol. They represent, for example, heaven and earth, above and below, night and day, hot and cold, male and female – without one element the other has no meaning.

Taken from a Daoist medical work, this woodblock print drawn in 1622 shows the balancing of yin *and* yang.

2 The *yin* and the *yang* are in constant flow, and thus maintain a constant balance.
3 Each element contains a part of the other: there is *yang* in *yin*, and *yin* in *yang*.
4 As they flow, the *yin* and the *yang* are constantly changing into each other.

It is from these principles that the universe is formed. This way of looking at everything in the universe lies at the heart of Daoist philosophy.

The character *yi* 易 comprises elements of the sun 日 and moon 月. It represents the changes of *yin* and *yang*, and the idea of life without end. In ancient times, *yi* was the art of divination, and its role was to seek the *Dao* ('way') of heaven in order to understand the human world. It was also applied to the study of philosophical thought relating to the *Dao* of nature, life and society.

The *Yi Jing*

The *Yi Jing*, 'Book of Changes' (also known as 'Source of the Great Way'), has had a huge influence throughout Chinese history. Thousands of commentaries make it the most revered and most annotated of all the Chinese classics.

According to legend, there were once three *yi* – the *Xia Yi*, the *Shang Yi* and the *Zhou Yi* – relating to the Xia, Shang and Zhou dynasties respectively. The divinatory symbols were created by Fu Xi, and later a character was ascribed to each symbol to express its meaning. The *Xia Yi* and *Shang Yi* were lost a long time ago. The only one that has survived is the *Zhou Yi*, studied, arranged and edited by King Wen of the Zhou dynasty (*c.* 11th century BC). Today when we talk about the *Yi Jing*, we are actually referring to the *Zhou Yi*.

Trigram	old character	name	nature	modern character	Pinyin
☰	乾	*qian*	heaven	天	*tian*
☷	坤	*kun*	earth	地	*di*
☳	震	*zhen*	thunder	雷	*lei*
☴	巽	*xun*	wind	風	*feng*
☵	坎	*kan*	water	水	*shui*
☲	离	*li*	fire	火	*huo*
☶	艮	*gen*	mountain	山	*shan*
☱	兑	*dui*	marsh	澤	*ze*

Table explaining the different divinatory symbols used by Daoist philosophers to find the Dao, the path to enlightenment.

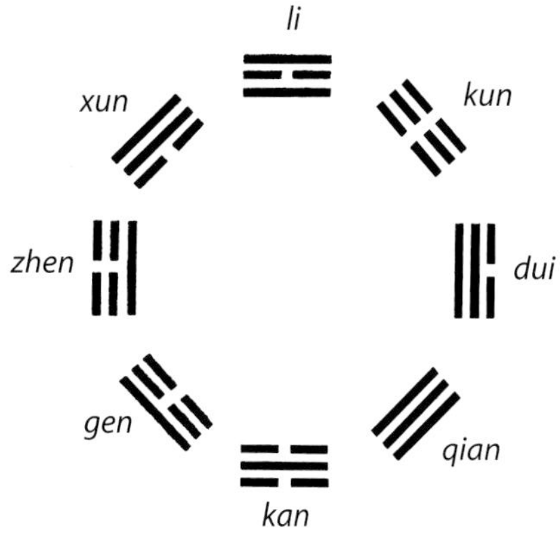

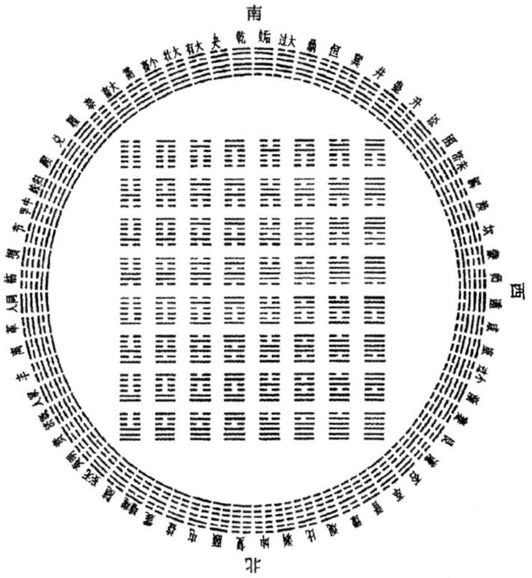

Far left Taiji *symbols as laid out in the* Yi Jing. *This diagram shows the 8 combinations of trigrams (three solid or broken lines) joined to form the hexagon of the* Yi Jing.

Left *More* taiji *symbols: the 64 combinations of hexagrams.*

The *Yi Jing* comprises 8 trigrams and 64 hexagrams. Each trigram is made from three lines, which are either broken or unbroken. It has its own form, its own name and associated character, and represents a particular aspect of nature. Each hexagram (two trigrams) has six lines, which are either broken or unbroken. Advances in science have revealed that the 64 hexagrams follow the same principle as the binary system.

The *Dao De Jing*

The *Dao De Jing*, traditionally written by Laozi (6th–5th centuries BC), is the main Daoist classic of the pre-Qin period (pre-221 BC) and Laozi is the most important Daoist figure (see p. 68). Legends tells us that he was from the state of Chu and was a contemporary of Confucius. In his time as an official at the Zhou court, Confucius had once visited him to pay his respects.

The *Dao De Jing* that we read today is the same one that was arranged by Laozi in the early Warring States period. There are 81 chapters, and over 5,000 characters in the book. Not only is this philosophy written in verse, it is also a penetrating account of the contradictions of human life and social issues, offering concepts and methods for considering and resolving these issues. Most of all, Laozi advocates abandoning sagehood, divesting oneself of knowledge, non-action, and cleansing one's mind until it is completely clear, for only then can one achieve a state of harmony and balance.

Below *A* taiji *master exercising in Beijing. In northern China, the predominant language is Mandarin and the pronunciation* taiji *is used, whereas the southern Cantonese say* taichi.

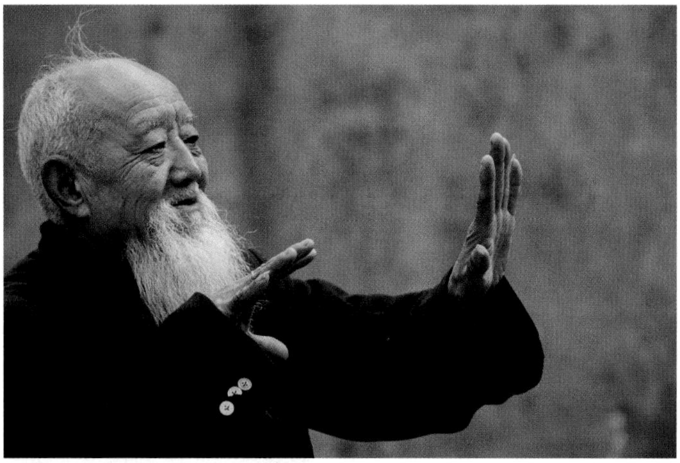

QU LEI LEI

16 Martial Arts

Train both Internal and External. External training includes the hands, the eyes, the body and stances. Internal training includes the heart, the mind, the spirit and strength.
MARTIAL ARTS MOTTO

武
术

The Chinese symbols for wu *(war) and* shu *(art).*

Though traditionally known as *kung fu*, martial art is nowadays called *wushu*. *Wu* means war/fighting, and *shu* means art/technique. The origins of *wushu* go back to ancient times when man wrestled with wild animals, fought sickness and disease and engaged with the enemy in physical combat. It has evolved over thousands of years, bringing together medicine and philosophy, and has gradually matured into a rich ensemble of forms, with regional and stylistic differences.

Today in China, there are five main forms of *wushu*: *quanshu* – the foundation for all *wushu* that includes *changzhang* (open hands), *taijiquan* (*taiji*) and *xingyi* (mind forms); *qixie* – which uses 18 different forms of weapons including knives, swords, guns and sticks; *duilian* – sparring with bare hands and weapons; *duikang* – defending, including freehand boxing; and *jiti* – group performances of *wushu*.

The Shaolin Monastery

The Shaolin Monastery lies deep in the woods on Shaoshi Shan, a mountain near Dengfeng in Henan province. It is one of the best known Buddhist temples in the world. The Shaolin Monastery was built in AD 495. In 527 the Indian monk Bodhidharma came to the monastery to teach Chan (Zen) Buddhism. Bodhidharma (*Damo* in Chinese) is regarded as the father of Chan Buddhism in China, and the Shaolin Monastery is known as the home of Chan Buddhism. The method of Chan Buddhism is known in Chinese as *biguan*, literally 'staring at the wall', and involves sitting calmly until one reaches enlightenment. Sitting cross-legged for long

A warrior monk displays his kung fu *skills in the forest of stupas at the Shaolin Monastery. Dengfeng, Henan province.*

Reconstruction of a silk chart of 168 BC excavated at Mawangdui. It shows 44 figures engaged in kung fu *moves.*

periods is very tiring, and the monks would practise martial arts to refresh and invigorate themselves. This is why the Shaolin style, known as *Shaolin quan*, is often said to have been created by Dharma. He studied the movement of the tiger, monkey, bird and snake, and put them together to form the *xingyi quan* (the mind forms) and *luohan shiba shou* (the 18 hand movements of the *luohan*, a magical disciple of the Buddha) and teach them to students.

Shaolin Monastery is known throughout the world for Chan Buddhism and *wushu*. Towards the end of the Sui dynasty, when Li Shimin (598–650) engaged in battle against Wang Shichong, 13 monks from the monastery gave their help, rescued Li Shimin and helped him to victory. When Li became the founding emperor of the Tang dynasty, he rewarded the Shaolin Monastery generously, and with his imperial support, it very soon became one of the most important Buddhist monasteries in the world, with over 2,000 monks. In the Song dynasty, Shaolin developed its own outstanding style and technique of *wushu*, known as the Shaolin School, with over 700 different forms of martial arts.

Inside the Shaolin Monastery, in the famous Hall of the Thousand Buddhas, there are two treasured wall paintings: 'The Five Hundred Luohans' and 'Forms of the Shaolin School'. To the east of the Monastery is the forest of stupas, or Buddhist monuments. With over 250 brick tombs dating from the Tang dynasty to the Qing dynasty, this is the largest group of stupas in China. A kilometre to the northwest is a little temple built in the Song dynasty, which is known as Dharma's Hut. Beyond this are the Wurufeng Mountains and Dharma's Cave, where the Dharma is said to have 'stared at the wall' for nine years.

The Shaolin culture, a synthesis of Chan Buddhism, martial arts and medicine, has emerged from an accumulation of history and culture of over 1,500 years.

Against a background portraying the main gate of Henan's Shaolin Monastery, Shaolin kung fu *monks perform in Kuala Lumpur.*

MICHAEL DILLON

17

Ethnic Minorities

Although there are a little over ten million non-Chinese in China, including Mongols, Manchus, Tibetans and Tartars, their number is small compared with the purely Chinese population, four hundred million in number, which has a common racial heredity, common religion and common tradition and customs. It is one nationality!

SUN YAT-SEN, *SANMIN ZHUYI* ('THREE PEOPLE'S PRINCIPLES'), 1924

On the surface, the people of China today might appear to be one single ethnic group as Sun Yat-sen, the father of the Chinese Republic, claimed. China's 1.3 billion citizens are no longer dressed in almost identical clothes as they were in the days of the Cultural Revolution, but they all seem to speak the same language and have a common culture. Dig a little deeper, however, and this facade of conformity and uniformity swiftly evaporates. China is a multiethnic, multilingual and multicultural society. It is true that the language and culture of the Han Chinese people dominate, especially in the public arena, but even among the Han themselves there are considerable cultural and linguistic differences. Spoken Mandarin and Cantonese are as different from each other as Portuguese is from Romanian even though they are sometimes referred to as dialects.

Zhuang woman in traditional dress. Ethnic minorities distinguish themselves through their clothing.

Beyond the Han, China is home to a variety of ethnic minority groups, who are categorized as Minority Nationalities (*shaoshu minzu*), a term derived from the system of ethnic classification that was used in the Soviet Union during the Stalin period. Their languages, cultures and religions in most cases have very little in common with the Han.

Minority people are found everywhere in China, including Beijing and the other major cities. They may work in the same kind of employment and live in the same areas as the Han, but the distinctiveness of their communities is most apparent in their historical homelands, some of which have been designated autonomous regions by the government of the People's Republic. The majority of these homelands are on the frontiers, notably on China's borders with Central Asia, but also in the southwest, particularly in the province of Yunnan.

Numbers

The Chinese state formally recognizes 55 minority nationalities, the most recently acknowledged being the Jinuo of Yunnan who were granted nationality status in 1979. The largest group is the Zhuang of Guangxi in southern China numbering 16 million. The smallest is the Lhoba of Tibet of whom there are fewer than 3,000. The minorities number more than 106 million, comprise 8.4 per cent of the total population of China but occupy 60 per cent of China's territory.

Mongols, Manchus and Tibetans

Some ethnic groups have played a more prominent role in Chinese history and society than others.

The 5.8 million Mongols who live mainly in Inner Mongolia and the northeast are closely related to the Mongols of (Outer) Mongolia, and more distantly to the Buryat Mongols of Russia. They are united by their language and culture, their nomadic heritage and their devotion to Tibetan Buddhism. During the Cultural Revolution, many of the Buddhist monasteries of Inner Mongolia were destroyed by the Red Guards or fell into disuse. Some have become museums but others are being restored.

The 10.6 million Manchus, originally from the northeast, were also originally tribal nomads, but when the Ming dynasty was on the point of collapse in 1644 they invaded China and put their own emperor on the Dragon Throne. The Manchus ruled China as the Qing dynasty until 1911 when they were replaced by a predominantly Han Chinese Republican government. Although they ruled in a coalition with Mongol bannermen and a Han Chinese elite, the influence of the Manchu was powerful and Manchu garrisons were established throughout China. The Manchu language, which is completely unrelated to Chinese but has some connection with Mongolian, gradually died out in common usage but remained as a language of the imperial court until the end of the dynasty. The Xibo (or Sibe) people of Xinjiang, descendants of Manchu troops sent to the region, speak a form of Manchu.

Many Tibetans would be uncomfortable with being classified as a Chinese ethnic minority and some would prefer to be citizens of an independent Tibet. There are 5.4 million Tibetans living in

Above *Tibetan dancers performing at the Chinese Ethnic Culture Park.*

Below *Two Manchu ladies in a rock garden in late 19th-century China.*

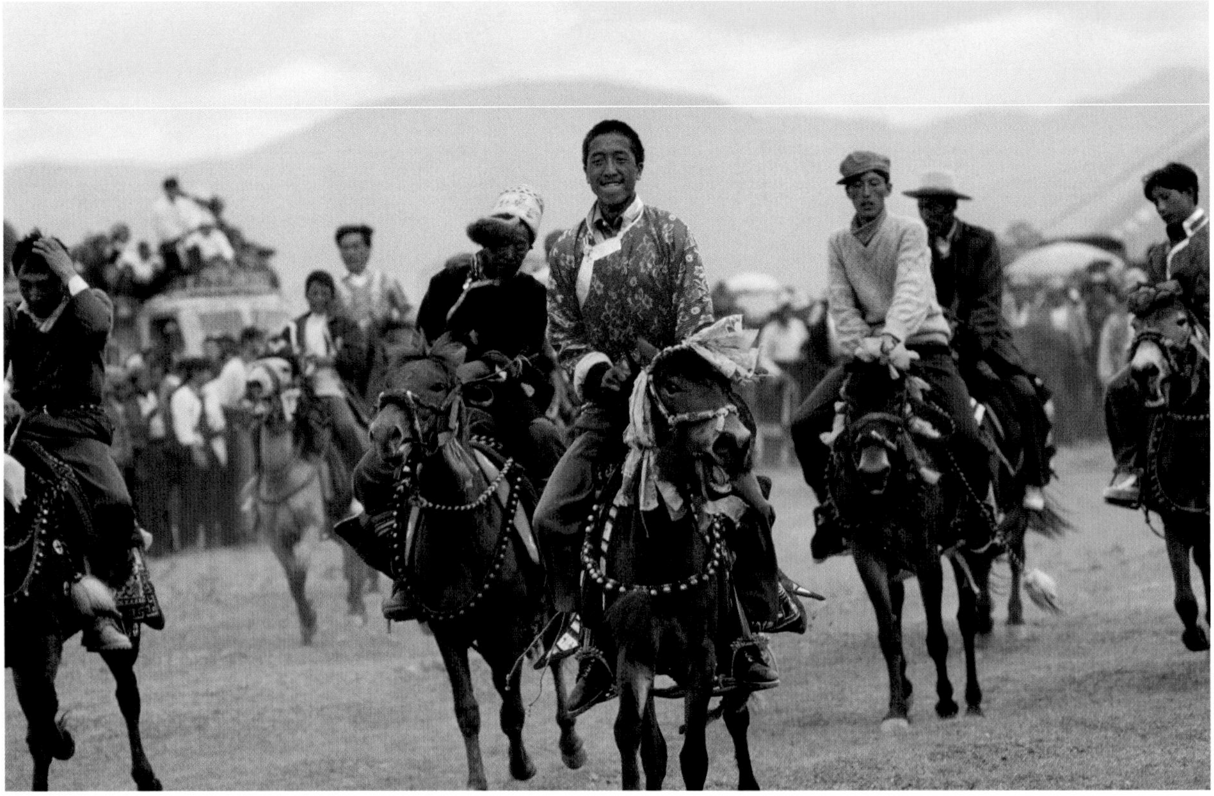

Tibetan men and boys ride horses fitted out with colourful woven bridles (Tibet Autonomous Region).

China, not only in the Tibetan Autonomous Region which is ruled by Beijing from its administrative centre, Lhasa, but in the provinces of Gansu, Qinghai and Sichuan, parts of which belonged to old Tibet which was independent between 1911 and the creation of the People's Republic of China in 1949. Tibetan Buddhism with its hierarchy of monasteries and lamas is quite separate from Buddhism as practised by the Han Chinese, and the Tibetan language uses a writing system derived from ancient Indian scripts.

Uyghurs, Hui and other ethnic groups

The 8.4 million Uyghurs of Xinjiang are a Muslim Turkic people and their language, religion and culture have far more in common with the Uzbeks in former Soviet Central Asia than with the Han Chinese. Frequently referred to as restive, and stigmatized as terrorists with very little justification by the Chinese authorities since 2001, they struggle to maintain their identity in a state that is bent on assimilating them to Han norms.

A Hui worshipper strolling through the courtyard of Da Qingzhen si, one of the most famous Chinese mosques (Xi'an, Shaanxi province).

The Hui are an interesting hybrid group in that they are Muslims of Central Asian and Middle Eastern ancestry but speak Chinese. They number about 10 million and have settled all over China, but they have had the greatest impact, both in terms of numbers and culture, in the northwest, particularly in Gansu province and Ningxia which is formally designated a Hui Autonomous Region. They speak the Chinese of their home region, but this is augmented by Arabic and Persian terms which have been incorporated for centuries to convey religious and cultural meanings.

Yunnan province (p. 48) on China's border with Burma and Vietnam has the most complex ethnic mix of any part of China. The different groups including the Dai, the Yao and the Nakhi (Naxi) are relatively small and widely dispersed. They speak languages related to Thai and Vietnamese and other languages of Southeast Asia. Unlike the minorities in the northern and northwestern border areas, no single group dominates the province. Chinese Communist Party officials attempting to classify the different cultures tended to regard them as primitive and indeed their economic level and social organization resemble types found in Asia many centuries ago.

The Communist Party's policy on ethnic minorities was based on the practice of the Soviet Union, but also drew on its own historical contacts with minority groups during the Long March at a time when it was consciously seeking to distance itself from the policies of the Kuomintang Nationalists who had neglected ethnic affairs.

On paper the policies are designed to give equality to minority groups and ensure at least a token representation in bodies such as the Chinese People's Political Consultative Conference. In practice, ethnic minorities and their cultures have suffered considerable discrimination, especially during periods of Maoist radicalism such as the Great Leap Forward and the Cultural Revolution. There is little sympathy among the majority Han population for expressions of minority ethnic identity and even less for demands for political independence by some Uyghurs and Tibetans.

A traditional musical gathering of the Nakhi (or Naxi) people.

VICTOR H. MAIR

18 The Tarim Mummies

Of all the Rong of the Western Regions, the appearance of Wusun is most peculiar. Those of the Hu today who have blue-green eyes and red beards and who look like macaques are their descendants.
YAN SHIGU, COMMENTARY TO *HISTORY OF THE HAN DYNASTY*, 7TH CENTURY AD

The far west of China is home to the world's largest and best preserved collection of naturally formed, prehistoric mummies. Hundreds of human corpses, many of them startlingly lifelike, have been recovered from dozens of sites located mainly along the eastern and southern edges of the Tarim Basin, Xinjiang.

This part of the world is perfectly suited for the preservation of organic remains. First of all, the Tarim Basin is filled by the Taklamakan desert, one of the largest and most arid sandy expanses on earth. Secondly, terribly cold winters slow down (or stop completely) the growth of bacteria, and very hot summers lead to rapid desiccation. Thirdly, many of the burial sites with the best preserved mummies are characterized by highly saline soils, which also acts to inhibit putrefaction.

Right *Ur-David, or the Chärchän Man.*

Below *View over the Taklamakan desert.*

History

The Tarim mummies date primarily to the Bronze Age and Early Iron Age, roughly the 2nd and 1st millennia BC, though a large number dating to the 1st millennium AD have also been found in the neighbouring Turfan Depression and elsewhere, mostly in the eastern part of the region. Some of these early inhabitants of the Western Regions were known to the ancient Chinese by such names as Rong, Wusun and Hu. According to extensive, detailed studies of geneticists and physical anthropologists, the earliest specimens are uniformly of west Eurasian extraction. During the 1st millennium BC, however, East Asian features begin to show up, and they gradually increase until, by the end of the 1st millennium AD, there are no more European-looking mummies. Nevertheless, the genetic contributions of the early inhabitants to the current populations persist, since the Uyghurs, Kazakhs, Kirghiz and others who live in and around the Tarim Basin today possess anywhere between about 30 per cent and 70 per cent European genetic characteristics.

A few of the mummies were first cursorily observed by

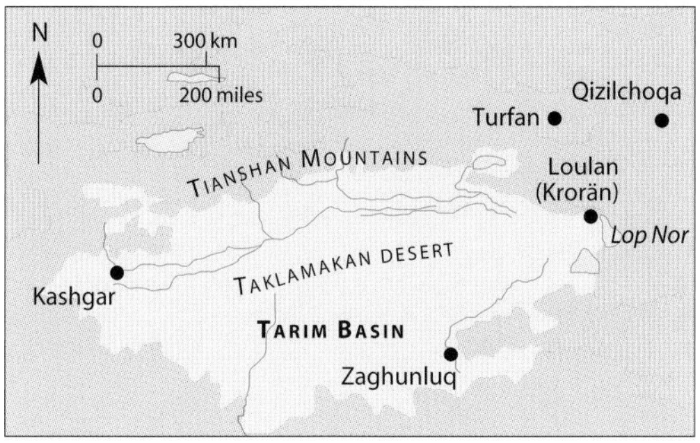

Left *The Tarim Basin area, Xinjiang Autonomous Region. Small River Cemetery No. 5 is about 160 km (100 miles) west of Lop Nor lake.*

European explorers in the early 20th century, but no serious studies were conducted. Around the same time, however, medieval manuscripts were found in the region, and their decipherment revealed that the dominant inhabitants were speakers of Indo-European languages, namely, Tocharian, Khotanese and Sogdian. All of these languages became extinct by the beginning of the 2nd millennium AD. They were displaced by speakers of Turkic languages from the east, who are still the chief occupants of the region, though Han Chinese from yet further east are gradually achieving parity in numbers.

Full-scale excavation

It was only in the late 1970s, with the initiation of massive construction projects in the region, that

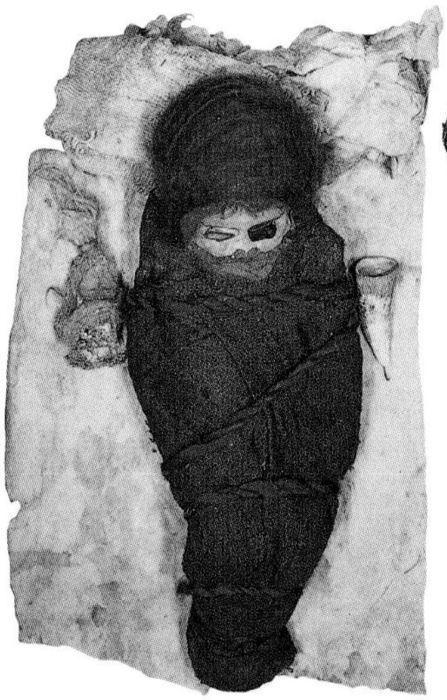

Above left *Little Baby Blue Bonnet, found with Ur-David.*

Above *The Beauty of Krorän.*

Left *Aurel Stein with members of his expedition and Dash II (one of his identically named dogs) at Ulugh-mazar, c. 1908.*

Two of the Tarim mummies, showing the amazingly well-preserved textiles that covered their bodies.

large numbers of mummies and skeletal remains began to appear. Chinese and Uyghur archaeologists and anthropologists carried out limited investigations on the mummies during the 1980s, but it was not until the 1990s that knowledge of the mummies became common throughout the world and an international research project was launched to study them in depth. Subsequently, some of the Tarim mummies achieved worldwide renown, including the Beauty of Krorän (Loulan) who dates to approximately 1800 BC, Ur-David or Chärchän Man from the village of Zaghunluq and dating to around 1000 BC, and Little Baby Blue Bonnet who was found next to Ur-David.

The most sensational event concerning the Tarim mummies in the first few years of the 21st century was the complete excavation of the Small River Cemetery No. 5, about 160 km (100 miles) to the west of Lop Nor. This yielded dozens of extremely well-preserved mummies and a multitude of revelatory artifacts dating to the early part of the 2nd millennium BC.

Linguistic discoveries

Among the results of these recent scholarly initiatives is the realization that some of the mummies undoubtedly spoke Iranian languages such as the predecessors of Khotanese and Sogdian, and others – perhaps the earliest ones – may have spoken Tocharian. The re-emergence of Tocharian is particularly important, since Tocharian is – next to Hittite – the oldest Indo-European language. In addition, if anything, it resembles western Indo-European languages like Celtic and Italic more than it does eastern ones like Indic and Iranian. The fact that Tocharian speakers were located right next to Sinitic (Chinese) speakers – at the end of the Gansu Corridor leading down into the East Asian Heartland – is of monumental significance.

Whereas scholars formerly had only an occasional hint of the impact of Indo-European upon Sinitic (for example, the Chinese word for 'honey' was recognized nearly a century ago as having been borrowed from Tocharian), they now have access to a broad array of historical, archaeological, mythological, and other types of evidence that substantiate the role of the Tocharians and other Indo-European peoples in linking eastern and western Eurasia already from at least the 2nd millennium BC.

Artifacts and clothing

Research on the Tarim mummies and their associated artifacts has already achieved impressive results. For example, it has been documented that diagonal twill plaids from the Qizilchoqa site near Qumul (Hami) dating to *c.* 1200 BC closely resemble roughly contemporaneous Celtic plaids from central and northern Europe. However, additional studies of the dyes and the wool (including the DNA of the animals that provided the wool) need to be carried out.

Not only were the Tarim Basin people pastoralists who possessed superb wool-weaving and felt-making skills, they were also agriculturalists who planted wheat. It is highly significant that both domesticated ovicaprids (sheep and goats) and wheat were transmitted from West Asia to East Asia before the Bronze Age reached China around the middle of the 2nd millennium BC.

The discovery of the Tarim Basin mummies and investigations carried out on them and their related artifacts during the 20th century and the start of the 21st century have completely transformed our understanding of the dynamics of Eurasian history. With continued multidisciplinary research on all aspects of the mummies, scholars are sure to learn even more about the nature and development of civilization during the crucial, formative years of the Bronze Age and Iron Age.

NI YIBIN

Circuses & Acrobats

19

His Majesty arrived at the Platform of Peaceful Joy ... watched the wondrous feats such as wrestling, cauldron-lifting, pole-climbing, sword-juggling, tightroping....

ZHANG HENG, *WESTERN METROPOLIS RHAPSODY*, AD 78–139

The circus and acrobatic feats were often collectively performed in ancient China at festivals and other mass gatherings and formed the bulk of *baixi* – 'a myriad of variety shows'. The earliest juggling props were excavated in Daxi-culture sites (6400–5200 BC): these clay balls are hollow with decorative scratches or stamped patterns on the surface and some later ones bear printed designs and can serve as a rattle to enhance the effects during performance because they enclose some small pebbles. Such balls also appear on stone carvings installed in tombs of the 3rd century AD.

Jesters

Classic texts reveal that retainers of the rich and powerful and jesters in court fare prominently in the budding stage of the Chinese circus. During the Warring States period (475–221 BC), Lord Mengchang managed to flee the Qin state with the help of his retainer, a bird mimicry artist whose vivid imitation of a cock's morning crow convinced the border guards to open the pass for them, believing it was time to lift the night curfew. Another anecdote tells how You Meng, a jester in the Chu court, was so skilled at mimicry that his impersonation of a deceased minister whose family had been neglected since his death prompted the king to honour the minister's widow properly.

Performing animals

Animal training also has a long tradition in China, the performing creatures including not only large ones such as elephants, tigers and lions, but also small ones like mice, fish and insects. Such circus spectacles were sometimes given a political twist, entertaining the audience as well as scoffing at the current political situation. In the Later Shu dynasty (934–965), located in the Sichuan Basin, Yang Yudu kept a flock of monkeys trained to wear costumes, ride dogs and mimic people of all trades. One of the masterpieces is the 'drunkard', in which a monkey appeared to be intoxicated, lying on the ground. Yang would call out, 'The constable is coming!' The monkey would not move. Then, he would raise his voice, 'The Inspector-General is coming!' The monkey still looked indifferent. At last, Yang would utter just quietly, 'Minister Hou is coming.' On hearing this, the monkey would scramble to his feet, nervously looking around and appearing very scared, prompting hearty laughter from the audience. This 'Minister Hou' was a particularly harsh and powerful official at the time.

Festivals

The scenes depicted on the brick from a tomb discovered in Shandong province in 1954 give us a glimpse of these festivals. An equilibrist is balancing a cross on his forehead, on which three figures are playing gymnastic stunts. In another section, one tightrope walker is executing a handstand in the middle of the rope with his legs suspended in a curve

This comic entertainer, probably a dwarf, would have sung stories while beating his drum (Eastern Han clay model). Jesters and jokers were a mainstay of popular entertainment.

Right *Acrobats date back to the most ancient times. This tomb brick shows some complicated circus acts involving men balancing on poles.*

Right *Early 20th-century print showing acrobats at a theatrical performance. Fight-play was much enjoyed at circuses in towns and villages.*

Below *Mongolian acrobats perform at the Tenth China Wuqiao International Circus Festival in Shijiazhuang, Hebei province.*

over his head to maintain balance. The other two are moving towards the middle of the rope from each end, swinging one or two stone meteors. What is more, the tightrope is suspended over a line of upended swords. In the third scene, an equestrian is leaping onto a galloping horse, reminiscent of the vault performed on a charging bull in a wall painting from ancient Crete.

At the turn of a new century, Chinese circuses are aiming to polish their skill and art yet further, and regularly exchange their craftsmanship with fellow artists from all over the world at Wuqiao International Circus Festival.

ROBERT ASH

Agriculture

20

Our ploughshares are sharpened – let us begin work on the southern fields ... Let us sow seeds of every grain! Wrapped up in them is life!
SHI JING ('BOOK OF SONGS'), 10TH–7TH CENTURY BC

Throughout history, agriculture has been critical in shaping China's social, economic and political development. For much of that history, national wealth was most obviously embodied in land, improved over centuries through the investment of labour. For governments, the maintenance of a harmonious relationship with farmers has always been a strategic priority. Failure often played a major role in the fall of dynasties. The Communist victory in 1949 drew greatly on the support of farmers. Today, the government and party face growing social frustrations in the rural world.

Food and population

China was one of the half dozen cradles of autonomous development of agriculture and civilization, where crop remains appeared by around 7500 BC. Some 3,000 years ago, at the beginning of China's imperial history, peasants living in the Yellow River valley (p. 36) relied on a form of slash-and-burn agriculture which had been practised for many centuries. Having cleared an area, they cultivated it for several years before moving on. Some wheat, barley and rice were grown, but the dominant crop was millet. Grain was mainly produced by dry farming methods, rice farming being restricted to undeveloped regions of the centre and south.

Not until the 7th century BC did a more settled system develop, based on cultivation of permanent fields. This had major social and economic significance: it encouraged new techniques of farming, carried out by smaller groups of people, and facilitated the emergence of a free peasantry, whose main economic responsibility was to pay land tax to the state, rather than giving a share of the harvest to a feudal lord.

The central economic problem faced by China from earliest times until almost the present day has been how to maintain a favourable balance between food production and population. Over almost 2,000 years of imperial history (AD 2–1887), a sevenfold increase in population was accompanied by a mere doubling in the area of arable land. Frequent local famines were caused by natural disasters while, at times, neglect of agricultural infrastructure generated shortages. Overall, however, the most remarkable achievement of successive Chinese governments was their ability to mobilize farmers to meet the needs of a rising population, and generate a surplus sufficient to support one of the greatest urban civilizations in the world.

Rice and water

The origins of this success lie in an economic revolution, which began in about AD 800 and continued for some four centuries. During this period, the twin process of invention and innovation occurred on such a scale and over a sufficiently wide area as to precipitate unprecedented economic expansion. The core of this was an *agricultural* revolution. In part, this reflected technical improvements enabling farmers to prepare and use soil more efficiently in the dry-crop

A 2nd-century BC Han pottery model of a grain silo, made to be placed in a tomb.

Right *A Qing-dynasty painting showing the emperor (in yellow robes to the left of the picture) driving an ox-plough during a spring agricultural festival in Beijing.*

Opposite *Water-filled rice terraces at sunrise in the mountain, Yuanyang, Yunnan province.*

Below *Figure of a farmer with spade and shovel. An Eastern Han ceramic excavated in Sichuan province.*

regions of the north. Much more importantly, it owed its impact to the mastery of wet-field (paddy) cultivation, opening up the previously underdeveloped, but very fertile, south.

Most important of all in this respect was the popularization of Champa rice from Vietnam (Annam), which let farmers extend double cropping and, through the reduced water requirements, facilitate the spread of rice into areas which had formerly supported less energy-intensive crops. In both cases, the result was significantly to increase food supplies and allow a major southward migration into the naturally fertile south of China.

The system of farming that emerged was based on the use of simple tools (wooden ploughs and hoes), organic fertilizers (grasses, straw, roots, animal manure and nightsoil) and, for traction and haulage, draught animals. It involved the application of large amounts of labour to small amounts of land, generating high yields by international standards, but with levels of labour productivity that were among the lowest in the world.

The abundance of labour also determined a key feature of Chinese agriculture: the nature of water control. Only at peak periods of the farming calendar – sowing, harvesting or transplanting a second crop – was the huge labour force fully employed. At other times, only a small proportion was needed, the rest being potentially available for farm capital formation. As throughout imperial history, and as recently as the 1960s, flood control, irrigation and drainage construction used mass under-employed farm labour. Some have argued that the coordination needed to implement such activities gave rise to an 'Oriental despotism' of power wielded by a bureaucratic oligarchy.

New crops

It is a measure of the success of China's 'medieval' agricultural revolution that between AD 800 and 1200, total population is likely to have increased more than fourfold. From the founding of the Ming dynasty (1368) until the end of the 16th century, population continued to grow rapidly; and in the first half of the succeeding Qing dynasty (1644–1911), rapid population growth was renewed. In the absence of further technical progress after around AD 1200, how did Chinese agriculture provide for such an increase in numbers and prevent the Malthusian trap from closing?

Part of the answer to this lies in the interruption of population growth by large-scale rebellions which brought high death tolls. More

significant, however, were two developments. One was the opening of the important agricultural resource frontier of Manchuria; the other lay in the introduction, from the 16th century, of maize and potatoes, after these New World crops had been introduced to Europe a century earlier. The ability of maize to grow in adverse conditions made it a popular crop in parts of the north. With intrinsically high yields, potatoes were a significant supplementary source – sometimes the main source – of energy for farmers.

In the early 20th century, conditions were becoming perilous for increasing numbers of farmers. During the Republican period (1912–49), things worsened. Tenurial practices were harsh and often generated a vicious circle of poverty, causing indebtedness and reinforcing agricultural stagnation. The invasion by Japan (1937–45) and the civil conflict between Nationalists and Communists up to 1949 made matters even worse. In the end, it was the Communists who got the support of China's peasants on their road to power.

The irony is that during the Mao era (1949–76), the government failed to capitalize on such support. Instead, it invoked dogmas and initiated policies that effectively neglected the agricultural sector, undermined farm output growth and left the farm population increasingly impoverished. Post-1978 reforms temporarily reversed this situation, although a recurring theme of recent years has been that of farmers' discontent and increasing frustration in the face of policies and behaviour which have discriminated against them.

Since 1978, the contribution of agriculture to GDP has fallen from 28 per cent to little over 12 per cent. But farming still accounts for around 60 per cent of total employment. The rise in protests by farmers, especially grain producers, against illegal land seizures and other forms of exploitation highlight the perennial fear of destabilizing political influences coming from the countryside.

A traditional adage has it that: 'Without farming there is no stability; without grain, there is chaos.' In the 1960s, a celebrated slogan added: 'Agriculture is the foundation of the economy.' For all the country's manufacturing growth, the farm sector is likely to keep its fundamental role in shaping China's development trajectory.

Planting rice below limestone karst mountains near Guilin, Guangxi Autonomous Region.

FUCHSIA DUNLOP

Food & Alcoholic Drinks

21

The transformations in the cauldron are so utterly marvellous and of such subtle delicacy, the mouth cannot put them into words, and the mind cannot comprehend them.

THE LEGENDARY COOK YI YIN, QUOTED IN THE 3RD-CENTURY BC TEXT
LÜSHI CHUNQIU ('SPRING AND AUTUMN ANNALS') BY LU BUWEI

Legend says that the cook Yi Yin impressed the founder of the Shang dynasty, King Tang, so much with his culinary skills that he was made prime minister. And when Yi Yin explained his views on governance, his words took the form of a long culinary metaphor, in which the combination of flavours in the cooking pot became an analogy for the creation of harmony in the state. Yi Yin's colourful exposition was not an eccentric one, however, because Chinese philosophers, poets and officials have long had a tendency to express important ideas in terms of food. Laozi, author of the *Dao De Jing*, suggested that ruling a kingdom was as delicate a matter as cooking small fish. Confucius is said to have rejected food that was improperly cut or lacking its appropriate sauce.

A general preoccupation with food has been one of the striking characteristics of Chinese culture since its beginnings. In ancient China, a

Mid-19th-century painting of a grocery store in old Canton (Guangzhou).

Right *A ding, bronze tripod from the Western Zhou period. This ornate cooking pot is decorated with a buffalo head and animal mask design. (Height 122 cm / 48 in.)*

kind of cooking pot, the *ding*, symbolized political power, and the rituals of government involved making sacrifices of food and wine. Vast numbers of staff in the imperial household were involved in the procurement and preparation of food for the emperor's table. The emperor, in turn, was duty bound to take care of his subjects, for whom food was of paramount importance (An ancient Chinese proverb is *Min yi shi wei tian* or 'To the people, food is heaven').

In ancient China, just as the business of government was often compared to the subtle seasoning of a stew, the maintenance of bodily health required a carefully balanced diet. Food was treated as medicine, and ingredients classified according to their effects on the vital energy of the body. In modern Chinese societies, people still respond to signs of illness by adjusting their diets, long before they pay a visit to the doctor.

The shared meal binds families together in many societies, but in China it also acts as a bridge between the living and the dead. The noblewoman buried at Mawangdui in Hunan province in the 2nd century BC was entombed with a meal on a tray that included several cooked dishes and a pair of chopsticks. According to tradition, hungry ghosts must be placated with offerings of food during the seventh lunar month, and, even today, ancestors are invited to share in a family's New Year's feasting through small dishes of food presented on living room altars and by the side of graves.

Despite its serious ritual and social functions, food in Chinese culture has also been a source of intense joy. Poets and scholars throughout the ages have written passionately about the pleasures of eating. Dining with family and friends is one of the most popular recreational activities in modern China, and food remains a favourite topic of conversation.

'A hundred dishes, a hundred different flavours' (*bai cai bai wei*)

Over the centuries and millennia, China has developed a cuisine that is one of the wonders not only of China, but also of the world. Though based on staple grains, it draws on a vast range of ingredients from all parts of the country and beyond, from the fruit-growing regions of the sub-tropical south to the northern grasslands; from the Tibetan borderlands to the lakes and rivers of the Yangtze delta. The international stereotype of the Chinese as 'eating everything' is

Right *Green lotus pods on sale in a Beijing market. You don't eat the pods themselves, merely the seeds inside them.*

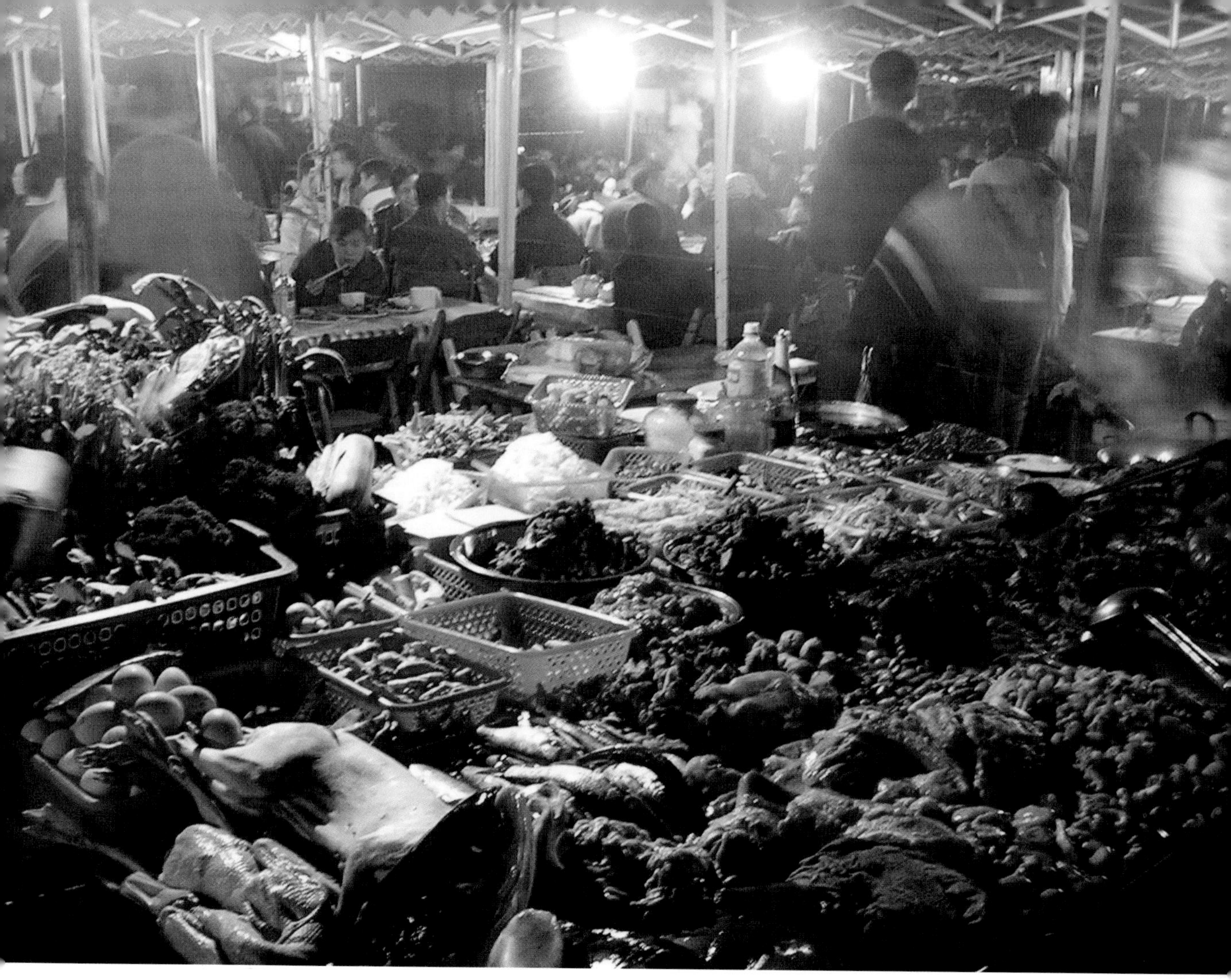

in some senses richly deserved; no other culture is as resourceful in making delicacies out of the most unlikely ingredients.

Professional Chinese chefs have a highly sophisticated system of cookery. Cutting is one of the fundamental kitchen skills – most foods are chopped into small pieces that can be cooked quickly and eaten with chopsticks. An extensive vocabulary describes the different ways of using the kitchen cleaver, and the shapes into which ingredients may be cut. At its most esoteric, the art of cutting can involve carving statues out of root vegetables, and arranging small pieces of multicoloured foods into elaborate collages.

Stir-frying is the best-known Chinese cooking method, but was not common until the Ming dynasty; steaming, another characteristic method, dates back to the Neolithic. These, anyway, are just two of a myriad cooking methods that are minutely categorized by professional chefs: one modern Sichuanese cooking encyclopaedia lists 56 different methods.

When it comes to the appreciation of food, while European gourmets pay attention to the colour, aroma and taste of food, the Chinese have an extra dimension: texture. 'Mouthfeel' (*kou gan*) is one of the essential pleasures of the Chinese table, and partly explains why tasteless ingredients with intriguing textures, such as shark's fin and jellyfish, are so highly prized.

Unity and diversity

Those aspects of Chinese food culture which have ancient roots, like artful cutting, steaming, the use of chopsticks, and a reliance on the soybean as a source of protein and flavour, suggest a certain continuity in its history. But the way Chinese people eat has also been shaped by foreign influences over more than two millennia. Ingredients such as pepper, spinach, garlic and

Food markets remain a staple feature of Chinese life. All kinds of wildlife are on sale at the nightly food market in Guilin, Guangxi Autonomous Region.

sesame came over the land routes from Central Asia from the Han dynasty onwards. New World crops such as maize, sweet potatoes and chillies, arriving in the late Ming, transformed the Chinese diet and helped to support a booming population. More recently, since the early 20th century, monosodium glutamate has become a ubiquitous seasoning.

Certain common themes unite Chinese foodways all over the country, but the regional diversities are just as striking. In the north, everyday diet is dominated by wheaten staples: ravioli-like dumplings, steamed buns, flatbreads and hearty noodle dishes. In the south, rice is the most important staple food, consumed at almost every meal.

Northern cooking shows the influence of nomadic cultures in cooking techniques such as boiling and roasting, and the use of mutton, while the country's finest ingredients and cooking skills were once woven together into an imperial cuisine in Beijing. In the east, cities such as Yangzhou and Suzhou are famed for their refined and elegant cuisines. Their dishes tend to be richer and sweeter than those in other areas; favourite cooking ingredients include sea- and river-food, dark soy sauce, sugar and Shaoxing wine. South, in Guangdong and the Pearl River delta, flavours are lighter and brighter; typical dishes include steamed seafood, crisp, refreshing stir-fries, and infamous exotica such as snakes and cats. Out to the west, Sichuan and Hunan are known for their lavish use of chillies.

Aside from the richly varied food traditions of the Han Chinese, dozens of ethnic minorities have their own culinary specialities. The Uyghur Muslims of northwestern Xinjiang share their noodle-eating habit with the Han, but their kebabs and nan breads link them more closely with the peoples of Central Asia. In southwestern Yunnan, various minority food traditions resonate with those of people across the borders of Southeast Asia.

Different food traditions

The complexity of Chinese society has also supported the evolution of different styles of eating. Haute cuisines in various provinces developed to

A New Year's Eve dinner today in a rural household in Hunan province. Dishes include home-smoked, home-reared pork, pig's intestines with Chinese dates, stewed dried radish, deep-fried glutinous rice puffs and 'golden needle' mushrooms.

satisfy the mobile elite of scholar-officials and wealthy merchants, and tend to be eclectic in their regional influences. Folk-cooking traditions are more limited in their scope, rooted in local ingredients and sometimes also in ideas about the importance of adapting diet to climate. Poorer people still exist on diets dominated by grains and vegetables.

Chinese Buddhist monks eat simple vegetarian food, and avoid pungent ingredients such as garlic, but the need to entertain their wealthy patrons at banquets also led to the creation of a specialist cuisine in which vegetarian ingredients are cunningly engineered to resemble meat, poultry and fish or seafood. The Hui Muslims who are scattered across China, but concentrated in the northwest, have their own variant Chinese cuisine, in which mutton and beef are used as substitutes for pork.

Aside from main meals, China has an extraordinarily varied tradition of snacks or 'little eats' (*xiao chi*). A famous scroll painting depicts all kinds of hawkers on the streets of the Northern Song capital, Kaifeng: such scenes were common in China until recently. Snack food varies widely across the country, from the Muslim noodles and pastries of the northwest, through the spicy dumplings of Sichuan, to the fried noodles and *dim sum* of the Cantonese south.

The appreciation of the alcoholic drinks known collectively as *jiu* is another important aspect of Chinese gastronomy. Made from cooked cereals to which was added a separate ferment, such drinks have been produced in China since the Neolithic. They were used in ancient sacrifices to gods and ancestors, and still play a part in marriage feasts and other banquets. In today's China, strong, clear liquors made from rice, sorghum and other grains are the preferred choice for ritual toasts, while beer is enjoyed as a more everyday drink.

The future

The last century has seen revolutionary change in all aspects of Chinese culture, including food. The early Communists frowned on fancy eating, and their policies contributed to a long decline in Chinese gastronomy. Since the start of economic reforms in the 1980s, there has been a dramatic recovery, and increased international contacts have brought new ingredients and new culinary approaches. Like the rest of the world, however, China now finds itself facing the consequences of rapid development and environmental degradation. Stocks of traditional delicacies like sea-cucumber have collapsed, pollution threatens the habitats of many edible species, and changing diets mean China now faces rising rates of 'Western' diseases like diabetes. At the same time, ironically, growing international awareness of the links between diet and health suggests that the rest of the world has much to learn from traditional Chinese food culture.

Steamed parcels of dim sum.

Parcel-gilt silver tea basket from the Tang dynasty, used to store tea leaves that had first been steamed then dried into bricks.

盧信隆德記洋貨
盧信隆德

Cities & Towns

Though it has always been, and remains, a predominantly rural nation, China contains some of the world's great cities. Today, the country counts 666 cities, 11 with more than 2 million inhabitants. Beijing (p. 116), has 15 million people and Shanghai (p. 126) 18 million. But the biggest is the new municipality of Chongqing, in Sichuan province, with 31 million.

Through the centuries, Chinese cities have been both governmental and commercial centres, each developing a specific characteristic but sharing common population pressure. A visitor to Beijing in the middle of the 19th century recorded streets filled with 'carts, porters, camels, chairs, peddlers, beggars, lamas, muleteers, horse-copers from Mongolia, archers on horseback, mandarins with their suites, small-footed ladies, great ladies in carts, closely veiled to keep off the gaze of the profane vulgar … not to speak of dogs and pigs'.

Today, the streets are filled, rather, with cars, buses, lorries – and bicycles. City centres are decked with flashing neon signs. Shanghai, Beijing and other metropolises house foreign luxury goods stores, and huge office and housing developments. The government is concerned about the gap between urban prosperity and the backwardness of rural areas. The emerging middle class lives, overwhelmingly, in the cities. As acres of concrete and glass tower blocks sprout, pollution grows, and easier communications reduce the separation between regions, the old character is fading – both Beijing and Shanghai are losing the traditional dwellings as

Traffic and pedestrians on Bonham Street in Hong Kong, c. 1900. Chinese streets are emblazoned with banners and signs.

the first redevelops for the 2008 Olympics and the second makes itself the showpiece of Chinese modernity and the site of the 2010 World Expo.

But echoes of the past are still present in the crowded streets, the jumble of housing outside the city centres, the noise, the local cuisine – and the history. Xi'an (p. 137) in northern Shaanxi province prides itself on its imperial heritage; it was the seat of the first Qin emperor – outside it lies his burial place with its army of terracotta warriors and many other early tombs that are, as yet, unexplored. Another former imperial capital, Nanjing (p. 141) lies on the wide Yangtze with broad avenues, the remains of huge buildings, monumental walls and, in the foothills of the Purple Mountain, the memorial mausoleum of the Nationalist father-figure, Sun Yat-sen. To the east, Shanghai has lived through two eras of startling expansion in modern times – the first spurred by foreign concessions wrested from China by Western powers in the 19th century, the second as a prime beneficiary of the market-drive growth since 1980.

Fine buildings from the 1920s and 1930s still adorn the former European concessions, while China's tallest building rises beside the Huangpu River. Down the coast, Hangzhou (p. 131), much admired by Marco Polo, is famed for one of China's most beautiful lakes, dug on imperial orders, while the eastern city of Suzhou (p. 134) is known for its canals and the intricate skill of its silk work.

In Beijing, the Forbidden City (p. 105) and the Summer Palace (p. 110) are among many reminders of 600 years of imperial history, broken only when the Nationalists moved the capital to Nanjing for two decades in the first half of the 20th century. The Communist party leadership compound lies behind the former home of the emperors, and a giant portrait of Mao Zedong adorns the wall of the Forbidden City looking out at Tiananmen Square – the world's biggest enclosed space where the embalmed body of the Communist leader lies in a memorial hall. Shenyang, 750 km (470 miles) to the north, counts more than a millennium of urban history as the home of the Manchus who went on to conquer China in 1644 and, in 1931, as the scene of Japan's grab of Manchuria which can be seen as the first step in the Second World War.

Today's cities may not display such a historical face as in the past, but they are emblematic of the way the country is changing. Tens of millions of rural dwellers trek each year to find work in urban areas. Most Chinese may still live on the land, but, so long as economic growth continues, China's future is likely to be increasingly city-based.

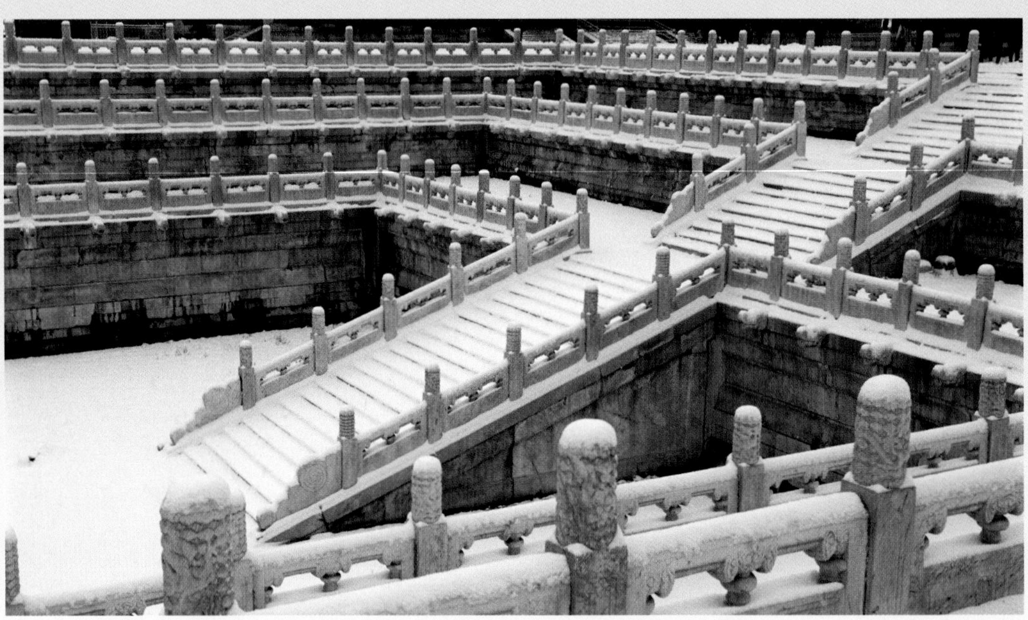

The snow-covered great steps and terraces of the Forbidden City, Beijing.

FRANCES WOOD

Imperial Beijing

22

I assure you that the streets are so broad and straight that from the top of the wall above one gate you can see along the whole length of the road to the gate opposite ... all the way down the sides of every main street there are booths and shops of every sort ... on every site stand large and spacious mansions with ample courtyards and gardens.

ATTRIBUTED TO MARCO POLO, 13TH CENTURY

Beijing as an imperial capital dates back to the beginning of the Mongol Yuan dynasty (1279–1368). There had been major settlements in the area since the Western Zhou (1046–771 BC), and the lakes that form today's Beihai Park were dug out by the Jin between 1125 and 1215. The city constructed for the Mongols, with its north to south orientation, regular checkerboard layout of streets, surrounding walls and central imperial palace, is the epitome of the Chinese city whose characteristic form dates back to the Shang dynasty (*c.* 1600 – *c.* 1046 BC). The rectangular plan, which emphasizes where state power lies by putting the ruler at the very centre, was not always possible to realize: Nanjing (p. 141), the first capital of the Ming dynasty (1368–1644), for example, was not rectangular in plan because the hills and waters of the site do not allow it. However, Beijing, on the North China Plain, is the perfect example of the imperial city plan. It also accords with geomantic beliefs, for it is protected to the north by the Western Hills and has a plentiful water supply led in from the lakes and springs there.

When Beijing was selected as the imperial capital by the Yuan, work began in 1267 and lasted for 20 years. The earthen walls enclosed an area about 50 sq. km (20 sq. miles) and was designed according to the *Zhou Li* or *Rituals of Zhou* (a 1st-millennium BC compilation thought to have been based on even more ancient texts) with an emphasis on centrality. Apart from the imperial palace at the southern end of the central axis, there were also Drum and Bell Towers on this central north–south line. These were significant reminders of government control, used to mark the hours of the day (drum) and the closing of the city gates in the evening (bell). The present Drum and Bell Towers date from the Ming and are not quite in alignment, with the smaller Bell Tower standing just to the northwest of the Drum Tower. Government offices were in the east of the city, as were the better markets (selling wine vessels, books, boots, fur hats and satin). The cheaper markets, including the livestock market selling camels, mules, sheep and oxen, were in the west.

The Drum Tower, Beijing, in 1874.

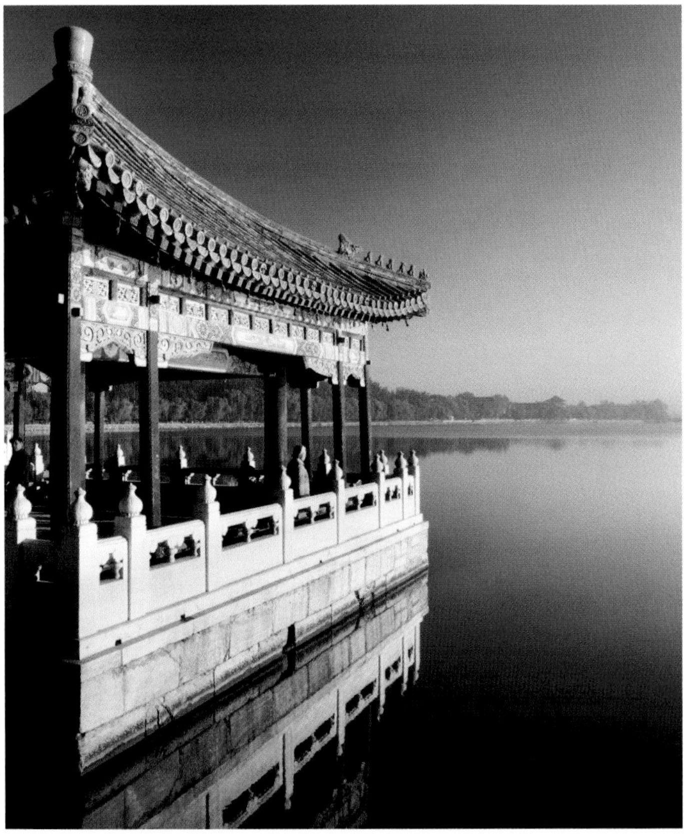

Above *A pavilion overlooking the lake in Beihai Park.*

Construction of a Ming imperial city

There was considerable destruction when the Ming dynasty overthrew the Mongols in 1368 and though repairs to the city wall, for example, were begun in 1370, it was not until 1403 that the Yongle emperor of the Ming (r. 1403–1424) decided to move his dynasty's capital from Nanjing to Beijing. His reasons were political – for the greatest external threat to China was still from the north, just beyond the Great Wall, and it was vital that political and military power be concentrated nearby to ensure supplies and support the loyalty of border troops – but they were also personal. According to the Chinese tradition of primogeniture, all imperial sons except for the first-born heir were sent away from the imperial palace and enfeoffed elsewhere. The Yongle emperor had been sent to Beijing, so it was his power base. He had to consult numerous specialists, historians and geomancers to make sure that the 'good luck' of the area had not been exhausted by the destruction of the Mongols. Assured that this was not so, the new capital began to rise, mostly to the south of the old Mongol city, consisting of three concentric walled 'cities', the imperial palace (Forbidden City) at the centre, surrounded by the 'imperial city' which included the Beihai Park area to the west, and the 'outer' city with its government offices, markets, temples and houses. In 1553 the area enclosed by the outer wall, now built of brick, was 62 sq. km (24 sq. miles) and there were nine gates in the wall, following the stipulations of the *Zhou Li*, and appropriate for an imperial city since nine was a number symbolic of the emperor.

To the east of the central axis of the city, on the southern wall, the Yongle emperor built the Temple of Heaven in 1420 and, during the Ming, it was used for sacrifices to both heaven and earth, until 1530 when the Jiaqing emperor built a separate Altar to the Earth outside the walls to the north of Beijing. The Temple of Agriculture, adjoining the Temple of Heaven, was used by the emperors to plough the first ceremonial furrow initiating the agricultural year. After the Qing dynasty overthrew the Ming in 1644, the Qing

Right *Qing-dynasty scroll of Emperor Kangzi's southern inspection tour.*

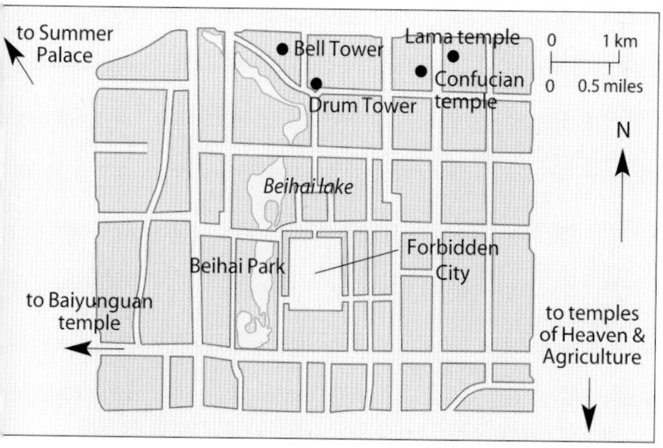

Simple plan of the centre of imperial Beijing. The Temple of Heaven and Fayuan si *(Temple of the Source of Law) are off the map to the south; the Baiyunguan Temple is off to the west. To reach the Summer Palace you would head in a northwesterly direction out of the city.*

emperors built further imperial altars to the moon and the sun to the west and east of the city. These large enclosures, supplied with altar sets of porcelain in different symbolic colours, their courtyards filled with massive thuja trees, were only visited once or twice a year by the Qing emperors and were otherwise firmly closed.

Apart from these altars and temples associated specifically with imperial ritual, with the emperor

'Bird's Eye View of the Capital' (Xu Yang, 1767). This painting shows the bustling streets of the shopping district in the foreground, the yellow roofed halls of the Forbidden City behind, and soldiers skating in formation on the Beihai lake (top left). Twenty poems on the theme of the coming of spring by the Qianlong emperor are also transcribed on the painting.

The gateway of the Baiyunguan Temple. The most important Daoist temple in Beijing, its annual fair has been revived recently. Grand gateways like this were to overawe the populace.

as the owner of the calendar, and heaven's 'representative' on earth, responsible for making an annual report to heaven on behalf of his subjects and to ensure heaven's favour, many Ming and Qing emperors and empresses became patrons of other, mainly Buddhist, temples in and around Beijing.

Life outside the palace

For the ordinary citizens of the imperial city, their ruler was an unseen presence. The Ming emperors rarely left the Forbidden City and its gardens (except for the rituals held around the New Year in the Temples of Heaven and Agriculture) and though the Qing emperors ventured out more often, travelling to their summer palaces or on tours of inspection of southern China, ordinary mortals were not allowed near the imperial route, and no portraits of the emperors were seen outside the Forbidden City which could only be entered by officials on government business. The annual round for ordinary citizens was focused on the New Year, a family occasion, or in visits to temples on the 1st and 15th of each lunar month or on special occasions like the birthday of a god or an annual temple fair when entertainers, shadow puppeteers, jugglers and stalls would fill the courtyards. Some temples had special attractions: people went to view the lilacs in the *Fayuan si* (Temple of the Source of Law) in April, other temples had beds of chrysanthemums or peonies to be viewed when at their peak.

Most people in Beijing lived in small courtyard houses entered from the tiny lanes that ran between the great avenues. A single family might occupy a single courtyard, a rich family would have a rambling complex of linked courtyards and the poor were crowded together in shared courtyards. Single-storeyed grey-tiled roof buildings, usually with three rooms to a wing, looked out onto a small paved courtyard which was usually planted with a deciduous tree to provide shade in summer without cutting off the slanting rays of the winter sun. As in the Forbidden City, the main hall was that which faced south: there guests would be entertained and the master of the house slept. These houses were completely private, surrounded by high walls, a tiny reflection of the three concentric walled enclosures that symbolized the imperial city.

FRANCES WOOD

The Forbidden City

23

Another rampart, in the same blood-red colour, and a large gate, decorated with faience, through which we passed: this time, the gate of the 'Forbidden City', that is to say, the gate to an area we had never visited, and it's as if that gate was announcing to me its enchantment and mystery....

PIERRE LOTI, *LES DERNIERS JOURS DE PEKIN* (*'THE LAST DAYS OF PEKING'*), 1903

The Forbidden City was the imperial palace of the Ming and Qing emperors, a great rectangular, red-walled, yellow-tiled complex in the centre of the imperial capital, Beijing. Earlier imperial capitals included Xi'an, Luoyang, Kaifeng, Hangzhou and the first capital of the Ming, Nanjing. The Mongol Yuan dynasty chose Beijing as the capital in 1279 but its imperial palace was destroyed when the Ming overthrew the Yuan in 1368. Traditionally Chinese capital cities were rectangular walled enclosures with the walled rectangular imperial palace at the centre. Though it is this red-walled rectangle that is the Forbidden City 'proper', the imperial family also made use of the lake and garden complex immediately west of the Forbidden City, now known as Beihai Park. And though there were imperial handicraft workshops within the Forbidden City, the imperial domains also included numerous farms, timber yards and silk factories

View of the Forbidden City from the south showing the surrounding moat with five marble bridges, the Gate of Heavenly Peace and the high Meridian Gate behind.

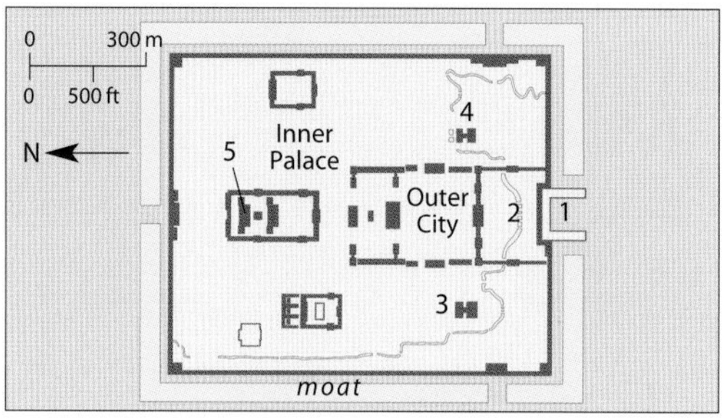

Plan of the Forbidden City showing the marble bridges (2) *just inside the main gate* (1), *the Hall of Military Eminence* (3), *the Hall of Literary Glory* (4) *and the Palace of Earthly Tranquillity* (5).

across China to ensure the supply of daily necessities to the several thousand inhabitants of the imperial palace.

How it was built

For mainly strategic reasons, the third emperor of the Ming decided to move the capital to Beijing from Nanjing and in 1406 he ordered the collection of building materials for his palace. Oak, elm, catalpa, fir and camphor were collected from Hunan, Hubei, Zhejiang and Jiangxi provinces and, for the solid main columns of the major halls, massive trunks of *Phoebe nanmu*, a coarse-grained hardwood, were shipped along the Yangtze and hauled up the Grand Canal. Timber was the main construction material in Chinese buildings and whilst columns in lesser buildings were often timber patchwork concealed beneath protective paint, the massive columns of the Forbidden City's halls were made from single trunks.

The halls of the Forbidden City were raised high off the ground on white platforms, made from marble quarried at Fangshan some 50 km (30 miles) west of Beijing. 'Mugwort marble', a hard white marble with a slight green tinge, was used for the huge 5,000 kg (11,000 lb) dragon-carved slabs over which the emperor was carried in his sedan chair, and 'white jade' marble was used for the carved balustrades surrounding all the terraces and bridges of the Forbidden City. Red clay to wash the walls and fix roof tiles was extracted and processed in Shandong province, yellow clay from Hebei was used to colour the walls of the great halls, and fine gold leaf, used in much architectural decoration, on red dragon pillars, gable decorations and elsewhere, came from Suzhou.

The great open courtyards between the halls were paved with fine-grained, hard-wearing 'settled clay bricks' from Linqing in Shandong, shipped up the Grand Canal. The interiors of the

High walls surrounded by a moat enclose the Forbidden City. There are yellow-roofed gates on all four sides with the main gate to the south. The towers at the angles of the walls have complex yet elegant roof profiles.

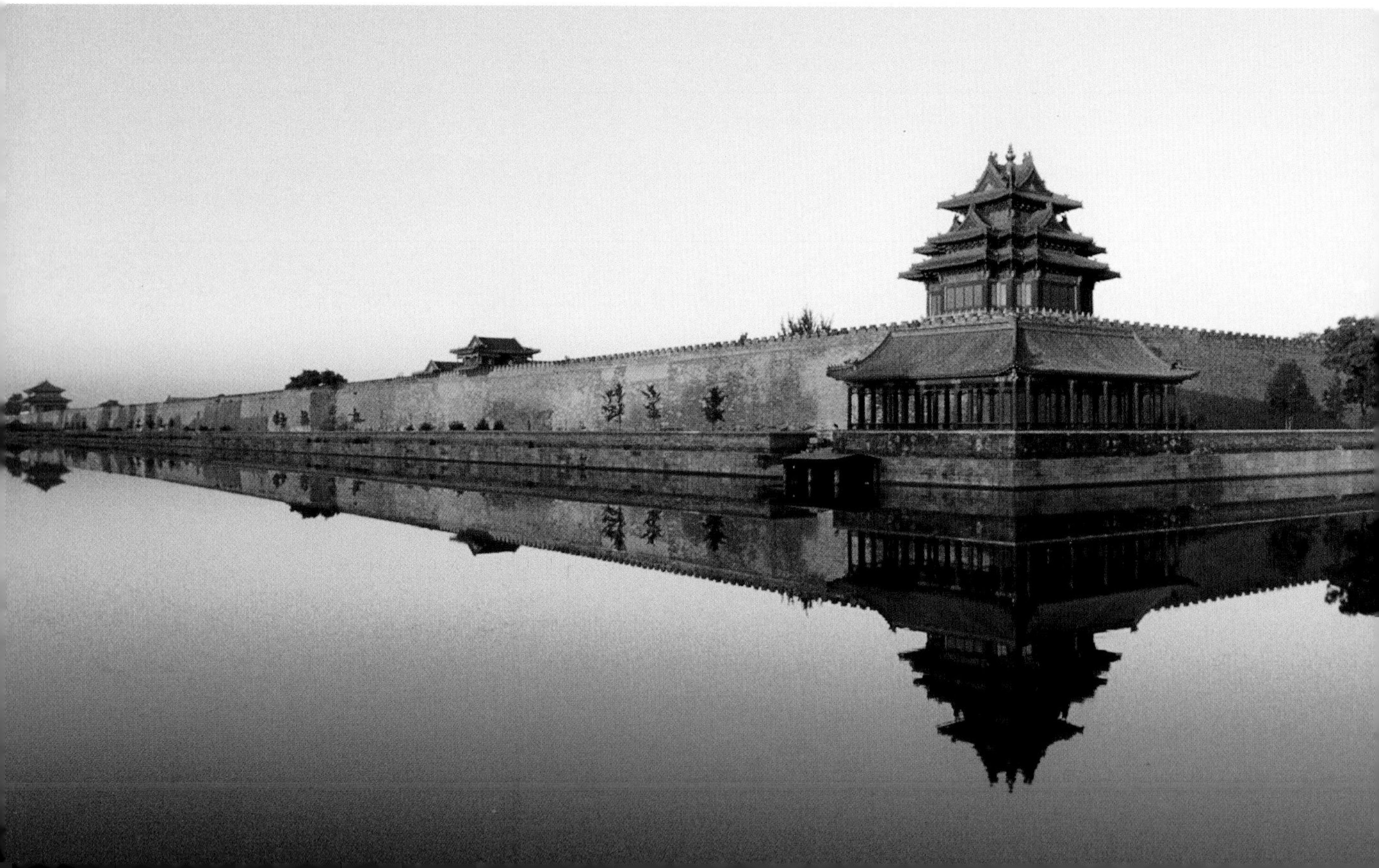

buildings were paved with dark grey 'metal bricks', the name deriving from the ringing sound they made when struck. These were produced in the Suzhou and Songjiang areas and also shipped up the Grand Canal.

The great variety of roof-tiles, yellow-glazed for the halls, unglazed grey for the smaller domestic buildings, were produced in Beijing. Extraction of clay to the southeast of the city created lakes which now form part of Taoranting Park. The first sets of glazed tiles were made in Liulichang ('glazed tile works'), later the centre of the antique and antiquarian book trade in Beijing.

The construction of the emperor Yongle's palace between 1417 and 1420 was supervised by an Annamese, Nguyen An (d. 1453), with a million convict and conscript labourers carrying out the heavy work on site whilst 100,000 specialized craftsmen worked on timber construction, decorative lattice-work and stone-carving. At the end of 1420, the Forbidden City was finished. Its red-washed walls encircled an area 961 m (3,153 ft) long and 753 m (2,470 ft) wide. Outside was the imperial city protected by a 52-m (170-ft) wide moat and a 10-m (33-ft) high wall.

Reception of Pieter van Hoorn's Dutch Trade Delegation at the Imperial Court of Peking (1668).

The complex was divided into two parts, the southern area known as the 'outer city' consisting of three axes with the three main yellow-tiled halls and gates raised on white marble platforms standing in vast courtyards on the central axis. The buildings of the western axis included the *Wuying dian* or Hall of Military Eminence where the Qianlong emperor (r. 1736–1795) had a printing and editorial office for the production of 'palace books'. On the east was the *Wenhua dian* or Hall of Literary Glory and the imperial library. To the rear of the enclosure was the 'inner palace' with its many lower yellow or grey-roofed halls where the imperial family and its retinue of maids and eunuchs lived amongst studies, temples and gardens. This division followed the stipulation of the *Li Ji* (Book of Rites), traditionally ascribed to Confucius, that 'court affairs should be to the front, sleeping quarters to the rear'.

The Chinese name for the palace is *Zijin cheng*, a contraction of 'Pole star forbidden city' since the Pole star was one of the symbols of the emperor who was known as 'the son of heaven'. Most aspects of the decoration of the Forbidden City were similarly symbolic. Many doors have rows of nine bosses, for the number nine was also a symbol for the emperor, as was the dragon which appears in marble carvings on floors and balustrades, on columns and painted ceilings. The phoenix, symbol of the empress, only appears in the inner palace.

Unusually, when the Manchu Qing dynasty overthrew the Ming in 1644, the Forbidden City was not badly damaged. It was common for the imperial palace, symbolic of the previous regime, to be destroyed, but the Qing emperor moved into the Ming palace almost immediately and, throughout the Qing, very little change was made to the basic plan, although several emperors ordered the construction of whole new complexes and interior design tastes changed. In 1955, it was calculated that of the 9,000 *jian* or 'rooms' of the original Ming palace, 8,662 were still intact. However, almost continuous repairs were needed owing to frequent and destructive fires caused by lightning strikes, firework displays and open braziers: particularly serious fires were recorded in 1679, 1740, 1758, 1783, 1797, 1869, 1870 and 1888.

The series of main halls on the central axis of the Forbidden City looking south from Coal Hill.

Imperial worship

The Ming emperors rarely left the Forbidden City, except to carry out annual sacrifices at the Temples of Heaven and Agriculture. Much imperial worship took place within the Forbidden City itself. Two shrines to Confucius were maintained within the Forbidden City, and the Yongzheng emperor (r. 1722–1735) ordered the construction of a temple to the City God in the northwestern corner of the Forbidden City in 1726. Annual rites were held in the main Daoist shrine within the palace, the *Qin'an dian* (Hall of Imperial Peace), the main building in the imperial garden at the northern end of the central axis of the inner palace. The Qianlong emperor ordered most of the religious buildings in the Forbidden City, favouring the Tibetan Buddhism of the Gelugpa sect, and it has been estimated that at the time of

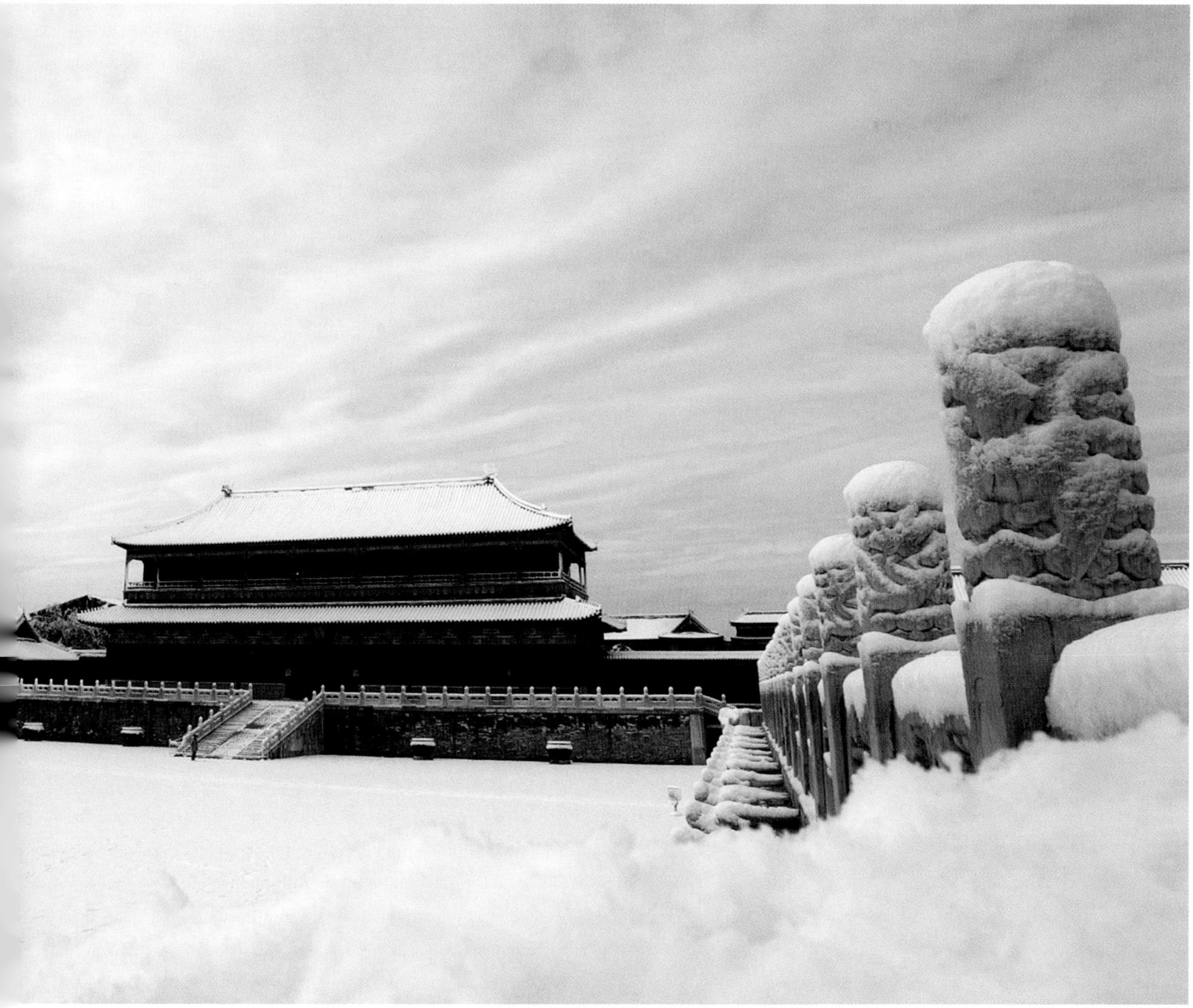

his death there were 35 Tibetan Buddhist halls with 10 smaller shrines within the palace.

Though the Manchu Qing emperors offered sacrifices in the Chinese tradition to Confucius, to their ancestors, to Daoist and Buddhist altars, as Manchus they were shamanists and they took over the *Kunning gong* (Palace of Earthly Tranquillity), formerly the residence of the Ming empresses, as the centre of shamanistic worship, installing cooking stoves for the daily preparation of meats offered to magpies and crows. The Manchus believed that they were descended from a magpie so every morning they hoisted pieces of meat to the top of 'spirit poles' to feed the birds.

The Forbidden City today

The beginning of the 20th century saw Western troops, sent to relieve the Siege of the Legations during the Boxer Rising of 1900, quartered in the Forbidden City. The imperial family returned and during the reign of the last emperor, Puyi (1909–1911), largely influenced by his Scottish tutor Reginald Johnston, Western innovations such as a telephone, bath-tubs and a bicycle entered the City. Some of its treasures were gone, sold off by eunuchs, and during the Sino-Japanese War the best of the imperial collections was packed up and is now on display in Taiwan. The Forbidden City, abandoned by Puyi in 1924, became a public museum in 1925.

Tourists visit the Forbidden City blanketed with the first snow fall of winter.

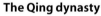

FRANCES WOOD

24 The Summer Palace

When summer is at its height, the lotus blooms for miles like a tapestry, its fragrance wafted afar by the breeze. Men and women gather by the flowing water, filling their wine cups to the brim. What can be more delightful?

YUAN ZHONGDAO, MING-DYNASTY POET

From the Zhou dynasty, if not before, rulers, and later emperors, enclosed vast tracts of land where they could hunt, keep exotic animals, entertain and construct gardens. Several of the rulers who occupied Beijing constructed summer palaces outside the city, in the Western Hills where the air was cooler in summer than on the plain below. In 1153, one of the Jin rulers of the area built a 'travelling residence' or temporary palace beside a small lake that lay under *Weng shan* or Jar Hill, now the site of the largest surviving summer palace in the Beijing area, the *Yihe yuan*, Garden of the Preservation of Harmony, often known as the 'New Summer Palace'.

A 19th-century painting showing some of the pleasure gardens built by the Qing emperors northwest of Beijing.

During the Mongol Yuan dynasty, the palace was abandoned. The site, with its hills, springs and pools filled with lotus and water chestnuts attracted the attention of the Ming emperors and a new palace was constructed, called the Garden of Wonderful Hills. Built up the side of the hill, the halls, pavilions and the lake below were described by the Ming literati painter Wen Zhengming (1470–1559), 'A spring lake in the setting sun, orchids moving with the gentle flow, buildings within the shadow of heaven tower above and below.'

The Qing dynasty

The scenery was compared to that of the beautiful West Lake at Hangzhou and this may have inspired the Qianlong emperor, who had travelled widely in south China taking a particular interest in its gardens, to build himself a summer palace here. Construction began in 1749 on the Garden of Clear Ripples, enlarging the lake (renamed *Kunming hu* after a legendary lake of the past) and building up mountains. Work on the palace, which comprised 3,000 bays or rooms, was completed in 1764 and many of the buildings (Hall of Benevolence and Longevity, Hall of Happiness in Longevity) and Jar Hill itself, which became Longevity Hill, were named in honour of the 60th birthday of the Qianlong emperor's mother in 1751.

The Qing emperors had other summer palaces nearby; there was the Kangxi emperor's

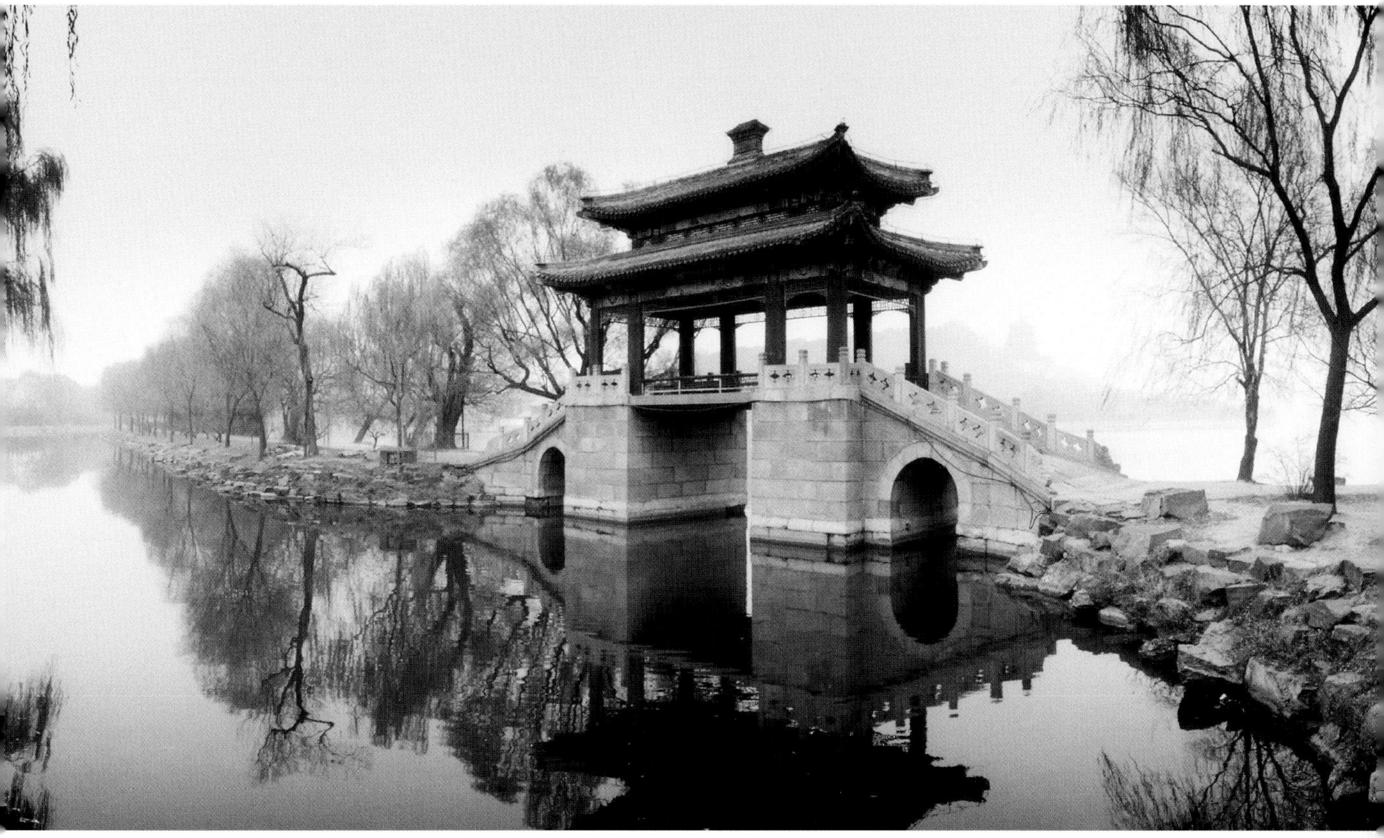

View over the lake at the Summer Palace, showing an ornate bridge.

Changchun yuan or Garden of Eternal Spring and the Yongzheng emperor's *Yuanming yuan*, Garden of Perfect Brightness, which was also enlarged by the Qianglong emperor who engaged European Jesuits to build 'European palaces' there between 1747 and 1759, with elaborate stone buildings and fountains. The Garden of Perfect Brightness and the 'new' Summer Palace were almost completely razed by British and French troops in 1860, an act of destruction recalled in a contemporary poem by Wang Kaiyun: 'Jade fountain laments and Kunming mourns, Alone, the bronze ox guards the thistles and thorns, In the hills of blue iris the fox calls in the night, Beneath the bridge of soft ripples fish weep at the sight.'

Retreat for the Dowager Empress

The 'new' Summer Palace was rebuilt in 1886 by the Dowager Empress Cixi, who gave it the name *Yihe yuan* or Garden of the Preservation of Harmony. In 1900, during the suppression of the Boxer Rising, it was again destroyed by foreign troops but Cixi rebuilt it again in 1902, making frequent visits to the site and demanding weekly reports. It remained her favourite residence and she returned to the Forbidden City and the 'Winter Palace' in Beihai Park with great reluctance. She would set out from Beijing with an entourage of about 1,000, either travelling by boat, which entailed clearing all the duckweed off the canal, or by road, which involved instant road repairs for a smooth journey. When she arrived in 1905, 458 eunuchs were lined up to meet her.

The main residential buildings were just inside the gate, and also served as government buildings for the continuation of the daily affairs of state. Cixi's clothes, many of which were embroidered with motifs that reflected seasonal plants such as peonies and wisteria for spring wear, lotuses for the summer and chrysanthemums for the autumn, were stored in 3,000 camphor chests in the Summer Palace. The kitchens produced 100 separate dishes for each of the two main

meals of the day and 25 to 30 smaller dishes for snacks in between.

Though the expanse of the lake, lined with elegant 'jade belt' bridges and a walkway covered with bright paintings, and the towering constructions rising up Longevity Hill are the most dominant features, the Summer Palace encloses many smaller halls and gardens. There is a recreation made for the Qianlong emperor of a famous garden in Wuxi in the northeast corner of the *Xiequ yuan* (Garden of Harmonious Interest), a tiny Fan Pavilion and, beside the lake, the famous Marble Boat, a gaudy stone recreation of a Mississippi paddle steamer, supposedly built by the Dowager Empress with money intended for the Chinese navy.

Cixi's main apartments where she stayed from spring to autumn most years, were in the Hall of Happiness in Longevity with two courtyards planted with fine magnolias, most of which were destroyed in 1900. A moon gate led to the apartment of the chief eunuch Li Lianying. The apartments were furnished with heavy, dark, carved wooden furniture and coloured glass chandeliers installed in 1903, the only distinctive Manchu touch being the wooden seating platforms that line the eastern chamber. It was customary for day-long performances of Beijing Opera to be performed for Qing emperors, and Cixi was fortunately very fond of opera. The theatre is beside the Hall of Health and Happiness, where Cixi sat on a gold lacquered throne before a screen decorated with hundreds of birds paying homage to a phoenix (symbol of the empress), with a pair of gilded cages with clockwork birds inside, a present from 'a foreign power'. There are three stages in the theatre: the main action took place on the central level, with angels and benevolent spirits descending from the upper stage and devils and evil spirits confined to the lower stage.

The Summer Palace became a public park in 1924.

Opposite *The Buddhist Sea of Wisdom Temple, made of glazed tiles, is one of the many temples decorating Longevity Hill.*

Below *A painting in the Long Corridor of the Summer Palace.*

FRANCES WOOD

25 The Temple of Heaven

The most important of all the religious structures in China ... I never felt under a more holy awe than when I was there.

JAMES LEGGE, MISSIONARY AND TRANSLATOR OF THE CHINESE CLASSICS, 1873

The emperor of China was known as the Son of Heaven (*Tianzi*), ruling with heaven's mandate, and part of the imperial annual ceremonial involved sacrifice to heaven. During the Ming and Qing dynasties, this took place in the enclosure of the Temple of Heaven, on the southern edge of Beijing.

Surrounded by a wall which is curved to the north, the enclosure is almost 6.5 km (4 miles) from north to south and contains three buildings linked by a raised, white stone walkway. The constructions are all circular in plan, for according to traditional Chinese cosmology, the earth is square but heaven is circular. Much of the enclosure is planted with fine thuja trees, arranged in neat rows like ranks of troops. Construction first began in 1420 under the Ming but the complex was enlarged under the Qing.

The Qinian dian, *or Hall of Prayers for Good Harvest.*

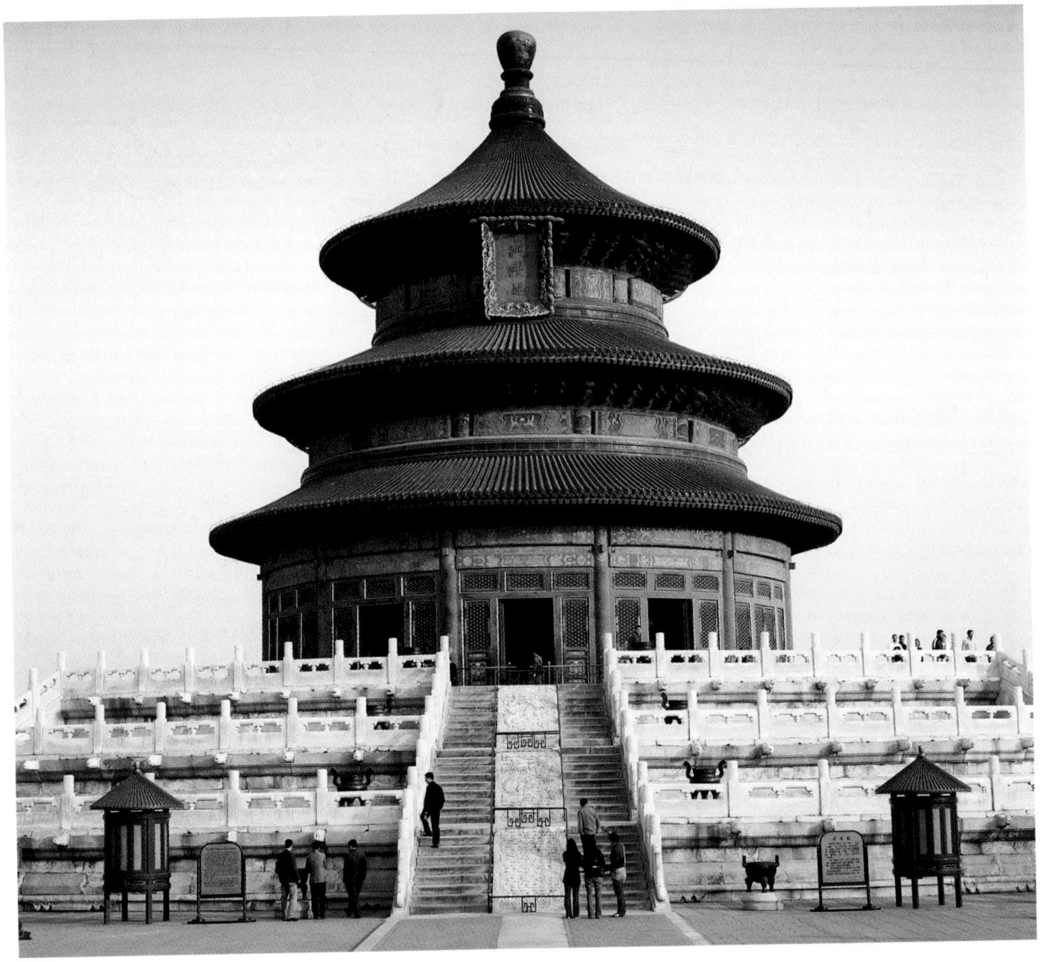

The altar and two sacred halls

The Altar of Heaven at the southern end of the enclosure is a triple-tiered circular platform with white marble balustrades. It is approached through four white stone triple gates with marble clouds decorating the tops of the marble pillars, and was first built with blue tiles (the colour of heaven) covering the outer walls. It was enlarged in 1749, when the blue tiles were replaced with white marble. The arrangement of the stone flags consists of multiples of 9 and 81, both considered 'lucky' numbers. The top terrace has a circular stone at the centre, surrounded by 9 stones, these, in turn, surrounded by 27 stone flags and onwards until the significant number of 81 is reached at the outer edge. It was here that pure white animals were sacrificed, and bales of silk burned in offering by the emperor on the first day of the winter solstice.

The two halls on the long white walkway are the *Qinian dian* (Hall of Prayers for Good Harvest) at the northern end and the smaller *Huangqiong yu* (Imperial Heavenly Vault) in the middle. Both stand on circular white marble platforms and are themselves circular in plan, with conical roofs covered with deep blue tiles. The 28 columns of *Phoebe nanmu* hardwood in the *Qinian dian* were arranged with four central columns representing the four seasons and the 24 outer columns, the 12 months and the 12 hours into which the Chinese divided the day. The roof beams were painted with dragons and phoenix, representing the emperor and the empress respectively, where the Forbidden City's halls have only the imperial dragon. The empress's symbol is presumably included because of the presence of the ancestral tablets in the Temple of Heaven.

The emperor visits

Ming and Qing emperors only visited the huge enclosure twice in the year. On the eve of the winter solstice, the emperor would proceed from the Forbidden City in his elephant-drawn chariot with a retinue of some 2,000, and enter the smaller *Huangqiong yu* to pray and burn incense in front of the imperial ancestral tablets that were kept there. As in ordinary homes, he reported the events of the past year to the ancestral tablets. After a night of fasting and meditation in a blue-roofed side hall, he went to the circular altar to make sacrifices and offerings, taking the imperial ancestral tablets to the ceremony, when he reported to heaven on the events of the last year. In the first month of the year, he returned to the larger hall, the *Qinian dian* where he prayed for heaven's favour in the New Year, and a good harvest.

Only four months after the Manchu Qing troops took the city of Peking in 1644, the seven-year-old Shunzhi emperor was escorted to the Temple of Heaven to make a special offering to heaven, in an indication that the Qing emperors acknowledged the mandate of heaven and were going to follow the ritual practices of the previous Ming dynasty. Until 1860, when foreign troops forced their way in, the Temple of Heaven remained a closed imperial precinct. When foreigners did get in, they were overwhelmed by its scale, forms and colours. James Legge (1815–1897) even removed his shoes to stand on its 'holy ground', an extraordinary act of reverence for a Protestant missionary.

Above *The magnificent painted ceiling of the* Qinian dian.

Below *The Altar of Heaven, the small* Huangqiong yu *and the* Qinian dian *are all linked by one long stone walkway.*

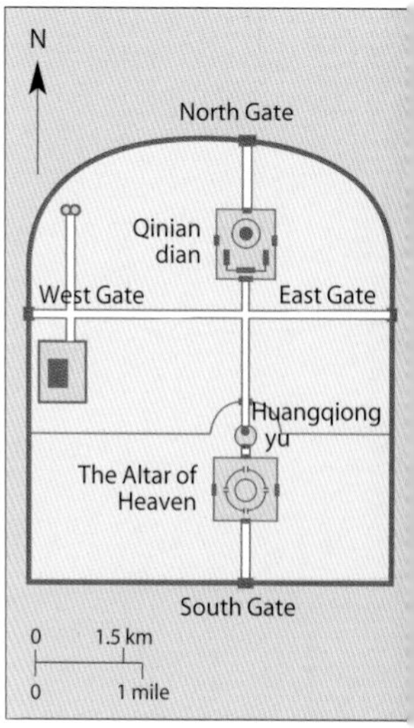

26 Beijing Today

China can stand up again.
MAO ZEDONG PROCLAIMING THE PEOPLE'S REPUBLIC IN TIANANMEN SQUARE, BEIJING, 1949

When China's empire fell in 1912, its capital city soon faced an uncertain future. The military strongman who took over the government, Yuan Shikai, insisted on Beijing remaining the capital, despite the claims of revolutionaries to move it southwards to Nanjing (p. 141). But, after Yuan's death in 1916, the governments which sat in Beijing lacked authority, and national power devolved to an array of warlords who ruled on a regional basis. Still, the modernizing, nationalist, iconoclastic movement launched by students on 4 May, 1919, which took its name from its date and provided 20th-century China with a liberal ideology, sprang from a demonstration in the capital, and intellectual life there remained vibrant. But the victory of the Nationalists over the warlords led to the capital being transferred to Nanjing in 1928. It was only with the triumph of the Communists in 1949 that Beijing regained its status as the political capital of China.

Under Mao Zedong, the city retained its great historical sites (p. 101). But much else changed, and the Cultural Revolution caused considerable damage to old temples, houses and monuments. The imperial walls were pulled down; factories were set up within the city. Then, as China moved into an era of high growth and market economics, Beijing was somewhat eclipsed by faster-growing cities such as Shanghai (p. 126) and the southern and coastal boom centres.

Olympics transformation

But, as it won the 2008 Olympic Games, the capital went through a major transformation process which, by some estimates, make it the biggest building site on earth. In the process, aspects of its old culture have been further destroyed. For instance, most of the typical one-storey *hutong* alleyway houses have been torn down to make way for modern blocks; however, one remaining alleyway treasure is the quiet home in Fruitful Lane of the great writer, Lao She, author of the classic account of the life of the city

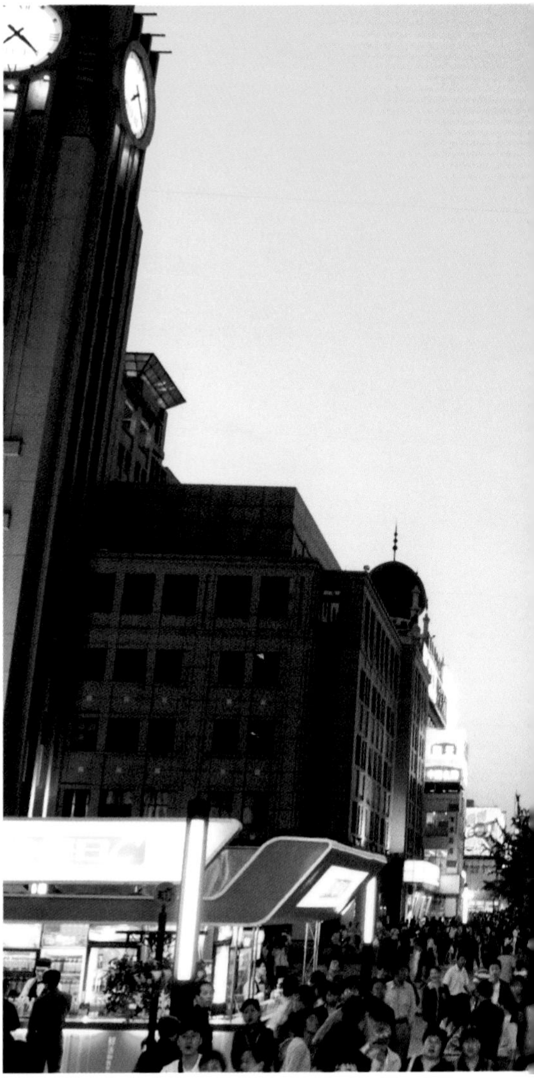

New office and retail buildings take the place of the old.

poor, *Rickshaw*, who died in the nearby Grand Peace Lake in 1966 – either drowning himself after being beaten by the Red Guards of the Cultural Revolution or disposed of by his tormentors.

Their shaky property rights prevented local inhabitants from halting wholesale development. Some see this as a symbol for the way modernization has transformed the culture of 21st-century China, but the great old monuments such as the Forbidden City and Temple of Heaven (pp. 105–109, 114–115) remain, along with historic parks, houses and gardens, and one place visitors do not reach – the Zhongnanhai compound, behind the old imperial palace, where the leadership lives amid lakes and lawns and graceful trees.

There is no doubt that the government is intent on making the capital a showpiece for the change that is taking place in China, and has taken the Olympic Games as the focus of that process. The Olympic Village will cover 517,000 sq. m (5,565,000 sq. ft) of modern accommodation. Avant-garde stadiums are going up, including the main one shaped like a classic bird cage. A major drive is under way to modernize communications and overcome the traffic jams that clog the city's roads. A new ring road is being driven through and an urban light railway system developed.

At the same time, expansion of Beijing's airport will result in a complex to rival the futuristic

Like many cities, Beijing is building, day and night.

Right *Shopping malls proliferate in modern Beijing.*

terminals at Shanghai-Pudong. Already the country's busiest airport, handling more than 30 million passengers a year, Beijing's third terminal is to have a floor area of 900,000 sq. m (10,000,000 sq. ft) on seven storeys.

New buildings for culture and technology

The Olympics are not the only spur to the hectic development. New modern complexes have already gone up along the main avenues to house offices, shops and smart apartments. A huge building is under construction for the main television service. Satellite cities housing millions of people have been built – or are under construction – round Beijing.

Below *Avant-garde architecture: model of the China Central Television (CCTV) headquarters.*

One of the most spectacular developments promises to be the new opera and theatre complex set on an island in a lake by Tiananmen Square and reached by tunnel. Designed by the French architect Paul Andreu, it will consist of a 2,500-seat opera house, a 2,000-seat concert hall, and two theatres with 1,200 and 520 seats apiece. In the east of the city, a big business district is fast taking shape, and the university is pushing ahead with a project to create a Silicon Valley for new technology on its expanding campus.

Above *Beijing Arts Centre.*

Below *A worker walks past the translucent wall of the National Aquatics Centre, dubbed the 'Water Cube', in Beijing.*

To go with all the modern building, Beijing has become a centre for avant-garde art, and streets have been turned into smart centres for galleries, bars and restaurants, including some which reach back to the imperial days to offer Qing-dynasty cuisine in courtyard houses, or, more recently Mao memorabilia.

Projects and development

All this means that in the last few years the capital of China has housed anywhere from 5,000 to 8,000 building projects, employing 2 to 3 million migrant workers. Total spending may reach $200 million. To the east, a major zone encompassing the old financial city of Tianjin and the port of Binhai is being developed, with the aim of matching Shanghai and the Pearl River cities of southern China. The area to the east is hoping to attract $20 billion in foreign investment by 2010 on top of $15 billion already put in to Tianjin.

There may be regrets for the passing of aspects of old Beijing as the population has raced ahead from its 1990s level of 6 million. If the inhabitants of satellite cities and peripheral towns are also included, this rises to as much as 20 million. But, for the people of the city, there are tangible benefits in modernization and the expansion of living space from 5 sq. m (55 sq. ft) each to some 13 sq. m (140 sq. ft) in the past 25 years. The official plan provides for life expectancy to rise to 75.4 years by 2010 as average per capita earnings go well above the national level to $6,000.

Under the empire, Beijing saw itself as the city of mandarins, the major centre for serious scholarship and classical ways. This remains the case, albeit under Communism rather than Confucianism. The government and the ruling party still give the city part of its character, as do the huge expanse of Tiananmen Square and the vast concrete official buildings including Mao's tomb and the Great Hall of the People.

As the suppression of the protest in Tiananmen Square in 1989 showed, Beijing is still a city where officialdom has the last word. But it is also racing to match the progress elsewhere in China and, in the process, is acquiring some of the most impressive urban features in the country, even if the price has been the destruction of the old.

A huge portrait of Chairman Mao still hangs on the main entrance to the Forbidden City in Tiananmen Square.

JONATHAN FENBY

Shanghai – 'Paris of the Orient' 27

Nothing more intensely living can be imagined.
ALDOUS HUXLEY, C. 1920

For the century before the Communist victory in 1949, Shanghai was the most advanced and largest city in China, a metropolis devoted to making money which also became the centre of progressive intellectual and political life. The concession areas which the British and French forced the imperial government to allow them to establish in the middle of the 19th century, complete with their own legal system and military garrisons, were the spearhead of modernization in the Middle Kingdom. Though deplored by Chinese nationalists, they introduced to China everything from modern banking to electricity, from a free press to motor cars.

By the 1920s, the ever-expanding city, strategically placed as China's bridge to the world by the sea and the mouth of the biggest river, the Yangtze, accounted for half the country's foreign commerce, contained half its factories, and attracted a third of all foreign investment in China. Its population increased by a million each decade to reach 3 million by the 1930s. Great corporate buildings lined the wide riverfront avenue of the Bund. European architects built Art Deco skyscrapers. The liberated middle-class youth

The Bund and Nanjing Road in 1893. As well as plenty of money, foreigners brought Western architecture and modern facilities to Shanghai.

Photograph of the Bund and Huangpu River taken in 1929. The riverside Bund was the main artery of the foreign concessions.

strode the streets in Western dress. Bankers and merchants came from all over China, and the city was home to a mass of small traders, shopkeepers and agents.

Many Chinese moved from the native city into the concessions – of the half-million people in the French area in the 1920s, only 19,000 were foreigners and, of those, only 1,400 were from France. For all his anti-imperialism, the 'Father of the Republic', Sun Yat-sen, had a home there, in the rue Molière, and it was in the French Concession that the Communist Party held its inaugural meeting. The concessions were havens for Chinese writers, artists and intellectuals, particularly left-wingers seeking shelter from the repressive Nationalist regime. The film studios made the metropolis the Hollywood of the Orient.

On their own or in association with the foreigners, leading Chinese businessmen built up fortunes like Charlie Soong, a converted Methodist who began as a Bible publisher and founded one of the most powerful families in China: one of his daughters married Sun Yat-sen, another wed the Nationalist leader, Chiang Kai-shek, and a third had as her husband the Prime Minister and Finance Minister, H. H. Kung. Charlie's eldest son, T. V. Soong, also served as Prime Minister and Foreign Minister and, as head of the Bank of China and an array of other companies, was said to be the richest man in the world in the 1930s.

Shopping and entertainment

'In the matter of mellow creature comforts of savoury fleshpots deftly served, no Croesus of America, North or South, can ever hope to attain the comfortable heights that Shanghai takes for granted,' wrote the correspondent of the London *Times*. As well as a 26-hectare (66-acre) racecourse in the centre of the city, there were three greyhound racing tracks, the largest holding 50,000 people. The department stores along the great shopping avenue of Nanjing Road were the last word in retailing, complete with restaurants, cinemas, ping-pong tables and massage parlours.

Left *Called the 'Haolaiwu (Hollywood) of the East', Shanghai's film industry prospered before the Japanese invasion of 1937.*

Below *The Sincere Company Ltd. was one of the giant Western-style department stores in Shanghai, selling the latest goods and offering a window on the world.*

Smart ballrooms could hold 2,500 people, and the French Club offered Asia's best-sprung dance floor. The future Duchess of Windsor said she felt she had 'really entered the Celestial Kingdom' as she danced to 'Tea for Two' at a hotel on Bubbling Well Road. Shanghai, she added, was 'almost too good for a woman'.

The most famous entertainment centre, the wedding-cake-shaped Great World, owned by 'Pockmarked Huang', who combined his gangster activities with a job as head of the Chinese detective force in the French Concession, got more outrageous as one ascended its six floors, the slits up the side of the dresses of the hostesses getting higher as one rose up the stairs. There were gambling tables, magicians, fireworks, acrobats, restaurants, barbers and earwax extractors, jugglers, ice-cream parlours, shooting galleries, massage benches, acupuncture, hot-towel counters, story-tellers, peep shows, a mirror maze, love-letter booths with scribes, marriage brokers and fire crackers.

Children as young as six years old were put to work in Shanghai's many cotton and silk mills.

Immigrant population

As an open city, Shanghai attracted shoals of foreigners and refugees, which gave it a special international character. The Japanese took an ever-increasing part in industrial development, particularly its cotton and silk mills. After the Bolshevik Revolution, tens of thousands of White Russians poured in, some working in commerce, others as bodyguards, prostitutes and dance-hall hostesses. Foreign visitors ranged from politicians and businessmen to the writers George Bernard Shaw and Aldous Huxley. Noël Coward wrote his play *Private Lives* in Shanghai, over a weekend while ill with influenza in his hotel room.

Jews from Iraq became great tycoons, among them Victor Sassoon, who ran a trading and property empire, but was equally famous for his parties, his pursuit of women, and his passion for the turf – 'There is only one race greater than the Jews,' he said, 'and that's the Derby.' Elly Kadoorie, another Iraqi Jew, indulged his passion for the tango in a 130-sq.-m (400-sq.-ft) ballroom lit by 3,600 bulbs at his white-painted Marble Hall mansion. Silas Hardoon, who started off as a warehouse watchman, lived with his Eurasian wife and ten adopted children in an estate in the centre of the city with three houses, pavilions, artificial hills, lakes and bamboo groves.

Poverty and crime

A celebrated novel of the city, *Ziye* (*Midnight*) by Mao Dun, opened with the image of a gigantic neon sign on the roof of the power plant beside the Huangpu River flashing out in flaming red and phosphorescent green the words (written in English in capitals) LIGHT, HEAT, POWER. But this vibrant city covering 50 sq. km (20 sq. miles) was, as a saying went, 'a thin layer of Heaven on a deep slice of Hell'. Most inhabitants lived wretched lives, toiling in mills for 10–14 hours a day, 7 days a week, sleeping in teeming tenements, if not on the street, on sampans or under river pontoons. Hygiene was non-existent, disease and crime endemic. The stink from the river and its creeks was inescapable, and Shanghai was three times as crowded as London.

The underworld Green Gang was enormously powerful, running drugs, protection rackets, kidnapping and labour extortion. Allying with the Nationalist leader, Chiang Kai-shek, it provided the foot soldiers for his 'White Terror' purge of the

Sampans (flat-bottomed boats, with the literal meaning of 'three planks') are moored on the Suzhou Creek. Beside the smart homes of the concessions, many lived in poverty.

powerful Communist and trade unions in 1927. Thereafter, the city was the main treasure house for the Nationalist regime that ruled China till 1949. The Gang's leader, opium-addicted 'Big Ears' Du, became the Shanghai Godfather, branching out in banking and legitimate business but still delivering coffins as warnings to those who refused his demands.

War

In 1932 Japan provoked a war in the city which ended with it forcing the Chinese government to agree not to station troops there. Five years later, as general fighting broke out across China, fresh conflict erupted in the streets and surrounding countryside, ending with Japanese occupation of the Chinese quarters – and then, after Pearl Harbor – of the whole city. The end of the Second World War in 1945 brought the liberation of Shanghai and the disappearance of the foreign concessions, but the city did not regain its previous vitality. As the Communist army approached in 1949, Nationalist troops fled to Taiwan without putting up a fight. A giant portrait of Mao Zedong was hung in front of the Great World as businessmen moved to Hong Kong.

In the first decades of Communist rule, the metropolis was regarded as an unwelcome symbol of the capitalist past. It became a byword for political orthodoxy and, during the Cultural Revolution, Shanghai became a radical centre, with Mao's wife operating from a mock-Tudor villa built in the 1920s by a foreign businessman for his mistress. It was not until the 1980s that the city began to return to its former glory, and the palatial buildings of its past were restored as offices, restaurants, bars and night clubs to produce China's most vibrant metropolis.

JONATHAN FENBY

28 Shanghai Today

The key issue is to further promote the city and increase the city's international awareness and influence.

YIN YICUI, DEPUTY SECRETARY OF THE SHANGHAI COMMITTEE OF THE COMMUNIST PARTY OF CHINA, APRIL 2006

Since China began its market-driven economic expansion in the 1980s, Shanghai has become the most visible standard bearer of modernity in this country of 1.3 billion people, as a major industrial, commercial and financial centre and a magnet for foreign investment. Its importance is shown by the way in which it contributes a quarter of total tax revenue received by the Chinese government. It was not, however, chosen by the patriarch, Deng Xiaoping, as one of the special development zones – those were located further south. But, from the early 1990s, it benefited from a combination of circumstances. First of all, there was its geographical location in the delta where the Yangtze River meets the sea. Then the policies of the municipal government and strong links with the central administration in Beijing boosted the city as an economic force. There was also, perhaps, the subconscious inheritance of its pre-Communist past (p. 121) and the traditional commercial acumen attributed to the people of Shanghai. All this make it China's most go-ahead city and the country's most populous metropolis with 18 million inhabitants – though both claims will be challenged by the development of the capital in the run-up to the 2008 Olympic Games (p. 116).

The city, which will host the World Expo in

Nanjing Road, Shanghai – a bustling commercial street of modern buildings.

A businessman makes his way towards the skyscrapers in Pudong district, the financial centre of Shanghai.

2010, has leaped ahead in a way that astounds visitors. One joke is that the street maps are out of date before they are printed. A constant theme of discussion is whether Shanghai will take over the long-standing role of Hong Kong (p. 281) as China's main bridge with the rest of the world, whether it will develop the legal and business methods needed to become a truly global metropolis – and whether the pace of growth seen in the last two decades can be maintained. Known for their self-confidence, Shanghai people have no doubt of the answer. The city's Communist Party leaders think there is still more to be done, though they were shaken by a major corruption scandal in 2006.

Shanghai counts some 4,000 skyscrapers, and plans another 1,000 in the coming years. The Oriental Pearl Tower, made up of three columns and topped by a TV transmitter, rises 486 m (1,600 ft) beside the Huangpu River. Nearby is the 421-m (1,400-ft) Jin Mao Tower, with a hotel perched on top. The business district of Pudong has been reclaimed from a swamp, which is now covered by wide streets and towering ranks of office and apartment blocks. The new international airport is one of the most advanced in the world, linked to the city by a magnetic high-speed train and an eight-lane highway.

The Donghai Bridge, the longest sea bridge on earth when it was opened in 2005, stretches

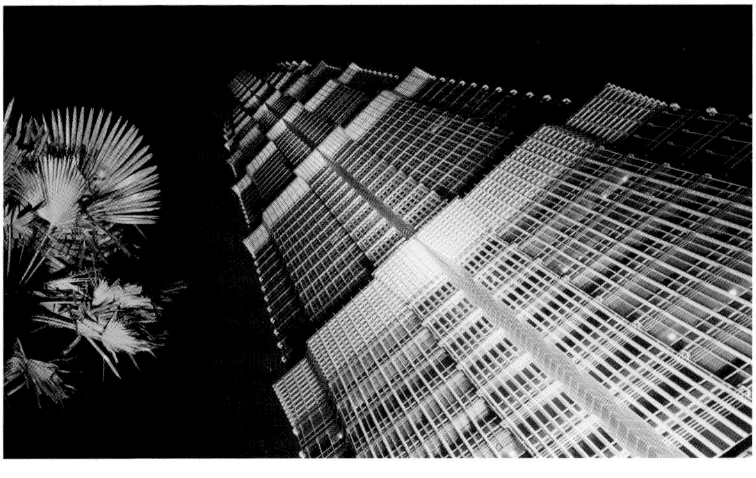

A dizzying view of the Jin Mao Tower.

for 32 km (20 miles) to the Yangshan Islands. Shanghai hosts a Grand Prix motor race and has an ultra-modern new stadium which is packed out particularly for visiting European soccer teams. The surrounding region, including the old silk city of Suzhou (p. 134) and new manufacturing centres in the Yangtze delta, make it an industrial hub, and its services sector has been expanding rapidly as well.

Elevated expressways are being constructed to reduce the traffic congestion. Lines are being added to the underground railway, and the city boasts a thousand bus routes. Its port has become one of the leading channels for goods in the world, playing a key role in the booming trade between China, Japan, Southeast Asia and the West. A state-of-the-art cruise ship terminal has been built on the river. Bullet train links will span out 160 km (100 miles) southwards to Hangzhou (p. 131) and 1,300 (800 miles) west to Beijing (p. 116). Shopping streets sport luxury global brands, and are jam-packed with crowds at weekends. Shanghai property developers are a byword for their activity. The region is a centre for China's burgeoning car industry. It houses one of China's two stock exchanges (the other is in the southern city of Shenzhen).

Links with the past

There are links with the past – now, as then, Shanghai is home to some of the country's top universities. It attracts writers, artists and filmmakers, and its night life and conspicuous consumption are celebrated. Gardens dating from the imperial age have been preserved, with their tea houses and arcades of shops selling traditional wares. The shrine of the school where the Chinese Communist Party held its first meeting has been renovated, close to an area of old houses which has been transformed by a Hong Kong entrepreneur into a buzzy restaurant, bar and night-club district. The homes of leading Communists, and other figures of 20th-century history, are carefully maintained.

But, as the city powers ahead, questions have been raised about Shanghai losing its character. Many of the traditional two- or three-storey houses with small courtyards or set behind brick walls along alleys with archways, have been pulled down to make way for modern apartment

Left *Some gardens and buildings of the past survive, as tourist attractions. China's oldest tea house in the old Chinese Quarter dates back to 1784.*

and office buildings. It is estimated that, by the time of the Expo in 2010, only 5 per cent of the old city neighbourhoods, with their street food stalls and markets, will remain. Still, the city authorities appear to have become more aware of the need to preserve the past alongside the gleaming concrete, steel and glass present. The big neo-classical buildings along the wide avenue by the river, the Bund, have been restored as homes for Chinese and foreign businesses.

The city houses one of China's finest museums, in a building with a square base and round top to denote earth and sky. Opened in 1996, its 11 galleries contain 120,000 pieces, collected not only from domestic sources but also including unique objects donated from Hong Kong and by Overseas Chinese (p. 288). It has an elegant modern opera house and theatre. The mansions of pre-Communist tycoons have been turned into municipal facilities; and the home of the Father of the Republic, Sun Yat-sen, is preserved on a quiet street in what was once the French quarter. Though the national tongue is spoken by virtually everybody under 60 years old, many inhabitants still use the Shanghai dialect which numerous

The Bund at night – Shanghai's famous riverside avenue flanked by historic buildings.

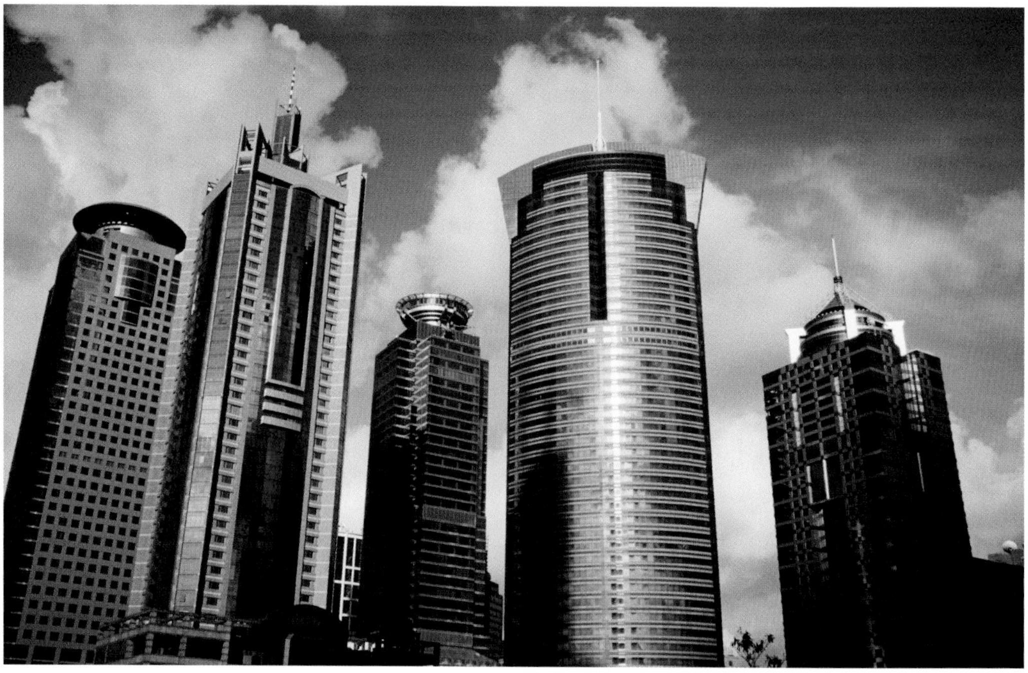

Skyscrapers rise by the month, funded by the booming economy and a growing middle class.

Chinese from other parts of the country cannot understand. The local cuisine thrives, particularly the speciality of dumplings.

The city as a magnet

As it was in its pre-Communist incarnation, Shanghai is a magnet both for Chinese people and for a growing foreign community. It attracts migrant workers from all over the country who provide low-cost labour for factories and construction projects. Some seeking work sleep in the street, a reminder that not everybody is profiting from China's economic miracle. There is also a steadily expanding middle class – both local and from elsewhere in China – which has fuelled the boom in property, retailing and the development of private education and health facilities. Some 300,000 people from the island of Taiwan are estimated to be living and working in the Shanghai region.

Though the importance of river transport has declined, the great Yangtze River remains a key route for China, linking the west of the country with the central valley round Wuhan and then going to the Nanjing (p. 141) region, and, finally, reaching the delta round Shanghai. Japan lies across the sea, and maritime routes connect Shanghai with both the traditional industrial area of northeast China and the fast-growing southern coastal zones.

As China undertook its path of expansion, led by exports to the West, prominent figures in the central government in Beijing had direct personal connections with the city. For a time after the Communist victory in 1949, Shanghai's past as a wide-open commercial centre known for its decadence and links with the previous, Nationalist, regime, made it politically suspect. It was kept under tight rein by Beijing. But then its former mayor, Jiang Zemin, became Communist Party chief and President and his successor as city leader, Zhu Rongji, was appointed Prime Minister in charge of economic reform. The Shanghai connection no longer applies as a new generation of leaders from other parts of the country has assumed power.

Some questions have been raised as to whether Shanghai will continue to receive favoured treatment, or whether the current policy of seeking to spread development more widely across China will affect it. But its size, prosperity and progress seem to guarantee the city on the Huangpu River a leading role in China's growth, and in its relationship with the rest of the world.

FRANCES WOOD

Hangzhou

29

Green mountains surround on all sides the still waters of the lake. Pavilions and towers in hues of gold and azure rise here and there. One would say a landscape composed by a painter. Only towards the east, where there are no hills, does the land open out and there sparkle, like fishes' scales, the bright coloured tiles of a thousand roofs.

JACQUES GERNET ON CHINA 1250–1276

Set beside the West Lake, at the southern end of the Grand Canal, the city of Hangzhou has been celebrated since the Tang dynasty (AD 618–907) for its natural beauty. The lake was formed when silt from the Qiantang River cut off an inlet and in the 6th century AD when the southern part of the Grand Canal was constructed to transport rice northwards, the small city was walled. It remained vulnerable to flooding, particularly during the autumn equinox when strong tides force the Qiantang waters inland, forming the famous Hangzhou bore, a wall of water some 7 m (20 ft) high. In the Five Dynasties period, when Hangzhou was ruled by the independent kings of Wu Yue, the Pagoda of Six Harmonies (*Liu he ta*) was constructed on the bank of the Qiantang River, in the hope of subduing the river.

Apart from the rice shipped up the Grand Canal, the silk industry was also important in Hangzhou, and tea produced on the local hills, particularly Longjing or Dragon Well green tea, is one of the most famous in China. The city became a major trading centre with ten great markets selling pork, cereals, fish, lotus seeds, 11 varieties of apricot, pears, shellfish, venison and other luxuries. It attracted traders and travellers, including possibly Marco Polo (13th century) and Odoric of Pordenone (14th century) and the first British envoy to China, Lord Macartney in 1793.

The West Lake

As a beauty spot, Hangzhou is one of the best examples of the Chinese aesthetic, which holds that nature, though beautiful in itself, is further enhanced by architecture. Construction on and around the lake, with temples and pagodas set in the surrounding hills began in the early 9th century. Some of the first constructions were both practical and aesthetic. The Bai causeway which links the sandbank island, *Gu shan* or 'Lonely island', with the lake shore, was built when the poet Bai Juyi (772–846) was serving as an official in Hangzhou, and incorporates locks to control the water flow. Allowing access to *Gu shan*, it also served to break up the expanse of water, a technique often used in garden design.

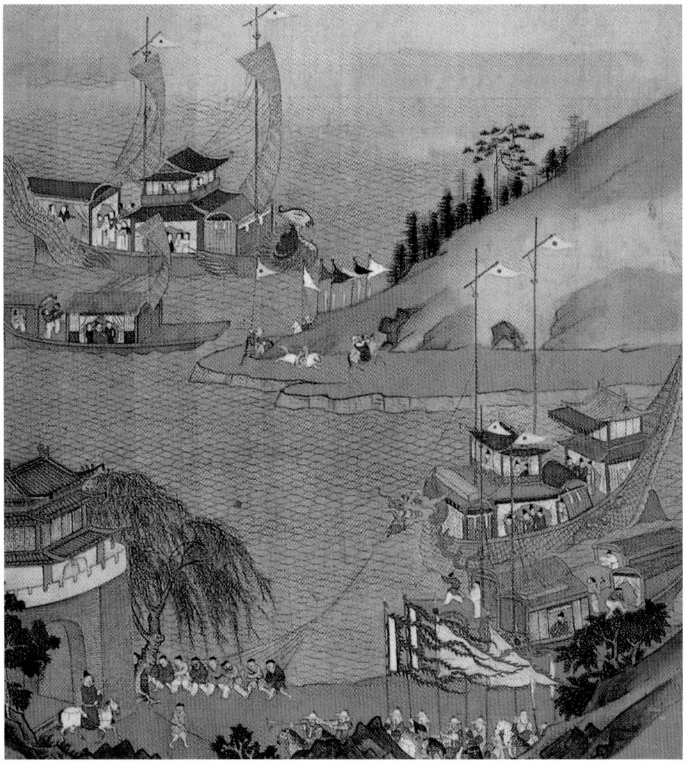

An 18th-century silk painting showing the emperor Yangdi inspecting the new extension of the Grand Canal at Hangzhou.

Above *As in a small garden, the West Lake is dotted with elegant waterside pavilions to frame views of the water and hills. It is one of China's most celebrated beauty spots.*

Below *The West Lake was once an inlet to the Qiantang River, but was then cut off from the river by silt deposits. The Grand Canal is off this plan to the northeast.*

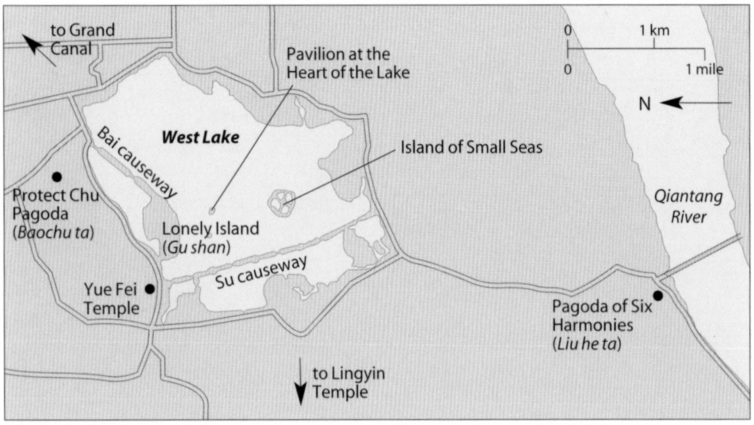

A longer dyke, which in effect created a 'western inner lake' was constructed when another famous poet, Su Dongpo, served as Governor of Hangzhou (1089–1091) and is named after him.

The surface of the lake is broken up by small artificial islets. The Pavilion at the Heart of the Lake, just beyond *Gu shan*, was first constructed in 1552 and the Island of Small Seas, with four pools enclosed by dredged silt, was made in 1607. Both have small pavilions on them and to the south of the Island of Small Seas is a group of stone pagodas set in the lake. They are said to have been placed by Su Dongpo, to warn against the planting of water chestnuts which threatened to clog the lake. When the moon is full, candles are placed within them so they look like three small moons joining the reflection of the full moon on the water.

Pagodas and palaces

Hangzhou was frequently visited by the Kangxi (r. 1662–1722) and Qianlong (r. 1736–1795) emperors on their tours of inspection of southern China. They built 'travelling palaces' around the town and on *Gu shan* island. There, Qianlong also built a library to house one of the sets of his 36,000-volume collectanea, *Siku quanshu* or 'Complete Treasury of the Four Storehouses', which was destroyed with most of Hangzhou's temples in 1860–1862 when Taiping rebels, led by a messianic leader partly inspired by Christian teaching, attacked the city.

Around the lake are the *Baochu ta* (Protect Chu Pagoda), built between 968 and 975 in an unusual tapering form, and the *Leifeng ta* (Thunder Peak Pagoda), built in 975 from bricks containing tiny printed Buddhist texts, which collapsed in 1924 but which has been very recently rebuilt, perhaps because of the legend of the White Snake. One of Hangzhou's most famous stories tells of a white snake which could turn itself into a beautiful woman to ensnare young men. The snake was finally trapped in the foundations of the pagoda and the story ends with a warning that when the pagoda falls, the Hangzhou bore fails and the West Lake dries up, the snake will be released.

To the west of the lake, in the hills, is the Lingyin (Spirit Retreat) Buddhist Temple, founded by an Indian monk in 326, and approached by paths lined with rock carvings dating from the

10th to the 14th centuries forming the most significant group of Buddhist rock carvings in southern China.

Beside the lake is a temple commemorating a local hero, General Yue Fei (1103–1142), whose loyalty to an effete ruling house is known throughout China and has elevated him to almost god-like status. The Song dynasty (960–1279) had been forced to move its capital south to Hangzhou in 1127 as the north of China was invaded by the Jin. Yue Fei led a successful campaign against them in 1140 and was keen to continue to recapture the north but he was ordered to return, as his army was seen as more of a threat than the Jin. He was imprisoned and executed, but in 1221 a temple in his memory was built near his lakeside grave. Characters which mean 'Ultimate loyalty to the country' which, according to legend, Yue Fei's mother tattooed on his back before he went north, are carved in stone by the Ming calligrapher Hong Zhu, and repeated elsewhere in the temple compound. This compound is also famous for the kneeling cast-iron figures of his persecutors that are spat upon by visitors.

The shrine of a local hero. A sculpture of General Yue Fei sleeping surrounded by lions rests in the Lingyin Temple.

Hangzhou today

Unlike many other Chinese cities, Hangzhou retains much of its beauty. High-rise buildings have largely been kept away from the lake and, though many grand villas have recently been built around it by the rich and powerful, they are mostly screened from view by trees and vegetation.

Pilgrims at the Lingyin Buddhist Temple. Traditional festivals have not been lost.

30

Suzhou

Above is heaven, on earth are Suzhou and Hangzhou.
CHINESE PROVERB

On the Grand Canal, in the south of Jiangsu province, Suzhou is famous for its silk and its gardens and was for over 1,000 years effectively the cultural centre of China. In the past, it was a small city criss-crossed by narrow canals, traversed by many elegant hump-backed bridges, the canal banks lined with white-walled, grey-tiled houses. During the Ming and Qing dynasties it became a favourite retirement place for officials who constructed fine house-garden complexes, created by local craftsmen and filled with elegant furniture, paintings and calligraphy. Where Hangzhou (p. 131) was celebrated for its natural beauty, the attractions of Suzhou were mainly man-made, reaching a peak of extravagant refinement. As the late Ming author Zhang Han noted, 'People from all over favour Suzhou clothing and so Suzhou artisans work even harder at making it. People from all over value Suzhou artifacts and so Suzhou artisans work even harder at making them. This drives the extravagance of Suzhou style to even greater extravagance, so how is it possible to lead those who follow the Suzhou fashion back to sensible economy?'

Album leaves from the 18th-century album 'Pictures of Tilling and Weaving' (Geng zhi tu).

In the late 18th century, John Barrow, comptroller to Lord Macartney, the first official British envoy to China, described Suzhou with less disapproval: 'The school of the greatest artists, the most well-known scholars, the richest merchants, the best actors, the most nimble acrobats, it is also the home of delicately made women with tiny feet. It rules Chinese taste in matters of fashion and speech, and it is the meeting-place of the richest pleasure-seekers and gentlemen of leisure in China.'

The silk trade

The town was created in the 6th century BC by a local ruler who dug canals to control the low water table and a moat to surround the walled town, but its economic position was assured by the expansion of the Grand Canal network between AD 605 and 611, subsequent improvements in the Tang dynasty including the construction of the Precious Belt Bridge (*Baodai qiao*) with its three high, elegant central arches enabling the passage of boats carrying quantities of Suzhou silk. During the Ming dynasty, when demand for silk was at its height, intensive production methods, involving hundreds of impoverished day workers, led to a strike in 1626, but conditions were not improved, for several stelae from 1715, 1734 and 1822 have been discovered carved with edicts forbidding the silk workers to strike.

Gardens

In contrast with the poverty and insecurity of the silk workers, rich officials constructed their characteristic southern gardens. Including domestic buildings as well as pools, rockeries and vegetable plots, these gardens often occupied a very tiny area. One of the most perfect, the Garden of the Master of the Fishing Nets (*Wang shi yuan*), first built in 1440 and rebuilt in 1770, occupies only one acre.

Suzhou gardens integrate dwellings and other buildings such as pavilions perched beside pools or on top of rockeries to afford a view, with water, rocks and, finally, plants. They are usually divided into different areas, each with a characteristic feature, which could be a pool, an elegant rock, stone-carved calligraphy set into the courtyard walls, raised beds surrounded by elegantly carved stone, or a single tree or plant. The walls dividing the spaces are often pierced with elegant openings, shaped like fans or leaves or filled with decorative lattice, enabling a glimpse of the view beyond. And just as the gardens themselves are never laid out to offer an open, unrestricted view, so the areas of water are rarely left completely bare but are divided by rocks or low bridges.

The earliest surviving garden in Suzhou is the *Canglangting* or Pavilion of the Blue Waves, named from a line in the 4th-century BC *Chu ci* (Songs of the South), 'If the water of the Canglang river is clean, I wash the ribbons of my official hat in it, if it is dirty I wash my feet'. The connection

The view across the pool in the Garden of the Master of the Fishing Nets is characteristically framed in carved lattice. Apart from a few waterlilies, the surface of the pool is clear, to allow reflections. Beside the grey tiled, whitewashed garden buildings there is restrained vegetation and a low rockery. Decorative openings, including a moon gate, offer glimpses of further garden courtyards.

Owing to the number of canals in the city, water transport was, until recently, very practical.

with officialdom is obvious for many gardens belonged to retired officials; washing the feet is a domestic detail, and many garden names reflect a form of modesty and domesticity (like the Master of the Fishing Nets), and the use of a quotation is characteristic. The naming of pavilions within gardens, the inscription of the name in fine calligraphy, made a visit to a garden a sort of literary and artistic crossword puzzle as visitors sought to recognize the source of a phrase. The layout of the Canglangting is as it was in 1044, a series of green 'rooms' with latticework windows, green bamboos, stone-carved landscapes and a 'borrowed view' of the canal outside, making the garden seem larger than it is.

The larger *Zhuozheng yuan*, Garden of the Artless Administrator, was built in the Ming dynasty on the site of an earlier garden. Its name refers to the statement by a discontented official of the 3rd century who said that gardening was the only form of administration suitable for untalented officials. Its central section is centred on a winding lake with side inlets and it is one of the few where changes in fashion in garden design over the centuries can be demonstrated, for while the Ming painter Wen Zhengming depicted natural, earthy banks along the pool, in the Qing dynasty (or more recently), the banks have been built up with craggy boulders.

A similar development in style can be seen in the *Shizi lin* (Lion grove), created in about 1336 for a Buddhist monk in the grounds of a temple. A scroll painting made shortly afterwards shows a fairly plain, rock-lined courtyard, whilst today the courtyard is crammed with strangely shaped rocks and crags, demonstrating in an extreme form the Chinese gardener's enthusiasm for club-shaped, deeply pitted rocks from Lake Tai in Wuxi.

Suzhou has lost many of its canals and is now criss-crossed by main roads, lined with modern shops designed to look like the old white-washed houses. Its fate is echoed in many of the picturesque waterside villages nearby such as Zhou Zhuang which are being developed as tourist sites, bustling with souvenir sellers by day, deserted by night.

ZHANG YINGLAN

Xi'an

31

In the middle of Shaanxi is the imperial capital of old.
DU FU, *AUTUMN FEELING*, TANG DYNASTY

Known as one of the six famous ancient cities in China, Xi'an in Shaanxi province has been the imperial capital of 13 dynasties since the 11th century BC, among them, the Western Zhou (*c.* 1046–771 BC), Qin (221–206 BC), Western Han (202 BC–AD 8) and Tang (618–907); these were the most strong and prosperous periods in ancient China.

In Chinese, Xi'an means 'Western Peace'; it also has some other names, such as Chang'an, which means 'Everlasting Peace'. Just like the meaning of these names, the natural environment of the Xi'an area is very agreeable. Located on the south bank of the Wei River, Xi'an was the cradle of Chinese civilization, thanks to the extremely productive and easily tillable soil of the Wei River valley. Archaeologists have found many Neolithic sites in this area, the most famous being Banpo.

The imperial capital

Xi'an's history can be dated back to the 11th century BC, when King Wen and King Wu of the Western Zhou made a capital at Fenghao near modern Xi'an city. In the 3rd century BC, the Qin state settled its capital here and named it Xianyang. Then Qin Shihuangdi, the first emperor of the Qin dynasty, planned and started the ten-year war in his palace here against the six other states, and finally unified the whole country. Although the Qin dynasty had only 15 years of history, it left many cultural relics here, such as the Epang Palace site and the terracotta army (p. 155).

The following Han dynasty also established the new imperial capital only a few miles northwest of present-day Xi'an, and named it Chang'an. It was the site of many luxurious palaces until about AD 25, when the Han capital moved east to Luoyang, another ancient city of China. The Xi'an area was relatively neglected during the period AD 220–581. In AD 581 when the Sui dynasty reunified China, the Sui emperor Wen established his capital in Xi'an, calling it Daxing (Great Prosperity).

A centre for trade

The Tang dynasty soon came to power; they enlarged the Sui capital and renamed it Chang'an to recall the glory of the Han dynasty. As the Tang capital, the metropolis flourished and became the most important cosmopolitan centre in Asia, and perhaps the largest city in the world at that time, with a population estimated at more than one million. Under the Tang, Chang'an formed a rectangle 10 km long and 9 km wide (6 x 5.5 miles) surrounded by an earthen wall, parts of which still remain. The imperial palace was located in the northern part of town, with the government offices just south of it.

Chang'an was a bustling cultural and commercial centre during the Tang dynasty. Chang'an was also at the eastern end of the trade routes from Central Asia, known as the Silk Road (p. 43), which since the 2nd century BC, had brought cultural and business contacts including foreign art, music, food and clothing. The Silk Road was especially active during the Tang period. The excavated ancient Chang'an marketplace, where thousands of travelling diplomatic envoys, students, clergymen and merchants lived, has revealed Chinese, Arabian, Persian and Byzantine coins; trade involved India and even Rome. The variety of temples shows the influence of Daoism, Buddhism, Nestorianism and Islam.

Pottery figure of a lady with a shawl. Excavated from a Tang-dynasty tomb in Xi'an.

The Silk Road was also the route travelled by the explorer Marco Polo, who arrived at the city in the 13th century.

After the Tang, Xi'an (as it was later renamed) went into a long period of decline, and never again served as the capital of China. It was partially rebuilt at the beginning of the Ming dynasty (1368–1644) but, greatly reduced from its former glory, occupied only one seventh of its Tang-dynasty area. During the Qing dynasty (1644–1911), Xi'an under Manchu rule was still noted for its beauty and historical artifacts, but was now only a small town.

The Drum and Bell Towers

Besides the world-famous terracotta army of the Qin dynasty, there are many ancient monuments, buildings and historical sites around Xi'an, due to its long history. The ancient city wall was built more than 600 years ago, with a circumference of 14 km (8 miles), covering an area of 11.5 sq. km (4 sq. miles), at 12 m (40 ft) tall and 12–18 m (40–60 ft) wide. In each side there are city gates, over which the various towers majestically stand. The South Gate is the most impressive. All together, the watchtowers, ramparts and 98 defensive towers form a very tight system for military defence of the city.

In the very centre of Xi'an city the symbol of Xi'an, a 36-m-tall (118-ft) Bell Tower is located, initially built in 1384, the 17th year of the Ming

The famous Bell Tower or Zhong Lou *in Xi'an, lit up at night.*

People stroll across the ancient city wall of Xi'an, which is flanked by 98 defensive towers. After recent restoration work, the city wall and its moat enclose a beautiful historical park.

Below *Modern Xi'an city. The City Wall, which was built 600 years ago, is located in the centre of the city, with Bell Tower, Drum Tower and Great Mosque within it. Daminggong Palace site, Big Goose Pagoda and Small Goose Pagoda of the Tang dynasty are around the city walls.*

emperor Hongwu's reign. In 1582 it was removed intact to its present position in the administration of Gong Xian, the imperial inspector of the time. The 15th-century, 2.5-tonne, iron bell that used to sound the hour now rests on the northwest corner of the tower, which now marks the intersection of four different streets around it.

Slightly northwest of the Bell Tower, the 27-m (90-ft) tall Drum Tower was also built under the Ming in 1380. In ancient times, drums were beaten from this tower for ten minutes before the city gates were closed for the night.

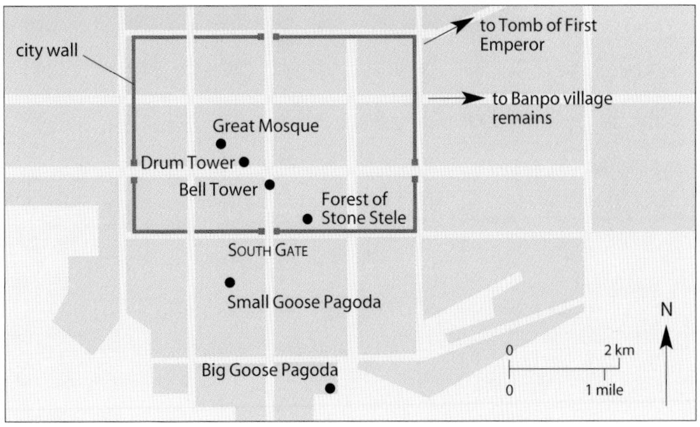

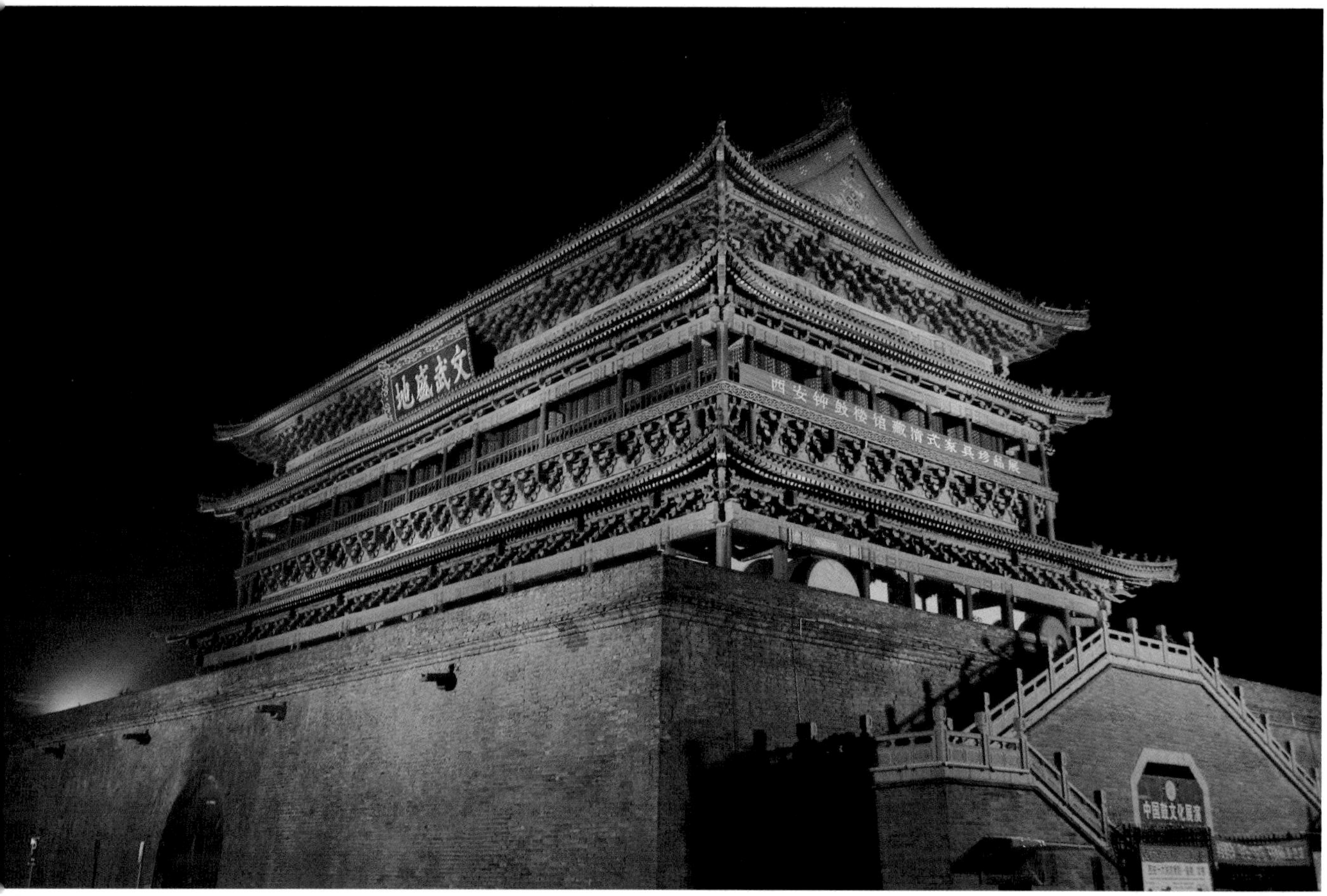

The Drum Tower stands 27 m (90 ft) tall. It was used to warn the people of Xi'an that the city gates were about to be shut.

The Great Mosque and other historical sites

Another attractive spot in Xi'an is the Great Mosque, which lies close by the northwest of the Drum Tower. During the Tang dynasty, large numbers of Muslims travelled the Silk Road to Chang'an, bringing Islam to China. They founded the Great Mosque in 742, with the support of emperor Xuanzong. The Great Mosque is a well-preserved example of cultural merging and exhibits the unification of foreign architecture. From the carvings and furniture inside to the eaved pagoda for the minaret, Chinese influence is apparent. However, Arabic and West Asian styles prevail in the Great Hall, which was constructed mainly in the 14th century. Inscriptions are in Arabic, but the characters are sometimes arranged like Chinese characters. The library includes many books in the Arabic style which were actually written in China.

There are also dozens of emperors' and empresses' mausoleums remaining around Xi'an. Archaeological excavations show us many unbelievable discoveries. Besides discoveries in Qin Shihuangdi's tomb, archaeologists have also unearthed thousands of naked pottery figures in the accessory burial pits of Yangling, the tombs of emperor Han Jingdi of the Han dynasty. Now a modern on-site museum has been built there, and visitors can go down the brand-new underground exhibition hall to touch the history.

In the long list of historical monuments and cultural relics found and preserved in Xi'an, we can add many other names, such as Daminggong Palace site, Big Goose Pagoda and Small Goose Pagoda of the Tang dynasty, and Forest of Stone Stele of the Song dynasty (960–1279). From them, we can almost follow every step of Chinese glory and imperial history. In fact, the height of Xi'an coincided with the prosperous period of ancient China.

JONATHAN FENBY

Nanjing

32

With Purple Mountain as twining dragon and Stone Wall as crouching tiger, Nanjing is a real home of emperors.

MING-ERA SAYING

Lying on the Yangtze River in the Jiangsu province of eastern China, and backed by mountains that give it good *feng shui*, Nanjing (*nan* 'south', *jing* 'capital') has seen some of the most dramatic and tragic episodes in Chinese history. It was a centre of learning and Buddhism under the Tang dynasty (618–907), famed for its poets, and for its Rainbow Terrace where, moved by a preacher's eloquence, Buddha dropped a shower of flowers that turned into agate pebbles. The Qixia monastery in the mountains was famed for its religious study – in the grounds, a stupa dating from 601 still stands near a rock face with carvings from the same century known as the Thousand Buddha Cliff.

The Nanjing region attracted several of China's rulers during the unsettled period that followed the fall of the Han in 220. A king from the Three Kingdoms period (220–265) was buried outside the city. The Jin emperor fled to the relative safety of the Yangtze when nomadic raiders occupied northern China in the early 4th century, and more than 30 sites have been found containing carved tombs of nobles and military leaders dating from the same era.

Under the Southern Song empire (1127–1197), Nanjing and the Yangtze valley came to play an important cultural and commercial role, and the city rose to glory when the first Ming-dynasty emperor, Hongwu (1368–1398), adopted it as his

Engraving of Nanjing Pagoda by Johann Bernhard Fischer von Erlach, c. 1721.

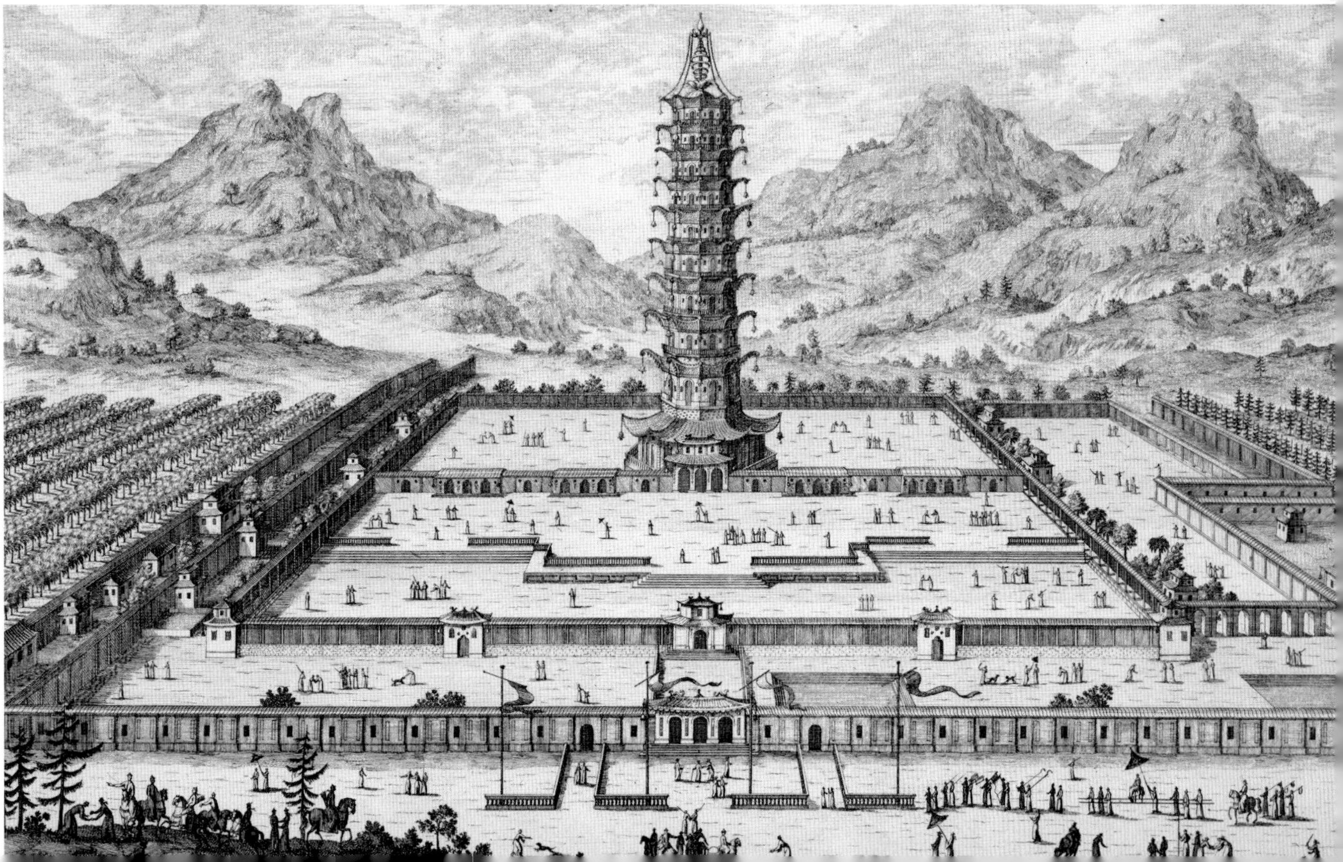

Hongwu, first emperor of the Ming dynasty. This portrait and his tomb are both in Nanjing.

capital under the name of Yingtianfu. The son of a poor peasant family, he built an enormous palace as a sign of his power. A high, thick wall – said to be the longest of any urban centre on earth – was constructed round the 129-sq.-km (50-sq.-mile) city, its 13 gates built with a mixture of paste, lime and rice gruel, some of which still stand.

Monuments

A hall was constructed which could accommodate 20,000 students as they sat for the imperial examinations (p. 64). On a peak outside the city, an observatory was built in which a Ming-era copy of an earthquake detector from the Han dynasty (206 BC–AD 220) can still be seen. The Bell Tower greeted the day with its chiming and the beating of a drum in the Drum Tower marked the closing of the gates at dusk – both have been preserved. In a novel architectural feat, the brick Linggu monastery was built in the Purple Mountains over a mound of earth which was then removed, leaving it without any supporting pillars.

When the first Ming emperor died at the very end of the 14th century, he was buried in a mausoleum 400 m (1,312 ft) in diameter below the mountains at the end of a spirit road lined with statues of scholars, warriors and animals who would accompany him to the afterlife. A hundred thousand labourers were said to have worked at the site which was surrounded by a 24-km (15-mile) wall and guarded by 5,000 soldiers. Though the third Ming emperor moved the capital to

Below *Gate to the Qixia Monastery.*

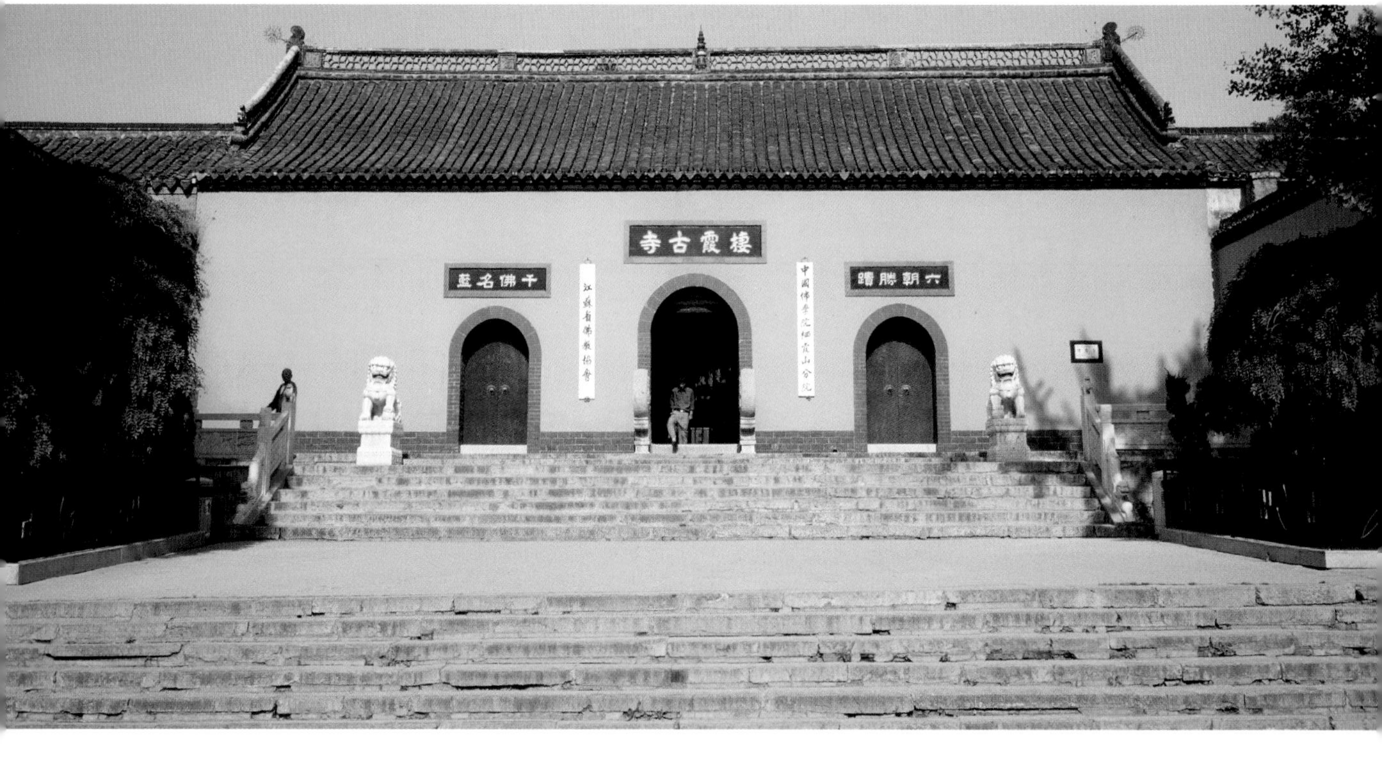

Beijing at the beginning of the 15th century, Nanjing remained the southern capital.

Politics and the Taiping Rebellion

It was still an important centre through the Qing dynasty which succeeded the Ming in the 17th century. Emperors included Nanjing on their provincial tours, one personally writing an inscription at the tomb of the first Ming. The city's strategic position on one of China's main river communications routes ensured that it would always be well guarded. But, in 1842, the British capitalized on their victory in the First Opium War by forcing the Qing to sign a treaty in Nanjing which ceded them concessions in Chinese cities as well as Hong Kong.

A decade later, the city became the capital of a messianic rebellion, the Taiping, led by a southern teacher who declared himself to be the son of the Christian God. In 1853, Nanjing was proclaimed the Heavenly City where the Taiping leader lived in a large palace while rebel armies roamed across China, at one point threatening Beijing. The Ming emperor's tomb was looted, and temples despoiled as the rebels pursued their crusade against the Manchu Qing empire and Confucianism. After 11 years, pro-imperial forces blasted their way through the walls and ended China's greatest rebellion of the 19th century which brought a death toll that has been estimated at anywhere between 10 and 20 million.

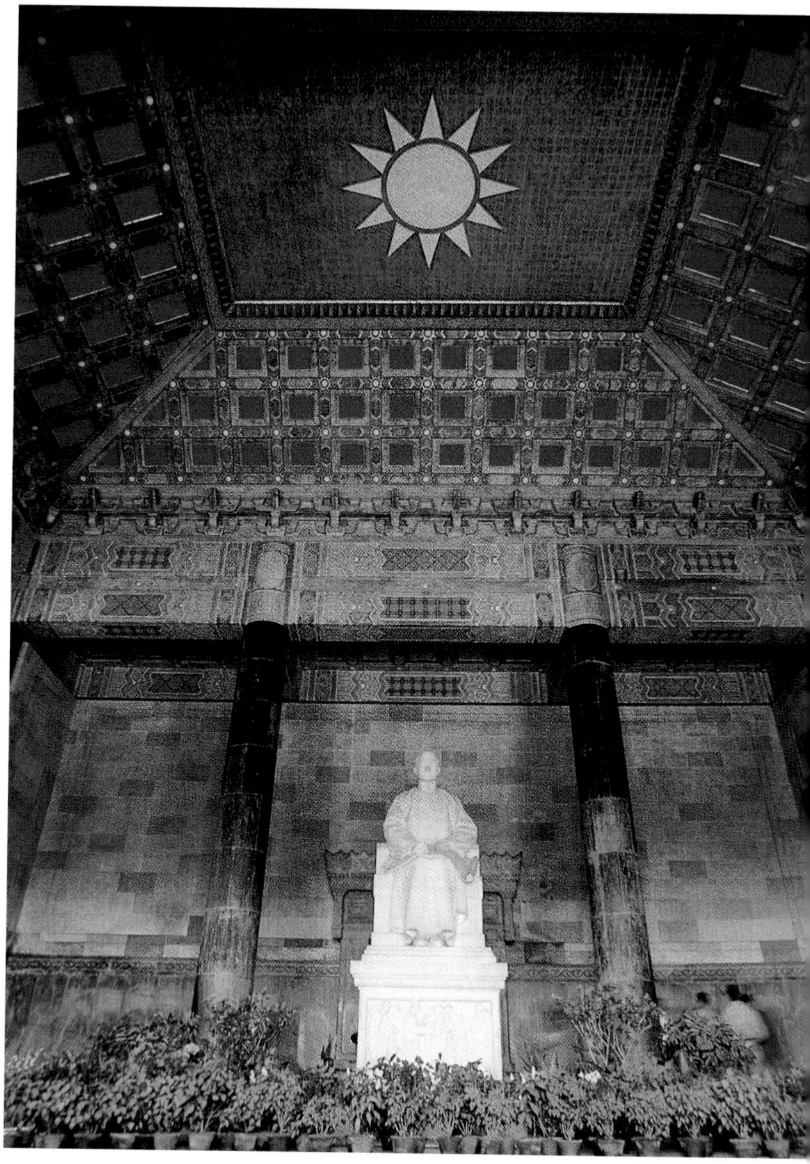

A large statue of Sun Yat-sen, the 'Father of the Republic', surveys his mausoleum.

Capital of the Republic

When the Qing were overthrown in 1912, the new Republic made Nanjing its capital. The first president, Sun Yat-sen, established his headquarters in an elegant late imperial garden complex, now a tourist attraction. But Sun soon relinquished power to a general based in Beijing and, as China descended into ten years of warlord fighting, Nanjing lost its status. In 1927, it was the scene of the Nanjing Incident where unruly troops killed foreigners, and set off an international storm. When Chiang Kai-shek, Sun's heir as head of the Kuomintang Nationalist party, led an army to unify China in the late 1920s and end the warlord era, he chose Nanjing as the national capital.

New government buildings were erected, combining traditional and modern styles. Western experts were appointed to advise on the modernization of China and its capital – one American suggested laying a road along the city wall. Sun Yat-sen's body was brought from its original resting place outside Beijing to an imposing mausoleum with a gleaming blue-tiled roof built at the top of 400 granite steps flanked by pine, cypress and Ginkgo trees. Over the gate at the top are inscribed Sun's words: 'The nation is the people's nation and everyone shall serve the nation selflessly.' Inside the 750-sq.-m

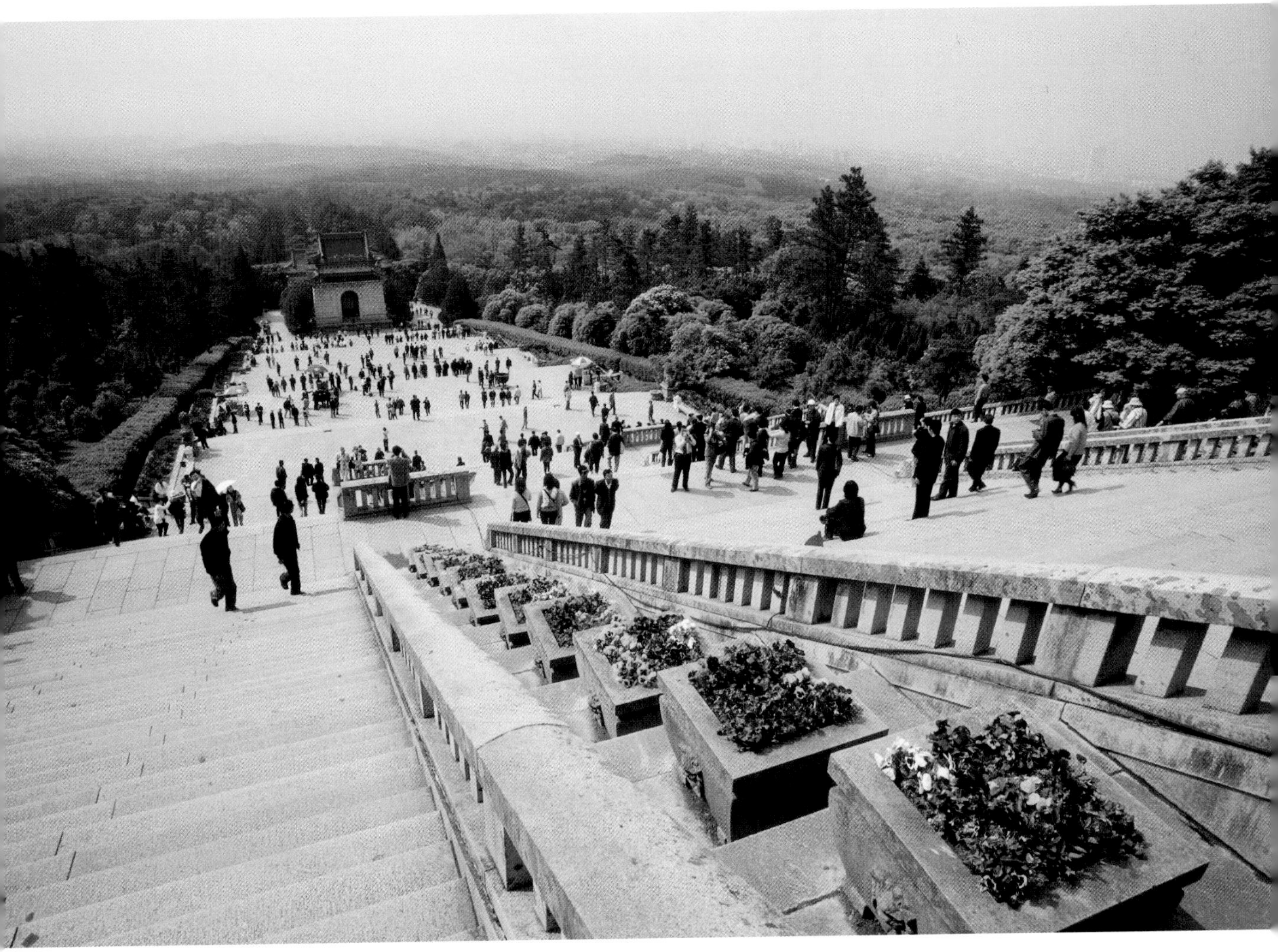

The long climb to the Sun Yat-sen memorial attests to the respect paid to him by his people.

(8,070-sq.-ft) hall is a white marble statue of Sun. In a bell-shaped vault to the north lies his body in a coffin also of white Italian marble.

The Second World War to the present

In 1937, after the outbreak of full-scale war, Japanese troops which had taken Shanghai moved in on Nanjing. Chiang Kai-shek flew out to establish a new capital further up river. After fierce fighting, bombing and an intense artillery barrage, the attackers breached the wall. As the Chinese soldiers fled, the Japanese perpetrated what became known as the 'Rape of Nanjing', killing, torturing and looting indiscriminately. Hundreds of thousands of Chinese, mainly civilians, perished in the most horrific ways. Some accounts put the death toll at 340,000. The atrocity does not appear to have been planned, but the Japanese commanders, the government in Tokyo and the emperor did nothing to halt it.

Nanjing became the centre of a collaborationist regime until Japan's defeat in 1945. After that, Chiang moved the capital back to the city, until the Nationalists fled to Taiwan in 1949 when the Communists took Nanjing virtually unopposed after winning a huge battle in the plains to the east. The capital was transferred to Beijing.

In 1968, the opening of a bridge over the Yangtze, which can widen to a mile in rainy weather, symbolized China's technical progress – previously all traffic had been obliged to cross the waterway on ferries. Most recently, it has flourished as the main city of Jiangsu province, one of the early leaders of China's economic expansion.

NANCY STEINHARDT

Shenyang

33

In the end the barbarians invite the civilized people into their palaces
and the civilized open their schools to the barbarians.

QUOTE CITED TO DESCRIBE THE INTERACTION BETWEEN NON-CHINESE CONQUERORS AND CHINESE IN CITIES SUCH AS SHENYANG

Located about 750 km (470 miles) northeast of Beijing, Shenyang is the capital and central city of Liaoning province and the largest urban region in the territory at one time called Manchuria. Within this prosperous industrial city whose population exceeds 7 million lies more than a millennium of Chinese urban past. The city's period of greatest flourishing was the early 17th century.

Seventeenth-century records trace the history of Shenyang to the prefectural capital Shenzhou, established by the Bohai (Parhae) kingdom of polyglot North and Northeast Asian population in the late 7th century. The archaeological record traces greater Shenyang's history several thousand years earlier, when the Neolithic Hongshan culture spread across Liaoning and into eastern Inner Mongolia. It is likely that in the last centuries BC the Han had a commandery on the Hun River, former name of the river Shen for which the city is named. The city Shenzhou fell to the Khitan dynasty Liao (916–1125) and then to the Jurchen dynasty Jin (1115–1234) and subsequently to the Mongols. Largely a military post and trading centre during those periods, it is believed that Shenzhou had been walled since Liao times. Each group, and the subsequent Ming dynasty which conquered the Mongols in 1368, had repaired city walls and built walls of their own.

The Manchu era

The most important period in Shenyang's history began in 1625 when the Manchu leader Nurhaci (1559–1626) moved his capital there. It was his fifth and last capital. The move signalled the intent of the Manchus to compete as an empire in the North and East Asian arena. Just a year later, Nurhaci died. He was succeeded by his son, Hung Taiji (Abahai) (1572–1643). In 1634, the city name changed to Shenjing, the second syllable one that had been used in China, Korea, and Japan for more than a thousand years to designate a capital. From Shenjing the Manchus overthrew the Ming in 1644, whereupon they transferred their centre of power to Beijing.

Shenjing, later known as Shenyang and as Mukden (Manchu for Fengtian), is thus associated primarily with a 20-year period and one ruler, for in fact most of the construction was left to Hung Taiji. Even after the establishment of the Qing dynasty in Beijing, Shenyang retained consider-

Qing-dynasty map showing the expansive Manchu version of the Chinese empire. China's borders include most of Siberia, stretch west to the Caspian Sea, and include Korea, a client state only nominally subject to the Qing court.

able prestige as the capital of the dynastic founders. Three major and several minor Manchu ancestral tombs are in the vicinity and treasures and regalia of the royal Manchu household are still kept at the Shenyang palace.

Palaces and other Manchu buildings

The Manchu palaces at Shenyang are sometimes considered a miniature Forbidden City (p. 105), but there are significant differences. One-sixth the area of the Beijing Forbidden City, the approximately 70 buildings of the Manchu palace divide into three parallel north–south sets. At the centre are four buildings. Great Qing Gate (the same name as its counterpart in Beijing) is the entry. There, one is told in Chinese, Manchu, Mongolian, Uygur and Tibetan to dismount. Behind are three halls, each with its own front courtyard. First is Eminent Administration Hall where Hung Taiji met foreign ambassadors, handled affairs of state, and held court. Next is Phoenix Tower, for a long time the tallest building in Shenyang. On exhibition today is a chair with antlers of a deer killed by Hung Taiji where he sat at banquets. Last is a building complex that shared its name with a residential compound of the Forbidden City: *Qingninggong* or Pure Tranquillity Palace. It was the living quarters of the emperor and empresses. In a back hall to the west, the emperor sacrificed to his dynastic ancestors. His concubines lived in the surrounding apartments; it was probably for this reason that the back courtyard

The Phoenix Tower, one of the four central buildings in the Manchu palace complex.

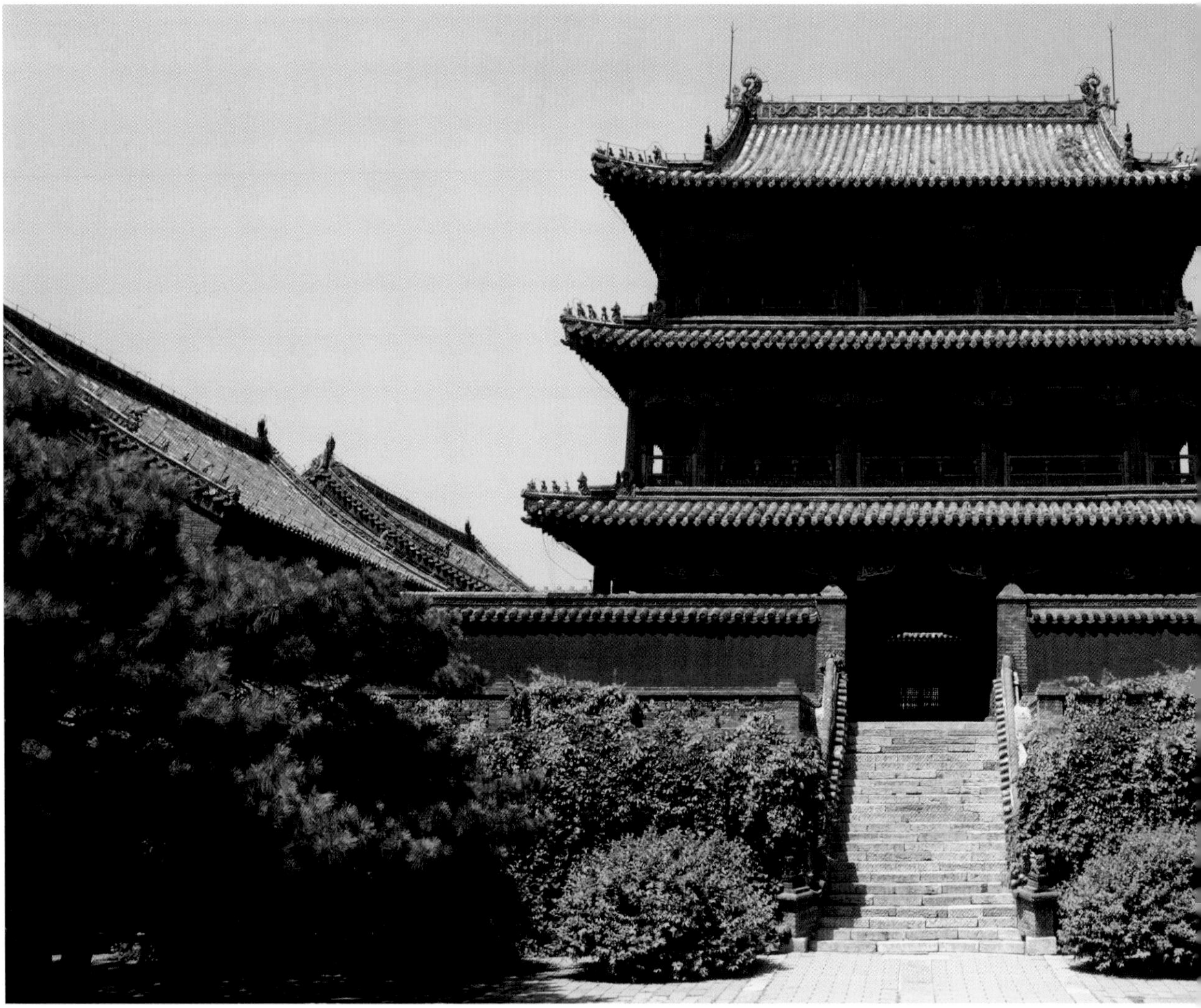

was only accessible through Phoenix Tower.

This area and the building group to the east, however, are unique and of a configuration that can be called Manchu. The octagonal Great Administration Hall, like an Eminent Administration Hall for imperial audiences, is the single focal point. Like eight of the small, squarish halls in front, its sides symbolized the unification of eight tribes by Nurhaci in the creation of the Manchu state. The halls closest to the octagonal hall were for the commanders of the left and right wings of the banners. The narrow building behind Great Administration Hall was a treasury.

The western part of imperial Shenyang was not constructed until the 18th century during the reign of the Qianlong emperor. Its focus is the multi-storey Imperial Library, built to house one of the rare sets of the *Siku quanshu*, an imperial compilation of more than 3,400 writings.

Ornate exterior of the Imperial Palace. The 'beaks' that project on either side of the pillars are typical of 17th-century Chinese architecture.

Imperial tombs

Other examples of imperial Manchu architecture in Shenyang include the tombs of Nurhaci and Hung Taiji. Already in 1598, Nurhaci had begun construction of an ancestral burial ground 125 km (77 miles) to the east in Xinbin. His own tomb, Fuling, shared with his wife, was begun in 1629 and completed in 1651. The tomb of Hung Taiji and his wife (Zhaoling or 'Luminous Tomb') was begun in 1643. Both have long approaches, triple-entry gates, pavilions, and offering halls that followed the pattern of the 13 Ming tombs near Beijing. Setting a precedent for Qing imperial tombs east and west of Beijing, Fuling and Zhaoling had curved walls enclosing mounds at the back ends.

Shenyang was the site of important battles during the Russo-Japanese war in 1904–05. The Mukden Incident of 1931 signalled the beginning of the Japanese conquest of Manchuria and eventual establishment of the puppet regime of Manchukuo (1932–1945). From 1946 to 1948, Shenyang was in the hands of the Kuomintang or Nationalists. Today Shenyang is a major Chinese city, but its non-Chinese heritage, primarily Manchu, is preserved at the city centre.

Monuments & Buildings

China's monuments were built with a purpose. Some, like the Labrang monastery (p. 171) in Gansu province in the west of the country and the Leshan Great Buddha in Sichuan province (p. 169), had a religious purpose. Elsewhere in Sichuan, the Dazu carvings (p. 181), with their Buddhist motifs, form part of the landscape as they stretch along cliff faces, in one place covering the entire side of a deep valley. Other great monuments, some dealt with in the previous section of this book, embodied a political statement, such as the Forbidden City in Beijing, symbolizing the power and divine majesty of the emperors. Overlooking Lhasa, the Potala Palace, one of the Great Monuments of Tibet (p. 174) – named after the mythical Indian home of the Buddhist deity, Avalokiteshvara – was designed to show the unity of Tibet under the Dalai Lama, while also evoking the roots of Buddhism, links with the Mongols and the decorative arts of China.

Two of the finest and most celebrated of monuments were to honour the dead, and ensure their well-being in the afterlife. The tomb of the first emperor, Qin (p. 155), outside Xi'an, contains the breathtaking terracotta warriors, arrayed in ranks to guard their master in the nether world. Excavations which have already taken place are impressive enough, but there are other tombs in the area which may yield equally great treasures. Outside Beijing, the tombs of 13 of the 16 Ming emperors (p. 165) stand in a sheltered valley, showing the Chinese belief in the spirit world beyond human life, and the link between earth and the heavens. The 'spirit road' leading to the

The Labrang Yellow Hat Monastery complex during the Tibetan New Year festival in Xiahe, Gansu province (see p. 171).

tombs is flanked by stone carvings of animals designed to depict a great, peaceful empire watched over by officials waiting to serve the emperor.

Some major monuments were more strictly practical, and there is also a myriad smaller architectural inheritances from the past in the form of classic Chinese houses and temples (p. 151) following similar patterns and constituting a distinctive theme running through history.

The most celebrated of all monuments, the Great Wall (p. 160) – more a collection of walls than a single project – was designed to keep out northern nomadic tribes. Militarily, it was not tremendously effective; both the Mongols and the Manchus penetrated it to take Beijing and found dynasties. More recently, the story that it is the only human construction seen from space has been exploded by a Chinese astronaut. But it remains probably the main symbol of China, giving its name to everything from a vineyard to a motor car company, and is seen by the Chinese as standing for their nation's greatness. In the late 18th century, Lord Macartney, leader of an abortive British mission sent to establish relations with the Chinese empire, declared it 'the most stupendous work of human hands'. Two centuries later, after walking along a stretch of it, Richard Nixon opined, 'This is a great wall and had to be built by a great people.'

The Grand Canal (p. 178), which Macartney called 'the greatest and most ancient of its kind', carried food to the imperial capital. Running through eastern China, it is part of a longer network of canals which bear witness to Chinese prowess in this form of engineering. Using some earlier stretches of waterway, and flowing in part over a canalized river, the main section was built by some 5 million labourers at the end of the 6th and beginning of the 7th centuries. The 1,000-km (600-mile) stretch from the Yellow River to the port of Tianjin was a vital unifying link in the centuries when water transport played a key role in China's economy – and in the movement of troops and people. Its decline in the 19th century symbolized the decline of the empire.

Many of today's new monuments are also highly practical (p. 183), devoted to boosting the economy through constructions of huge dams, highways, high-speed train links, airports and forests of tower blocks in cities across the nation. Some of these carry concerns for the environment, which will be a continuing preoccupation of China's headlong development – not a problem the builders of the Great Wall, the Grand Canal or the imperial tombs had to take into account.

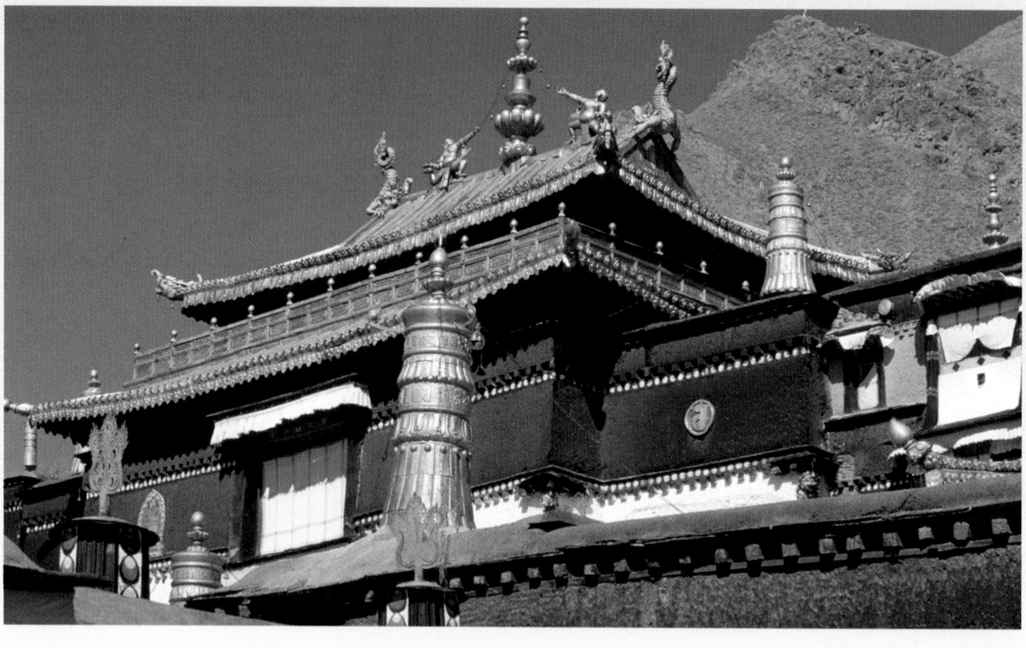

Upper floor of the Tashilhunpo Monastery, near Shigatse, one of the Great Monuments of Tibet (p.174). It is one of the largest Buddhist monasteries of the Gelugpa sect.

FRANCES WOOD

Domestic & Religious Architecture 34

Those who restored the temples always followed the original plan.... Generally this is very similar and resembles in many ways that of a secular residence ... we find the same series of rectangular courtyards running from north to south with the principal edifice in the centre and the lesser buildings at the sides.

JULIET BREDON, *PEKING*, 1920

Since the Chinese have relied upon timber, susceptible to fire and natural rotting, as the main structural component of buildings since at least 6000 BC, reconstructing the buildings of the past is difficult. A further difficulty in reconstruction has been a tendency to re-build because of the frequent destruction of timber-frame buildings. In contrast with Japan, where the maintenance and repair of sacred structures means that Tang-dynasty-style buildings have survived without alteration to plan or form for some 1,500 years, in China it was the site that was sacred, not the structure, so major temples, founded nearly 2,000 years ago, may have been rebuilt many times, reflecting changes in architectural styles.

Archaeological evidence

The remains of the foundations of buildings with evident post-holes reveal the use of upright timber columns from the Neolithic period through to the Han dynasty (206 BC – AD 220). During the Han, various other pieces of evidence for the shape of the timber structure enable historians to reconstruct vanished forms. These include the stone gate towers, built in imitation of timber and tile constructions, which stand in front of some Han tombs; the ceramic tomb bricks which line some Han tombs, showing buildings, gardens and towers; and the ceramic models of houses, farms and towers which were placed in tombs, together with ceramic models of people and animals.

This new evidence reveals three major areas in buildings: the foundation, the pillar structure and the roof, the last two linked by an increasingly complex bracketing structure set above the columns to support the eaves and the roof. Foundations, whether of pounded earth or stone, raised the building above the ground for practical reasons, preventing rising damp, and indicated

A 71-cm (28-inch) tall clay tomb model of an elaborate Han-dynasty, rural manor house, found in Hubei province. Note the courtyard, gatehouse and watchtower.

status, for the higher the foundation, the more significant the building. Timber columns, often set in stone pillar bases, frame the building while the roof, usually covered with rows of cylindrical or semi-cylindrical tiles running from the ridge down to the eaves, was supported on a series of W-shaped brackets which, during the Han and through to the Tang (AD 618–907) dynasties stood on top of the upright columns. The roof ridges were often decorated with ceramic animals and the eave tiles finished with circular end-tiles. Lattice windows with simple diamond lozenge patterns anticipate a major area of decoration in later times.

The earliest surviving timber-frame halls

Though some stone and brick pagodas survive from the Tang dynasty, the most significant early surviving buildings are two temple halls, discovered in the Buddhist centre of Wutai Shan in Shanxi province. The east hall of the Foguang Temple, built in 857, was rediscovered in 1937 by China's foremost architectural historian Liang Sicheng (1901–1971), and the small hall of the tiny Nanchan Temple, built in 782, was rediscovered in the early 1950s and restored quite sensitively with reference to contemporary wall paintings from Dunhuang. The construction of the two Tang halls was similar. Timber columns set in plain stone bases on a high brick platform supported the eaves with bracketing set on top of the columns and intercolumnar brackets in the form of inverted Vs. The bracketing of the Foguang hall is complex, with four tiers of cantilevers to support the considerable eaves projection. The grey-tiled roofs have incurved 'owls' tails' at each end of the ridge.

By the Tang, temple complexes had already developed their characteristic layout, in a series of rectangular courtyards, ideally oriented north–south with the main halls on the central axis, facing south. Lesser buildings stood to the east and west of the courtyards. Behind the main halls, at the greatest distance from the main gate, were the private apartments of the monks. This principle of building courtyards in a series, sometimes

Temples, houses, markets and gardens form a picture of life inside the city wall of Nanjing in this Ming woodcut.

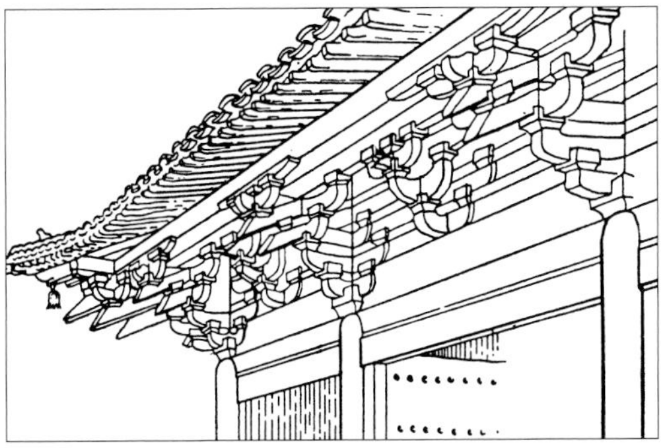

Far left *Section and elevation of the timber-framed east hall of the Foguang Temple on Wutai Shan. The roofs have 'owls' tails' at the end of each ridge.*

Left *Detail of the bracketing and eaves of the same Foguang Temple hall, showing the four tiers of cantilevers and intercolumnar bracketing.*

with several axes but the main buildings on the central axis, was also followed in palaces and private houses, as was the practice of siting the most private, intimate areas farthest from the main gate. The residential part of the Forbidden City is at the northernmost end of the complex. In domestic buildings, which might consist of a single courtyard rather than the series of courtyards in a temple complex, a guest could measure his intimacy with the residents by how far into the courtyard he was allowed: tradesmen were seen at the gate but family friends might be entertained in the main, northernmost hall.

Development of styles

The development of architectural styles throughout the succeeding dynasties saw considerable progress, both in bracketing and in roof decoration. The great halls of the Forbidden City have long friezes of bracketing, no longer restricted to the tops of the columns, and, instead of the simple owls' tails, the roof ridges have glazed-tile gaping dragon heads at either end, as well as many little ceramic animal figures running down to the eaves end. These, apart from their decorative function, were intended to protect. Dragons in China are associated with water and, in buildings constantly threatened by fire, their watery associations were protective. Much building magic involved protection: circular end tiles were impressed with snarling lion faces to frighten evil spirits and 'spirit walls' or screens were built opposite the main gates or temples or inside the gate of private dwellings to keep out evil spirits who were believed to be able to fly only in straight lines and thus unable to negotiate barriers.

Sumptuary regulations restricted the decoration of private houses. In Beijing, only temples could have glazed-tile roofs; houses had to have grey, unglazed tiles and were also forbidden painted ceilings, although such rules were often ignored. It was the roof style and decoration of temples that showed the greatest regional

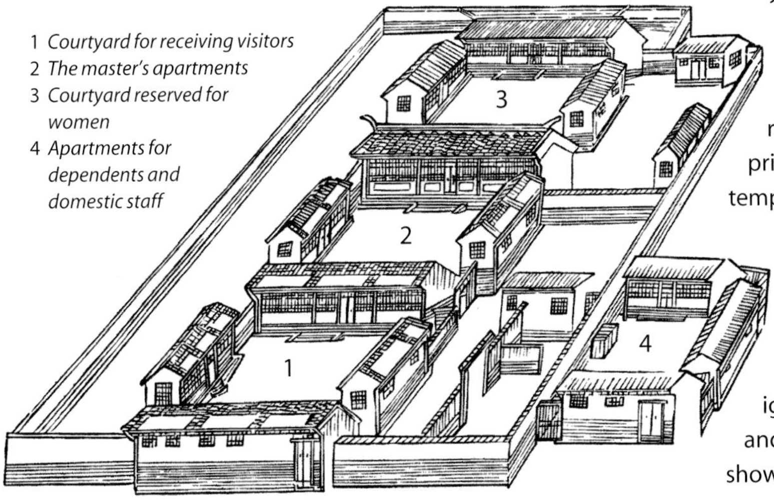

1 *Courtyard for receiving visitors*
2 *The master's apartments*
3 *Courtyard reserved for women*
4 *Apartments for dependents and domestic staff*

Left *The layout of a typical Qing-dynasty courtyard house, Beijing, showing how the innermost areas were reserved for the most important people.*

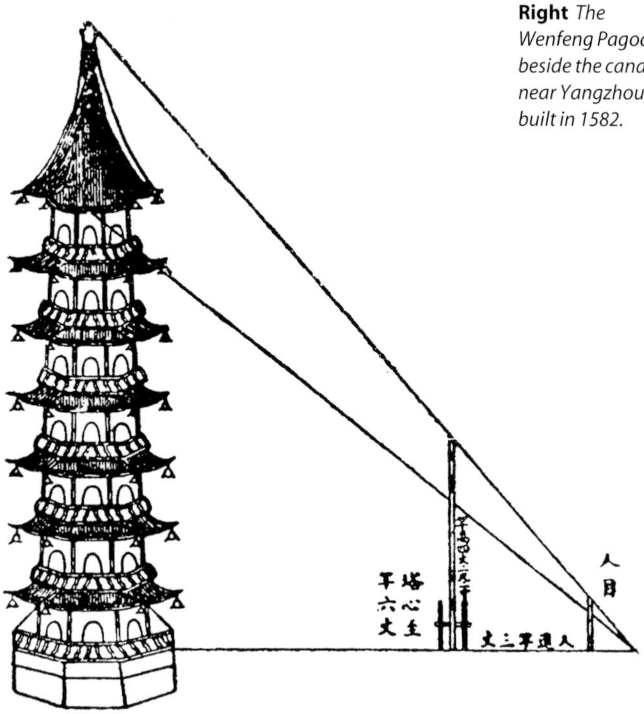

Above *Illustration from a 3rd-century AD mathematical book showing how to use trigonometry to measure the height of a pagoda.*

Right *The Wenfeng Pagoda beside the canal, near Yangzhou, built in 1582.*

variation, for their plan remained fairly constant throughout China. In Fujian province, temple roofs might soar in a series of sharp triangular gables, all adorned with ceramic figures of gods and heroes, in Guangdong province, entire operatic scenes in glazed ceramics fight their way across roofs, while in Sichuan they are decorated with grey tile ornaments.

Domestic regional variety

Domestic architecture used to show the most dramatic regional variation. Though all based on the courtyard plan, courtyards in northern China were open to make the most of slanting winter sun, while southern courtyards were almost entirely roofed over to avoid hot summer sun and higher rainfall. Black-and-white half-timbered buildings were characteristic of Sichuan, and gable end walls in stepped or arched 'cat's back' forms were seen across south-central China. In the Jiangnan area, house-garden complexes in Suzhou and Yangzhou had lattice windows, like houses across China, but their decoration was more delicate and imaginative than elsewhere. In northern Fujian, houses had heavy roofs uplifted at the eaves, whilst in southern Fujian, the eaves uplift was increasingly exaggerated. Unfortunately, the increasing wealth of peasant families has seen the construction of new houses throughout the countryside whose eclectic borrowings of moon gates, additional storeys, Disney fairy palace roofs and gold bauble roof finials have largely destroyed the sense of local diversity which was so characteristic of traditional domestic architecture.

ZHANG YINGLAN

The Tomb of the First Emperor

35

We were witnessing one of the most spectacular excavations of this century.
AUDREY TOPPING, 1978

In 1978, when Audrey Topping of *National Geographic* visited the terracotta army sites for the first time, confronted with the sight of thousands of life-size, 2,200-year-old pottery warriors, she stood in the rain and was moved almost to tears.

But in fact, the terracotta army is only a small part of the 180 burial pits of emperor Qin Shihuangdi's mausoleum. So far, within the area of 56.25 sq. km (21.72 sq. miles), archaeologists have found millions of square metres of palace ruins, hundreds of accessory tombs and burial pits, unearthed thousands of terracotta warriors and horses, dozens of pottery acrobat figures, bronze birds and stone armours, and two sets of bronze chariots, as well as large numbers of other rare artifacts. All these treasures were unknown for thousands of years until the archaeologists' trowels cleared the soil covering them. It was no surprise that Peter Hessler wrote: 'There's so much history here that it literally rises out of the ground.'

History

Emperor Qin Shihuangdi (259–210 BC), the 'First Emperor' of China, conquered the other six states after ten years of war, and in 221 BC founded the first unified feudal empire in Chinese history. He promulgated a uniform code of law and standardized currency, weights and measures, the written language and the axle-length of wagons and chariots. He also built a vast network of roads radiating from the Qin capital, Xianyang, and joined up the previous separate defensive walls of states into the Great Wall (p. 160). For his personal glorification, besides building a number of elaborate palaces near his capital, emperor Qin Shihuangdi also built an underground palace for his afterlife.

Qin Shihuangdi's mausoleum lies 35 km (22 miles) east of the city of Xi'an, Shaanxi province. The tomb was 38 years in the making, having been begun only one year after his coronation. There are several reasons why the emperor chose Lishan Mountain as his burial place. The geomagnetic omens for this area were ideal, with mountains in the south and the Wei River in the north. Also the tombs of Qin Shihuangdi's ancestors were located here. The emperor's tomb mound, now 76 m (250 ft) in height, and 1,250 m (4,100 ft) in perimeter, was originally enclosed by rectangular inner and outer walls respectively 4 and 6 km (2.5 and 4 miles) in perimeter.

We get a few clues from written records about the underground palace of the tomb, although

Above *The 'First Emperor' of a united China, Qin Shihuangdi.*

Below *Mound under which the emperor may be buried. The actual gravesite has not been excavated.*

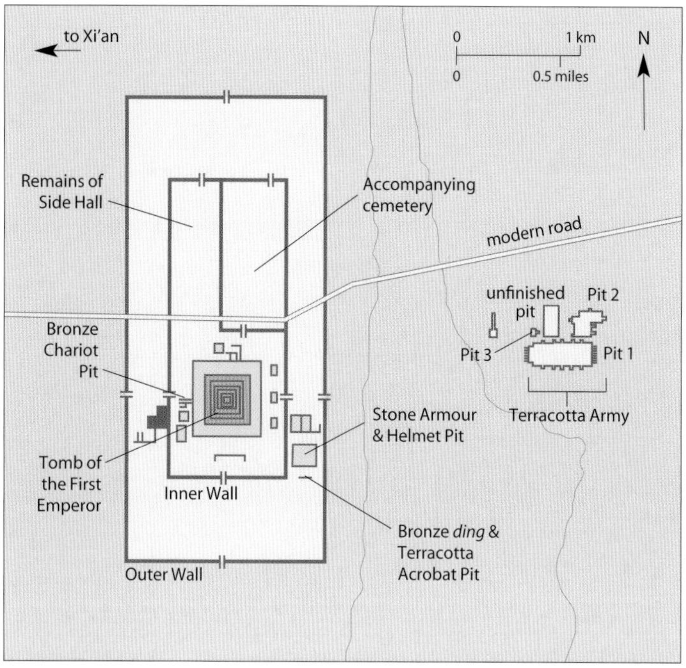

Above *Plan of the First Emperor's mausoleum and underground terracotta army pits. The city of Xi'an is to the west of this burial site.*

the entire mausoleum remains to be explored and excavated. According to Sima Qian, who wrote his *Records of the Grand Historian* some 100 years after the emperor's death, the ceiling of the tomb chamber is a model of the heavens and its floor a topographical map of the empire, with circulating mercury to represent the waters of the earth. Jewels and other treasures buried within are guarded by crossbows triggered to release arrows at any intruder, and the workmen who installed the finishing touches were buried alive to ensure that the secret of the entranceway died with them. While we are uncertain about the truth of the description, a geophysical survey in the 1980s proved that there was an area of 12,000 sq. m (130,000 sq. ft) of unnatural concentrations of mercury in the area under the tumulus.

During the following 2,200 years, although there were many legends about the mausoleum, the truth was not revealed until this extraordinary discovery of the terracotta army.

Discovery

In March 1974, local villagers unearthed a number of fragments of terracotta warriors and horses when they dug a well in a field 1.5 km (1 mile) east of the mausoleum, the area now called Pit 1. After the discovery of Pit 1, Pits 2 and 3 were found in May and June 1976 respectively. Excavations show that all three pits of life-size pottery figures were originally roofed over and lined with a framework of earth and wood, which collapsed long ago. All the pits were damaged, the first two burnt, possibly by the rebel forces under General Xiang Yu. As a result, most of the pottery figures were reduced to fragments.

Pit 1 is 230 m (755 ft) from east to west, 62 m (103 ft) from north to south, 5 m (16 ft) deep, and covers an area of 14,260 sq. m (153,500 ft). Rows of wooden pillared corridors were covered with woven mats and earth up to ground level. The floors are paved with bricks, and both the corridors and the earthen partition walls are roughly 3 m (10 ft) wide. The terracotta army stands within these corridors. To date, archaeological excavations have brought to light more than 1,000 pottery warriors and 24 pottery horses, but it is estimated that there were in fact about 6,000 terracotta warriors and horses buried in total. The serried ranks of 1.8-m-tall (5.9-ft) warrior figures are divided into teams of four, facing east. Wooden chariots with four horses were deployed between them.

In the front end of Pit 1, the 210 warriors carrying crossbows or bows formed the vanguard

Pit 1 of Qin Shihuangdi's burial mound, containing over 1,000 life-size, terracotta figures of warriors and horses. Another 5,000 or so are also thought to be lying unexcavated.

Above *Soldiers from the main formation, some now damaged, flank the chariots in defence of their emperor.*

Above right *One of the kneeling archers found in Pit 2.*

of the main formation. Immediately behind them are 38 columns in 11 groups facing east, which consist of infantrymen and charioteers. The two sides of the formation are flanks, which face north and south respectively. On the west end of the pit, there are rear guards facing west.

Most of the warriors in the main formation wear armour. They originally wore swords at their waists and held spears in their hands, and though the wooden parts of these weapons have long since disintegrated, the soldier's fingers are still curled to grasp them. The bronze swords and spearheads were found at the figures' feet. These warriors escorted war chariots in the same manner that a modern infantry escorts tanks.

Pit 2 is located 20 m (65 ft) north of the east end of Pit 1. It is shaped like an inverted 'L', stretching 124 m (407 ft) from east to west, and 98 m (322 ft) from north to south. Pit 2 is similar to Pit 1 in construction, but it contains an even greater variety of terracotta warriors. In addition to infantrymen and charioteers, there are also cavalrymen and archers. The cavalrymen are leading their saddled and bridled horses; the archers carry either longbows or crossbows. Standing and kneeling archers manned the front lines, while the chariots occupied the right flank and the cavalry stood on the left. In the centre was a rectangular formation of interspersed chariots and infantrymen.

Pit 3, the smallest of the three at only 520 sq. m (5,600 sq. ft) in size, contains 68 warriors and 1 chariot with 4 horses, and is thought to be the headquarters commanding warriors of the first two pits.

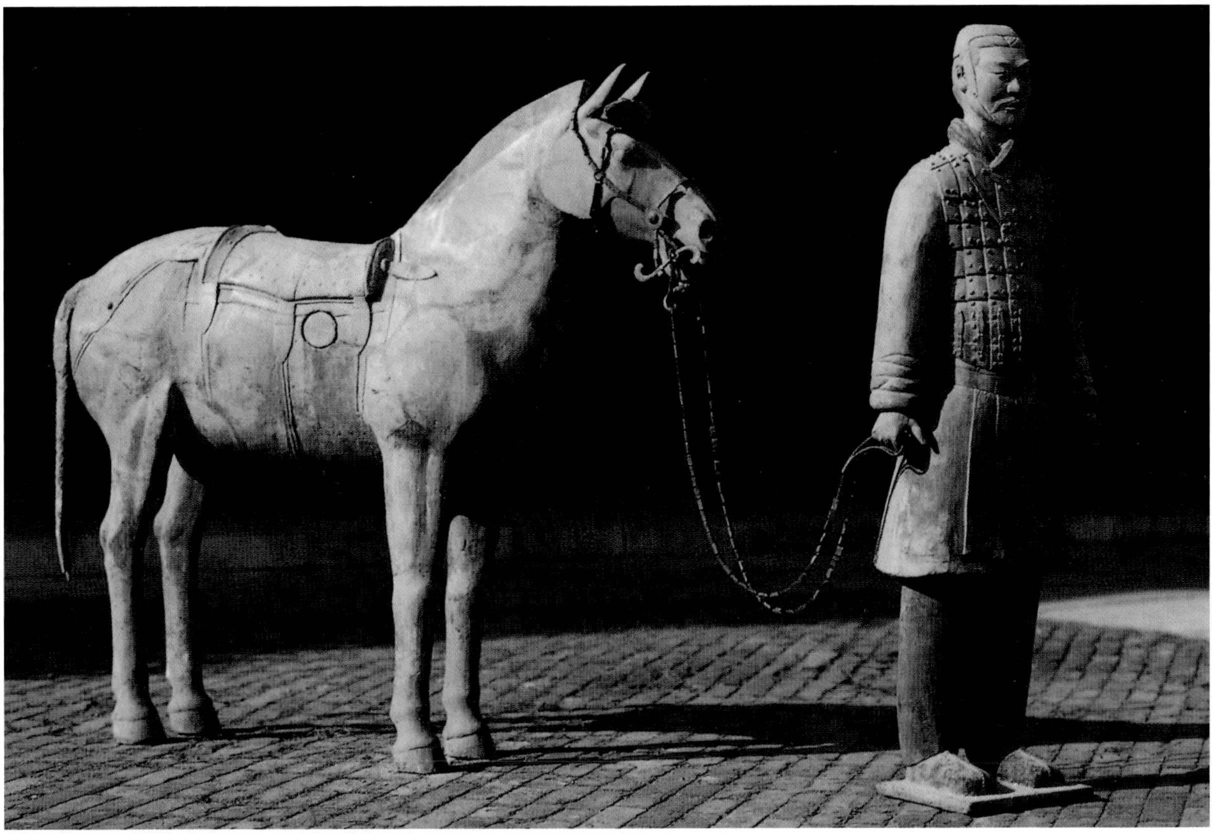

A cavalryman stands to attention with his horse, ready for battle.

Historical importance

This underground army represents the imperial guard of the emperor Qin Shihuangdi, who hoped they would protect him in the afterlife. But he didn't foresee that these terracotta warriors and horses would offer us an invaluable source of material for the study of Chinese history. We can learn a great deal more about the culture, politics, art, metallurgy and many other achievements of China based on the cultural relics unearthed here.

The variety of bronze weapons, for example, still sharp and shining despite 2,000 years underground, demonstrate the advanced level of Qin metallurgy. Chemical analysis has revealed that the swords and arrowheads are primarily bronze and tin with traces of rare metals, and that their surfaces were treated with chromium.

Besides the terracotta army, there were many new discoveries within the area of the emperor's mausoleum. In 1980, two sets of bronze chariots and horses were unearthed near the mound of the mausoleum. Built at half life-size, these bronze chariots were buried here as the imperial transport for Qin Shihuangdi.

In recent years, archaeologists have unearthed many new objects in the field excavation, including hundreds of pieces of stone armour and helmets in the stone armour pit, located near the tomb's mound. In another burial pit nearby, dozens of life-size pottery figures of acrobats give us a visualized description of imperial entertainment in the Qin dynasty. Bronze birds and pottery musician figures found in 2001 also give us a picture of the imperial garden of that period.

No Chinese archaeologist could tell you when the next astonishing discovery in the emperor's mausoleum may be and what may be unearthed, for there were so many imperial secrets buried there 2,200 years ago. Although we cannot excavate the emperor's actual tomb for conservation reasons, the huge number of cultural discoveries around it will be enough for generations of archaeologists to spend a whole lifetime excavating.

NANCY STEINHARDT

36 The Great Wall

It is probable that no existing monument of human intellect and skill has so captured and held the imagination of people of all nations as has the Great Wall of China.
L. NEWTON HAYES, *THE GREAT WALL OF CHINA*, 1929

Long before the first decades of the 20th century, there was no doubt in the minds of young or old that China was a country of walls or that her greatest man-made achievement was a 5,000-km-long (3,000-mile) brick wall that stretched from end to end of her northern border. By the end of the 20th century, other facts about the wall were widely known: at no time in history did a continuous wall extend from Gansu province in the west to former Manchuria in the east; the circuitous line that marks the location of the Great Wall on maps at no time coincided with China's northern border; the wall is not, as had often been said, visible to the naked eye from the Moon; the wall was the ultimate symbol of enclosure of pre-modern, sedentary China from the world of the barbarian nations outside; in Chinese, the Great Wall is called the 'Long Wall of 10,000 *li*' (5,000 km / 3,000 miles).

Every remaining piece of the wall has been studied and analyzed. Treks along it have become fashionable destinations for bold travellers. The height, width, size and composition of bricks, number of layers from bottom to top and across, position and configuration of watchtowers, way in which troops were quartered, and warning signals varied according to the terrain and anticipated manner of attack at each pass and each wall portion between.

A northern defence for the Qin dynasty

The first piece of wall associated with the Great Wall is believed to date from the 7th century BC, the time of China's Spring and Autumn period (770–476 BC). During the next several centuries, contending states constructed their own defensive barriers, often joining disparate wall parts and watchtowers that existed from earlier times. Each of the seven states, Chu, Qi, Wei, Han, Zhao, Yan and Qin, that would be unified into the first Chinese empire, and many of the smaller kingdoms, had its own mud-brick wall. In the 4th century BC, the threat of invasion and pillage by the Xiongnu and other Northern tribes was so intense that fortifications of Zhao, Yan and Qin became more systematic, but each wall was still individual to the state.

With unification in 221 BC under China's first dynasty, Qin, by the man who called himself First Emperor, Qin Shihuangdi, our current concept of the Great Wall came into being. Together with unity of written language, currency, weights and measures, and a national communication system on horseback, the First Emperor promulgated the connection and strengthening of walls of those states he had conquered along China's northern border, sometimes tearing down pieces and

Right *Sketch of the 'First Emperor' Qin Shihuangdi, whose safety concerns over the northern borders of his newly united China led to the idea of a defensive wall on these frontiers.*

Opposite *A restored section of the Great Wall just outside Beijing.*

reconstructing them more sturdily than before. New wall parts and towers were added with the goal of a continuous barrier to protect China's northern frontier. Just one of innumerable building projects – including palaces in replica of those of conquered states and the First Emperor's own infamous mausoleum east of modern-day Xi'an (p. 155) – initiated during the emperor's 11-year reign (221–210 BC), masses of conscripted labourers died in its construction.

The wall's progress after the Qin

Completion of the Great Wall was not an ambition of the 400 years of Han rule (206 BC – AD 220 with a 14-year interregnum in the early 1st century AD) that followed Qin, but portions were added, in some cases in parallel sets, along China's northern border to aid in defence against the ever-present northern tribes. Most dynasties, states or kingdoms that ruled north China between the 3rd and mid-13th century repaired or amended wall parts or built walls of their own, but none with the vigour of Qin or even Han.

One exception was the Tang (618–907), which at its height in the 7th and 8th centuries extended its influence to territories that had formerly posed a threat to China, and thus did not seek division from them. Another exceptional dynasty in terms of wall construction was the Mongols, who made no significant changes or additions to the Wall. This was in contrast to the northern non-Chinese dynasty Jin (1115–1234), which had built fortifications to prevent the encroachment of other northern tribes; and Jin's predecessor, the Liao dynasty (916–1125), which had maintained parts of the Wall and added sections at China's farthest northeastern points in Heilongjiang to block the advance of the groups including those who formed the Jin dynasty.

The century of Mongolian rule (1263–1368) is associated with one Wall structure. Cloud Terrace (Yuntai) was erected and carved in 1345. The white marble archway, originally part of a larger fortification, stands 9 km (5.5 miles) south of the strategic pass through the Wall, Juyongguan, and the Badaling Mountain range just beyond it. The underside of the archway preserves relief sculpture of Buddhist deities, passages from Buddhist sutras, and an inscription in the six most common languages of the Mongolian empire: Chinese, Sanskrit, Tibetan, Mongolian, Uyghur and Tangut, the last the language of the Xi Xia kingdom which ruled North Asia from 1038 until the Mongolian conquest.

The next dynasty after Qin that engaged in serious construction and rebuilding of the Great Wall was the Ming (1368–1644). Like Qin, their purpose was strategic defence. Also like Qin, the Ming had an official pro-Wall construction policy. Building of a stronger wall than had existed in

Below left *Map showing the nine garrisons that were organized in the Ming dynasty to maintain and rebuild parts of the Great Wall.*

Below right *Tools vital for building a border wall are shown in this Ming-dynasty sketch of workers at a kiln.*

earlier times was ordered by the first Ming emperor, Zhu Yuanzhang (r. 1368–1398), and continued in earnest for nearly another 150 years. Ming military organization, in fact, placed significant focus on the Great Wall. According to the imperial order, a continuous wall of approximately 6,300 m (20,000 ft) was to be built at China's northern border, from the Hexi Corridor in Gansu to the Yalu River in the northeast. The territory was divided into nine regions, each with its own fortresses, watchtowers and strategic passes, each under the supervision of a military commander who received reports from subcommanders and who himself reported directly to the emperor's Minister of Defence. The closest China came to a continuous wall was at this time, each piece of Wall averaging 1 m (3 ft) in breadth and 5 m (16 ft) high – which, if placed end to end, would exceed the equator in length. The majority of Wall that still exists dates from the Ming period.

The last Chinese dynasty, the Manchu Qing dynasty (1644–1911), also had an official policy concerning the Wall, but a very different one. The second Qing ruler, the Kangxi emperor (r. 1662–1722), promulgated conciliation with the numerous northern peoples and tribes, of whom the Manchu themselves were one. Neither the Kangxi emperor nor his successors built or repaired the Wall.

The famous gate and wall at Shanhaiguan, a pass across the eastern part of the Great Wall near Liaoning and by the Bohai Sea.

Famous spots, infamous defence

The fortresses and other architecture at strategic passes (*guan*) along the Great Wall punctuated China's northern defence system through 2,000 years of warfare and provide the captivating imagery that has made the Wall famous. About a dozen are universally known, in China by name and image and outside of China, by image, at least. Most famous are Shanhaiguan at the eastern end and Jiayuguan in western China.

Under Northern Qi rule (550–577), a fortress stood at Shanhaiguan, near Hebei province's border with Liaoning and the Bohai Sea. The famous gate and adjoining wall seen today were begun in 1382 with additions in 1551 and 1571. Shanhaiguan is also famous as the starting point of the Barrier of Willows or Poplars, 1,950 km (1,200 miles) of trees planted by the Qing as a symbolic deterrent through Liaoning and Jilin provinces for non-Manchu tribes in the far northeast. Its greatest fame, however, is anachronistic. Lady Meng Jiang went to the Wall in search of her husband, a conscripted labourer, only to learn that he had died in his toils. Her tears caused the wall to crumble, and from the rubble emerged her husband's corpse, allowing her to take him home for proper burial. This legend may date to the Spring and Autumn period, and was not recorded until the Tang dynasty. In the Ming, the story was placed at Shanhaiguan, where a temple and tomb were built for Lady Meng.

The Great Wall of China winding across a hilly region of the country.

Jiayuguan was also constructed in the Ming dynasty, but near 2nd-century-BC wall remains from a Han commandery. Pieces of a Han fortress can be seen alongside this best-preserved portion of the Ming defence system: surviving at Jiayuguan are the citadel with defensive pass; *wengcheng*, or additional defence battlements attached to the wall and beyond it as a protective curtain for a gate; *loucheng*, an outer wall (a term also sometimes used for the enclosure of a city) beyond the main wall that must be penetrated before the main defence region can be encroached; and watchtowers, intended to stand every 10 *li* (5 km / 3 miles) along the wall, so that smoke or other signals of approaching attack could be sent forth. Sometimes equally exotic, and in all cases well-preserved (if not as extensive), are Wall remains at Beizhen in Liaoning, Gubeikou, Badaling and Yulin in Hebei, Datong and Yanmenguan in Shanxi, Huhehaote (Hohhot) in Inner Mongolia, Sanguankou in the Helan Mountains, the Guyuan fortification of Ningxia, and Yumenguan in Gansu.

Immutably, the Great Wall is the structure through which China has defined herself to the world beyond her borders.

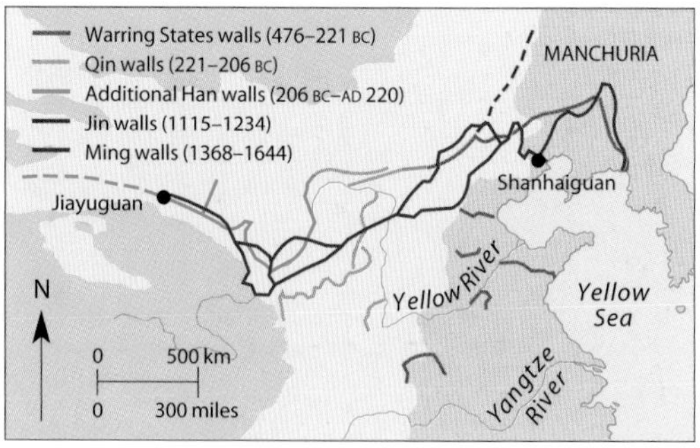

Right *Map showing the extent of the Great Wall (or Walls) at various times in history.*

ANN PALUDAN

The Ming Tombs

37

The Ming Tombs in Ch'ang-ping undoubtedly formed one of the largest and most gorgeous royal cemeteries ever laid out by the hand of man. They yield the palm to the Egyptian pyramids in point of bulk, but certainly not in that of style and grandeur.
JAN JACOB MARIA DE GROOT, 1894

The tombs of 13 of the 16 emperors of the Ming dynasty (1368–1644) lie in a sheltered valley 45 km (*c.* 30 miles) northwest of Beijing. These are the earliest Chinese imperial mausolea with surviving surface buildings and as such, they provide a unique illustration of traditional Chinese beliefs concerning the relationship between the living and the dead. The imperial system was based on the idea that the emperor was the Son of Heaven. As the link between heaven and earth, it was his duty to create or maintain order and prosperity. In the Ming tombs we can see how clearly imperial complexes reflect the belief that human society could only flourish when it was in harmony with the greater forces of the cosmos. Everything from choice of site to the smallest decorative motif was designed to provide contact between the deceased emperors and the spirit world.

The first Ming emperor was buried in his capital, Nanjing. The second disappeared in a war of succession and it was the third, Yongle, after moving his capital north to Beijing, who chose a new dynastic burial ground. The valley conforms to Chinese ideas about geomancy or *feng shui*; the shape of the valley emphasizes the unity of

Stone sculptures along the spirit road leading to the 16th-century tomb of the Ming emperor Jiajing's parents. Zhongxiang, Hubei province.

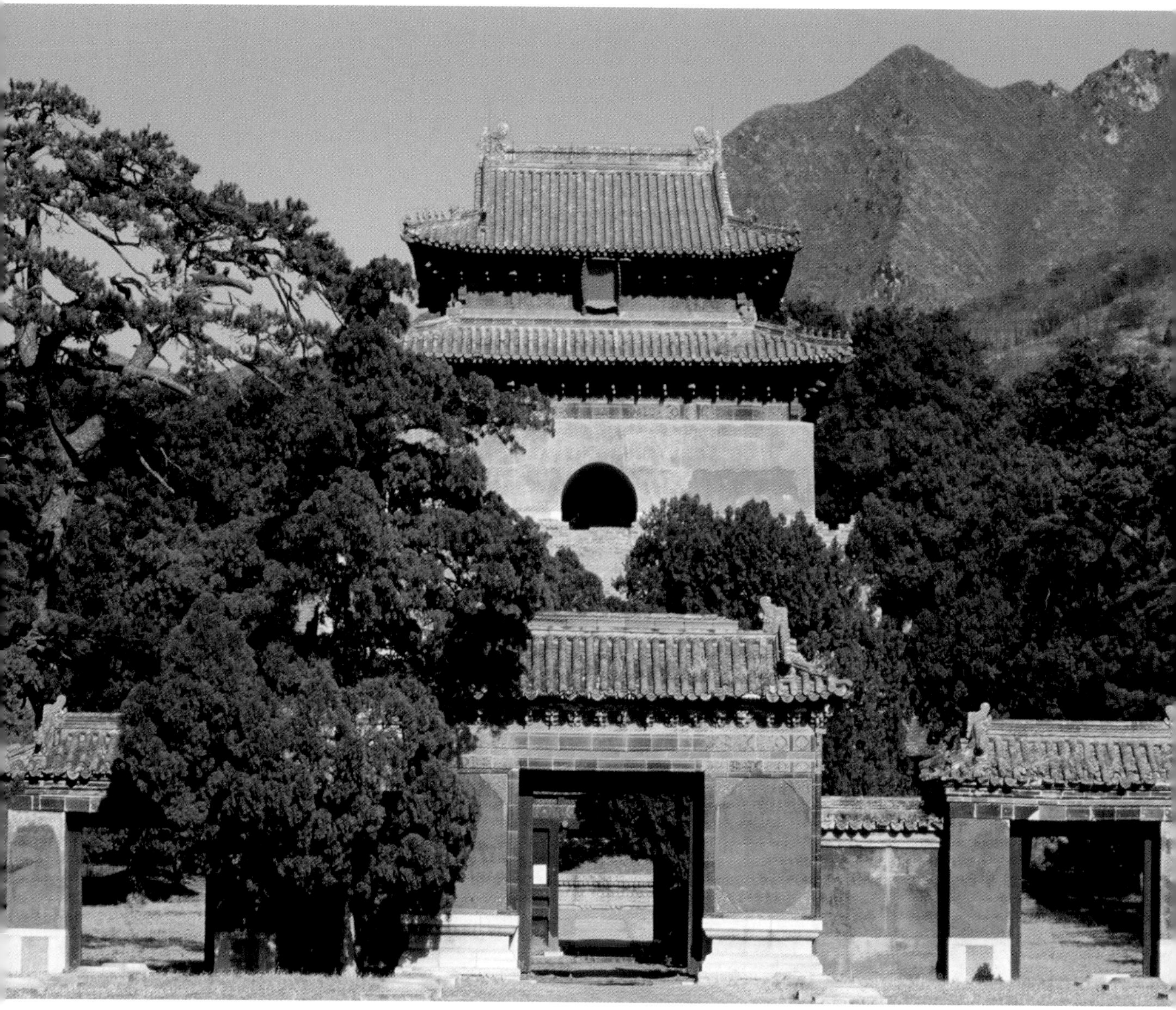

The Dingling tomb of Emperor Wanli (d. 1620) is the only one of the Ming tombs to have been excavated.

the empire, and the tombs are protected from the cold northern winds by mountains whilst being open to the warm south. The approach to the tombs is heralded by a large memorial archway; from there the way leads to a stone stele, 10 m (33 ft) tall, on a tortoise base. The dedication to Changling, Yongle's own tomb and the first in the valley, with its references to the virtues 'of the great dynasty of Ming', underlines the permanence of the dynasty irrespective of emperors who may come and go. Beyond this, the 'spirit road', an avenue of stone figures, leads northward to Changling. Later tombs, set in the hillsides to the east and west of the first tomb, are reached by small ways leading from the central avenue like branches on a tree.

The spirit road

Since the Han dynasty (206 BC–AD 221), spirit roads had played an important part in the Chinese burial system. Each dynasty redesigned the avenue to show the nature of their rule, and where necessary, to seek help from the unseen powers. The Ming, succeeding the Mongol Yuan dynasty, were determined to re-establish links with China's great past as if the alien occupation had never taken place. Their imperial spirit road expresses the idea of a large unified, peaceful and well-run empire with its roots in China's ancient history. After a pair of stone beacons, the statuary consists of two pairs each of six animals, three real and three fabulous, shown first sitting (to rest at night) and then standing. The fabulous beasts illustrate the nature of the new dynasty: lions (treated as mythical beasts in China) for military security and two mythological creatures symbolizing wise, peaceful government and justice. The real animals denote the extent of the empire with elephants for the south, horses for the west and camels for the north. Beyond the animals, six pairs of standing officials represent ideal military commanders and imperial advisers, identified by the detailed carving of their clothing. Together the statues informed not only human visitors to the tombs but also those in the unseen world about the nature and power of the Ming empire and its clear difference from the warlike Mongol rule.

The spiritual role of the tombs was underlined by a complete change in decorative motifs. Statuary on the tombs of earlier dynasties included stone reliefs of real subjects – birds, animals and plants – but in the Ming valley all relief carvings portray fabulous creatures in their believed habitat of sea, mountains and clouds.

Tomb architecture

The tomb plans were based on the ancient saying 'heaven round, earth square'. For the first time, this was expressed architecturally with a clear division between the square, or rectangular, first part of the tomb with its great halls where the rites were performed, and the round or oval mound covering the underground burial chamber. The worldly sections are replicas of contemporaneous palace architecture; the halls are built in traditional manner with red wooden weight-bearing pillars and brightly coloured walls and tiles set in walled courtyards. The largest hall, the Hall of Heavenly Favours in Changling, is an exact replica of the largest hall in the Forbidden City, the Hall of Supreme Harmony (or Imperial Peace); until the early 20th century these were the two largest buildings in China.

Behind this, in the last courtyard is a stone altar with five stone replicas of the ritual objects used in sacrificial rites. This altar, never used, was a reminder that in the distant Chinese past sacrifices were held in the open.

Military official in the spirit road leading to Changling, the first tomb in the valley.

The tomb

The way from the square earthly to the heavenly round part of the tomb lies through a tall pavilion containing a stele dedicated to a deceased emperor. Entering the tomb section is like coming into another world. Gone are all the colours. Here everything is of unadorned stone. The tree-covered mound is enclosed by stone ramparts with a view of the mountains. The only excavated tomb, Dingling, tomb of the emperor Wanli (who died in 1620), consists of a series of vaulted chambers leading to the room where the coffin lay. The doors and walls are made of white marble, with slabs fitting so tightly that the interior was completely dry after 250 years. The contents of the tomb, now mostly on display in the Forbidden City museum, included valuable clothing and headdresses of the emperor and his two empresses, numerous jade objects, models of furniture, fine porcelain and a very large collection of Ming textiles.

Marble thrones and blue and white urns in the sacrificial chamber of the tomb of Emperor Wanli (d. 1620).

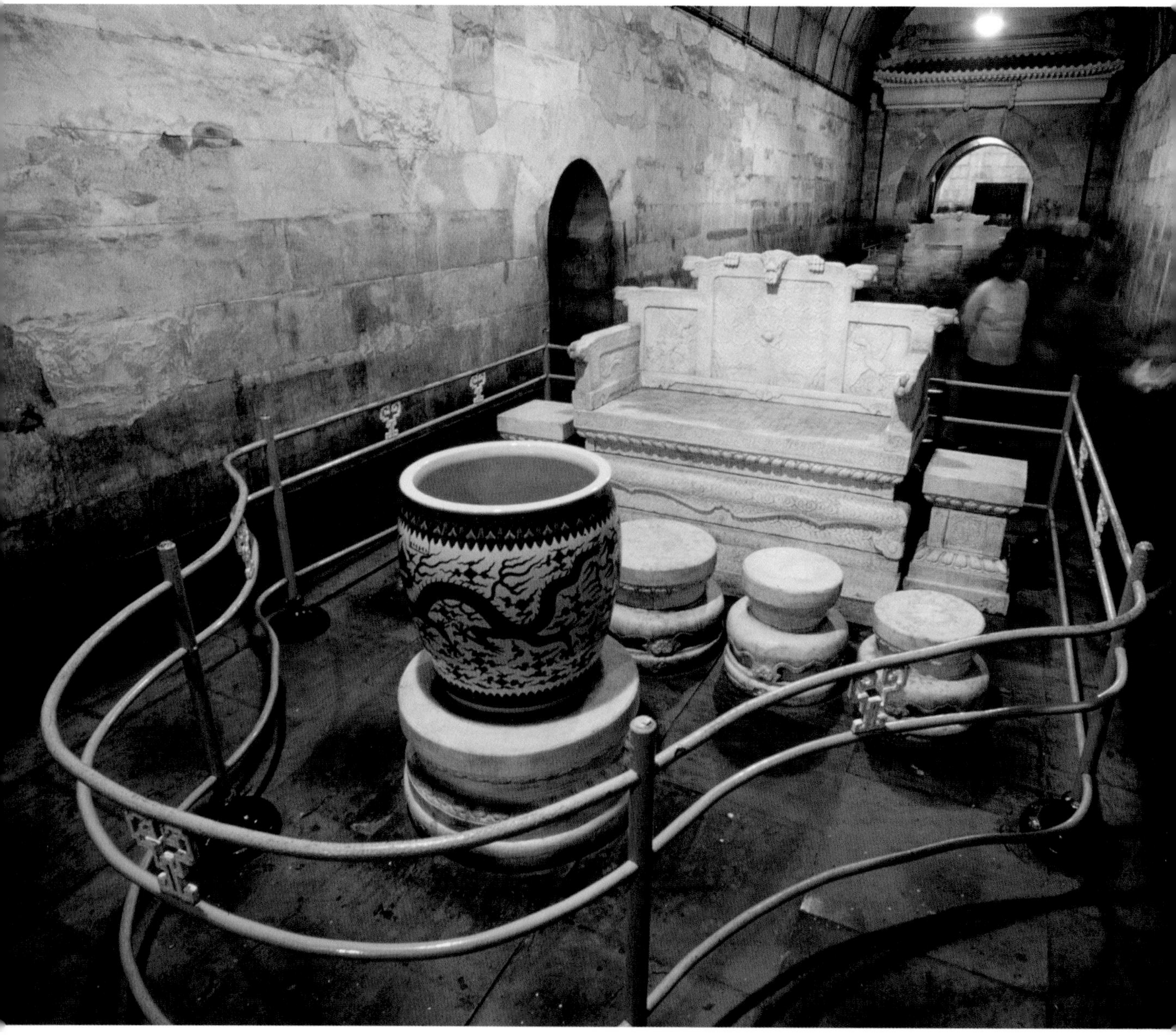

FRANCES WOOD

Leshan Great Buddha & Caves

38

The mountain is a Buddha, the Buddha is a mountain.
LOCAL CHINESE / SICHUANESE SAYING

In the southwestern province of Sichuan, not far from the Buddhist holy mountain Emei Shan, dedicated to the worship of the Bodhisattva Samantabhadra, a giant Buddha figure is carved into a reddish, tree-covered cliff at Leshan. The site is dramatic for three rivers, the Dadu, Qingyi and Min, converge at Leshan. The giant Buddha sits against a cliff on the bank of the Min River. Carved during the Tang dynasty between 713 and 803, the figure is that of Maitreya, the Buddha of the future, rather than the historic Buddha, Sakyamuni. Sakyamuni is often depicted either standing or sitting cross-legged on a lotus throne whilst Maitreya is usually shown, as here, seated as if on a chair, with feet on the ground. Smaller Maitreya figures show the hands in the preaching *mudra* or gesture, held up in front of the chest, but the size of the figure and weight of the Leshan Buddha mean that its hands rest firmly on its knees.

The Leshan Great Buddha was clearly modelled on earlier giant Buddhist carvings seen by Chinese pilgrims to South Asia. Faxian, a monk who travelled to India in the early 5th century, wrote an account of his visit to the 3rd-century giant figures of standing Buddhas at Bamiyan, cut deep into a cliff face. The larger of the two Bamiyan Buddhas was 53 m (174 ft) high, the Leshan Buddha is 71 m (233 ft) high and not standing, but seated. So it may well be true, as the Chinese claim, that the Leshan Buddha is the largest stone-carved Buddha in the world. It has been recently designated a World Heritage site, which should help to preserve it from the fate of the Bamiyan Buddhas that were blown up by

Previous page
The Leshan Buddha surveys the Min River from his cliff.

officers of the Taliban Ministry for the Prevention of Vice and the Promotion of Virtue in March 2001. The Leshan Buddha is impressive rather than beautiful, with a head nearly 15 m (50 ft) high – covered in tightly carved curls of hair – and 7-m (23-ft) earlobes, for all Buddha figures have long earlobes, dragged down by earrings.

Pagodas and subsidiary statues

Above and behind the Buddha, on the top of the cliff, are temple buildings and a pagoda. These are much later in date than the Buddha and have been frequently restored. The Lingbao (or Spirit Treasure) Pagoda, built in brick, was first constructed during the Song dynasty and restored in the Ming and Qing. Local legend holds that the site was chosen at the confluence of the rivers in an effort to prevent flooding, and that funds were raised for the Buddha's construction by a local monk, who gouged out one of his own eyes to impress potential donors. A series of narrow steps with nine turns is carved into the rock on the right side of the Buddha, leading down to the feet at the riverside, each one said to be large enough to accommodate 100 people. On both sides of the cliff beside the Buddha's knees and ankles, smaller niches containing multiple Buddha figures have been carved over the centuries. Visible only from the river or the opposite bank are the two standing guardian figures carved into the cliff on either side of the Buddha. Such attendant guardians are commonly seen at other great rock-carved Buddhist sites in China like the Longmen caves near Luoyang. Some 20 m (66 ft) tall, they are more delicately modelled than the Buddha.

A little further east of the giant Buddha are a number of tombs built in natural caves in the cliff. One dates from AD 159 and has a roughly carved Buddha figure in a roundel on the lintel. This is a particularly significant carving, probably the earliest Buddha image in China, for it dates from the very first years of the introduction of Buddhism from India and it is surprising to find it in Sichuan, so far from the Silk Road or the capital city.

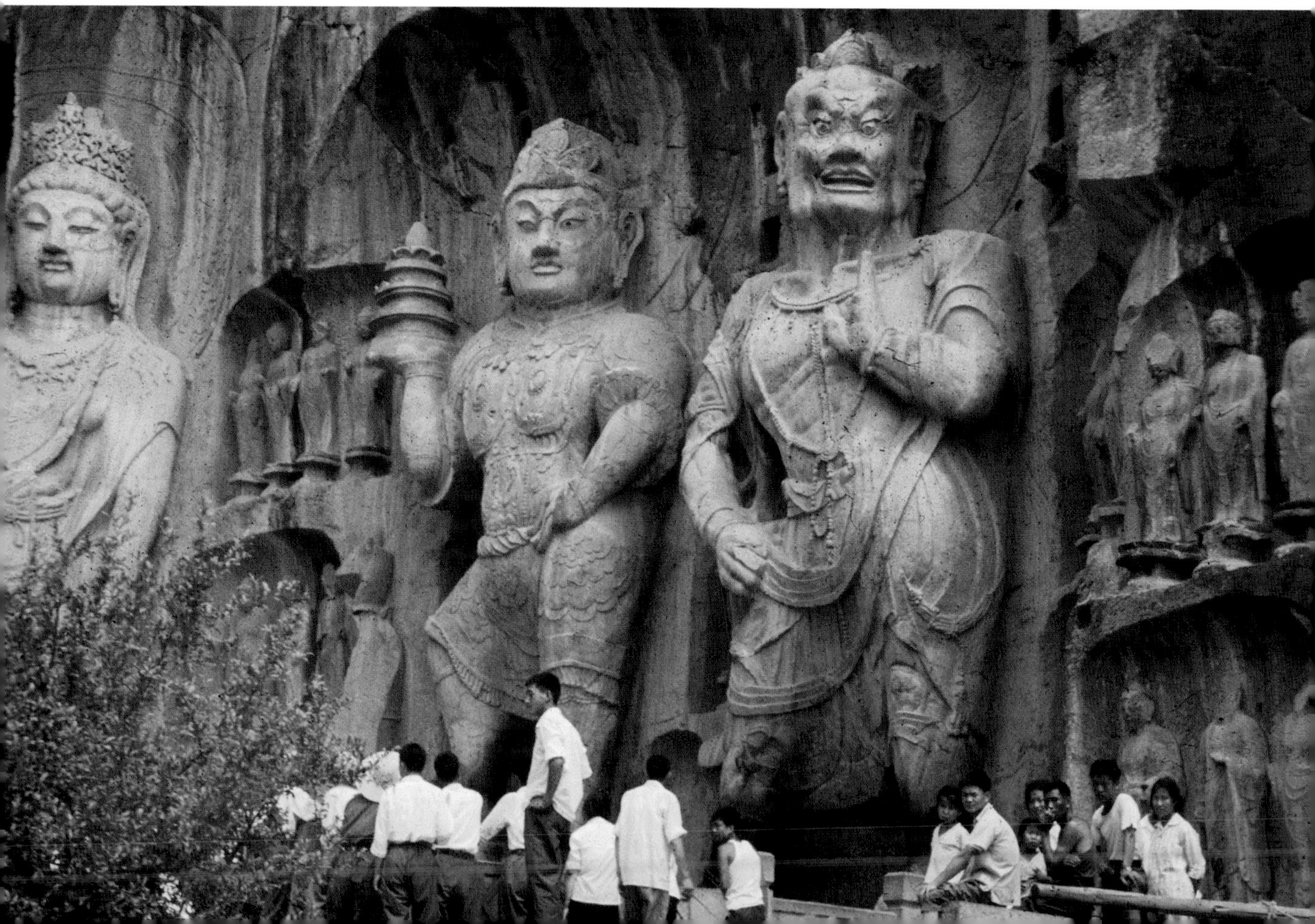

View of the Longmen caves, near Luoyang.

PHILIP DENWOOD

Labrang Yellow Hat Monastery

39

In 1703, Jamyang Shepa received the whole set of Buddhist scriptures from the Mongol prince Ardinijunan. The latter asked him to return home to propagate Buddhism. To this he replied, 'Suppose I go back home, could you help me in building as good a monastery as Drepung?' 'It would be somewhat difficult to build one like this,' the prince replied, 'but I shall try my best to fulfil your wish.'

ADAPTED FROM LI AN-CHE, *HISTORY OF TIBETAN RELIGION*

The 300-year-old Labrang Monastery is one of the largest monasteries of the Yellow Hat school of Tibetan Buddhism. The monastery and town of Labrang (Sangchu county, Gansu province) straddle a trade route running along the narrow but level floor of the valley of the Daxia River (Tibetan Sangchu) between steep hills on either side. The river flows from the bleak Tibetan plateau to the west into a zone of formerly forested hills and cultivated valleys, the site of Labrang being at the junction of nomadic and settled areas.

To the west the hinterland of Labrang is occupied largely by Tibetan nomads, who share a

Ancient map of the Labrang Monastery complex in Gansu province.

Right *Labrang Monastery from the west. In the foreground is the Gunthang Stupa, restored in 1992, with some of the main temples in the background.*

Below *An ethnic Tibetan pilgrim lies prostrate in prayer on the grounds of the Labrang Monastery, which looms up in the background.*

common language and religious culture with the settled Tibetans in the immediate vicinity and to the east, though following a very different lifestyle. Also in the nomadic areas live the descendants of the Mongol tribes who were politically dominant at the time of the monastery's foundation, many of them now Tibetanized in varying degrees. Some 40 km (25 miles) to the east and north, Tibetan culture gives way to Han Chinese and Muslims (Hui and Salar). Labrang, despite its firm affiliation to the Yellow Hat, or Gelugpa, school of Tibetan Buddhism, has since its foundation been a focus of complex religious, cultural, economic and political relations between these and other groups, as well as Manchu, Nationalist and Communist governments. Economically the Monastery has depended on the revenues from taxes, lands and trade derived from the local population.

History

At the time of Labrang's foundation in 1709 the region was controlled by Erdeni Jigong, grandson of the Qoshot Mongol whose installation of the Fifth Dalai Lama in 1642 had led to the building of the Potala Palace in Lhasa (p. 174). The religious initiative came from the first Jamyang Shepa, a native of the area and an incarnation third in rank after the Dalai and Panchen Lamas. The local Mongol aristocracy continued to play a leading political role in this rather turbulent frontier area down to the mid-20th century and were the main sponsors of the development of the Monastery. Not until 1950 did China in the form of the Communist Government take firm control of the region. After a period of neglect until after the Cultural Revolution, monastic life has been re-established.

By the early 20th century the Monastery occupied an area about 1 km (0.6 mile) in length and 500 m (1,600 ft) wide along the north bank of the river, with all the main buildings facing south. The outer buildings present a continuous perimeter wall to the outside. Concentric circumambulation paths thread through and around the complex. Two roads traverse the monastery from east to west. This general layout is typical of Gelugpa monasteries throughout the Tibetan cultural area. Like most large Tibetan monasteries, it is the product of a long period of growth.

First to be built was the assembly hall, in 1709–11, replacing a tent with a community of just five monks. The first Jamyang Shepa also founded the Gyume Tratsang (Lower Tantric College), the Sokshing Chora (College of Dialectics) and the Jokhang (Buddha) Temple. Many other buildings were added during the 18th century, including the Serkhang Chenmo or Great Golden Temple, and the Dukhor Tratsang (Kalachakra College). Others followed in the 19th and 20th centuries.

These buildings, their functions and contents, reflected the collegiate organization; the academic programmes including dialectics, debate, astrology and medicine; and the ritual and iconographic preoccupations of the great Yellow Hat monasteries near Lhasa, particularly Ganden and Drepung. By the 20th century there were 'six sutra halls, forty-eight Buddha temples, thirty-one palaces for the Jamyang Shepas and the senior lamas, thirty mansions for the incarnate lamas, eight government buildings, six big kitchens, one

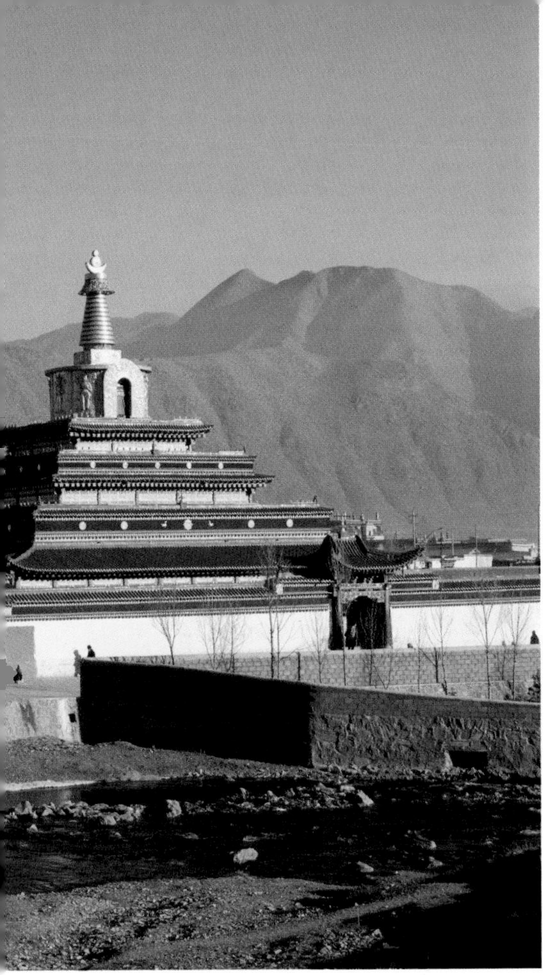

printing house, two main meeting halls, over five hundred prayer-wheel rooms, and more than five hundred common monks' cells.' (Quote from a book by Huang Jengqing, 1989.)

Architecture

The architectural style of the buildings has been aptly described as 'an example of the Tibetanization of Amdo architecture'. While in many Amdo monasteries Chinese building materials (baked brick and tiles), plans and aesthetics are prominent, albeit mixed with local features, the overall plan of Labrang is inspired by that of Drepung in central Tibet. The temples are in the central Tibetan 'Gelugpa' style and the monks' houses are in the local flat-roofed style with a central light well (some of them replacing more Chinese-like dwellings after the Cultural Revolution). The main building materials are stamped earth (adobe) and stone, with inward-sloping outer walls and, internally, the standard painted Tibetan wooden columns and elongated bracket capitals. The Gelugpa style in turn itself incorporates a few Chinese elements, principally small pitched roofs on the flat roof terraces of important temples. The rough exterior surfaces are painted in white and, in the case of temples, red, with the typical brushwood parapets at terrace level, and vertical windows outlined with black trapezoidal borders.

The architectural and religious core of the Monastery is still the assembly hall, completed in 1711, enlarged in 1772, accidentally burnt down in 1985 and rebuilt to the same design in 1990. It is entered through the Thosamling College, which consists of an entrance hall roofed with green-glazed Chinese tiles, leading into a large cloistered courtyard. The assembly hall itself is a clear space accommodating up to 4,000 seated monks, whose flat roof is supported by 140 columns. To the rear is a two-storeyed temple building with three chapels on the ground floor. Its upper storey looks onto the cloistered roof terrace and bears a small Chinese roof. Thus in general terms the design follows that of many important central Tibetan temples, such as the Jokhang in Lhasa and Shalu near Shigatse, with entrance courtyard, assembly hall and temple to the rear, though without any side chapels to the assembly hall.

There were between 3,000 and 5,000 monks in residence until the Communist takeover, and there are now about 2,000 monks, mostly recruited from the surrounding regions of Amdo. Labrang is once again a bustling centre for pilgrims, traders and now tourists, as well as being a fully functioning Tibetan monastery.

An old man at the monastery makes use of the prayer wheels.

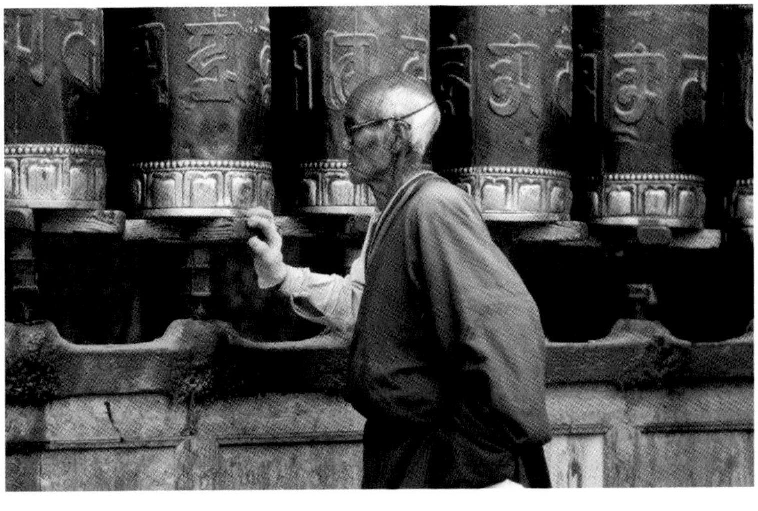

PHILIP DENWOOD

40 Great Monuments of Tibet

The roadway was but a gully, and we had to dismount and pass through in single file. But once through, what a sight lay before our eyes!... Immediately to our left we were face to face with the gigantic structure of the Potala Palace, which covered the whole of the hill....I halted almost dumbfounded before its splendour.

W. MONTGOMERY MCGOVERN, 1924

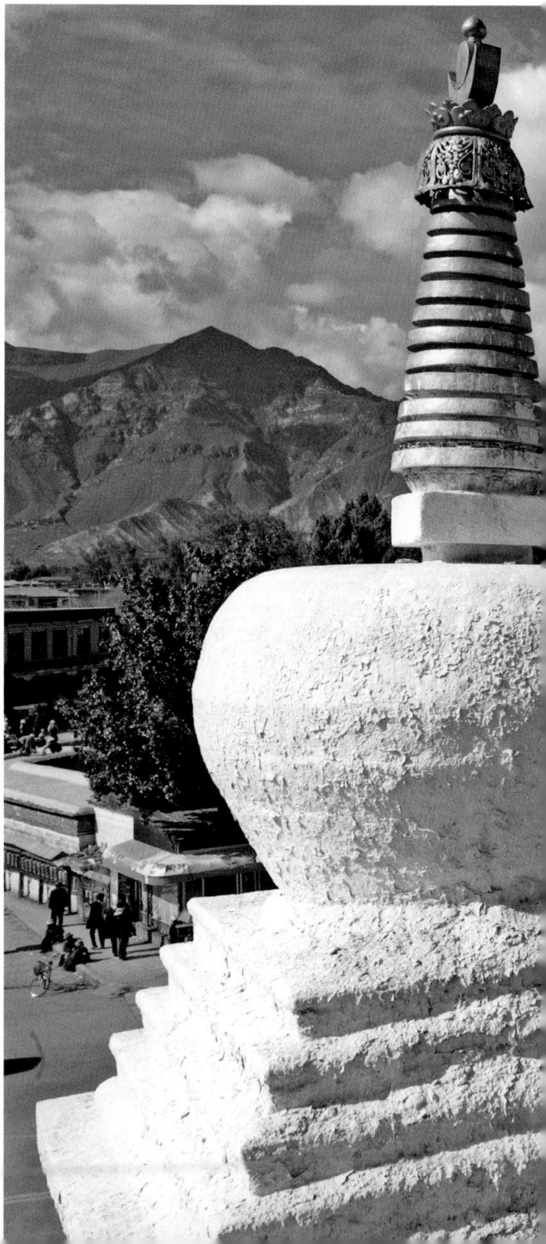

Right *View of Potala Palace from the southwest. The stupas in the foreground mark the main western entrance road to the old city, considerably widened in recent years.*

The Potala Palace was conceived as a symbol of the Tibetan polity at a time when the country was newly united under the rule of the Buddhist Dalai Lamas. It has admirably fulfilled that function, its image having been displayed by diverse groups in their claims of control over or affiliation with Tibet, while it also provides the quintessential visual symbol of Tibet for outsiders. At the same time it evokes the Indian roots of Tibetan Buddhism, the practical Mongol backing which made its construction possible, and Chinese modes of architectural embellishment.

Named after the mythical south Indian palace of Tibet's patron Buddhist deity Avalokiteshvara, the Potala is built on the alleged site of a small palace erected by the 7th-century AD founder of Tibet, King Songtsen Gampo, who like the instigator of the Potala the Fifth Dalai Lama (r. 1642–82) is reckoned as a reincarnation of Avalokiteshvara.

The Potala runs along the crest of a low ridge overlooking the town of Lhasa to the south, and is part of a fortified complex which includes a rectangular walled precinct at the ridge's foot. Its core comprises two main elements, the White Palace to the east and the Red Palace to the west.

After being installed as ruler of Tibet by the Mongol Gushri Khan in 1642, the Fifth Dalai Lama constructed the White Palace between 1645 and 1648 and made it his official residence. His last regent, Sangye Gyatsho, built the Red Palace between 1690 and 1694 to incorporate the Dalai Lama's mausoleum.

Both the White and the Red Palaces are ultimately a development of ancient Indian monastic design. A rectangular ground-floor assembly hall is surrounded by inward-looking cells over which are superimposed two or more storeys of further cells to leave a galleried and open central inner terrace over the hall. The internal spaces are mostly dedicated as chapels, monastic rooms, Dalai Lamas' living apartments or their funerary shrines.

The tomb of the Thirteenth Dalai Lama (r. 1895–1933) is housed in a western extension to the Red Palace built between 1934 and 1936. Peripheral buildings such as monastic living quarters at the western end, storerooms and outer fortifications seem mostly to go back to the late 17th century, though many minor modifications have been made over the years. Access is by narrow defensible gateways reached by a number of stepped ramps whose gentle gradient is easily negotiable by a loaded horse.

The crest of the hill seems to have been levelled into a terrace by cut and fill, a standard Tibetan technique, the outer walls of the buildings descending below the terrace to various levels, giving the impression of growing out of the ridge.

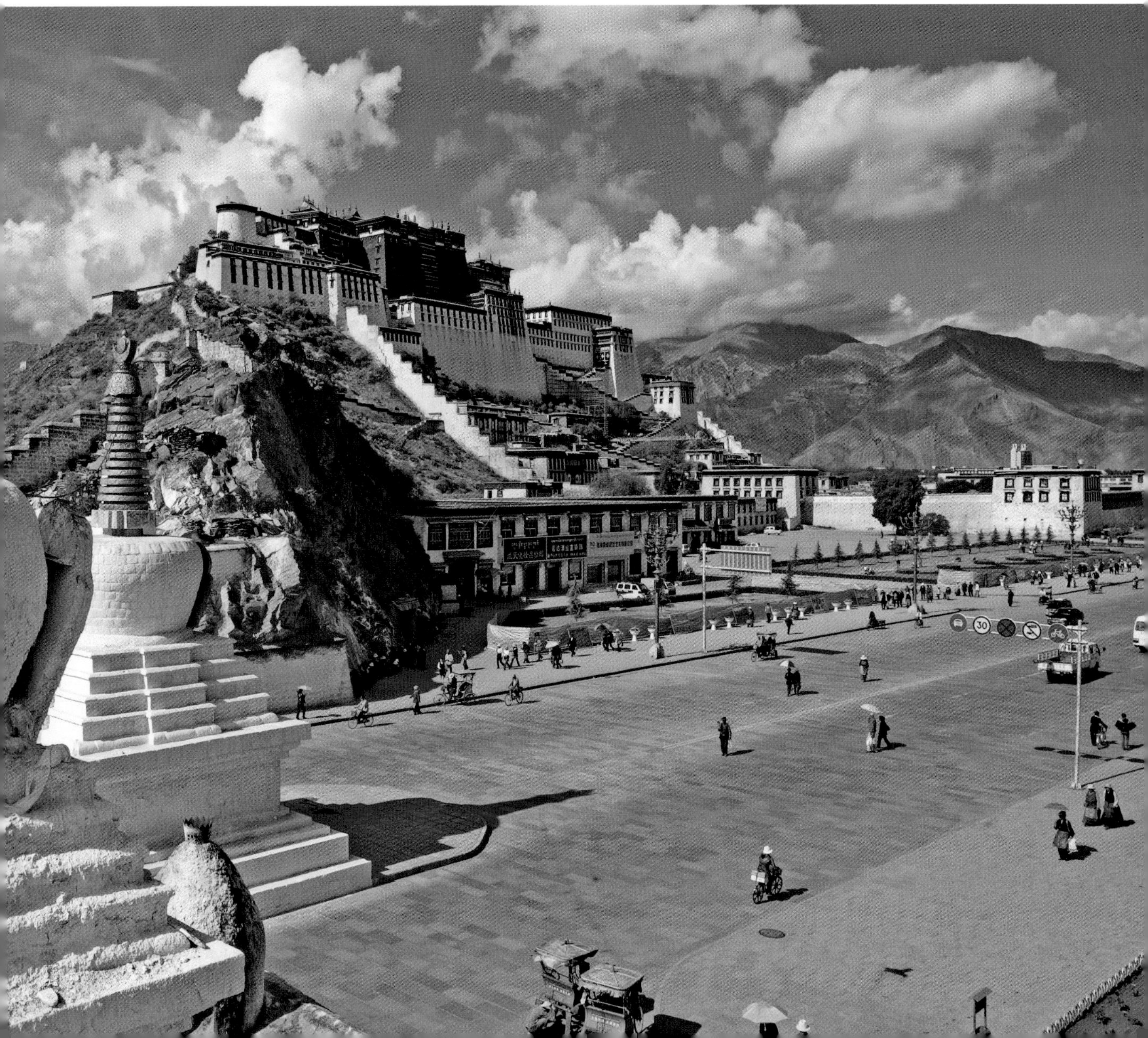

In technology and use of materials, the Potala differs hardly at all from the ordinary Tibetan farmhouse: not surprising since the bulk of the workforce can only have been recruited from the local peasantry. The structural technique is one of heavy outer loadbearing masonry walls – in this case of roughly dressed stone mortared with mud – into which are set heavy wooden ceiling beams which in turn support wooden joists. Internally the beams are supported by wooden columns via long brackets. Thus masonry on the outside gives way largely to timber on the inside.

Much of the stone was transported from sites upstream to the northeast of Lhasa on the backs of porters and by coracle, while the mud was largely dug from immediately behind the site, leaving pits which were later converted into an ornamental lake. The inner and outer skins of the walls are made of horizontal courses of stones, separated by thin layers of much smaller, flattish stones packed with mud to form a level bed for the course above.

Typical of Tibetan architecture is the inward slope or batter of 6–9 degrees from the vertical of the outer walls. The inward slope of the walls is visually counterbalanced by columns of timber-framed windows, slit-like in the lowest tier and widening out sometimes to balconies in the upper tiers. Their lintels are capped by projecting joist-ends and mud canopies. The flat roofs are bounded by parapets, vertical rather than battered, into whose outer face is set a stack of willow or tamarisk brushwood, ends outwards and painted red. This is a fossilized version of the stack of fuel still heaped round the roofs of Tibetan farmhouses. The walls are decorated by a wash of lime or red ochre. The rough texture of the outer surfaces at close quarters reinforces the rustic feel of the building.

Internal woodwork and wall surfaces are heavy with painted and carved decoration. The most important points within the complex are marked at the highest level by small gilded roofs of Chinese type and gilded ornaments of Indian origin, almost certainly made by Chinese and Nepalese craftsmen respectively and another departure from the farmhouse style.

Gyantse religious complex

The Pelkhor Chode or religious complex of Gyantse comprises the side of a rocky outcrop overlooking an important trade route leading from Bengal and Sikkim to central Tibet. The complex is surrounded by a wall with a fortress at its highest point, completed on earlier foundations by the local prince Phakpa Pelzangpo in 1365. Within this fortified enclosure were built the Tsuklakhang, or main temple, and the Kumbum Stupa between 1418 and 1439, as well as a number of other structures. The town of Gyantse sits on the valley floor outside the fortification.

The centre of the Tsuklakhang is a large assembly hall whose flat roof is supported by 48 wooden columns. It is entered by a porch and entrance hall to the south, opposite which is the main sanctum, which contains three large Buddha images and is surrounded by a circulambulation corridor. To east and west are two further chapels, lending the whole plan the outline of a Buddhist mandala. A small upper storey on the terrace roof has five chapels round a central gallery. The building is in typical central Tibetan style with inward-sloping outer masonry walls, roughly finished and painted dark red, topped by a whitewashed frieze and black brushwood parapet.

The 38-m (125-ft) high Kumbum ('One hundred thousand images') is by far the most impressive stupa in Tibet and ranks among the foremost in the world. Unusually, the five-storey base, laid out

Right *Gyantse city fortress was built in a staggering location, its outer walls continuing downhill to enclose the whole of the old town and its temples.*

The Kumbum Stupa at Gyantse, one of the largest and most impressive stupas in Tibet.

on a 20-cornered plan, is hollowed out into a total of 68 chapels, accessible from the surrounding terraces, with a further seven chapels inside the dome and spire. The iconography of the images and wall paintings displays an upward progression through the pantheon of the four classes of Buddhist tantras, as well as the important lineages of Tibetan Buddhism. Thus the concepts of the stupa (an iconic symbol of the Buddha and his enlightenment) and the mandala (symmetrical array of divine forms), both with their elaborate symbolism, are integrated in a single structure in a way seldom achieved elsewhere.

Tashilhunpo Monastery

Tashilhunpo Monastery outside Shigatse was founded in 1447 by the First Dalai Lama. Like other great Gelugpa monasteries such as Labrang (p. 171), it has grown progressively to take the form of a loosely arranged row of major temples and mausolea of the Panchen Lamas (tutors to the Dalai Lamas), facing southeast over a river valley with their backs to a rocky outcrop; other monastic buildings and monks' housing is to the front. The whole area is surrounded by a defensive wall which incorporates a massive blockhouse, usable as a last redoubt and over whose southern face a huge textile *thangka* (image of the Buddha) is draped during major festivals. The buildings are in the typical central Tibetan 'Gelugpa' style, the temples mostly painted red and topped by gilded Chinese roofs; other buildings are whitewashed.

The mausolea of the Panchen Lamas were destroyed in the 1960s, except for that of the Fourth (the Kudung Lhakhang), but the Tenth incumbent constructed a new one (the Dungten Tashi Namgyel) to house the relics of his five predecessors in the 1980s, and he was himself entombed in a magnificent mausoleum built after his death in 1989. Their design is paralleled by that of many of the temples. Tall buildings, they contain several storeys of galleries surrounding a high central space, occupied in the case of the Jamkhang Chenmo by the world's largest gilded metal image of Maitreya (26 m / 85 ft high); and in the case of the Tenth Panchen Lama by a gigantic metal stupa.

Below *Pilgrims at Tashilhunpo Monastery.*

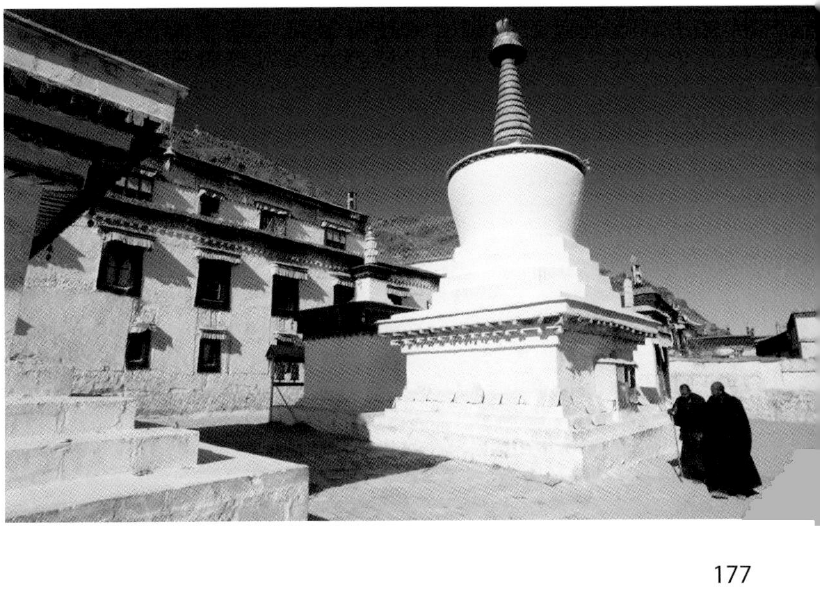

FRANCES WOOD

41 The Grand Canal

At Lin-sin-choo, the yachts quitted the Eu-ho which ... is here joined by the Imperial or Grand Canal.... This enterprise, the greatest and most ancient of its kind ... was found to extend in an irregular line of about 500 miles, not only through heights and over vallies but across rivers and lakes.

LORD MACARTNEY, 1794

Though Lord Macartney, the first British envoy to China, speaks of the Grand Canal in the singular, and means the part of the canal running northwards from Hangzhou to Linqing on the Hebei-Shandong border, known in Chinese as the *Da yunhe* or 'Great Canal', it is only a part of the great canal system constructed in China from as early as the 5th century BC.

Historically, transport of heavy goods by water was 50 times more efficient than the use of a pack-horse and, since China's main rice-growing area was in the south, canals were needed to help transport grain northwards to the imperial capital. It was not just for food and for storage in state granaries against times of hardship, but most of the revenue required for the running of the bureaucratic state was collected in the form of grain.

The major river systems in China, those of the Yellow River and the Yangtze, run from west to

Watercolour of the Grand Canal by William Alexander (painted 1792–94).

east, thus most of the canals run roughly south to north, linking river systems and lakes. The Grand Canal was constructed partly on the basis of earlier, shorter canal systems such as that connecting the Yellow River with the Huai valley and linking with a very old canal leading southwards to Yangzhou.

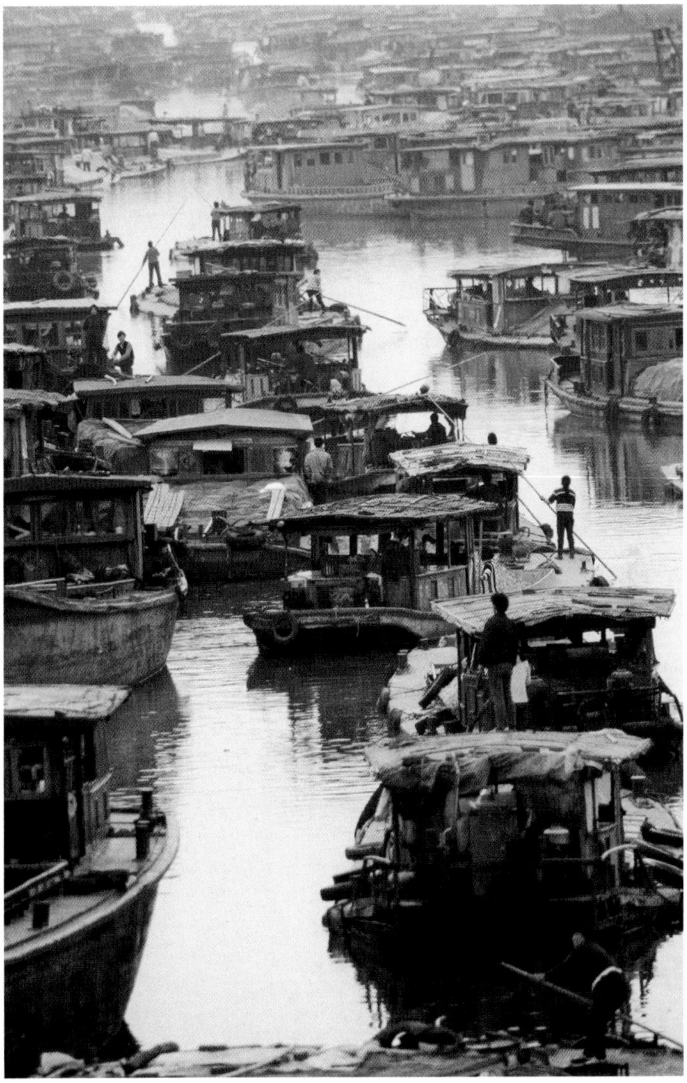

Barges line up on the Grand Canal near Suzhou.

Construction

Most of the early work, involving more than 5 million male and female labourers, was done during the short-lived Sui dynasty (AD 581–618). It was economically imperative to link the capital at Luoyang with the fertile lower Yangtze delta and also to be able to move troops about the country fast to establish control. The section of canal almost 1,000 km (620 miles) long, running from the Yellow River via the (canalized) Wei River and reaching close to Tianjin, was one part of the Grand Canal that was newly constructed in the Sui. Despite the efficiency of the transport system (a 9th-century Japanese monk talks of mile-long flotillas of salt boats, lashed three- and five-abeam), conservative Confucian historians were critical of the cost of canal-building under the Sui.

In the subsequent Tang dynasty, further canal building was undertaken, to link the capital, Chang'an (modern Xi'an), with the system, but it was during the Mongol period, when China's capital was established in Beijing, that the last great canal-building effort took place. In 1293, Beijing was linked with Tongzhou, some 80 km (50 miles) away, by a section of canal requiring some 20 lock-gates, and the northern part of the old canal was moved eastwards. In 1327, the Grand Canal had attained its final length of about 2,574 km (1,600 miles). There was still room for improvement, and a Ming engineer helped the flow of the canal at its highest point in 1411 by building dams and reservoirs to collect water and sluice gates to control its flow.

Canal building involved canalizing parts of rivers, dredging and damming, all techniques that had been developed since the 7th century BC in efforts to control the silt-laden Yellow River. But to enable ships to pass along a waterway that varied in height above sea level from 8 to 55 m (26–180 ft), it was necessary to construct various types of water gate and slipways. Sluice-gates were first mentioned in Chinese literature in 36 BC and flash-lock gates were used at the same time, though it was not until the 10th century that pound gates, which improved the speed of canal travel, were introduced. Many of the pound locks seem to have fallen into disuse during the Yuan dynasty when a greater volume of southern produce was sent north by sea and smaller vessels were used on the Grand Canal. These could more easily be hauled over weirs and upstream, or winched up over slipways as was depicted in many drawings made by members of Lord Macartney's Embassy to China in 1792–94.

ANN PALUDAN

42 Buddhist Cliff Carvings at Dazu

Should you enquire about the meaning
Of the illusion-like manifestations,
Then it is similar to the wildflowers and
Luscious grasses growing together.
INSCRIPTION BESIDE THE OX-HERDING CARVINGS, BAODINGSHAN, DAZU

In Dazu, sculpture is part of the landscape. In this remote mountain region of Sichuan some 60,000 carvings have survived from the 9th to the 13th centuries, and in 1999 it was declared a World Heritage Site. The two major centres, Beishan and Baodingshan, not only contain some of the finest sculptural work in China but clearly demonstrate the extent to which Buddhist doctrines had been assimilated into a system of popular Chinese beliefs.

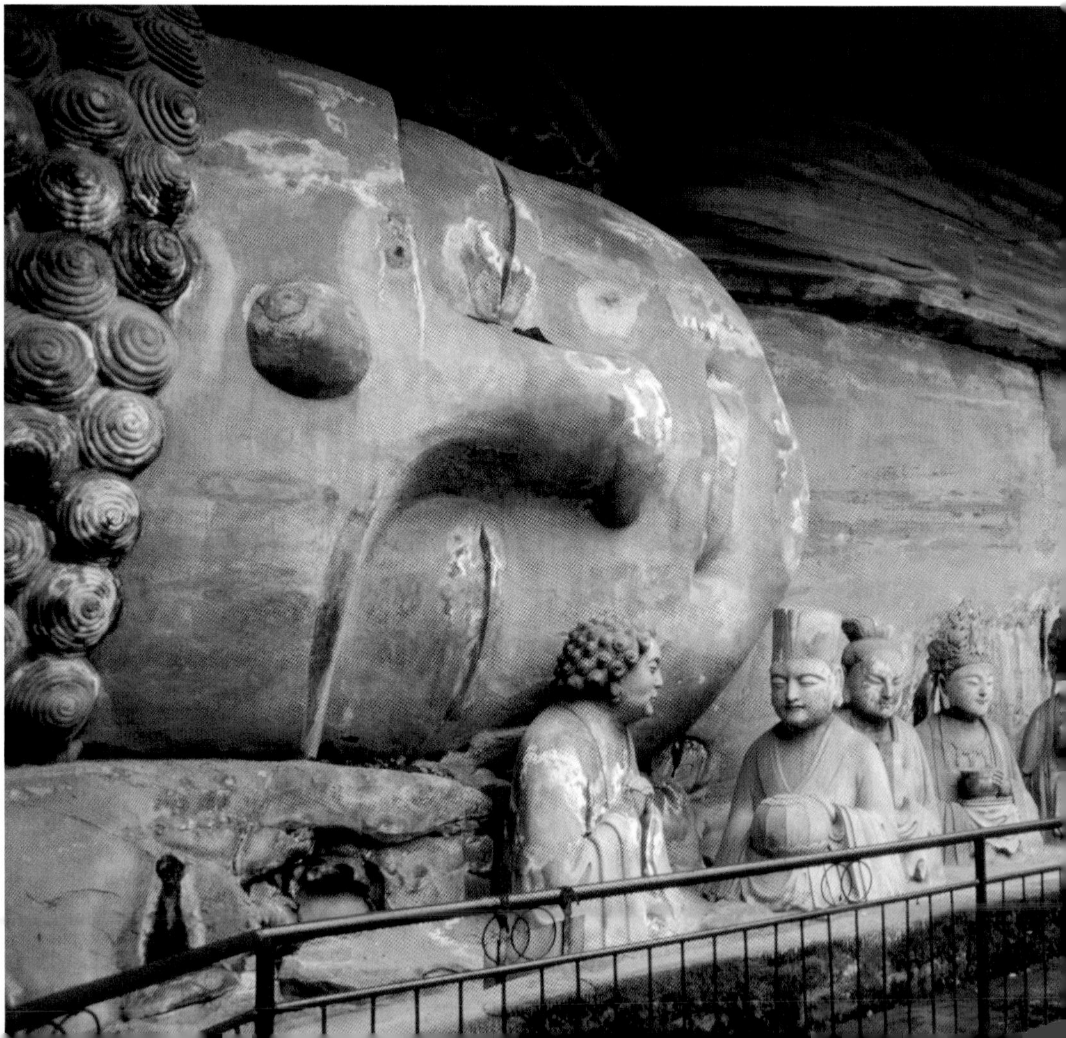

Buddha entering nirvana with mourning figures, Baodingshan. (Height 7 m / 23 ft, length 31.6 m / 103 ft.)

Beishan is a typical mountain site with shrines carved apparently haphazardly, along a 300-m (985-ft) cliff face, often 7 m (23 ft) high. The most spectacular shrine depicts the Western Paradise, a blessed land which believers who called on the Amitabha Buddha with complete sincerity could enter after death. Paradise is portrayed in Chinese terms with palaces, pagodas and balconies complete with officials; earthly beings climb the palace walls, viewers pack the balconies while musicians and spirit figures fly above. Smaller shrines, such as the Guanyin of the Rosary, are portrayed with the delicacy of a painting.

Baodingshan

The jewel of Dazu is, however, Baodingshan, a hairpin valley whose entire cliff sides were carved 500 m (1,640 ft) long and 14 m (45 ft) high, in a continuous period (1179–1249) under the guidance of the Tantrist monk, Zhao Zhifeng. Unique among Chinese shrines, there is no repetition. Carvings along the first part of the valley demonstrate major Buddhist doctrines including a Wheel of Life showing the process of attaining salvation. On the far side, educational scenes with explanatory inscriptions demonstrate traditional Buddhist and Confucian virtues and the horrific punishments awaiting sinners. Finally the unfinished carvings of towering guardian figures record the abrupt ending of the project with the arrival of the Mongols.

The Wheel of Life is one of thousands of complex Buddhist works of art sculpted into the cliffs at Dazu.

Sculptural skills

Little is known about Chinese sculptors; their profession was regarded as a manual task outside the scope of official records. At Baodingshan, however, we can see that the men who created this valley were highly skilled craftsmen with knowledge ranging far beyond carving to the techniques of geology, architecture and water control.

A dominant theme in the site, Buddhist enlightenment, the gradual process of man's liberation from worldly ties, is expressed in the treatment of the stone. Along the upper regions, Buddhas are carved almost free from the cliff;

Right *The Three Sages sculptures represent the consummate skill of the sculptors who worked at Dazu.*

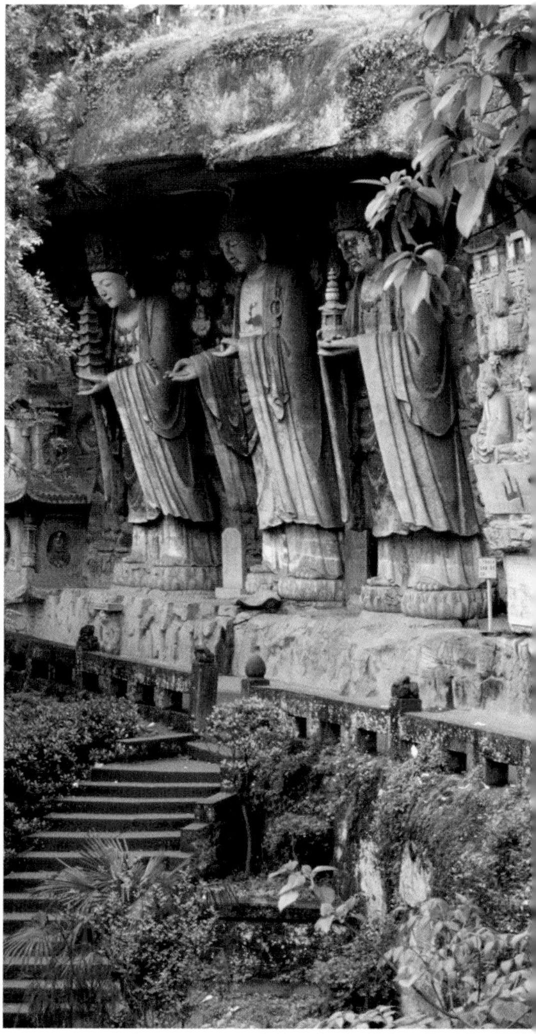

beneath them, semi-divine figures are in high relief but still visibly attached to the rock. At the lowest levels, human figures are firmly attached to their worldly background, often taking their form from the natural contours of the rock. Even a visitor ignorant of Buddhist doctrines can read and understand the message.

A scene depicting the Three Sages of the Huayan School of Buddhism appears to defy gravity. Over 8 m (26 ft) tall, leaning 20 per cent forward from the cliff, each of the outer figures carries with outstretched arm a 2-m (6.5-ft) tall pagoda weighing 400 kg (14,000 lb). By using architectural methods for making balconies, the sculptors have carried the weight of the overhanging section through the robes, thus creating a diagonal support down to the base and for over 900 years, these apparently unsupported figures have survived undamaged.

Skills in water control are combined with brilliant ability to adapt nature for their purposes. A natural stream has inspired a possibly apocryphal episode where the young Buddha bathes, protected by nine Chinese dragons. Contrasting illustrations of the way to enlightenment are carved in fundamentally different styles, thus emphasizing the difference in doctrines. In the carefully designed Cave of Enlightenment, a suppliant kneeling before three enthroned Buddhas is dramatically illuminated by natural light. The cave is completely dry; water from a roof gutter flows into a fruit held by a monkey and passes through his body into the ground. In stark contrast, nearby illustrations of the parable likening the way to enlightenment to the taming of wild oxen are carved as an integral part of the cliff. The oxen and herders are part of the rock; their background of streams, bamboos and a flute player are all inspired by the natural formations.

Finally, the carvings show that the sculptors were men with a certain independence. Illustrating the sin of breeding animals for food they carved a plump, happy woman tending pheasants with young peeping out from a basket. Unthinkable that she should be destined for hell.

Below *Work on these guardian figures carved into one of the grottoes was broken off at the arrival of the Mongols.*

JONATHAN FENBY

Modern Buildings & Infrastructure

43

When the sleeping dragon awakes, the world will be amazed.
NAPOLEON, C. 1800

Imperial China was famed for its major constructions, which are featured elsewhere in this book. Today, the government in Beijing and the ruling Communist Party, along with provincial administrations, have encouraged a spate of building on a scale that even the most glorious emperors could not have envisaged. China has become not only the workshop of the world, but its biggest construction site, stretching from a huge new city round Chongqing in Sichuan province in the west, and the Three Gorges Dam, to the gleaming towers of Beijing (p.116) and Shanghai (p. 126).

Major cities are being developed across the country, not only in the fast-growing coastal belt, but also in inland regions, such as the municipality of Chongqing, which has 12 million people living in the metropolis itself, and another 19 million spread over outlying areas. A huge project is under way to bring water to parched regions of north China along three canals covering 1,370 km (850 miles). It is expected to take 50 years to complete at a cost of £33 billion.

Hong Kong has long been a by-word for modern urban development, but, as economic growth has taken off, Chinese cities have seen some of the most intense construction on earth in recent years, leading to the joke that the national symbol should be the crane. In 2003, the country became the world's biggest producer of cement and its demand fuelled a steep rise in world steel prices. Four of the tallest buildings in the world are in China – in Hong Kong, Shanghai and the southern cities of Guangzhou and Shenzhen. While Shanghai takes pride in the 420-m (1,380-ft) high Jin Mao Tower, the former British colony

Looking down onto one of the lobbies of the Hyatt hotel from an upper floor inside the Jin Mao Tower, Pudong, Shanghai.

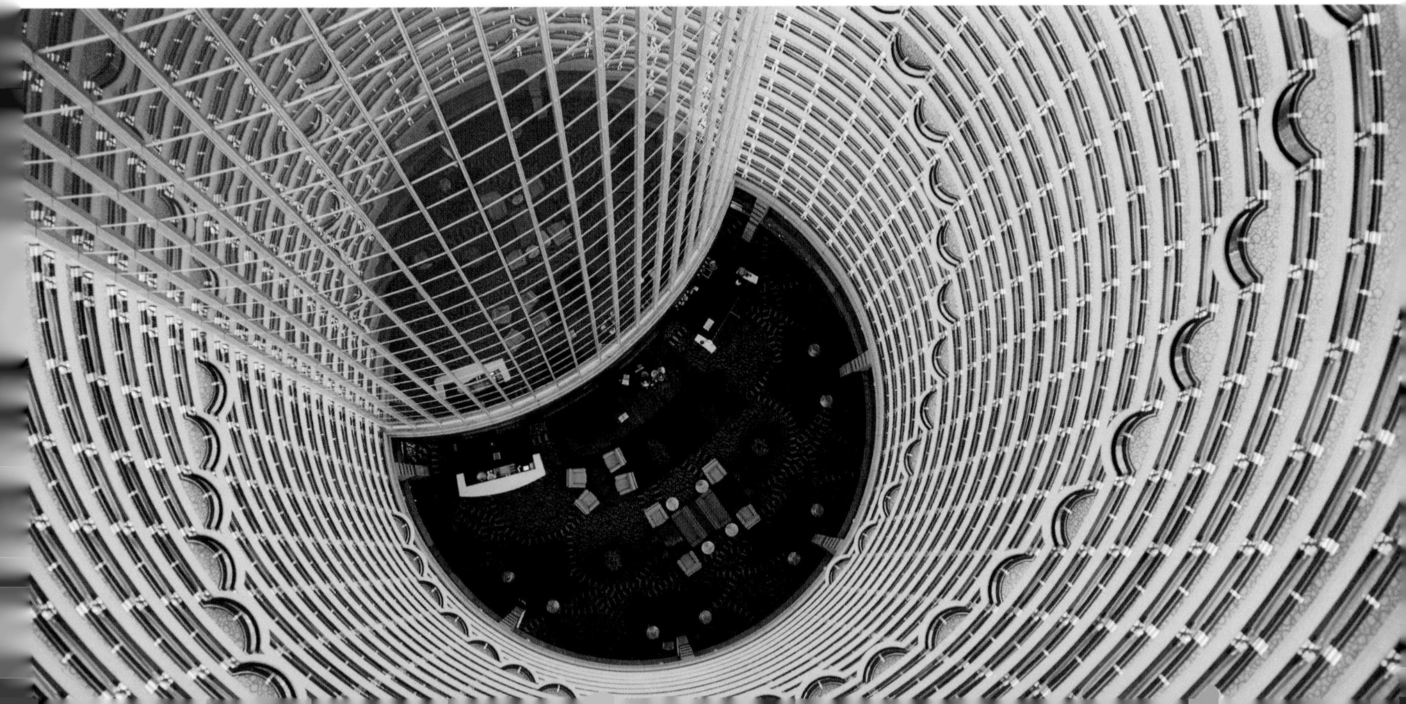

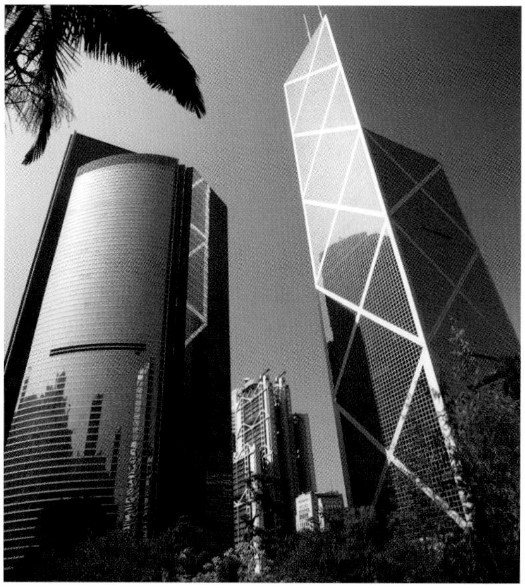

Reaching to the sky: the Bank of China, the Citibank Tower and the HSBC building, Hong Kong.

points to what must be two of the finest bank buildings in the world – the Bank of China in its Central District by the Chinese American architect, I. M. Pei, and the nearby Hong Kong and Shanghai Bank offices designed by the British architect, Norman Foster.

Transport

Airports have sprouted across the country, including the ultra-modern, architecturally accomplished installations in Shanghai and Hong Kong. Around another 50 airports are on the drawing board.

The departure hall of Pudong International Airport, Shanghai, is a good example of cutting edge, modern Chinese architecture.

Tens of thousands of miles of highways are planned, along with major new high-speed railway lines such as the one destined to link Beijing and Shanghai. In 2006, China opened the world's highest railway between the capital and Tibet which runs over a plateau 5,450 m (18,000 ft) above sea level. As befits the country which pioneered bridge-building (p. 264), the world's longest arched bridge, the Lupu Bridge, spans the Huangpu River outside Shanghai, carrying a six-lane highway over a 520-m (1,700-ft) main span. It is one of four bridges over the river that runs through China's biggest city. Another major transport link, combining a 16-km (10-mile) tunnel and a 9-km (6-mile) suspension bridge, connects Shanghai to outlying Chongming Island. In another sign of its modernity, Shanghai has installed a German-built magnetic-levitation railway to whisk passengers to and from its new airport at speeds of up to 435 km (270 miles) an hour.

The Three Gorges Dam is the largest water control project in the world, its construction work lasting 13 years.

Such huge investments in infrastructure have been a major driving force in pushing China's economic growth. Some economists worry that it may be too high, making the country too dependent on such projects and causing economic imbalances. Big environmental concerns have also been raised about some of the projects, and the pollution caused by the expansion of air travel, industry and motor transport.

Three Gorges Dam

The hydro-electric dam in the Three Gorges of the Yangtze River, on which work started in 1993, is the biggest project of its kind on earth, 2.4 km (1.5 miles) wide and more than 180 m (600 ft) high. It will create a reservoir stretching back nearly 640 km (400 miles) along the river. The locks through which shipping will pass are 280 m (920 ft) long, 35 m (115 ft) wide and 5 m (16.5 ft) deep, designed to handle barges with cargoes weighing up to 10,000 tons.

Its backers point to its role in lessening the country's serious energy shortage, with only small effect on air pollution – it is due to provide 10 per cent of energy needs by 2009, or as much as 18 nuclear power plants. They also say it will help flood control and meld in with the policy of encouraging economic growth in inland provinces by facilitating shipping along the river. Though historic treasures have been moved to higher ground, the building of the dam has involved the displacement of more than a million people and the flooding of some 1,300 archaeological sites, while altering the landscape of the Three Gorges by raising the water level.

Ecologists worry about the effect on wildlife along the Upper Yangtze, and others are troubled by the effect of silt carried down China's biggest river, which could reduce the power output from the dam while also affecting the fertility of the lower Yangtze by cutting the amount of silt washed down to provinces to the east.

The Arts

China's arts are wide and deep. They cover an enormous range, and have a profound history, stretching back millennia to form an integral part of the world's oldest continuous civilization. The story of Chinese arts is, in part at least, the story of the country as it moved through different stages of development under the overall umbrella of the imperial system (p. 64).

There is beauty in everything, Confucius taught, but not everyone sees it. In the case of the wonders of Chinese arts, this is hardly the case. Many were made to attract attention, to demonstrate extreme degrees of workmanship and refinements – and to bear witness to the owner's social status. Imperial patronage was always important, as was the respect of the scholar-gentry class which formed the backbone of the nation. The elaborate court ceremonial in the Forbidden City included the finest works the country could provide. Imperial garments, notably those made of silk, and objects, such as those made of jade, reflected the exquisite skills of Chinese artists and of artisans who rose to supply the country's rulers, usually anonymously.

The last dynasty, the Qing, though from Manchuria beyond the Great Wall, had a keen appreciation of how to use art to spread the message that it presided over a multi-cultural domain stretching from the nomadic lands of the northern steppes to the intense rice cultivation of the south. The search for modernity in the 20th century was amply reflected in literature and the visual arts. The Maoist era saw art pressed into the service of the new state.

Today, as China sets out on its new road, iconoclasm and invention sometimes bordering on nihilism accompany the march to the market

A modern-day stone carver in Yunnan province creates a lion using traditional methods. The 'spirit road' leading to the famous Ming tombs is lined by sculptures which were to act as guardian spirits of the emperor's final resting place.

Bronze mask decorated with gold leaf, found along with several other remarkable Bronze Age artifacts (c. 1200–1000 BC) at the site of Sanxingdui (literally 'three star mound') in Sichuan province at the end of the 20th century. (Height 48.5 cm / 19 in.)

economy, but there is also a widespread appreciation of the value of past achievements, even if perhaps the biggest single collection lies across the sea in Taiwan, where it was taken by Chiang Kai-shek's Nationalists in 1949.

Arts like porcelain (p. 217), silk (p. 231) and lacquer work (p. 222) also served significant commercial purposes as sources of export income. Significantly, all three come from humble ingredients and epitomize the way in which human ingenuity can make something fine and lasting out of virtually nothing. Jade (p. 194) was another much prized natural resource, hard to sculpt but used in everything from belt ornaments to the ink pots on a scholar's desk. The great Qing emperor, Qianlong (r. 1736–1795), was said to have brought together a collection of 30,000 jade objects, having poems he wrote inscribed on some of them.

Calligraphy (p. 198) always held a prominent place. Fine manipulation of the brush was prized not only for its visual appeal but as a sign of learning; some of the most successful graduates of the imperial examinations that selected the top bureaucracy were known for their expertise. The literary tradition (p. 204) can be traced back 3,000 years, with the succeeding centuries bringing Confucian analects, the verses of the Tang era (618–907) and the dramas of the Ming (1368–1644). Working of bronze (p. 189) also began early, with examples having been found that date back to 4000 BC. The Shang dynasty (*c.* 1600–1046 BC) saw both extremely refined bronze objects and very large pieces, weighing up to 875 kg (2,000 lb), and the tradition developed further under the first great Qin emperor and the succeeding Han dynasty, but then appears to have run out of invention.

In everyday life, well-off Chinese took pleasure, and pride, in two other characteristic art forms – furniture (p. 236), which evolved through the dynasties, and the beauty of Chinese gardens (p. 240) with their pavilions and rocks.

Chinese painting (p. 212) is probably best known for its depictions of rural scenes, putting humans in a natural setting, sometimes highly realistic, at other presenting swirling imaginative visions of mountains, rivers and skies. The earliest-known surviving scroll painting, *Admonitions of the Court Instructress,* probably dates back to the 3rd or 2nd century BC; made in a 'gossamer thread style', it depicts how the empress and concubines should behave. After centuries in which different approaches to painting ran through Chinese art, the Italian Jesuit, Giuseppe Castiglione, who sought vainly to convert the Qianlong emperor, introduced Western techniques, he himself working in a mixture of Chinese and European styles which, for all its introduction of perspective and shading, still reflected the universalist worldview of the Chinese empire.

ZHANG YINGLAN

Bronze Work

44

Although there were independent cultural traditions developing from diverse cultural centres, the cultural system characterized by the Shang and Zhou cultures in the Central Plains always maintained the leading position in Bronze Age China.
PROFESSOR LI BOQIAN, 1998

Bronze is an alloy of copper, tin and lead. In any civilization the use of bronze is a major watershed, for it requires a settled, specialized and tightly organized community.

Chinese bronze work has a long history; it was seldom equalled and never surpassed in any other ancient civilization. Its origins in China can be probably traced back as far as 4000 BC (Yangshao period of the Chinese Neolithic). By 2000 BC, China had entered an actual Bronze Age. From then until the reign of the Qing dynasty's last emperor, bronze was widely used, and played an important role in ancient Chinese society.

Bronzes handed down or unearthed so far suggest that Chinese bronze work developed as an independent system. Compared with other civilizations, in which the making of bronze tools and agricultural implements was the main signifier of the Bronze Age, the symbols of this epoch in China were bronze ritual vessels and weapons. Ancient China also differed from other ancient civilizations by using casting rather than forging as a bronze-making technique. Late in the Bronze Age a second technique of bronze casting, usually called the lost-wax method (or 'cire perdue') came into use in China. The fact that Chinese artisans used the complicated piece-mould and core method for most of their history suggests that their bronze industry developed independently from that of the West, where lost-wax bronze casting appeared by 3500 BC.

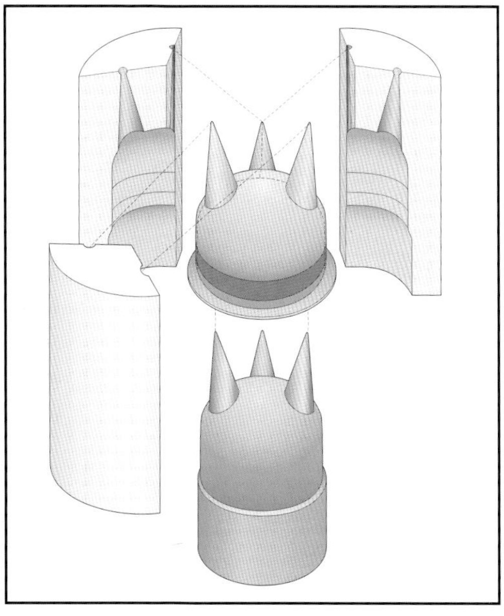

Far left *A three-legged bronze vessel (jue) for storing wine, 13th–12th century BC.*

Left *Diagram showing the 'piece-mould and core' method of casting bronze used in China, in this instance for a tripod vessel.*

Right *Highly detailed bronze dragon.*

History

Why was it that bronze-making developed so rapidly in ancient China? First, by the end of the Neolithic period Chinese artisans had already mastered exceptional technical skills through the making of ceramics. Secondly, bronze was an extremely precious commodity in ancient China; its use and distribution seems to have always been a monopoly of the ruling class. So, from the beginning, bronze was used to create majestic vessels that played central roles in state rituals and ancestor worship.

During the Xia (*c.* 2070 – *c.* 1600 BC), Shang (*c.* 1600 – *c.* 1046 BC) and Western Zhou (*c.* 1046 – 771 BC) dynasties, along with the development of the Chinese ritual ceremony system, bronze-making grew quickly. Up until the late Shang dynasty, decoration in bronze work was very refined and complicated. Some huge bronze works of this period suggest that the making of bronze was a consummate skill. One good example is the Si muwu square tripod, which is 130 cm (51 in.) long, with a total weight of 875 kg (1930 lb), and named after the three Chinese characters on its inscription.

Below *The giant Si muwu square tripod, unearthed in Anyang, Henan province, a Shang-dynasty ritual vessel.*

From the Western Zhou until the Spring and Autumn period (*c.* 770 – 476 BC), the decoration of bronzes followed the previous tradition with few changes. But during the late Spring and Autumn period, the decoration altered considerably. The dragon came to dominate the popular animal mask details, and gilded, geometrical patterns and true-life drawing were used in the decoration of bronze work. Although casting was the dominant technique, the lost-wax method was applied in bronze-making for the first time.

During the Warring States period (476–221 BC), the development of economic exchange meant that great numbers of bronze coins were in demand, forcing the rapid development of mass production.

Although bronze was used until the 20th century, the Qin and Han dynasties were the final resplendent stage of Chinese bronze work. There were some magnificent pieces made in this period, such as the bronze, colour-painted chariots unearthed in Emperor Qin Shihuangdi's mausoleum (p. 155), and the Changxin Palace bronze lamp found in the Mancheng Han tomb in Hebei. Since the Han dynasty there have been few technical innovations in bronze work.

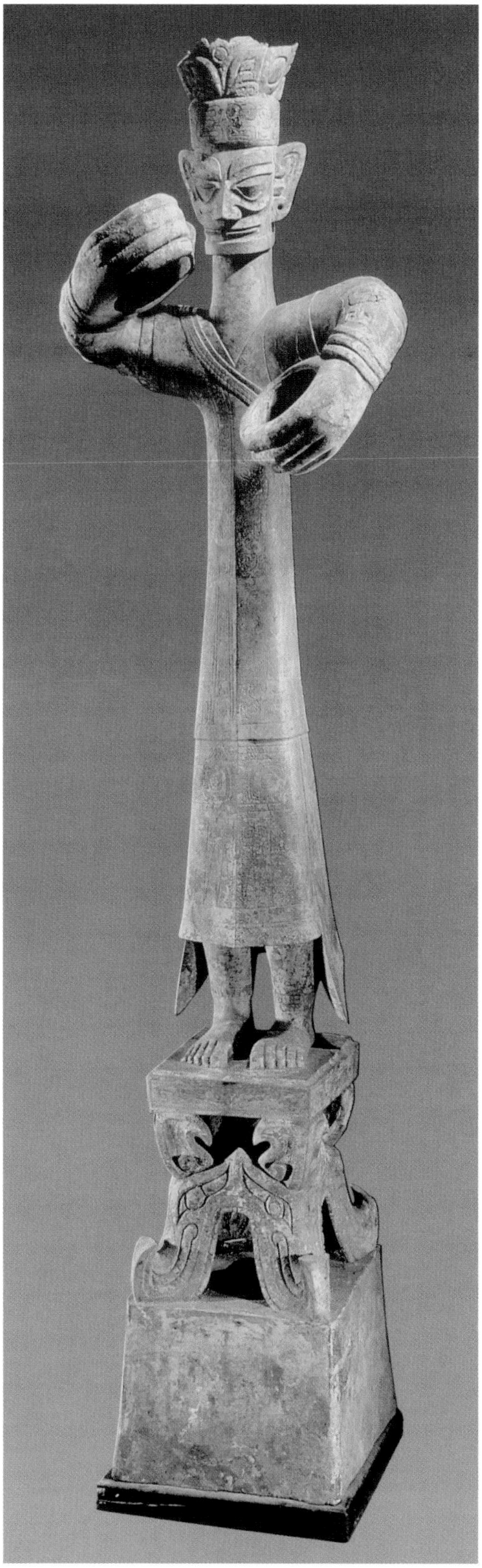

Far left *The beautifully made Changxin Palace bronze lamp was found in a tomb in Hebei province (Han dynasty).*

Left *Shang-dynasty figure found in Sichuan province, standing 2.6 m (8.5 ft) high.*

Bronze tripods and other vessels

In China, the difficult technique of bronze-making does not seem to have hindered the ancient craftsmen from making vessels of enormous scale almost from the start. An ancient Chinese book, *Kaogongji*, records the directions for making bronze products, explaining the six kinds of bronze alloy known as *liuji*, and gives us detailed descriptions of the different compositions of bronze work for different purposes.

Of the many bronze objects used in ancient China the tripod is the most distinctive and important, for it was always regarded as the symbol of the state. Bronze tripods were usually used by the rulers to hold offerings of food and wine that were presented to royal ancestors and deities; in this way they became expressions of power and legitimacy. In a famous Chinese legend Huangdi, the traditional first emperor, cast nine monumental bronze tripods symbolizing the nine provinces of his realm. When his dynasty fell, these precious ritual vessels were claimed by the new rulers, the Shang. And in turn, with the defeat of the Shang these symbols of the state were taken over by their conquerors, the Zhou. Besides the tripod, there were many other kinds of bronze work, such as wine containers and weapons.

Right *Large and intricately decorated wine jar,* or fang hu, *found with its pair in a Spring and Autumn-period tomb in Xinzhen, Henan province.*

Centre *The set of bronze chime bells found in the tomb of Zenghou Yi, Hubei province (shown here with reconstructed frame), have been dated to the Warring States period, c. 433 BC.*

Below *Inscription on a bronze vessel.*

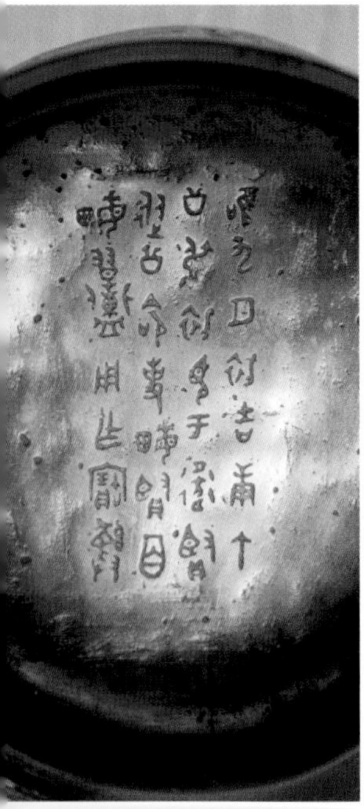

Decoration

The decoration of early Chinese bronzes was an integral part of the object. The Chinese craftsmen preferred to cast the entire vessel in one pour, but complicated decoration was sometimes cast separately and added to the object later. Apart from their vital function in ancient China, ritual bronzes can also be extremely important historical documents due to the inscriptions that many of them bear. Cast into the surface of a vessel, these inscriptions were first seen during the late Shang dynasty as identification of the vessel's owner, or the ancestor to whom it was dedicated.

During the Western Zhou period, inscriptions appear in increasingly greater numbers and at longer lengths, extolling the achievements and recording other contemporary events. Bronze inscriptions are first-hand sources that often serve as a check against the accounts of early events preserved in later histories. From the inscription, technique and decoration of bronze work, we can verify famous historical affairs and research the history of long-lost sites.

Bronze bells

The Bronze Age officially comes to an end in China between the 6th and 5th centuries BC, when cast iron began to take over. Despite this loss of prestige, the bronze tradition continued at a reduced scale and was still used, for example, in making bells.

There are no clear records about the origin of Chinese bronze bells, but we have found them in some archaeological sites of the Xia dynasty. During the 16th–11th centuries BC, the Shang craftsmen could already manufacture many different kinds of bronze bell, and the examples unearthed in Anyang can be divided into several categories according to the style.

Above *The King of the Bronze Bells: the Yongle Bell in Beijing is one of the most famous examples of Ming-dynasty bronze work.*

In the Zhou dynasty, bronze bells were thought of as top-class musical instruments, used during the ritual ceremonies and palace banquets to perform *Yayue* (Music of Elegance). The chime bells found in the tomb of Zenghou Yi are perfect examples of this kind of bronze bell. Since the Han dynasty, the round-edged shape of the India bell followed the introduction of Buddhism into China. These bells were made widely in China, and thought of as holy vessels, representing the king and divinity. So bronze bell-making developed rapidly in the following dynasty. In the Ming and Qing dynasties, this technique reached the peak of its development, and was used widely in sacred places such as temples and palaces. The 500-year-old Yongle Bell is a good example of a bronze bell during this period.

The Yongle Bell hangs in the bell tower of the Dazhong (Big Bell) Temple in Beijing. It was made in the Yongle period of the Ming dynasty by Emperor Zhuli and was usually rung at festivals. Made from an alloy of copper, tin and lead, this bell is 6.94 m (22.7 ft) tall and weighs 46.5 tons. On the surface of the bell, there is a 230,000-word inscription that includes over 100 sutras in Chinese and Sanskrit. It has the greatest amount of inscription on a single bronze object in the world and it took scholars over four years to complete the rubbing. Until modern noise intervened, its sound could be heard as far away as 40–50 km (25–30 miles), hence its other name: King of the Bronze Bells.

CAROL MICHAELSON

45

Jade

Anciently superior men found the likeness of all excellent qualities in jade. Soft, smooth and glossy, it appeared to them like benevolence; fine, compact and strong, like intelligence; angular, but not sharp and cutting, like righteousness; ... its flaws not concealing its beauty, nor its beauty concealing its flaws, like loyalty; ... esteemed by all under the sky, like the path of truth and duty.

Li Ji ('Book of Rites')

Jade is a material inextricably associated with the Chinese, though they are by no means the only culture that has worked it. It has been fashioned longer in China than anywhere else, for probably 8,000 years, and has long been revered in that land. Confucius praised it as a material reflecting all the good qualities of the perfect gentleman. In a country where gold and diamonds were never valued in the same way as in the West, jade was and remains at the top of the Chinese hierarchy of valued materials.

Jade is in fact a generic term for two distinct minerals: nephrite and jadeite, both referred to as *yu* in Chinese but having different physical characteristics. However, until relatively recently the jade used in China was almost entirely nephrite. This was originally available in the north and eastern parts of China, though these sources were basically exhausted by the end of the Neolithic period. After this time nephrite was mined in what is now Xinjiang province in western China and access to the material depended largely on the control the Chinese had over this territory. Jadeite, from Burma, only came to be used extensively from the 18th century AD.

Working jade is very difficult. Jade is harder than metals such as bronze and iron, so that it cannot be shaped with metal tools alone. The material is also extraordinarily tough and difficult to break. Although we refer to the 'carving' of jade, it has to be worked by time-consuming abrasive methods. Traditionally, fine sands or ground natural minerals, such as quartz, garnet and corundum abrasives that are all harder than jade, were used. The abrasive was mixed with water and applied with various iron or steel tools.

Right *This coiled dragon is an example of a 'pig-dragon', which may have been derived from the slit ring, or* jue. *Many jade artifacts that survive from c. 3500 BC were used as pendants and some seem to have been attached to clothing or to the body. It incorporates the pig's snout and the snake-like body of a dragon.*

Neolithic period

Archaeological evidence suggests jade was first worked in the northeast of what is today China, in present-day Liaoning province and Inner Mongolia as early as 5000 BC. During the Neolithic period we can of course only guess at its significance for the people who so patiently and laboriously carved it. There are no written records to explain either its function or attraction for these peoples. Some of the earliest shapes included earrings – *jue*.

The Hongshan culture, centred around Liaoning province and dating to about 3500–3000 BC, and the slightly later Liangzhu culture (*c.* 3000–2500 BC), centred in Jiangsu and Zhejiang provinces in southeast China, are the two earliest jade-working cultures for which we have substantial evidence. There might be up to about 20 jades in any one elite tomb of the Hongshan, including the so-called 'pig-dragon' (a semi-circular jade with a pig's snout and a snake-like body) and chest and hair ornaments. In the Liangzhu culture there might be as many as 300 jades in

any one elite tomb, including the quintessential Liangzhu jades, the so-called *bi* and the *cong* – the round disk and the hollowed-out tube – the latter often decorated with a mysterious fierce mask in relief, the iconography of which is still not understood. The tube shapes were often found aligning the body in the grave and the disks placed prominently on the chest and stomach of the deceased, but the significance of these jades is unknown. Jade axes were also buried, many with beautifully decorated fittings as well as necklaces, awls and many beads. Jades have also been found in many other Neolithic cultures within China. Many axes and tools were fashioned in jade rather than stone and their gleaming polish distinguished them from their more utilitarian prototypes. These were probably for ceremonial and ritual use.

Shang, Zhou and Han dynasty jades (*c.* 1600 BC–AD 220)

One of the most dramatic finds in the 20th century was that of the unrobbed tomb of a consort of a Shang king, who flourished around 1200 BC. Fu Hao was buried with 750 jades. Many of these were pendants, with holes for suspension, some in human or animal forms, though we have no idea if they were worn during her lifetime or made specifically for her to take to the afterlife. She was also buried with some Neolithic jades that by her lifetime were already 2,000 years old,

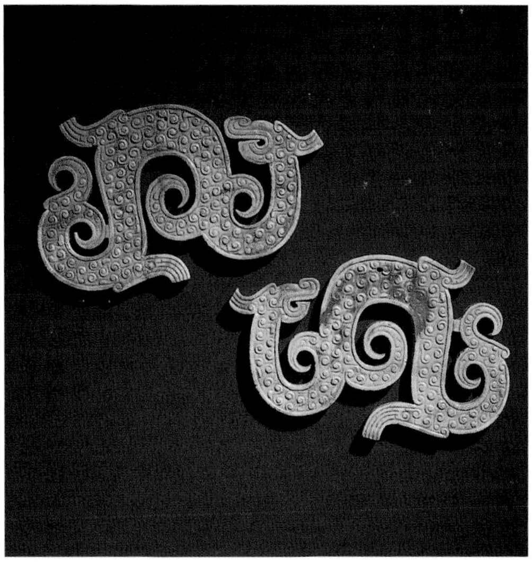

showing the extent to which jade was already clearly prized.

Particularly beautiful jades in the subsequent Zhou period (1046–221 BC) were often valued and used as trophies to be exchanged between rulers. It was during this period that the idea of the incorruptibility of jade as a material, because of its hardness, seems to have begun to be linked with the idea that if it was used to cover the body in death it would stop the body's disintegration and leave it whole for the afterlife. Many bodies have been discovered where the faces were covered with small jades shaped like the facial features, sewn onto textiles placed over the face. Then the body, from the neck to the knees, was covered in long and elaborate pendant sets and with halberds and awls. Such an association of jade and the incorruptibility of the human body culminated in the use of the jade suit during the Han

Far left *A jade cong (hollowed-out tube), 6.8-cm (2.6-in.) high decorated with a monster mask design. Found in Fuquanshan, Shanghai. Neolithic period.*

Left *Dragon-shaped jades make a sudden appearance among the range of jades used in pendant sets in the 5th century* BC. *Matched pendants of this quality are rare and made only for the elite.*

Below *This burial suit found in the tomb of Prince Liu Sheng, son of emperor Jing of the Han dynasty, was made from almost 2,500 pieces of solid jade. The stone's legendary toughness was believed to prevent the body from decaying. The pieces are tied together with gold thread.*

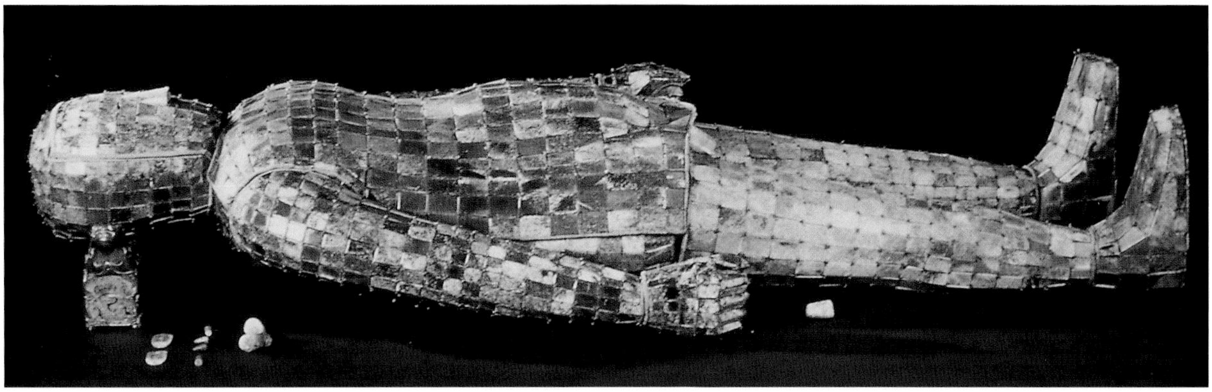

This impressive figure of a horse is one of a relatively small and distinct group of creatures, carved on a scale much larger than had been usual in jade. The group is traditionally dated to the transition period between the Ming and the Qing. (Height 12.75 cm / 5 in.)

dynasty (206 BC–AD 220). Other notable jades of this period include sword fittings, some vessels and three-dimensional animal figures.

Post Han dynasty jades (AD 220 onwards)

From the end of the Han to the Tang, AD 220–618, very few jades have been discovered archaeologically and we know relatively little about the jade production of this period. They would seem to have been passed down from generation to generation and worn or used rather than being buried for the afterlife. During the Tang dynasty (AD 618–907) many hoards were buried at times of unrest and fortunately for us not recovered until the last century. These include jade belt sets which were a marker of the highest rank according to the then prevailing sumptuary laws. There were also hair and dress ornaments for women. Vessels modelled on the more popular metal shapes of the period were also produced at this time.

During the Song period (960–1279) the emperors, as custodians of the imperial art collections, printed catalogues of them. These were

subsequently used by various craftsmen as pattern books. Thus many archaic shapes, even those made in other materials such as bronze, were copied in jade, the stone so prized still by the Chinese.

It was during the last two imperial dynasties, those of the Ming (1368–1644) and the Qing (1644–1911), that jade was worked most extensively and the majority of the jades we prize today are from these two periods. Mined jade was more easily available because of technological advances and supplemented the river jade pebbles used from the earlier periods. This meant that larger jades could be worked, and improved tools and abrasives made jade carving easier and quicker.

During this period many items for the scholar's desk were made, including brushrests, brushpots, paperweights and seals. The decoration particularly on brushpots testifies to the skill the jade workers had acquired in being able to work designs in 3D that had originated in two dimensional (2D) drawings. The acme of jade production can be ascribed to the reign of the Qianlong emperor, who reigned from 1736 to 1795. He was an ardent jade lover and was supposed to have amassed a collection of over 30,000 jades during his reign. His military campaigns included the conquering of the jade-producing area of Khotan and he received tribute from the Mughal jade workers whose works he admired and had copied at his court. He oversaw production of the imperial jades and wrote many poems that were then inscribed onto them. During his reign many so-called auspicious jades were made, incorporating the punning rebuses that are a feature of the Chinese language. The Qianlong emperor promoted a renewed interest in archaistic jades. Many decorative pieces survive from this period including male belt accessories and ladies' hair ornaments and jewelry. Large, even huge, jade boulders were commissioned depicting the stories and legends of Chinese history. Jadeite from Burma also began to be used for jewelry and exquisite carvings incorporating jades of brilliant hues.

Towards the end of the Qing dynasty, with growing political unrest in China, jade working suffered a major decline. Today jade continues to be worked and a high level of artistry can still be seen occasionally but many jades are mass-produced. Jade is still seen today as containing properties that promote good health, luck and protection, and many older Chinese will have some jade about their person.

Left *Belt hooks like this one found in Henan province were made in the Warring States and Han periods. Some 18.7 cm (7 in.) in length, this gilded bronze example is inlaid with jade and glass beads.*

Below *An 18th-century jade brush pot. Jade workshops often used conventional painting themes in their work, treating them like hand-scrolls whose surfaces should be subdivided. Here the detailed relief shows two farming scenes. (Diameter 19 cm / 7.5 in.)*

SHANE McCAUSLAND

46 Calligraphy

How could a person's reputation be in any way separate from his calligraphy? Calligraphy is a picture of the mind.
ZHAO MENGFU, *ESSAY ON WANG XIZHI*, *c.* 1300

The art of Chinese calligraphy is closely linked in time with history and in place with East Asia. Dependent on writing for its forms, calligraphy begins as history does in China, with what we know as epigraphy: the rune-like inscriptions carved on oracle bones (like ox scapulae) and tortoise plastrons by diviners to the Shang kings (*c.* 1600 – *c.* 1046 BC). Ruling in the 'cradle' of Chinese civilization, the Yellow River valley, they sought to sustain prosperity in this world through communication with their deceased ancestors dwelling in the afterlife. Later, in the Zhou dynasty (*c.* 1046–221 BC), inscriptions moulded into the surfaces of bronze vessels by early casters commemorated enfeoffments, political alliances and ties.

A tortoise plastron from Anyang, Henan province, shows an example of the earliest type of calligraphy – carved inscriptions and numbered divination cracks.

This arch-politicization of calligraphy is a fact of Chinese history that remains evident to this day. The typography of mastheads of newspapers announces their values and authority the world over; in China, the masthead of the *People's Daily*, the mouthpiece of the Chinese Communist Party, is still printed in the calligraphy of Chairman Mao Zedong, the 'great helmsman'. Culturally and politically at the heart of China's self-definition, calligraphy is collected across the globe, as the diverse provenance of the accompanying illustrations attests.

From Confucius to the elite

Considered the highest of the visual arts in dynastic China, even above painting, calligraphy has its own development of scripts and styles, its own traditions of collecting and connoisseurship, and was the means by which many of the great role models defined themselves. The sage Confucius (551–479 BC) lived five or six centuries before calligraphy was considered an accomplishment of the learned man, an 'image of the [cultivated] mind', but his precept that writing should strike a balance between style and substance shaped the later development of calligraphy.

China's First Emperor, Qin Shihuangdi (r. 221–210 BC), standardized the various forms of writing as 'seal' script following the first political unification of China under the Qin dynasty in 221 BC, and under the subsequent Han dynasty (206 BC–AD 220), 'clerical' and cursive scripts, used mainly

A calligrapher in a modern Chinese studio uses the same tools – ink stick, ink stone, brushes – as the ancient artists.

by scribes, were developed. From the late Han and into the subsequent Period of Disunion (220–581), calligraphy gradually became a learned accomplishment of the educated elite, as brushes, ink and paper became more common, if still luxury media. Calligraphy retained its social role: its practice was morally justified as contributing to transformation of the self, and hence all of society.

The classical tradition

Traditionally, it is in the liberated and stylish cultural climate of the Eastern Jin dynasty (317–420), one of the short-lived southern regimes between the Han and Tang empires, that the full expressive potential of the new medium was discovered, and that the 'classical tradition' begins. Lines and character forms which had previously been overwhelmingly emblematic (seal) or lateral (clerical) began to thicken and thin, apparently turning in space like ribbons in new script types: 'running' and 'standard' scripts. Brush traces reflected the accomplishments of the individual calligrapher, and contributed to the public good. From the 4th century, collectors vied to own the calligraphy of upstanding talents like Wang Xizhi (*c.* 303–*c.* 361), 'Calligraphic Sage' and author of the *Orchid Pavilion Preface* (see next entry), and his unconventional son, Wang Xianzhi (344–386).

Tools

Some of the finest writing from China's early historical period survives in the form of inscriptions in bronze vessels (p. 189). An inscription of this kind was written by a scribe using a stylus into the soft clay mould for the vessels before the molten bronze was poured in. In recent years, the rubbish pits of Han-dynasty military garrisons have revealed that by then, writing in ink on slips of bamboo was commonplace. The bamboo slips were tied together with string and could be rolled up in a scroll for convenience. The scribes were using brushes, probably ones with bamboo shafts stuffed at one end with the stiff hair of an animal.

Traditionally, ink for writing and painting in China was made from the natural pigment lamp black, mixed with glue (perhaps from fish bones), and with a fragrance, such as powdered sandalwood. This mixture was compacted into sticks, which when ground with a little water on an ink stone, could conveniently be turned into ink. By the late Ming dynasty, deluxe ink cakes for collectors were marketed in fine woodblock-printed catalogues.

Style mirrors technology

Intriguingly, styles and types of calligraphy developed in parallel with the technology for making and reproducing it. The forms of characters in 'seal' script reflected the rounded forms of the stylus moving through clay. Early brushes of the Han dynasty were rather stiff, judging by the flat, blunt appearance and pointed strokes that characterize the 'clerical' script used at the time. What enabled the transformation of calligraphy from mere writing to the highest form of artistic expression in China, however, was the invention of paper (p. 253). Made in the late Han dynasty from hemp and other organic materials, and later from bamboo, paper actually absorbed the ink; at the same time, brushes became more sophisticated with the use of more responsive, springy hair tips. The individualistic 'men of culture' of the Jin dynasty were the first to recognize and appreciate the nuanced shapes and pulsating linear energy of their peers' 'running' script and 'cursive' script calligraphy.

The Tang to the Qing

By the early Tang dynasty (618–907), when a new 'standard script' was pioneered at court to reflect the reunification of the state, all the scripts were complete. From mid-Tang on, for calligraphers at the cutting edge, the art form was about personal discovery, about self-expression through reinvention and visual referencing of past styles. The brush traces of the great neo-Confucian thinkers, men like Zhu Xi (1130–1200) and Wang Yangming (1472–1529), as well as of emperors and statesmen, were also collected. Intriguingly, the finest calligraphers were not all ethnic Han Chinese, notably under periods of non-Chinese rule like the Liao, Jin, Yuan and Qing dynasties.

Although the *Orchid Pavilion Preface* writer Wang Xizhi was said to have been taught by a Madam Wei, later critics rarely mentioned women's calligraphy. Femininity was seen as a flaw – the hand of the Yuan-dynasty master Zhao Mengfu (1254–1322) was mockingly described as 'girlish and pretty'. Incidentally, his wife, Guan Daosheng, is one of China's best-known – but little studied – woman artists.

The towering figures of the tradition of Chinese calligraphy during the Yuan, Ming and Qing dynasties were, however, also great statesmen and 'men of culture', like Zhao Mengfu, Wen Zhengming (1470–1559) and Dong Qichang (1555–1636), who garnered comprehensive knowledge of past styles through their activities in collecting and connoisseurship, but also developed their own distinctive styles to become models for their own and future generations.

Calligraphy in the modern world

Following the fall of the Manchu Qing dynasty in 1911, as classical Chinese language and learning

Emperor Huizong of the Song dynasty was an accomplished poet, painter and calligrapher. This is his work Five-Coloured Parakeet on Blossoming Apricot Tree.

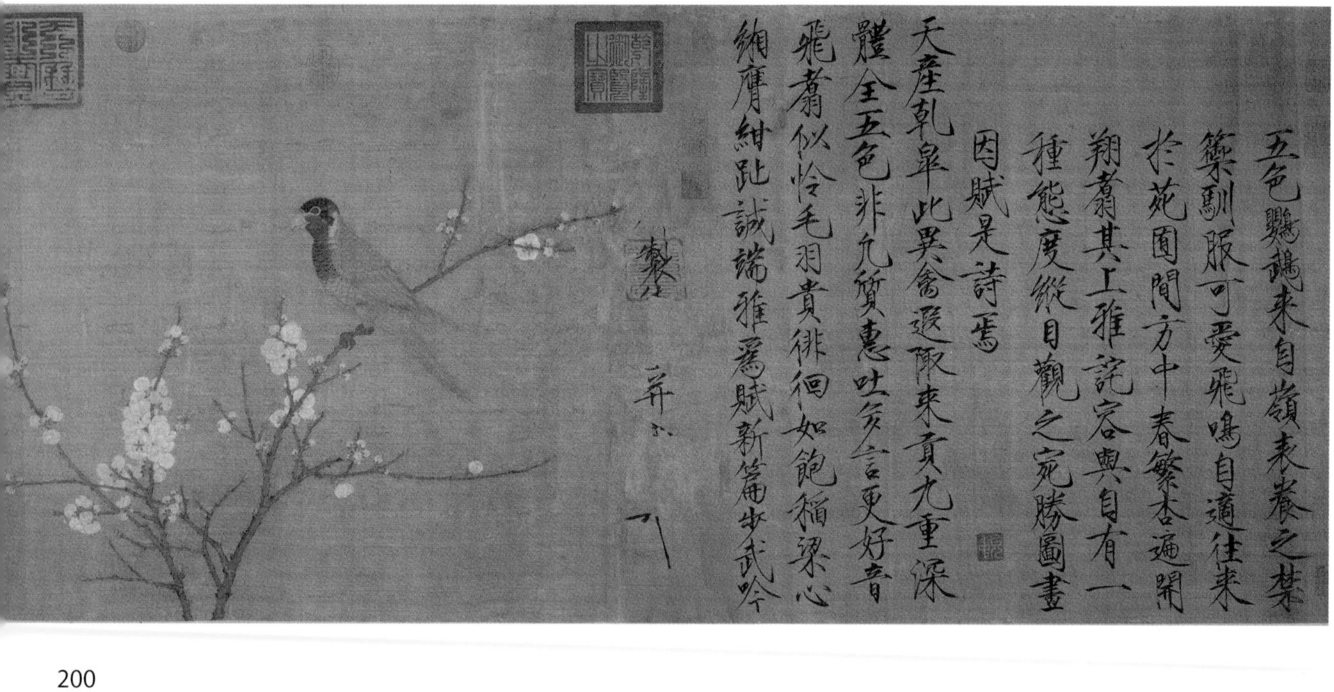

Wanluan Thatched Hall *by Dong Qichang (1597). Hanging scroll, ink on paper, with 19 inscriptions by the Qianlong emperor.*

were replaced by vernacular and scientific equivalents, the traditional training in brush calligraphy became obsolete. However, Chinese calligraphy has retained its remarkable power to define a particular Chinese culture. In a 1960s campaign to increase literacy, thousands of characters were simplified by the CCP in the mainland, in the first major reform of the written language since the Tang dynasty. In some cases common simplifications used in cursive writing replaced more complex standard characters, but others were more arbitrary. Singapore adopted the changes, whereas Hong Kong and Taiwan have retained the 'traditional' forms. Japan has made its own simplifications of Kanji (Chinese characters). Korea and Vietnam, meanwhile, have all but replaced Chinese characters in their written languages with Hangul and Roman alphabets, respectively.

Today, contemporary Chinese artists balk at the traditional power of the language – which finds its highest visual expression in calligraphy – to shape the lives of more than a billion people. The ironic, meaningless writing in the work of some contemporary calligraphers, like the émigré Xu Bing (b. 1955), seems to suggest how this marriage of history and calligraphy may now be coming to an end.

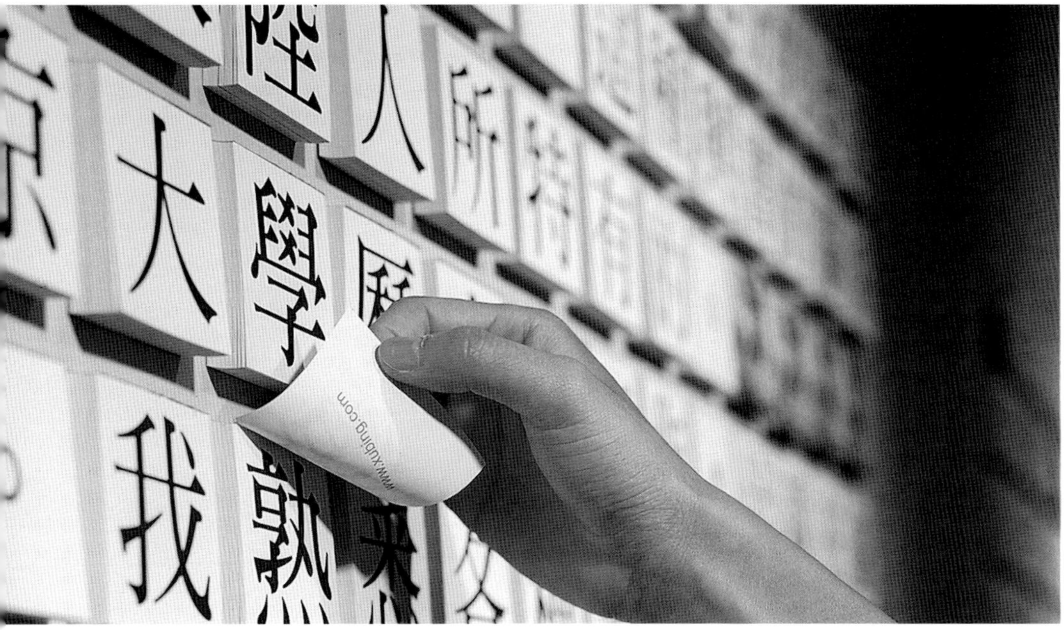

Xu Bing's modern take on calligraphy was unpopular with his more conservative critics. Each pad of paper in this work, Statement, *contains various words. The audience is invited to peel off the top sheets from the pads, changing the words, and creating an ever-changing exhibition.*

SHANE McCAUSLAND

47 The Orchid Pavilion Preface

This is the work of calligraphy in which Youjun [Wang Xizhi] truly attained his intention. One who studies it ceaselessly would be unfortunate not to surpass others.
ZHAO MENGFU, *THIRTEEN COLOPHONS TO THE ORCHID PAVILION PREFACE*, 1310

The *Preface to the Orchid Pavilion Collection* is the most celebrated work in the history of Chinese calligraphy. This is despite – or perhaps due to – the loss of the original manuscript of 353, written by the 'Calligraphic Sage' Wang Xizhi (c. 303–361) to head a set of poems composed at a famous literary gathering. It describes the beautiful setting near modern Shaoxing and conjures up the general ambience of a cultured and refined event: 'The pavilion divided the flowing water into two winding brooks, and all the guests were sitting side by side; although we lacked the boisterousness of a live orchestra, with a cup of wine here and a reciting of poetry there, it was sufficient to allow for a pleasant exchange of cordial conversations....'

The *Preface* is so unique partly because, as the quote above suggests, Wang Zixhi 'truly attained his intention', in other words it was a true image of the (cultured) mind and the physical trace of a genuinely sagacious mind at its peak – a model for all ages. It is also celebrated because the great early Tang-dynasty emperor Taizong (r. 626–649) resorted to stealing the *Preface*. An official called Xiao Yi obtained it for him by means of a ruse from the Buddhist monk who kept it, and the emperor is said to have taken the *Preface* with him to the grave. Championing Wang Xizhi's 'classical' calligraphic style, Tang Taizong had had it copied by his court calligraphers, however, and it has thus been known across East Asia over the past millennium and a half through these copies – or, more accurately, through the myriad copies of these copies in the form of freehand manuscript copies and transcriptions, punctilious tracing copies, ink rubbings from stone engravings, woodblock prints and, more recently, photographic, lithographic and digital reproductions.

Written in the Eastern Jin dynasty (317–420), an age renowned for unconventional and freethinking individuals, the *Preface* was the work in which Wang Xizhi was said to have perfectly expressed his intent through the expressivenuances of the thickening and thinning, ribbon-like forms created by brush and ink on paper, then new media. Understood as an 'image of the mind' of the sagely master, the style of the *Preface* became the perennial model for calligraphers in later Chinese art history, and embodied the 'classical tradition' of Chinese calligraphy.

This gilt-bronze beast was decorated with precious turquoise stones and used as a container for one of the 'Four Treasures' of the scholar: an ink stone.

Zhao Mengfu

A measure of its significance is the way that a commentary of 1310 by the later pivotal master, Zhao Mengfu (1254–1322), on a Song-dynasty (960–1279) ink rubbing of the so-called Dingwu stone engraving of the *Preface*, is regarded as Zhao Mengfu's own calligraphic masterpiece. Mengfu's *Thirteen Colophons to the Orchid Pavilion Preface* was damaged in a palace fire in the reign of the Qing-dynasty Qianlong emperor (r. 1736–95) – himself another imperial champion of Wang Xizhi's *Preface* and the classical tradition it stood for. The charred remains of Zhao Mengfu's *Thirteen Colophons* do survive today in Japan; intriguingly, the original had already been copied in woodblock print form in the Ming dynasty (1368–1644).

The *Preface* in modern China

Over the last two centuries, the central position of the classical tradition of Chinese calligraphy in Chinese culture and the traditional power of China's rulers to control culture and determine history through writing, symbolized so poignantly by the *Preface*, has come under fierce attack in the increasingly sceptical climate of scholarship. The contemporary avant-garde calligrapher Qiu Zhijie's performance of *Writing the Orchid Pavilion Preface One Thousand Times* – done on the same sheet of paper until it turned black – is a seemingly nihilistic gesture that appears finally to have severed the link between calligraphy and history. If this is the case, we now live in a post-historical age.

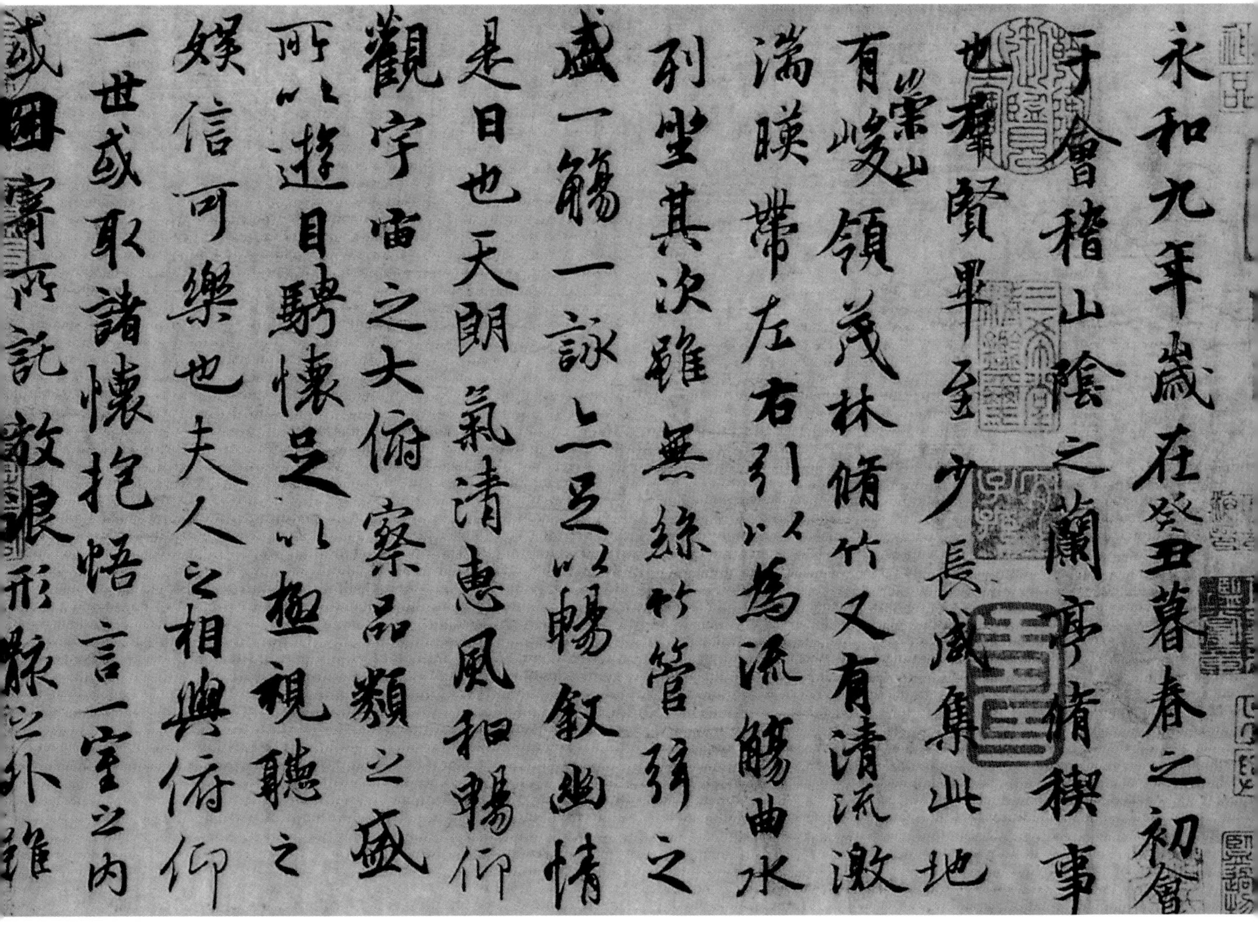

A detail of the first half of the famous Preface, meticulously copied at the Tang court.

VICTOR MAIR

48 Literature

Without going out of doors,
One may know all under heaven;
Without peering through windows, one may know the Way of heaven.
Laozi, *Dao De Jing* ('Classic of the Way and Virtue'), *c. 300 BC*

With a history of roughly three millennia, Chinese literature boasts the greatest longevity of any literary tradition in the world. The Chinese writing system began *c.* 1200 BC when it was used for short, oracular inscriptions carved on cattle scapulae or turtle plastra. These were followed by brief, commemorative inscriptions on ritual bronze vessels. By around the middle of the 1st millennium BC, what might be called 'literature' proper began to emerge with the formation during the succeeding five centuries of such foundational works as the *Poetry Classic*, *Book of Changes*, and the *Analects of Confucius*. During the 3rd century BC, there arose shamanistic verse known collectively as the *Elegies of Chu*, designated by the name of the great southern state with which it was associated. The most famous exemplars of this type of poetry were *Encountering / Departing Sorrow* and *Heavenly Questions*, both attributed to Qu Yuan (*c.* 340–278 BC), and the latter displaying clear affinities with Indo-European riddle texts.

This storytelling scroll from Dunhuang has pictures on the front and verses on the back. The story is that of the Buddhist saint Sāriputra defeating the Six Heretics.

Early genres

Also connected with the south is the Daoist philosophical tradition of Laozi and Zhuangzi. Both of these thinkers are shadowy figures, and the works attributed to them are composite in nature, with strong indications of accretional composition. Indeed, it is quite likely that there never was a single individual styled Laozi ('Old Master'), but rather there seems to have accumulated during the 4th and 3rd centuries BC a body of gnomic wisdom possessing traces of oral transmission that collectively were ascribed to a putative author who was given that name. Not much is known about Zhuangzi either, although he is said to have lived between *c.* 355 and *c.* 275 BC. One thing is certain, however, and that is the fact that the book attributed to Zhuangzi contains wildly disparate, and sometimes even contradictory, intellectual strands.

Still, a core body of material reveals Zhuangzi to be the most creative and inventive thinker of ancient China, one who exerted an enormous influence on writers for the next 2,000 years and more. The little volume of around 5,000 characters attributed to Laozi, *Classic of the Way and Virtue* (*Dao De Jing*), is one of the most frequently translated and influential books in the world. The much lengthier and more complex work ascribed to Zhuangzi, called simply the *Zhuangzi*, but also known in English as *Wandering on the Way*, is widely read for its stimulating, provocative ideas and for its witty, whimsical prose.

It was not until the Han dynasty (206 BC– AD 220), however, that the formal genres which would characterize Chinese literature for the next two millennia started to appear. The first, and most enduring, of these quintessential forms of Chinese writing was that of history *(shǐ)*, with Sima Qian's (*c.* 145 – *c.* 85 BC) *Records of the Grand Historian* constituting the basic model for the 24 dynastic histories that would follow during the succeeding 20 centuries.

In stark contrast to the staid, serious productions of the official historiographical enterprise, one other genre born during the Han period revealed a more private, florid authorial impulse. This was the rhapsody or rhymeprose, with its lush verbiage and rich description. Another literary giant surnamed Sima, this one Xiangru (179–117 BC), wrote elaborate accounts of imperial hunts and royal capitals, establishing the benchmark for the rhapsody against which all later writers were measured.

The effect of Buddhism

The most important development in Chinese literature after the fall of the Han dynasty was the arrival of Buddhism. This complex Indian religion

The Yongzheng emperor reading a book, with a stack of six fascicle containers to his left. Painted by an anonymous court artist.

brought with it a wide variety of texts and concepts that had a profound impact upon numerous aspects of Chinese literature. Among the most obvious was the introduction of thousands of new words, many of which are still employed in common parlance today. The structure of argumentation and analysis was made more logical and rigorous, often with the inclusion of lengthy numerical lists of points or attributes which were lacking in pre-Buddhist discourse. From the 3rd to 6th centuries, the Chinese predilection for strange tales manifested itself, with substantial influences from the vast repository of Indian stories, many of which were incorporated in the Buddhist scriptures that were systematically being translated into Chinese. During this politically unstable period of major division between north and south, the foundations of Chinese literary criticism were laid and aesthetic principles that would govern art and literature until the modern age were formulated, with evident impetus from Indian sources.

A golden age of literature

The Tang dynasty (618–907), when China was once again reunited, represents the apogee of traditional Chinese culture, including Chinese literature. If one had to choose a single genre that

A schoolhouse scene from the Dream of the Red Chamber, *one of the greatest Chinese novels. It was completed in c. 1760 by Cao Xueqin.*

best exemplifies the genius of the entire Chinese literary tradition, it would have to be the short, lyric verse (one or two quatrains) called *shī* that flourished above all in the Tang (more than 50,000 such poems survive from this period). Here, normally in a minimum of 20 syllables or a maximum of 56 syllables, Chinese poets displayed their devotion to exquisite craftsmanship and sensitive depiction. Men such as the exuberant romantic Li Bo (701–762) and the restrained Confucian Du Fu (712–770) are still revered as the supreme laureates of verbal expression in Chinese. The most demanding poetic form of the period was *lüshi* ('regulated verse'), which borrowed and adapted arcane rules from Sanskrit prosody. A thousand years later, poets continued to slavishly imitate the most exacting tonal configurations and rhymes of the Tang, long after the language had evolved to such an extent that they were no longer operative.

Heptasyllabic and pentasyllabic quatrains and double-quatrains were thus the premium literary genres of the age. But the Tang was also a crucial moment of countercultural experimentation. On the one hand, the tales of anomalies from the preceding period of disunion were perfected and refined as classical language short stories – *chuanqi* (literally, 'transmission of the strange') – which afforded writers and readers an outlet into a realm of eroticism and exoticism that was off limits to the more austere world of *shī*. Still more radical, however, was the emergence of partially vernacular, prosimetric (alternating between prose and verse) narratives called 'transformation texts' and related genres that were fostered by the demotic impulses of Buddhism.

While it would take more than a thousand years before vernacular writing came into its own and achieved public, official recognition, it was during the Tang that the cataclysmic gulf between classical (or literary) and vernacular (or colloquial) styles of writing first emerged. From this moment forward, Chinese literature progressed along two vastly dissimilar tracks – though the vernacular was always coloured by classical elements to a greater or lesser degree.

The lyric meter

Upon the arrival of the less cosmopolitan, more introspective Song dynasty (960–1279), a reaction to the excesses of Tang versification set in, and a completely new form of poetry came to attract many of the best voices. This was the lyric meter (*ci*), a type of verse that was intimately tied to popular songs which had their origins among courtesans of the demi-monde and entertainers from the border regions. In allowing lines of varying length, lyric meters broke free from the blockish (5-5-5-5 or 7-7-7-7) structure of *shī*. They also enormously enlarged the limits of permissible diction by employing colloquial expressions and vernacular grammatical structures.

Under the Mongol Yuan dynasty (1279–1368), the ethos of lyric meters was broadened into suites of cantos (*qu*) and further incorporated into China's first full-fledged dramas – *zaju* (literally, 'miscellaneous plays'). These were earthy, rambunctious productions that permitted Chinese authors sidetracked from official careers to give full vent to a range of expression and sentiments to which they were hitherto unaccustomed. The most memorable and extraordinary of these dramas is *Injustice to Dou E*, which tells of the posthumous vindication of a heinous wrong done to a young widow, by the renowned playwright, Guan Hanqing (*c.* 1240 – *c.* 1320).

The Ming and Qing dynasties

The Ming (1368–1644) and Qing (1644–1911) dynasties witnessed the perfection of traditional Chinese drama, with Tang Xianzu's (1550–1617) *The Peony Pavilion* an acknowledged masterpiece about the supernatural power of love – even over death – that has recently been successfully staged several times in the West. While poetry during this long, late imperial period was largely devoted to the emulation of Tang and Song models, there were notable exceptions such as Wang Shizhen (1526–1590), a prolific *shī* poet who dominated the literary scene during the late Ming, and the young Manchu nobleman Nara Singde (1655–1685), an acclaimed exponent of lyric meters.

The Ming-Qing period also spawned a diverse assortment of fine essays and saw the culmination of the classical language short story in works such as Pu Songling's (1640–1715) *Strange Tales from Make-Do Studio*. But it was the full-length novel that captured the imagination of the age, with the perfection of the genre being realized in such masterpieces as *Romance of the Three Kingdoms, Journey to the West, Water Margin / All Men Are Brothers / Outlaws of the Marsh, Gold Vase Plum, Dream of the Red Chamber / Story of the Stone, Unofficial History of the Literati* and *The Travels of Old Derelict*, all but the first being decidedly vernacular in nature. These great novels ranged from the picaresque to the pornographic, from the historical to the heartrending. The greatest of them all, however, is *Dream of the Red Chamber*, the tragic love story of the singular, hyperactive Baoyu and his delicate, over-emotional cousin Daiyu, which has rightfully taken its place in the canon of world literature. At the same time as the flowering of the full-length novel, the vernacular short story was being perfected, with hundreds of captivating gems being gathered in the collections of two outstanding advocates of the genre, Feng Menglong (1574–1646) and Ling Mengchu (1580–1644).

Among the galaxy of 20th-century writers, no star shines brighter than that of Lu Xun (1881–1936). His *Diary of a Madman*, with unashamed apologies to Gogol, was the first Chinese vernacular short story to use modern literary techniques, and his *The True Story of Ah Q*, with its searing dissection of the Chinese psyche, is a monument of sharply penetrating insight and profound compassion. Lu Xun was a radical who went so far as to advocate the abolition of Chinese characters in favour of a more convenient alphabetic script, but he also cared deeply for his fellow citizens. Another 20th-century short story writer who captured the thoughts and feelings of the common man was Lao She (1899–1966), who is well-known internationally for his Peking novel *Rickshaw Boy* and his revealing three-act play *Teahouse*.

Now, in the early 21st century, with China a booming economic behemoth, Chinese writers have begun to experiment with completely new forms of literature, such as on-line novels and poetry circulated by cellphone as short text messages. There can be little doubt that Chinese literature will undergo remarkable metamorphoses in the coming decades, and the world will take due note of the wonders that will unfold.

Some 300,000 sutras are stored on wood-carved printing boards at the Tibetan Derge Parkhang (Printing House) in Derge.

NI YIBIN

49 Music & Beijing Opera

Music is joy, an emotion which people cannot help experiencing at times. Unable to resist feeling joy, people must find an outlet through voice and movement.
XUNZI, 2ND CENTURY BC

The same Chinese character is used for both 'music' and 'joy', which inspired the philosopher Xunzi to write the above quotation pointing to the intrinsic relationship of the two in Chinese society.

A 9,000-year-old playable flute

Intangible as music is, we are now able to share with our ancestors living 9,000 years ago the tune played by a flute ingeniously carved out of the wing-bone of a red-crowned crane; the flute surfaced in an archaeological excavation in Jiahu village, Henan province, in the 1980s. The very material of this flute recalls the Chinese legend about the immortal Xiaoshi, who would play the flute to attract cranes and phoenixes dancing around him, and his romance with the daughter of the Duke of the Qin, who was drawn to him, being herself a flute fan. Seven finger-holes had been evenly drilled along the bone, with a tiny one added to the seventh to adjust its tone from G-sharp to A, achieving the whole octave. The flute, twenty centimeters long and one of the three dozen found together with about four hundred human burials, sounds like the high-pitched human whistling and is still capable of producing multinote music. Obviously, the community that created this oldest extant instrument

Brick carving from a Song/Jin-dynasty tomb, portraying a female entertainer playing a flute.

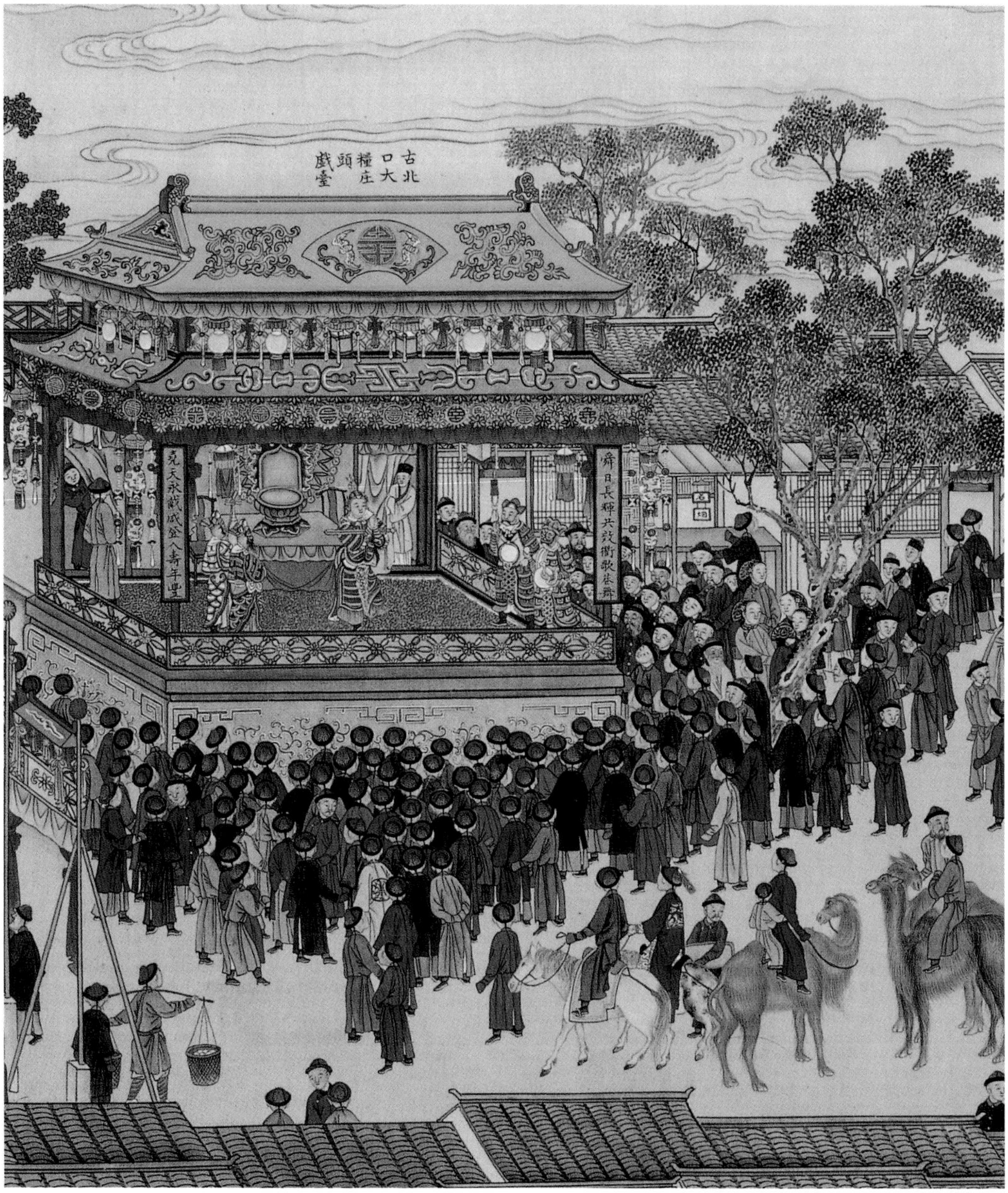

Detail of The Kangxi Emperor's Sixtieth Birthday Celebration Scroll One. *Late 18th-century colour on silk by anonymous court artists.*

enjoyed a high level of civilization, as evidenced by the large variety of animal bones and possible pictograms inscribed on tortoise shells lying nearby. Further speculations about the flute include the significant function of music in rituals and government in this structured society.

The role of music in China

In fact, *Yue Ji* ('Book of Music', *c.* 1st and 2nd centuries BC), part of the Confucian classic *Li Ji* ('Book of Rites'), advocates the tradition of education of people through music as a way of organizing the society to make communal life harmonious: music and rites were devised by ancient kings and sages to teach people to weigh likes and dislikes in the balance and lead them to what is proper. Music, which would connect people with the spirits of their forefathers and rulers with the power of heaven, was highly developed in ancient China as an essential component of the rituals at grassroots level as well as in court. With music, commoners

Actors playing the Emperor Ming Huang and his consort Yang Kuei-fei enjoy the flowers in The Pavilion of Concentrated Fragrance. *This illustration from a 1930s publication on Chinese drama portrays Mei Lanfang in the role of the consort.*

sought blessing and protection and rulers exerted authority. As early as 1058 BC the Zhou court had set up a government department in charge of collecting and monitoring music and songs performed in the different strata of society, which culminated in the anthology *Shi Jing* ('Book of Songs'), allegedly compiled by Confucius (551–479 BC). Three hundred and five lyrics survived in this book, including odes and hymns performed in court as well as love songs and ballads of sorrow sung by ordinary folk.

The earliest work preserved in musical notation for the scholars' favourite instrument, *qin* (a seven-stringed zither), is *Youlan* ('The Secluded Orchid'), composed by Qiu Ming (493–590) and hand-copied in the Tang dynasty. The notation suggests how the strings are to be plucked, tapped or stroked, and how the left-hand fingers should glide over the strings to produce subtle variations in timbre. It also suggests what poetic images are being expressed by combinations of touching the strings. For instance, a sliding sound may evoke an association to 'a flying seagull touching down' and a press by the left finger 'echoes in an empty canyon'.

The rise of musical theatre and Beijing opera

While court music continued to perform its ceremonial and political functions in the high echelons of society and some instruments such as the *qin* and *xiao* (end-blown flute) were favoured by scholars and reclusive philosophers, various string and percussion accompaniments flourished in popular musical theatre in late imperial China.

Traditional Chinese theatre is characterized by stylized role types, stage movements, pantomimic gestures, costumes and makeup, and by a unique combination of recitation, songs, dances, acrobatics and music. All these elements were epitomized in the culmination of this tradition – 'Beijing opera', known as *jingju* or *jingxi* in Chinese. In 1790, during the Qing emperor Qianlong's 80th birthday celebration, troupes from Anhui province thrilled the audience in the capital by staging innovatory performances incorporating the *erihuang* music mode and sensational acrobatic feats.

This event marked the birth of Beijing opera. From then on, a new variety of Chinese theatre, in competition with the currently dominant *kunqu* (literally 'musical theatre of Kunshan', Jiangsu province), gradually evolved into a nationally adored entertainment. However, its full maturity would still take 60 more years, when the Anhui theatre successfully integrated the Hubei troupes who later came to Beijing with their distinctive *xipi* music mode. Actually, the name *jingxi* (literally 'musical theatre of the capital') was established only after the popular Beijing troupes whirled onto the Shanghai stage in the late 19th century.

Compared with the highbrow *kunqu*, this new musical theatre was easier to understand and thus welcomed by a much wider audience. Its repertory drew from dramatic tales in popular history and vernacular literature which to the audience were familiar as well as fascinating because the plots exemplified titillating themes such as love, betrayal, revenge, retribution, reward for loyal deeds and triumph of justice. Different plays often focused on different aspects of Chinese theatrical art, attracting varying types of audience. For example, *The Three-Pronged Crossroads* belongs to the category of combat plays because the two protagonists, pretending to be in total darkness, fight with amazing acrobatic skills from beginning to end. On the other hand, in *Picking Up the Jade Bangle* the actress would use all her skills to portray a maiden falling in love, the entire play consisting of her deliberating whether or not to accept her admirer's gift, classifying the performance as a virtuosic acting play.

There were four major role types in Beijing opera: *sheng* (male), *dan* (female), *jing* (painted-face) and *chou* (comedian), with subcategories such as *laosheng* (mature male) or *wudan* (female acrobat). Each role is characterized by a set of distinctive speaking, singing, and dancing or acrobatic skills. Informed audiences could identify particular roles by the pitch, volume and enunciation of their singing and speech. The instrumental music in Beijing opera consists of two sections: melodic and percussive. It is the percussion ensemble, a set of drums, gongs and cymbals, that is responsible for punctuating actors' movements and singing and, fundamentally, integrates different elements of a play, e.g. arias, gestures, change of scenes, change of actor's emotions, etc. into an organic whole. With 60-odd conventional rhythmic patterns, large and small percussive instruments could induce various atmospheres as required during a play, helping to form a vivid mental picture of the appropriate situation in the audience's mind and complementing the minimalist setting.

Modern times

By the mid-19th century Beijing opera had eventually taken over the national popularity of *kunqu*. With the cultivation of the sophisticated theatre-goers and imperial patronage, it prospered in both the traditional Beijing and Westernized Shanghai. Beijing opera won international acclaim when its towering figure, Mei Lanfang, toured America and Russia in the 1930s. His roles as beautiful women moving demurely on stage were legendary and his performance influenced Bertolt Brecht and V. E. Meyerhold, among others, in their innovative work in Western theatre.

Performers of the Beijing Opera Troupe on the opening night of The Carp Fairy of the Green Pond *in Beijing. Beijing opera is an art form which has entertained audiences for over 200 years. While it is still widely regarded as the highest expression of Chinese culture, different contemporary forms of entertainment have flooded China in recent years.*

SHANE McCAUSLAND

50 Painting

If a painter seeks breath-resonance [vital force] in his painting, physical likeness will naturally be present in his work.
ZHANG YANYUAN, *LI DAI MING HUA JI*, 847

Like its fellow brush art, calligraphy (p. 198), the art of painting has a long and distinguished history in China. A characteristic of this history is a remarkably continuous set of theoretical ideals over almost two millennia, chief among them the notion of *qiyun shengdong* – that a painting will have vitality when it achieves 'breath-resonance' with its subject, rather than by achieving a likeness using visual techniques to deceive the eye. By identifying a sequence of great artworks, however, and trusting those works to throw light on history, it is possible to see distinct phases of stylistic development which undermine that impression of continuity.

Tools

The tools for painting are largely the same as for calligraphy. The media include paper of various kinds, *xuan* being the finest, as well as silk and the more tightly-woven and technically challenging satin. In addition to ink made from lamp black (see p. 198), organic and mineral pigments are used, including ores like cinnabar (mercuric sulphide) for vermilions, malachite and azurite (both forms of copper carbonate) for greens and blues, and gamboge (a gum resin) for yellows. Paintings are typically mounted in handscrolls or albums for personal viewing, or in hanging scrolls for display on walls. When a mounting wears out, the artwork is simply remounted.

Early scroll-paintings

Probably the earliest surviving scroll-painting ascribed to a known artist, and thus a window on the origins of one of the world's great painting traditions, is the *Admonitions of the Court Instructress* handscroll (now in the British Museum). Although it is attributed to the founding father of figure painting, the Eastern Jin master Gu Kaizhi

Fishermen *scroll by Xu Daoning, c. 1049.*

A scene of the emperor rebuffing 'the beauty who knew her own beauty' from the famous Admonitions of the Court Instructress *scroll attributed to Gu Kaizhi.*

(*c.* 344 – *c.* 406), this is likely to have been painted a century or two after him, but in his lyrical, 'gossamer-thread'-like style. Its nine scenes illustrate tracts of a moralizing poem about how the emperor's wives and concubines should conduct themselves, written by the polymath and statesman Zhang Hua in 292, possibly after the ruler was poisoned by a spurned empress. A time of dramatic cultural development and religious and intellectual exchange, this Period of Disunion (220–581) is also noted for political rivalries and short-lived dynasties. The body language, bearing and facial expressions of the beauties in the *Admonitions* are minutely observed and elegantly finished in swirling outlines, which points to the artist's personal experience of life at one of these courts. It is almost possible to see, from the self-assured way the painter breathes new life into this rather stuffy, archaic subject, how the art of painting was born in China.

The *Admonitions* is a remarkable survivor; very few other scroll paintings remain from the Tang dynasty or before, although we read about great masters who painted genre scenes, horses and early landscapes. Some works survive from the Northern Song dynasty (960–1127), the era of monumental landscape painting. Among them is Xu Daoning's *Fishermen* scroll, which portrays the archetypal hoary vista of classical Chinese landscape painting. Plotted over successive movements of a handscroll, as unrolled from right to left, this emotive landscape invites the viewer to roam among scenery that is highly suggestive of mood and outlook. Tiny figures, dwarfed by the grandeur of cliffs, travel in the deeply cut ravines on shoaling waters or over plank bridges; at every turn, the landscape seems to reveal the majestic power of nature. The monumental landscapes of the Northern Song came in no uncertain terms to symbolize the figure of the emperor as the 'son of Heaven', and of the wider moral order of the Song polity (see p. 200).

Changes in the 11th century

A wide range of explanations must account for why such links were all but severed during the 13th and 14th centuries, as painting took what might be called an inward turn. In the 11th century, the unity of the feudal state was challenged by the rise of a new social class, the literati, or scholar-officials, who championed China's great tradition of statecraft. Their interests did not always coincide with those of the Song monarchy.

Also, China was no longer politically unified after the Song lost the northern half of China to the Jurchen Jin dynasty in 1127 and suffered the humiliating capture of the emperor Huizong. Once again, the country became home to rival Chinese and non-Chinese powers – few paintings made under non-Chinese regimes survive. The Southern Song (1127–1279) staked a claim, corroborated by later historians, to have retained the 'Mandate of Heaven', and, for a time, a refined Chinese courtly culture flourished, surviving in the form of an elegant, if brittle style of classical calligraphy, bucolic nature poetry and fan paintings.

The reunification of China by the great Mongol ruler Kubilai Khan (r. 1260–94) in the late 1270s, however, precipitated a pivotal shift in Chinese

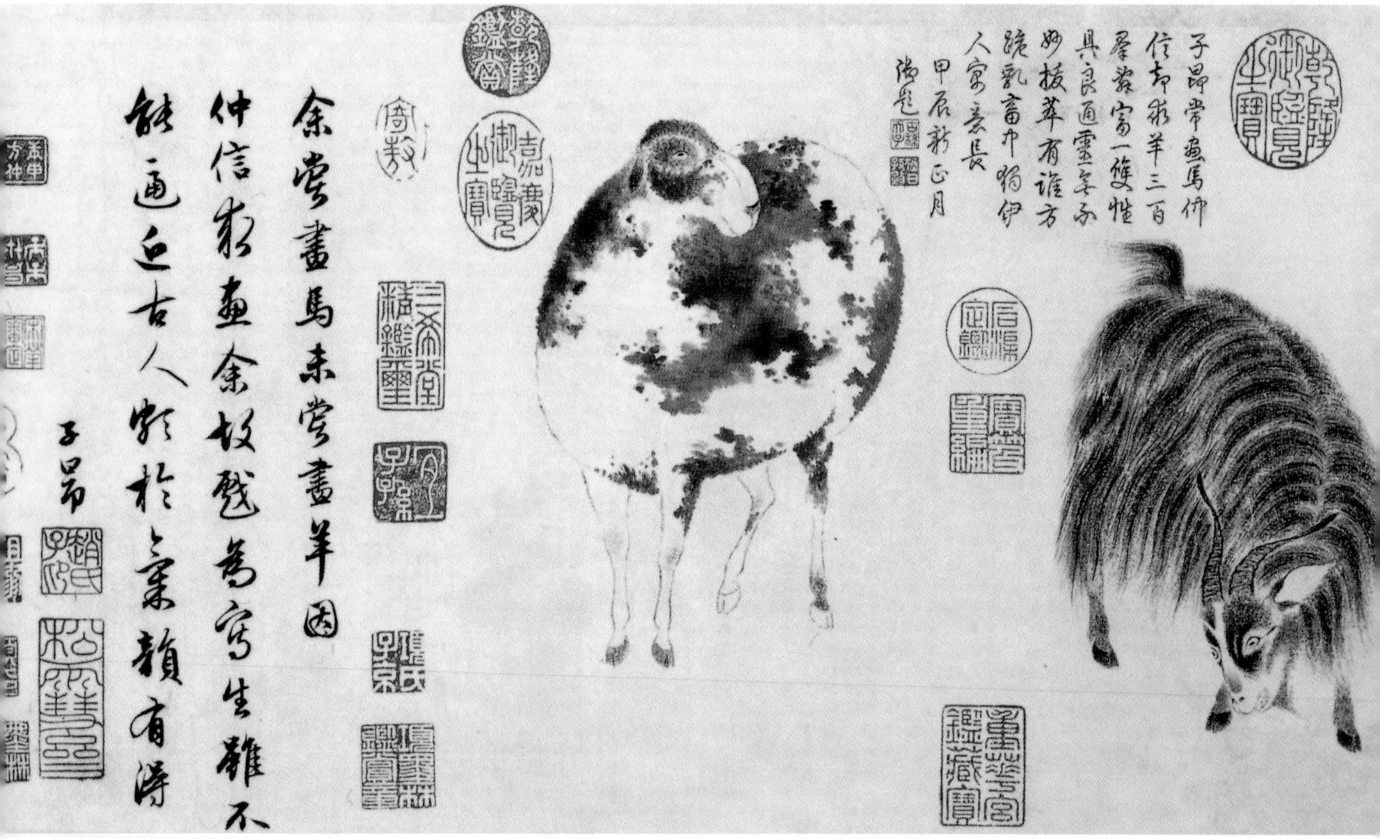

A sheep, a goat and a three-line calligraphic inscription combine in one of the Yuan master Zhao Mengfu's finest works.

painting history, as artists, led by Zhao Mengfu (see also p. 198), engaged in a comprehensive reform of the artistic canon, combined with a fundamental re-disciplining of painting in terms of the learned art of calligraphy.

The Ming and Qing dynasties

Such transformations broadly determined the subsequent literati tradition of painting, which reached early maturity under the native Ming dynasty (1368–1644) in the art of the magisterial Shen Zhou. A work of both calligraphy and painting, *Night Vigil* exemplifies the development of this 'amateur', lyric tradition (the Wu School), which vied critically with the art of court, academic and professional painters (the Zhe School). Recording Shen Zhou's meditations through a wet but moonlit autumn night in 1492, the painting may be read as a kind of manifesto of literati beliefs about art, its relation to nature and its practice as self-cultivation.

By the 17th century, the insistence of literati critics on distinctions between the art of lofty amateurs and 'vulgar' professionals was wearing thin. The painting of the lovable eccentric Chen Hongshou (1598–1652), a failed scholar-official but a famous professional painter, is laced with irony about his role and status, first in late Ming times and then early Qing (1644–1911) society. His acknowledged masterpiece, *Lady Xuanwen Giving Instruction on the Classic*, 1638, is headed by a lengthy inscription about Confucian learning in the Period of Disunion, which only a literary man could have written, and yet the painting is executed in a 'professional' collaborative style together with his studio assistants.

Like Chen Hongshou, the Qing monk-painter Bada Shanren was a 'left-over subject' after the fall of the Ming and during the gradual establishment of the Manchu Qing dynasty. A minor prince of the Ming royal family, Bada Shanren sought refuge in the Buddhist church after 1644. His painting is noted for its stark, mysterious images of rocks, fish and birds, which he combined with often opaque poetry. Even into old age, he dwelt on his fate as a kind of émigré in his own country.

European connections

Bada Shanren's generation was probably the last to have practised the art of painting before, with the growing power of European nations, knowledge of Western art became fairly widespread in China under non-Chinese Qing rule. At first, Western painting was championed at the Manchu court, as successive emperors from Kangxi and Yongzheng to Qianlong,

An anonymous court painting entitled The Qianlong Emperor as a Chinese Literatus and Art Lover, Playing the Zither in Front of a Painting in his Own Hand, *probably dated to 1766.*

retained European men of learning. The Italian Jesuit master Giuseppe Castiglione, who is known in Chinese as Lang Shining and spent almost his entire life at court in the vain hope of converting the Manchus to Christianity, was the Qianlong emperor's favourite court artist, a liking in part based on his early masterwork, *One Hundred Horses*. By the 1730s, Castiglione had developed an extraordinary hybrid style, combining Chinese painting media of brush and ink on paper or silk with Western painting techniques of vanishing-point perspective and *chiaroscuro* or shading, and embodying the pragmatic, universalist world-view of the emperor he served.

Painting in modern China

After the fall of the Qing dynasty in 1911 and the establishment of the Republic, a period of modernization began. In the 1920s, many artists travelled to Europe to train in Western styles, including in oils, and to Japan, an obvious role-model to China where both Asian and European styles and techniques had been taught since the Meiji restoration of 1868. In spite of Japanese militarist ambitions in China and throughout Asia from the 1930s up to 1945, the legacy of this exchange is clear to see in the work of Chinese painters who studied in Japan. One such is Fu Baoshi, a traditionalist and master in the style known in China as 'national painting' (*guohua*). Illustrating a line of Chairman Mao's poetry, *This Land So Rich in Beauty*, painted by him with Guan Shanyue for the Great Hall of the People in Beijing in 1959, clearly reworks similar Japanese images from the early 20th century. This huge painting is shown in situ below in a photograph taken on the occasion of US President Richard Nixon's visit to China in 1972.

Traditional and oil painting continues both in China and among the diaspora, but it is the artists and showmen of the avant-garde who often capture headlines. Standing out from the crowd is the Fujian-born artist Cai Guo-Qiang, whose works with gunpowder, both on paper and as performance art, have garnered international critical attention.

This Land So Rich in Beauty, *painted by Fu Baoshi and Guan Shanyue in 1959.*

STACEY PIERSON

Porcelain

51

The beautiful porcelain which is a vivid and sparkling white, and of a beautiful and celestial blue, all comes from Jingdezhen.

PÈRE FRANÇOIS XAVIER D'ENTRECOLLES, IN A LETTER FROM CHINA DATED 1712

Porcelain is one of the most successful products ever created in China. As a domestic ceramic, porcelain historically was used in China for the production of hard-wearing, mass-produced tablewares, specially commissioned imperial ceramics, and figural sculptures. As an export product, Chinese porcelain was an important trade item and a major source of government revenue from the 8th century onward.

Porcelain can be said to have been invented in China when the Chinese started using local white clay for high-fired, instead of low-fired, white ceramics. It is today so closely associated with China that the popular term for porcelain vessels and figurines in general is 'china'. As a ceramic material, porcelain is admired for its pure white colour, its hardness that resonates like glass when struck and for its translucency, allowing light to pass through and illuminate the material. Before the advent of Chinese porcelain, this material was unknown in other cultures but once encountered, it had a profound impact on world ceramic consumption, including the development of a taste for hard, white ceramics, especially the 'blue and white' porcelain for which China came to be famous.

History

Porcelain was first produced in China in the Sui period (581–618) in forms that related to foreign silver vessels such as drinking cups from Sassanian Persia. In the succeeding Tang dynasty (618–907), three main kilns began producing porcelain on a wider scale: Gongxian in Henan province, and Xing and Ding in Hebei province. These kilns made a wide range of wares in porcelain including small dishes which were popular for export as well as porcelain decorated in underglaze cobalt blue, the earliest 'blue and white' in the world.

The earliest Chinese porcelains were made in north China but in the Song dynasty (960–1279), kilns in south China also began to produce porcelain. One of the most important and successful southern types of porcelain from this period is known as *qingbai* (bluish white) ware. This ware

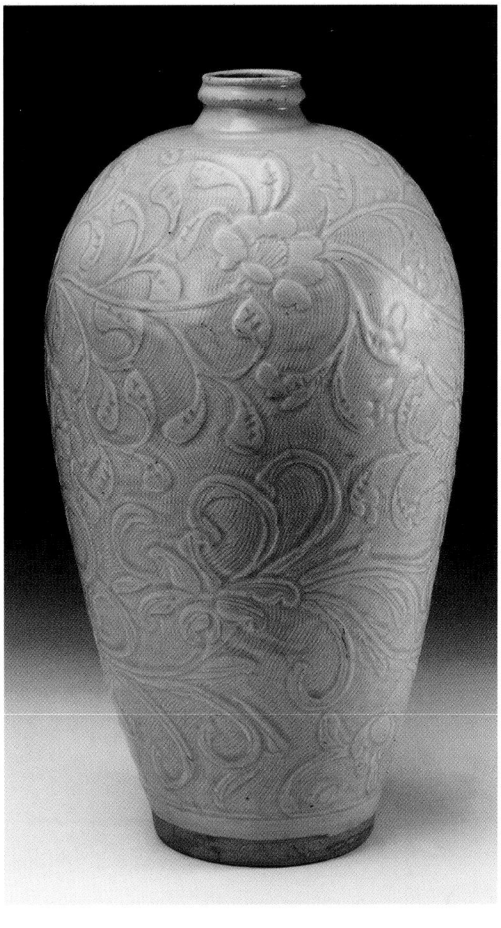

Found in Sichuan province, this Song-dynasty vase has a qingbai *glaze. (Height 41 cm / 16 in.)*

Vase produced at Jingdezhen in the Yuan dynasty. Its blue underglaze narrates a Han-dynasty story, and the characters are pictured among typically Chinese surroundings – bamboo, pine trees and plum blossoms.

was first made at Jingdezhen in Jiangxi province which came to be one of the largest and most successful porcelain-producing areas in China, if not the world. In the Yuan dynasty (1279–1368), court porcelains were commissioned from Jingdezhen and this continued in the Ming (1368–1644) when part of Jingdezhen was designated for imperial production. Specially commissioned wares were made for the court and often had the name of the dynasty and the emperor for whom they were made inscribed on the base. These inscriptions are today known as 'reign marks'.

In the 17th century, China experienced considerable political and economic turmoil and this affected production of porcelain, including that of Jingdezhen. When court patronage of the factory ceased in 1608, Jingdezhen began producing porcelains for the export markets on a much greater scale than ever before. The imperial factory was heavily damaged in this period, but after rebuilding in the 1680s, official production resumed under the new Qing dynasty (1644–1911) and the Kangxi emperor's (1662–1722) interest in technology had a great impact on developments in porcelain production at this time. One major development was the opening of porcelain painting workshops in the palace itself so that blank porcelains from Jingdezhen were sent there for painting by specialist painters. This resulted in some of the most beautifully painted porcelains in Chinese history.

Technology and decoration

Chinese porcelain is composed of two materials: kaolinitic clays and porcelain stone, which is also known as *baidunzi* or 'petuntse'. Both materials are found in south China but very little porcelain stone is found in the north of the country. At the primary porcelain factory in China, Jingdezhen, the porcelains were made with both materials in varying proportions, with the earlier examples tending to contain more porcelain stone than kaolin clays. Like most other porcelains, Chinese porcelain is very high fired, historically up to 1,320° C (2,410° F), and translucent. Some examples are so thin that they are described in Chinese as being 'bodiless'.

Chinese porcelains from the north were generally fired with coal fuels, which were abundant in the northern porcelain-producing areas. In the south however, wood fuels were more common and at times, so much wood was consumed in the making of porcelain that entire areas were deforested as a result. Glaze materials were derived from the body materials plus glaze ash, and these were sometimes coloured with mineral pigments which could be used to produce red and green glazes (copper), blue glazes (cobalt or iron), yellow (iron) or black (iron) glaze colours.

Making porcelain, as shown on an 18th-century painting.

In terms of decoration, a wide range of techniques were used, with underglaze cobalt painting the most common. This was first developed in the late Tang dynasty but continued to be used as a decorative technique in the Yuan, Ming and Qing dynasties. Today it is even used for contemporary Chinese studio porcelains. Underglaze blue was often combined with overglaze painting using low-fired enamels. This combination first appeared in the 15th century when the technique was used to produce what are known as *doucai* (juxtaposed colours) wares. These have

Chinese porcelain, doucai *bowl and dish from the Qing dynasty.*

Opposite *Two Qing-dynasty vases from the second half of the 18th century, with matching snuff bottle and stopper. These bear the reign marks of the Qianlong emperor.*

designs painted with fine blue lines under the glaze and then after a first firing, the outlines are filled in with overglaze colours and the piece is fired again. A simpler version of this technique was introduced in the 16th century but it was not until the late 17th and early 18th centuries that new colours were added to the enamel palette and new techniques of painting were introduced. One of the most popular new colours was pink which was used in combination with other colours in a palette known today as *famille rose*.

Forms and functions

Porcelain is used to make a wide range of objects in China and these, in turn, are used for an equally wide range of functions. The most common porcelain product in China is tableware, from dishes and bowls for eating to cups and ewers for drinking. Such tablewares were made for both ordinary consumers and the Chinese court, and many of these court wares are highly admired today as collected objects. Other uses for porcelain in China include religious ritual, such as vessels or figurines for Buddhist practices or altar wares for temples, which often have dated dedications. Architectural tiles were made of porcelain in the Ming dynasty, with the most famous example being the white tiles made for the 'Porcelain Pagoda' of the Yongle period (1403–1425) in Nanjing (see p. 141).

The earliest porcelain forms took their inspiration from foreign silver; this practice continued into the Ming dynasty when some forms were copied from Near Eastern glass. Foreign styles were also adopted for Chinese textiles at this time including motifs such as a dragon chasing a flaming pearl, which came to be associated with China but which originated in Central Asia. A number of porcelain forms were inspired by Chinese metalwork such as ancient bronzes of the type made in the Shang and Zhou periods. This kind of influence, when combined with designs inspired by ancient bronzes, is known as 'archaism', an important stylistic development in Chinese art beginning in the Song dynasty when the court's collection of actual ancient bronzes was first catalogued.

In the Qing dynasty forms were both simple and complex, with simple forms developed to be used as a canvas for more elaborate decoration. The more complex forms often featured a number of archaistic references from ancient bronzes to Tang poetry and Song ink painting, often on one piece. A number of these archaistic porcelains were used in court ritual. New forms were also developed such as hanging vases for sedan chairs, water pots for use in calligraphy and porcelain lanterns, which benefited from the transparency of later Chinese porcelain.

Worldwide influence

Chinese porcelain was first exported in the Tang dynasty. Archaeologists have found Chinese porcelains of this date in Samarra (Iraq), Fustat (Egypt) as well as east Africa. In the Yuan dynasty, Chinese porcelain, especially blue and white, was exported in great quantities to the Near East and Southeast Asia as well as Japan where plain white porcelains were preferred. In the Ming dynasty, exports continued with Europe entering the market in the 16th century. In fact, the first European country to specially commission Chinese porcelains was Portugal, and in the succeeding century hundreds of thousands of Chinese porcelains were exported to Holland, England, Sweden, Germany and other European countries.

Chinese porcelain provided a model for white ceramic production in many of the countries where it was consumed. In Turkey, for example, local Iznik wares were made in close imitation of Chinese porcelains in the 16th century and in the 17th century, Dutch 'Delftware' copies of Chinese porcelains began to be made from tin-glazed earthenware. In Britain, Chinese porcelain inspired the production of bone china and the development of the popular 'blue willow' pattern which was thought to be a Chinese original by early consumers.

Today, Chinese porcelains are still being imitated by studio potters, who tend to copy the shapes and glazes of Song porcelains, and larger ceramic factories such as Wedgwood who make Chinese-style dinner services and tablewares in porcelain.

ROSEMARY SCOTT

52 Lacquer Work

Ancient or modern carved red lacquer should be judged by the thickness of the lacquer, the fresh red colour, and by its strength and weight. The pieces on which are carved sword ring patterns and grass scrolls are especially fine.
CAO ZHAO, *GE GU YAO LUN* ('ESSENTIAL CRITERIA OF ANTIQUITIES'), 1388

The Chinese seem to have been the first to discover and exploit the properties of lacquer. The lacquer produced in China comes mainly from the so-called lacquer tree *rhus verniciflua*, which is indigenous to the country and is found today in central and south China, although in previous times it grew over a much larger area.

The sap of the lacquer tree was harvested as a viscous grey substance; an oil in water emulsion, the essential constituent of which is urushiol. On exposure to oxygen this spontaneously polymerizes (forms molecules of much higher molecular weight) and this results in a material somewhat resembling a natural plastic. It can be applied to both organic and inorganic materials and is resistant to water, to acids, to heat and to termites. It can be used as an adhesive and is even electrically insulating. Indeed in East Asia in the 20th century it was still sometimes used to provide a coating for laboratory benches and conservation worktables. It is also quite strong and therefore an excellent material to use as a protective coating for organic materials such as wood or leather. As well as these practical uses, when applied properly it will take on a beautiful glossy sheen; it can be combined with certain pigments to produce dramatic colours; it can be used to paint designs; and, when applied in many layers, it can be intricately carved.

The Neolithic and Bronze Age

The earliest lacquered object so far discovered in China comes from the Neolithic site of Hemudu, *c.* 3000–5000 BC, near Hangzhou in Zhejiang province. Even on this rough wooden bowl, the lacquer has been coloured red so that it provided both protection and decoration. There are only a limited number of pigments that can be combined with lacquer, and red and black have remained the most popular colours for lacquer up to the present day. During the early Bronze Age the use of lacquer became more widespread and more decorative. Excavations at the Shang-dynasty (*c.* 1600 – *c.* 1046 BC) site of Taixicun in Hebei province revealed fragments of a platter or tray covered in red lacquer, with black lacquer used to pick out a design that is almost identical to those seen on contemporary bronzes.

Right *One of the three coffins belonging to Lady Dai, excavated at Mawangdui, Changsha, Hunan province. The multicoloured painted lacquer design on the sides of the coffin depicts immortals and creatures from the spirit world amongst swirling clouds. Some details of the design have been rendered in raised lines for additional emphasis. Western Han dynasty.*

From the Zhou (1046–221 BC) and Han (206 BC–AD 220) dynasties there is a wealth of material that indicates lacquer being used on vessels, implements of warfare and funerary paraphernalia, although it should be remembered that lacquer was an expensive luxury item that contemporary literature indicates was more expensive than bronze. Lacquer provided both strength and decoration for shields and for armour, used by both soldiers and horses. Both the shields and armour were made of leather, which was given several coats of lacquer and then had multi-coloured designs painted on the surface in lacquer. Excavation of the mid-2nd-century BC tomb of Lady Dai at Mawangdui, Changsha, Hunan province, revealed wonderfully well-preserved lacquer wares and silk textiles. As well as vessels and boxes, the tomb also contained three lacquered coffins, one inside the other.

The Tang dynasty (618–907)

With the establishment of the Tang dynasty came a period that is regarded as one of the highpoints for the arts of China. The range of techniques used to decorate lacquer objects in the Tang greatly expanded, as did the kinds of items to which lacquer was applied.

There are three decorative lacquer techniques which are particularly associated with the Tang period. These are lacquer wares with inlaid mother-of-pearl decoration, lacquer with gold and silver inlays, and the so-called 'bodiless' or 'dry lacquer' technique. When mother-of-pearl was used to decorate Tang-dynasty lacquer objects – such as the backs of bronze mirrors or musical instruments – the pieces were usually relatively thick and whitish in colour, often from the shells of *turbo cornutus* or *turbo marmoratus,* and decorative details were incised into the upper surface of the shell. The inlay of precious metal foils had been used with lacquer in the later Bronze Age, but the Tang-dynasty examples were much more complex, sometimes covering the whole surface with a single sheet of gold foil, for example, into which a design had been cut, and occasionally combining areas of different coloured metals. Decorative details were sometimes incised into the surface of the metal foil. Records indicate that the 'bodiless' or 'dry lacquer' technique was established in the Han period for vessels, and for sculptures in the Eastern Jin (317–420). A clay core provided the shape of the image, onto which fabric and then lacquer was applied. The clay was then washed out, leaving light but strong objects. It became a popular technique for making Buddhist images in the Tang dynasty in the south of China.

Below *This carved red lacquer box, 24.4 cm (9.6 in.) in diameter, shows two herons in flight.*

Song and Yuan dynasties (960–1368)

Some of the most beautiful lacquer wares of the Song and Yuan dynasties are plain black or red. However, several decorative techniques, originally developed in earlier periods, also became popular. These included incising fine lines into the lacquer surface and then sticking gold leaf or metallic powder into the grooves to create a contrasting design. Alternatively, contrasting coloured lacquer could be applied to the grooves. A technique in which layers of lacquer in contrasting colours were applied to the surface of a vessel also came to prominence. In some cases the layers were applied to an uneven surface, which was then polished to reveal the differently coloured layers unevenly in a technique sometimes called 'rhinoceros skin' in Chinese. A more common multi-coloured technique had scrolling designs cut through the layers leaving wide grooves, which revealed the different coloured layers. This is often known in the West by its Japanese name *guri*, a reference to the design of a sword pommel. This technique was widely used on items from brush handles to mirror cases.

Mother-of-pearl inlay continued to be used in the Song and Yuan dynasties, but the pieces of mother-of-pearl became smaller and thinner as well as more iridescent and colourful, coming from the inner layer of the *haliotis* shell. The designs on such pieces became more complex, often pictorial, and began to be applied to furniture as well as items such as boxes and trays. However, the most important feature of Song and Yuan lacquer work was the establishment of deeply carved lacquer with pictorial designs, an art for which China would become world famous. This required many layers of lacquer, which each had to be applied very thinly and thoroughly 'dried' before the next was added.

Ming and Qing dynasties (1368–1911)

The 14th- and early 15th-century carved lacquers are the most prized by connoisseurs, and indeed records exist of Chinese lacquers sent as official gifts from China to Japan in the Yongle reign (1403–1424). However, fine carved lacquers were made throughout the Ming and first half of the Qing dynasty, ranging from tiny seal-paste boxes

A magnificent carved lacquer throne made for the Qianlong emperor. Records suggest that the throne came from one of the audience chambers of the Duanhe Travelling Palace in the Southern Park, a large imperial park about 10 km (6 miles) south of Beijing.

Workers hand-painting a lacquer screen in a modern workshop.

to magnificent thrones. These two dynasties saw a greater interest in multi-coloured lacquers, often with yellow, green and brown as well as red and black, on items in which the contrasting colours could be painted, inlaid or layered.

All the major techniques had been developed by the Qing dynasty, but one group of lacquer wares, so-called 'Coromandel' lacquer, is particularly associated with this period. These are mostly large screens, and their name comes from the fact that many came to Europe via the Coromandel Coast of southeast India. The wooden base for these lacquers was given a thick coat of a special ash mixture before several layers of black lacquer were applied. The surface was then deeply carved to create a design which could be filled with oil colours and gold.

Late Qing to the present day

In the late Qing period, although the imperial lacquer workshops in Suzhou closed down, lacquer wares continued to be made elsewhere in China. Lacquered items with painted gold decoration were made for export to Europe and America in workshops in southeast China, such as those in Fujian and Guangdong provinces. Today lacquer ware is still made in many of the areas of China traditionally associated with the craft. While the modern carved lacquers rarely reach the high standards of the finest earlier pieces and prospective buyers should beware of synthetic imitations, experimentation with new forms and new variants of traditional techniques means that lacquer remains a lively industry in modern China.

ANN PALUDAN

53 Sculpture

To the east there opens the jade Image Hall,
Where white Buddhas sit like serried trees.
We shook from our garments the journey's grime and dust,
And bowing worshipped those faces of frozen snow
Whose white cassocks like folded hoar-frost hung,
Whose beaded crowns glittered like a shower of hail.
We looked closer; surely Spirits willed
This handicraft, never chisel carved!
BAI JUYI (PO CHU-I), *THE TEMPLE*, 772–846

China is a land of sculpture. The range of sculptures, from solemn tomb figures or gigantic Buddhist cliff images to clay figurines, terracotta armies and delicate jade figures, can be bewildering. For Westerners, distinguishing between religious and secular subjects, the different forms appear to have little in common. These problems disappear once the statuary is seen against the background of early Chinese beliefs.

The nature of Chinese sculpture was formed in the period before and soon after the unification of the Chinese empire in 221 BC. It was based on beliefs in the inter-relationship of all parts of a cosmos in which there was no clear boundary between the visible and unseen worlds; events in one sphere influenced those in other spheres. Architecture and sculpture were used to achieve harmony with the heavenly spheres. Cities, palaces, temples and graves were carefully sited into the overall pattern of the universe since error in one area would disturb the others. In this context, sculpture was not an art. As in the European Middle Ages, a sculptor was an anonymous craftsman whose work was designed for a particular site and purpose, to convey a moral educational message intended to influence those in the seen and unseen worlds.

In Neolithic China, different forms of sculpture developed in different regions, with numerous forms of pottery and jade carvings reflecting local beliefs. During the Bronze Age, the most striking artifacts were large bronze vessels designed to establish contact with the spirit world after death, small jade carvings and a growing number of clay models created to serve the deceased after death. Certain materials acquired symbolic meanings. Bronze, used for weapons and ritual vessels, became associated with power and status. Jade was associated with purity; ownership of a jade object implied possible contact with the immortals. Stone was associated with permanence or eternity. Bronze Age ritual stone bells and steles, like inscriptions 'written in metal and stone', were intended to create a permanent link with the unknown future.

Imperial sculpture

The unification of China in 221 BC by Qin Shihuangdi, the First Emperor, bringing together the techniques and ideas of the previously independent kingdoms, gave sculpture a role at the heart of the state. Above ground the emperor's palaces included twelve vast bronze figures made from melted weapons of defeated states. Below ground, within and without his tomb, models such as the army of terracotta warriors were designed to serve the emperor after death (see p. 155).

Recent excavations of 2nd-century BC Han-dynasty tombs reveal a similar picture. At

Yangling, joint tomb of Han Jingdi (188–141 BC) and his wife, reliable estimates suggest that nearly 100,000 terracotta figures were made. Whilst the majority were painted models like the earlier terracotta warriors, a small group of men, women and eunuchs were modelled nude with flexible wooden arms; each figure was then clothed in silk, gauze or hemp according to its role. Seldom can the underlying belief in the creational powers of sculpture have been made so clear.

In the early 1st and 2nd centuries AD, a dramatic change in tomb arrangements gave stone sculpture a dominant role in imperial burials. The underground world of the Qin and Western Han with their vast pits outside the central tomb was now concentrated within the tomb complex. Above ground, an avenue or 'spirit road' of stone men and/or animals provided status and protection; below, within the underground palace, terracotta figurines recreated the known world of the deceased, whilst wall reliefs and paintings placed the tomb correctly in a world of spirits. This new pattern lasted until the fall of the empire in 1911. Each dynasty redesigned the content of its spirit road to give a desired picture of its rule and seek protection or help from the other world, and the believed powers of stone were harnessed by authority for political, educational and spiritual purposes.

A terracotta figure of a dancing lady from the Western Han dynasty. She stands 47 cm (18.5 in.) high.

The arrival of Buddhist sculpture

After the fall of the Han, during the Period of Disunion (220–581), Buddhism spread through both parts of a now divided China. In the north, non-Chinese rulers introduced Indian ideas of cliff shrines at Yungang, near their capital, Datong, Shanxi. Under guidance of a Chinese

Aerial view of the west side of Longmen Caves, Henan province. Fengxian Cave, pictured above, is the large shrine with a huge seated Buddha sculpture carved from the cliff face. AD 672–675.

monk, Danyao, the first five imperial caves were dedicated to the ancestors of the first Northern Wei ruler, thus associating Buddha and Buddhism with traditional Chinese ancestor worship. In the south, whilst the imperial tombs were guarded by magnificent traditional stone beasts, intellectuals were attracted by Buddhist doctrines dealing with subjects ignored in traditional Chinese philosophy.

To commission or make an icon earned merit for oneself, and with the introduction of new sites and Buddhist iconography there was a dramatic explosion in sculptural production. Like the indigenous statuary, the new carvings were created to have an effect: to praise, teach and provide contact with the unseen. The process was similar to that of grafting a new vigorous strain of apple onto an old apple tree. The new part may well produce more fruit but it depends on the roots of the original tree.

Sui to Song dynasties

Under the Sui, Tang and Song dynasties (581–1279) prosperity, foreign contacts and the growth of commerce and a middle class provided the chance to explore every branch of sculpture. The first Sui emperor commissioned 100,000 new images in gold, bronze, sandalwood, ivory and stone. Tang emperors sponsored Buddhist and Daoist temples and shrines at Longmen and elsewhere; statuary was used in architecture, gardens and civic works.

Subjects were chosen for their symbolic power. Huge oxen, traditional symbols of water control, were cast in solid iron to anchor the first permanent bridge across the Yangtze River, whilst their iron herders, chosen from different minorities, stressed the unity of the empire. Behind the anchors, seven pillars for the Great Dipper, the fixed point in Chinese astronomy, anchored the bridge to the cosmic forces.

In the field of tomb figurines, technical advances produced the prized Tang three-colour figures with prancing horses, dancing girls and foreign musicians on camel-back.

Tang and Song emperors used portrait statues of themselves and their ancestors in temples and processions to increase their popularity. Buddhism, like Daoism, became increasingly absorbed into a popular religion in which local gods and nature spirits played a part and the gap between the supreme figures and mankind was lessened; bodhisattvas were portrayed as court women rather than beings with supernatural natures.

Bodhisattva holding a lotus leaf-shaped tray bearing an inscription to Emperor Yizong. Found in the underground chamber of the Famen Temple, Shaanxi province, and made of gilt-silver.

The Yuan to Qing dynasties

The Yuan dynasty (1279–1368) brought major changes in attitudes towards small sculptural works. Craftsmen imported from the West introduced new techniques. Ignorant of, or indifferent to, local belief in the power of images, these skilled workers paid greater attention to detail, technical skill and appearance than to the meaning of the figure, and the choice of medium ceased to express a decisive part of the message. Under the Ming and Qing dynasties (1368–1911), sculptural production increased but its status fell. Spirit road statuary retained importance but the age of great cliff shrines was over.

Buddhism no longer supplied the necessary magnificence, and contacts with the unseen world were confined to temples, small local shrines, household altars and the traditional Chinese altars to Heaven and Earth. Small carved objects, used to convey messages through their symbolism, became increasingly popular with intellectuals. Collectors valued intricacy as in small concentric balls or a cabbage with coloured insects carved from single pieces of ivory or jade.

Right *Ming-dynasty figure of Buddha Sakyamuni. (Height 62.6 cm / 24 in.)*

Below *One of the many statues of Chairman Mao Zedong that are still seen throughout China. This example greets visitors at a square in Fuzhou, Fujian province.*

Modern developments

Chinese 20th-century sculpture closely reflects political developments. Immediately after 1911, there was considerable French influence, but the civil and foreign wars which followed halted sculptural activity. In 1950 sculpture received official recognition as an art taught in the Central Academy of Fine Art in the Peoples' Republic. For nearly 30 years sculptural work was dominated by Social Realism, with large group memorials to revolutionary martyrs and to ubiquitous statues of Mao Zedong. His figure, with hand raised in victory, proclaimed the new state.

Change came after the Cultural Revolution. It began with civic statues like the Peony Queen in Luoyang, linked with legendary or symbolic figures rather than political messages. Giant abstract metal works were placed in city squares or on new buildings. In the 1990s, the pace quickened with the emergence of individual sculptors known by name and becoming internationally known. Furthermore, sculpture is regaining its former prestige with international symposia, attracting foreign sculptors whose projects are carried out by artisans from traditional stone- or metal-working areas.

SHELAGH VAINKER

Silk Work

54

One hundred days weaving the coloured threads,
one morning the loom's shuttle stops.
In the loom is a double phoenix
transformed to a garment for heaven's edge.
BAO RONG, TANG-DYNASTY POET

Silk, along with tea and porcelain, has defined China to much of the world, in many periods. It was first made and used there some 6,000 years ago, and has been exported for more than two millennia. To the Romans, its production was a mystery and they paid huge sums for it; in Byzantium and Persia in the 4th–6th centuries, raw silk was imported and local industries developed. By the 14th century, Persia itself produced raw silk and exported it to southern Europe and there, over the ensuing centuries, a silk industry was established.

The spread of silk production was slow partly because it required several stages and because the cultivation of mulberry trees did not adapt easily to different climates. The reeling of silk from wild silkworm cocoons was understood in various places, India for example, for some time before a silk industry was established yet in China, the silkworm *bombyx mori* was domesticated as early as the Neolithic period. The long continuous threads that were reeled from the cocoons were wound to form raw silk, which was then twisted into yarn ready for weavers to make into silk cloth. This was done on industrial scales, and also at the level of rural domestic production; silk was traded both abroad and within China as raw silk, yarn, bolts of cloth and as finished goods.

Early uses of silk

The few surviving fragments of Neolithic silk appear to belong to belts or ribbons, while the first systematic use that can be identified is the wrapping of precious objects in silk during the Shang dynasty (*c.* 1600 – *c.* 1046 BC). Bronze ritual vessels and ceremonial jades have been excavated from tombs in north, south and east China, and quite often bear traces or even fragments of silk that show the weave and texture of the original cloth. Some are woven with fairly elaborate geometric motifs. Other evidence of silk from this early period is also indirect: jade carvings in the form of silkworms, and sheep or ox bones bearing

An album leaf from the Qing-dynasty volume Agriculture and Sericulture, *depicting people involved in the process of silk weaving.*

Above *A painting on sillk by an anonymous court artist from the late Kangzi period (1709–1723), showing a woman at leisure.*

divinatory inscriptions that refer to silk. In the Zhou dynasty (1046–221 BC) silk became a material for writing on, and several early manuscripts survive. The alternative writing material was narrow slips of bamboo, which were written on in a single column then lashed together and rolled up to form a scroll, just as silk manuscripts were. The earliest work of literature in Chinese is a Han-dynasty (206 BC–AD 220) record of Zhou-dynasty songs, and though no Zhou silk version of it survives, many of the poems refer to mulberry groves and silk clothes.

Silk in art and literature

Silk is mentioned frequently in poems and novels throughout China's literary history, either as an object of praise in its own right, or in passing descriptions of clothes and furnishings. It also played a practical role, for the use of silk for writing documents was extended to calligraphy and painting. Though paper was invented during the Han dynasty, it was not until the 11th century AD that it became the usual material for ink paintings, favoured for its absorbency and responsiveness to the brush. Silk contined to be used, however, particularly for more colourful paintings, and from the 12th century onwards techniques of tapestry weaving (*kesi*) were so refined that woven silk pictures were created in close imitation of painted works. In the Ming dynasty (1368–1644), albums of pictures and calligraphy were produced in embroidery, and became as highly sought after as albums of paintings. Silk brocades and tapestry weaves were used for wrapping scrolls and books.

Silk clothing

The earliest complete silk robes date from the 5th–4th centuries BC, and were found in a tomb containing neatly wrapped bundles of silk garments at Jiangling in Hubei province. They wrap to the left from the shoulder, just as later robes do, but without the toggles. Early garments also included cap, jacket, skirt, trousers and shoes, and were made of silk gauzes, lenos (a type of gauze), damasks, brocades, braids and embroideries. Some of these techniques were highly complex, and all continued on later silks. The drawloom, a

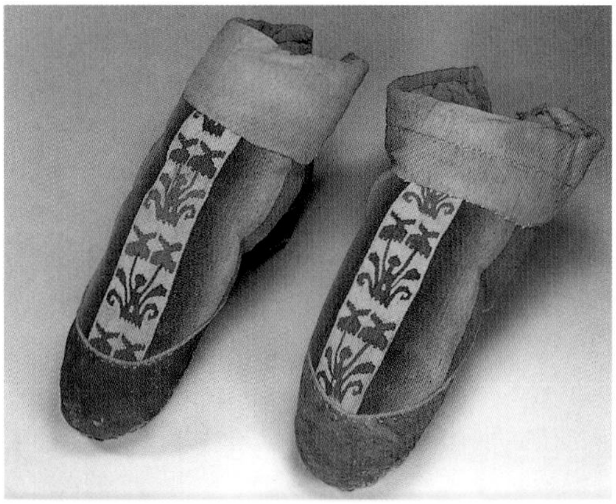

Right *A pair of silk shoes found at Niya, Minfeng (Eastern Han / Jin period).*

huge, complicated piece of textile equipment that accounted for sophisticated early weaving, is thought to have been in use by the Han dynasty. The most significant subsequent innovation was the introduction of weft patterning shortly before the Tang dynasty (618–907). Patterning in the weft rather than the warp allowed much greater versatility in ornament, and the intricate, multi-coloured designs of many Tang fragments and garments from the Silk Road bear vivid testimony to this. The period also saw developments in clothing style, with the influx of westerners and luxuries via Central Asia. The fashion for riding meant women began to wear trousers and short jackets. In the Song dynasty (960–1279), robes tended to be of quite loose cut, and patterned with scattered floral decoration rather than the repeated medallions and roundels of Tang weaves. A 13th-century tomb belonging to a young married woman, at Fuzhou in the southeast, contained more than 200 silk items, many of them exquisitely delicate. The gauzes used for summer jackets and robes were woven with large, well-spaced flowers on a background of fine transparent gauze;

One of the many silk items found in the tomb of Huang Sheng at Fuzhou. This lady's robe dates to the Southern Song period and has a height of 125 cm (49 in.).

Above *Six volumes of a Buddhist sutra with assorted gold brocade covers. The sutra was printed in 1584 but the silks are earlier, and include examples of Nanjing cloud brocade, or* yunjin.

trousers were in a denser weave that still created a light, fluid fabric.

Clothes from Ming-dynasty tombs are also made of silks patterned in the weave, with geometric designs as well as motifs with auspicious symbolism, such as bats (prosperity), children and seasonal flowers. At this time the garments were often made of shiny silk satins, a new technological development. It was also in the Ming dynasty that velvet began to be produced on any scale, though occasional examples of pile fabrics are known from as early as the Han dynasty.

Dragon robes

The best-known clothes from China, however, are the 'dragon' robes of the Qing (1644–1911) dynasty, so called after their association with the emperor and his court. Particular designs – 12 auspicious symbols, and frontal dragons – were restricted to the robes of the emperor himself, and different colours were worn according to rank, season and occasion. Rank was denoted by a square badge on the front and back of the robe woven or more usually embroidered with the appropriate bird, animal or other motif derived from nature (see example on p. 64).

Courtiers, civil and military officials had different styles of robes, formal and informal, and the rulings on them were extended to their wives. In addition, local officials in the 18th century encouraged official styles of dress for formal occasions in the lives of ordinary people. Given the growth in prosperity in that period and the increasingly widespread use of silk, large numbers of robes are evident, even if few have direct links with the imperial court. The finest imperial robes, however, are known to have taken more than a year to make, and incorporated gold threads and kingfisher feathers into the weaving.

In the early 20th century, clothing in China adopted a more international style. Ladies' robes became shorter, and the *qipao* or *cheongsam* (very fitted, straight dress with stand-up collar) became the fashionable dress up until the foun-

Right *Qing-dynasty brass and silk satin saddle with velvet trim.*

Silk hanging scroll portraying the Qianlong emperor (c. 1739–1758), painted by the artist Giuseppe Castiglione, whose Chinese name was Lang Shining (see p. 212).

dation in 1949 of the People's Republic of China with silk, as ever, the most favoured fabric.

Silk is light in weight, warm in cold weather and cool in hot, and these properties were exploited for furnishings as well as clothing. Bed hangings and covers, curtains, table and chair covers, which often constituted wedding gifts or trousseaux made by the bride herself, might be of embroidery, tapestry weaves, gauzes, satins or velvets. In the public sphere, silk was used for temple hangings and religious attire, and for opera and theatre costumes. Silk was used in diplomacy and for paying taxes: indeed its trade and production played as important a role in China's agriculture and economy as its utility, beauty and prominence have played in the country's cultural life.

NICHOLAS GRINDLEY

55 Furniture

The men of today make them in a manner which merely prefers carved and painted decoration to delight the vulgar eye, while the antique pieces are cast aside, causing one to sigh in deep regret.
WEN ZHENHENG, *ZHANG WU ZHI* ('A TREATISE ON SUPERFLUOUS THINGS'), *C.* 1615

Like most of the peoples indigenous to ancient East Asia, the Chinese people, in earliest times and at all levels of society sat or reclined on the floor, or less frequently on low platforms. An Eastern Han (AD 9–220) pottery tomb relief found near Chengdu, Sichuan, shows formally dressed students seated in the kneeling posture on long rectangular mats, whereas the teacher is on a raised, low platform leaning on an armrest. This is a typical depiction of the complex hierarchical structure of seating that existed throughout Chinese history. In the centuries following the fall of the Han dynasty (AD 220), more and more depictions exist of figures, both religious (particularly Buddhist) and secular, seated not only on raised platforms but also on forms of what we would now identify as chairs with fixed, rather than folding frames, with legs pendant.

Tang to Song dynasties

By the Tang dynasty (618–907) there are depictions of figures seated on stools playing *shuanglu* (a board game similar to backgammon) and a wall painting from a tomb in Nanliwang, Changan county, Shaanxi, depicts figures shown cross-legged or with one leg hanging down from long benches at a table laden with food. Important evidence of this chair-level mode of living is shown in a handscroll generally considered to be a 12th-century copy of a painting attributed to the 10th-century painter Gu Hongzhong entitled *The Night Revels of Han Xizai*, in which high tables for eating as well as suitably proportioned chairs and couches are represented. The tables depicted with their inset legs joined by stretchers are of a form which continues throughout the history of Chinese furniture. Also in this painting are yoke-

Detail from The Night Revels of Han Xizai, *believed to be a copy of a 10th-century handscroll. It is a valuable historical source on early Chinese furniture design.*

back chairs and large couches (*chuang*), the design of which changes little until well into the Qing period. By the Song dynasty (960–1279) there are many depictions of chairs of other forms, including roundback (horseshoe chairs) and folding chairs of both horseshoe and yoke-back form.

Early Ming dynasty

Little furniture has survived from the late Yuan (1279–1368) and early Ming (1368–1644) periods, although there are literary references to furniture at this time which seem to indicate a predominance of lacquered furniture either with incised and filled-in gold decoration (*qianqin*) or inlaid with mother-of-pearl. An important group of both miniature models and full-scale furniture has nevertheless survived from the excavated tomb of Prince Zhu Tan, who died in the 22nd year of the Hongwu reign (1389). The full-size furniture includes a red-lacquer and gold-decorated chest with dragon and cloud designs, a recessed-leg table with everted flanges, four deep-side tables, and four red-lacquer deep-side tables with stone panel tops. The miniature furniture shows a cross-section of forms that we have come to associate with hardwood furniture of the later Ming period. It includes a low-back couch with a freestanding superstructure, a tall square stand usually referred to as an incense stand, a recessed- leg table, a basin stand, a clothes rack and various other trunks and benches, all of which are now preserved in the Shandong Provincial Museum.

No inscribed pieces, that is those bearing reign marks or datable inscriptions, are known to have survived from the early Ming period, but by the mid-15th century there are two examples of lacquered furniture with Xuande (1426–1435) reign marks. The first of these are a pair of square corner cabinets with incised and filled-in gold decoration of dragons and clouds on the lacquer base in the Palace Museum in Beijing, the second a spectacular carved lacquer table (pictured below) with three drawers, also bearing a Xuande reign mark, in the collection of the Victoria and Albert Museum, London. This unique table, probably made for a ceremonial or religious function, is decorated with dragons, phoenix and floral motifs in a style typical of the mid-15th century (although normally associated with much smaller objects such as boxes and dishes). Both of these pieces with Xuande reign marks can be attributed to the imperial lacquer workshops established by the Yongle emperor (1403–1424).

Below left *Red lacquer folding table with incised and filled-in gold decoration (late 14th / early 15th century).*

Below *Carved red lacquer table with drawers, Xuande period (c. 1426–1435).*

Above *A pair of horseshoe armchairs made from* huanghuali *wood and woven cane.*

Late Ming dynasty

Furniture production, along with lacquer manufacture and general patronage of the decorative arts, especially for the court, appears to have been in decline during the latter part of the 15th century and the early years of the 16th century-only to be revived under the emperor Jiajing (1522–1566). Decorative arts were not entirely stagnant during this period as the production of porcelain, for example in the Chenghua reign (1465–1487), demonstrates, but imperial patronage, particularly in the so-called 'minor arts' (everything but painting and calligraphy), diminished. During Jiajing's reign the decentralization of government (resulting in a rise in the wealth of large cities and towns especially along the coast, such as those in the Jiangsu and Zhejiang areas) created important centres of production for furniture and other decorative arts. In 1567 the longstanding ban on foreign trade was lifted and the prized hardwoods we associate with furniture of the late Ming started to be imported, and it is this following century that has become known as the 'classic' period of Ming furniture.

The late 16th and early 17th centuries represent the high point of 'classic' Ming-style furniture. Much furniture was made in hardwoods such as *huanghuali* and *zitan*, but many other woods were used. The Chinese terminology for the classification of woods can be confusing in that the term 'hardwood' refers to woods of the tropical variety whose denseness and hardness as well as their imperviousness to insects qualify them as being 'hard'; all other woods are grouped as 'softwood', but these include woods of deciduous nature which would be termed hardwoods in the West. Wen Zhenheng, writing the *Zhang Wu Zhi* ('A Treatise on Superfluous Things') around 1615, suggests that other woods such as *wumu* (ebony), *tielimu* (ironwood), *nanmu* (similar to cedar) and *huangyangmu* (boxwood) were all considered woods suitable for making furniture for a man of taste and refinement. Wen goes on to describe the arrangement of the furniture, and the styles in which it should be made.

Much of the furniture made in the late Ming was exceptionally elegant and refined, with a paring-down of design and decoration which we have come to associate with design of the 20th century, and indeed did influence modern furniture makers such as Hans Wegner in Denmark in the 1950s.

Right *A* huanghuali *inset-leg, bridle-joint table from the early 17th century. 'Bridle joint' is a construction term where the apron passes through a slot in the top of the leg.*

Qing dynasty

When the Manchus overthrew the Ming government in 1644 little change occurred in the manufacture of furniture, and by 1662 when the Kangxi emperor ascended the throne, traditional Ming forms of furniture were still popular although new, more decorative styles started to develop. A series of paintings produced in the late Kangxi period by anonymous court artists entitled 'Twelve Beauties at Leisure Painted for Prince Yinzhen, the Future Yongzheng Emperor' give us a very good idea of the style of furniture being produced in the early 18th century, at least for the court, with a range of new designs in lacquer, bamboo and rootwood as well as pieces inlaid with mother-of-pearl or with decorative marble panels.

Throughout the late 18th and 19th centuries furniture became more decorated and less functional, at least in the households of the rich merchants, although it would appear that the Ming style lingered on as the taste of the more literati class. The advent of Communism in China has seen a rejection of the traditional forms of furniture and an adoption of Western furniture designs.

Above left *One of the 'Twelve Beauties' sitting at a heavily decorated chair (Kangxi period).*

Above *Pair of softwood, black and gilt lacquer armchairs from the 18th century.*

ALISON HARDIE

56 Gardens

I will guard simplicity and return to my fields and garden.
TAO QIAN (TAO YUANMING), 365–427

The appearance of Chinese gardens is very different from the gardens of Europe, although many of their purposes – aesthetic pleasure, relaxation, closeness to nature, the production of food – are similar. A notable feature of Chinese gardens is the extent to which architecture is incorporated into the garden, with pavilions, covered walkways and so on. These may be used simply for shelter from sun or rain while enjoying the scent of flowers or the sound of rain on banana leaves, or as a study, living room or place to sleep; elevated buildings beside water were often used for coolness in the hot and humid summers of southern China. Another essential feature of Chinese gardens is the presence of rocks, often in fantastic shapes, and water, forming mountains and lakes or rivers in miniature. Plants, although important, do not enjoy the supremacy which they do in European gardens.

In the Chinese cosmological 'triad' of Heaven, Earth and Man, one can see the rocks and water as representing Heaven or the cosmos of *yin* and *yang*, the negative and positive principles, plants as representing the Earth from which they grow, and buildings as representing the presence of Mankind. Chinese gardens are often regarded as microcosms, incorporating all aspects of the universe in miniature. As such, they also incorporate the cycle of the four seasons and ideally should provide something to enjoy in every season, such as snow on the evergreen pine-tree in winter, or the scent of lotuses in the pond in summer.

Plants often have specific associations, not only the obvious seasonal ones such as evergreens with winter, prunus blossom with early spring, lotuses and peonies with summer, or the highly scented osmanthus with autumn, but also symbolizing particular moral qualities: bamboo for gentlemanly integrity, lotus for Buddhist enlightenment, the pine, bamboo and prunus as the 'three friends in winter' for endurance. The garden should suggest an expanse of space greater than its actual dimensions, for example by the use of separate but interconnecting 'space cells', or of 'borrowed views' from beyond the garden's boundaries. The use of allusive names for the garden's features, and the inclusion of calligraphic inscriptions, also link the individual garden to the whole cultural heritage of literature and art.

Origins

The origins of Chinese gardens go back to imperial hunting parks in the Zhou (1046–221 BC) and Han (206 BC–AD 220) dynasties, such as the Shanglin Park (*Shanglin yuan*) of Emperor Wu of Han (Han Wudi), celebrated by the poet Zhang Heng (78–139). This emperor, who was much obsessed by the search for immortality, had his park configured with a lake and three islands to represent the Islands of the Immortals in the Eastern Ocean, in the hope that real Daoist immortals would take up residence there and reveal the secrets of immortality to him. The inclusion of three symbolic islands in a pond became a standard feature of later gardens, not only in China, but also in Japan, Korea and Vietnam. The land-owning aristocratic families were soon imitating the imperial gardens on their own estates.

During the Period of Disunion following the collapse of the Han dynasty, many members of the upper classes turned to Buddhism, and used landscape and gardens as an aid to spiritual understanding, a tendency particularly associated with the poet Xie Lingyun (385–433). At about the same time, more modest ambitions

were embodied by the 'pastoral' poet Tao Qian (or Tao Yuanming, 365–427), who rejected an official career in favour of cultivating the land and growing chrysanthemums, becoming an iconic figure for later generations of garden-lovers, up to the present day.

The flourishing of aristocratic culture during the Tang dynasty (618–907) saw the creation of many splendid gardens, such as the Level Spring Garden (*Pingquan yuan*) of Li Deyu (787–850), although poets such as Du Fu (712–770) and Bai Juyi (772–846) also wrote about their more lowly garden dwellings. As the literati class (scholar-officials, mandarins) took over administrative power from the aristocracy during the Song dynasty (960–1279), the growing influence of literati culture meant that a more modest, elegant and restrained style of garden became the ideal, as described by the historian Sima Guang (1019–1086) in his *Record of the Garden of Pleasure in Solitude*. Elaborate gardens came to be seen as decadent, and the collapse of the Northern Song empire was even attributed to the emperor Huizong's extravagant garden construction. The 11th-century writer Li Gefei explicitly linked the rise and fall of dynasties to the

Parts of the Yi pu *(Garden of Cultivation), Suzhou, may date back to a 16th-/17th-century garden on this site belonging to one of the leading local gentry families.*

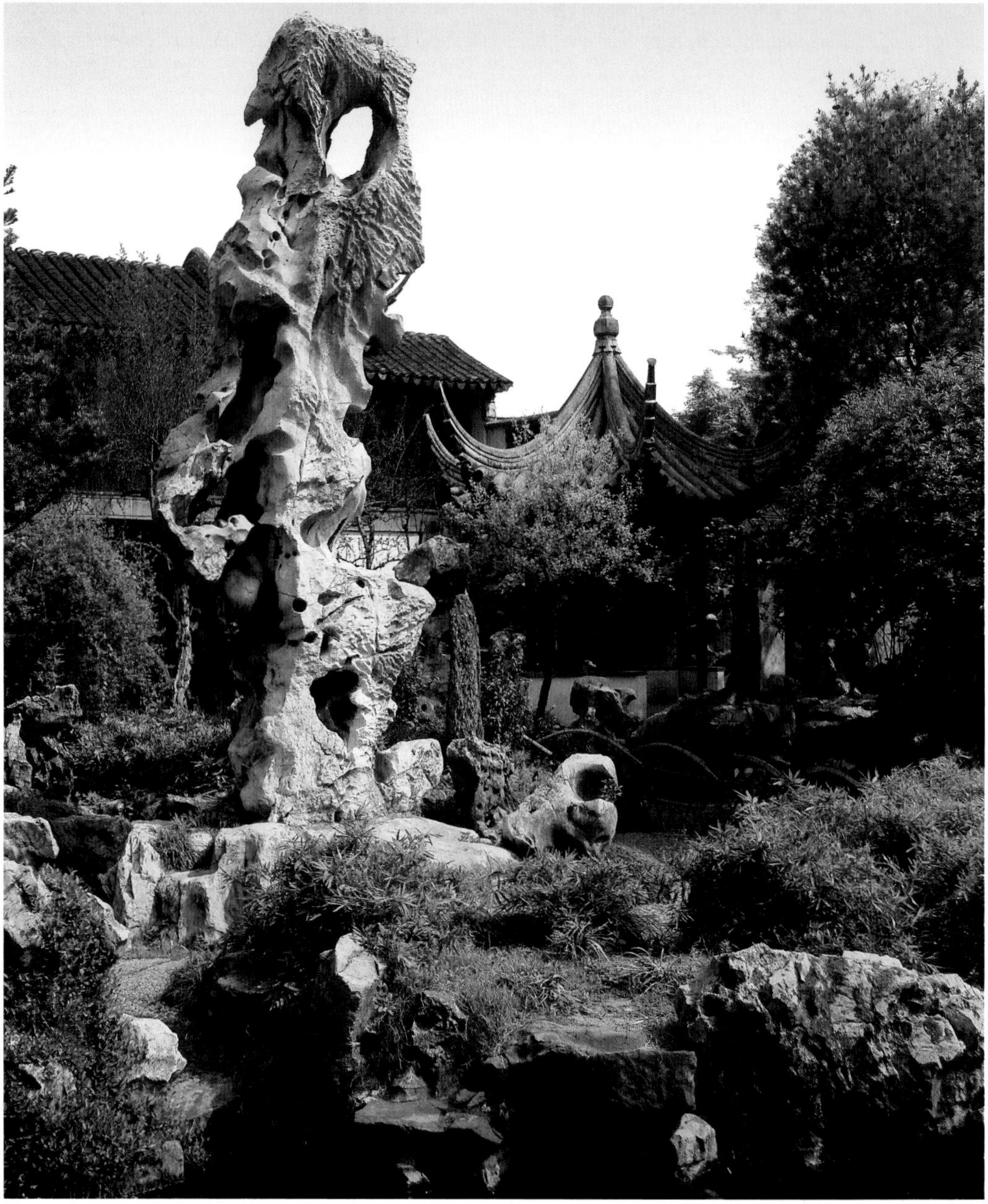

Liu yuan *(Garden for Lingering) in Suzhou, on the site of a garden built by a wealthy scholar-official in the Ming dynasty. Today it is regarded as one of the four most famous gardens in China. The rock called the Cloud-Capped Peak, in the foreground, was originally shipped from Lake Tai, 40 km (25 miles) away.*

splendour and decline of gardens in his well-known *Record of the Celebrated Gardens of Luoyang*.

Culmination

The Ming dynasty can be seen as the period when the literati garden developed to its most classical expression in Jiangnan, the wealthy Yangtze River delta area, with its high concentration of scholar-official families; the ideals of this garden style were of elegant simplicity and cultural sophistication. A flourishing print culture spread descriptions and images of gardens throughout China and abroad (particularly to Japan). It is likely that this led to a greater unity of style among gardens in different parts of China, despite their diversity of climate, flora and vernacular architecture. The Jiangnan garden style became a standard to aspire to, although regional variations still persisted, as did the more elaborate style of the aristocratic and imperial gardens.

As the economy expanded, the increasingly wealthy merchant class created gardens as a way to demonstrate their participation in elite culture. The traditional elite fought to maintain their special status by setting up ever more exacting standards of 'elegance' and 'taste'. This contest was reflected in the growth of 'connoisseurship literature' in the form of manuals either setting impossibly high standards of elegance in gardens, household furnishings and works of art (such as Wen Zhenheng's *Treatise on Superfluous Things*, *c*. 1615–20), or outlining how those less sure of their own taste might achieve an elite lifestyle (of which Ji Cheng's *The Craft of Gardens*, *c*. 1635, is most probably an example).

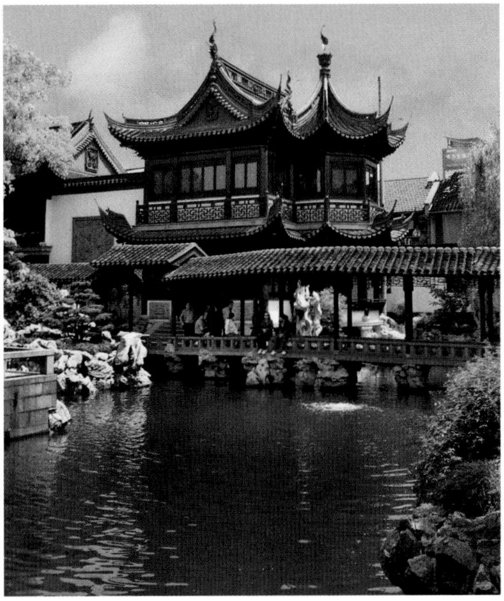

View of the Yu yuan *(Pleasing Garden), located in Shanghai old town. Originally begun in 1559, it covers an area of 20,000 sq. m (215,300 sq. ft) and now consists of an inner and outer garden.*

Hybridization

The Ming garden style or styles persisted into the beginning of the Qing dynasty (1644–1911). But the remarkable prosperity of the 18th century led to ever greater elaboration, and by the late 19th century gardens were often crammed full of ornate buildings, extravagant rockeries and showy vegetation, and had lost the practical function of providing some foodstuffs for the household. The distinction between imperial or aristocratic and literati garden styles had largely broken down, particularly as a result of the Qianlong emperor's enthusiasm for the gardens of Jiangnan, which he had reproduced in his own gardens in and around the capital and in the imperial summer retreat at Jehol (Chengde). The Qianlong emperor also wished to indicate the extent of his power by incorporating European-style architecture and artistic techniques into his surroundings, particularly in the 'Western buildings' (*Xiyang lou*) section of the Summer Palace (the *Yuanming yuan*), designed by Jesuit missionaries at the imperial court. The glowing accounts which some of the missionaries gave of the imperial gardens, and the engravings which they sent back to Europe, helped to give rise to the development of the naturalistic 'English' landscape style, replacing the geometrically designed gardens which had dominated Europe since the Renaissance. During the 19th century, particularly in south China, growing Western influence led to the adoption of European features into the vernacular style of architecture and gardens, resulting in a distinctive Cantonese garden style; European features can also be seen in the late 19th-century merchant gardens of Yangzhou in the Yangtze delta.

Today, many old imperial and private gardens have been restored and opened to the public, and elements of traditional garden style are still used in modern parks, but the social conditions in which the Chinese garden tradition developed have gone for ever.

An engraving by the Jesuit Matteo Ripa in 1713 showing the Imperial Gardens at Jehol (Chengde), the summer retreat of the Qianlong emperor.

Inventions & Achievements

In their time, China's inventions and inventiveness put the country far ahead of the rest of the world in a wide variety of domains. Some date far back into history. Together they contained a corpus of knowledge which probably outdid the achievements of any other civilization. One of the great questions of Chinese history is why such a nation found itself overtaken by the West in the 19th century.

Some inventions bolstered the empire, not just gunpowder in times of war (pp. 268–271), but also the pursuit of astrology to find heavenly confirmation that a dynasty enjoyed divine favour. The full range of science (p. 247) was in place by AD 100, centred in imperial offices and including mathematical calculation as well as astronomy (p. 250), which was seen as particularly important to produce accurate calendars.

The decimal system (p. 259) produced an easily grasped relationship between numbers that facilitated calculations. Alchemy was pursued to try to cultivate the self into eternal life. *Feng shui* sought to track the *qi* – the energy essential – to find the best places to build houses, or locate imperial tombs like those of the Ming. From this sprang the development of compasses (p. 261), which were being used with a needle pointer by the 4th century AD.

Other inventions were closer to everyday life (p. 272). From wheelbarrows to chopsticks and fishing reels, China led the way. It produced the first umbrellas around the 4th century AD, followed by matches and playing cards. Tea (p. 275) originated some 3,000 years ago in the western

Astronomy: A 15th-century copy of an armillary sphere (a copy of one produced c. 1280) at the Purple Mountain Observatory, Nanjing. Pivoting circles and a sight tube relied on the naked eye to read positions of any celestial body.

basin of Sichuan province, and would become China's major export in the 18th and 19th centuries, establishing a link with Europe that was to lead to foreign invasions as the British pressed opium on China from its Indian empire to help balance the tea trade deficit.

The origins of Chinese medicine (p. 256) lie before the beginning of imperial history in 221 BC, drawing on man's relations with the heavens, weather and seasons. Its practice has developed over the subsequent millennia to produce a body of knowledge which is being increasingly adopted by other parts of the world, from acupuncture to the use of plant roots.

Classical Chinese bridges (p. 264) were things of beauty and advanced engineering achievements, developed on empirical lines using varied materials. They pre-dated such constructions elsewhere in the world, forming an integral element in the rural and urban landscape to provide what the historian of China's science, Joseph Needham, has called 'a subtle combination of the rational with the romantic'.

One key invention was paper (p. 253), attributed to a eunuch around AD 100, who refined earlier procedures by using fibres derived from hemp, tree bark, rags and nets. It enabled the emperors to set down their decrees and dispatch them from the Forbidden City throughout their domains, and also encouraged calligraphy. Thin and durable, Chinese paper was used for other purposes than writing – as window covering or in the manufacture of three other Chinese inventions: lanterns, umbrellas and kites.

Paper led naturally to printing (p. 253), which was probably developed in China eight centuries before it emerged in the West. The earliest woodblock-printed relics which have been discovered, mainly in the form of Buddhist texts, date from the 7th century AD. In the Tang dynasty (AD 618–907) printed paper money appeared. Movable type followed at the start of the 2nd millennium, but the range of Chinese characters meant that the old woodblock form continued in wide use as being more convenient.

That, in its way, was symptomatic of why China did not capitalize on all its inventions to establish a technological advance in the modern era, and had to borrow from the West. Its inventions, great and useful though they were, served the purposes of an imperial society which simply wanted to go on as it had for centuries. Achievements were not linked to advances to produce a platform for further progress. Learning was highly prized, but there was little spirit of rational inquiry, or thirst for change as in the Western Enlightenment. Great achievements remained as monuments of China's past, rather than opening a door to the future.

Late 18th-century woodblock print showing Wan-nian Qiao Bridge, Suzhou.

NATHAN SIVIN

Science

57

Many historians of ideas and culture still blandly assume that the Asian civilisations 'had nothing that we should call science'. . . . My own experience has shown that it is comparatively easy to produce a whole series of bulky volumes about the scientific and technological achievements which the Chinese are supposed not to have had.

JOSEPH NEEDHAM, 1969

Modern science depends for its power on rigorous experimentation or observation using logical deduction and, usually, mathematics. Before modern times, no civilization depended on systematic experiment or quantification for its knowledge of Nature. To understand the evolution of science, therefore, we have to define its early forms simply and loosely: observation ordered by abstract concepts seeking (without necessarily finding) objective patterns. Religion could account for the things and processes in the universe in ways that satisfied most people. New explanations that did not depend on the wills of divine beings made science autonomous.

Ancient peoples generally noticed that in the world outside human society every individual being or thing is changing, quickly or slowly, but Nature as a whole remains the same. What is responsible for this constancy within unending mutation? Before 200 BC, the Chinese evolved two strategies for answering this question.

First, everything in the physical world, even human consciousness, is composed of a substance called *qi*. It holds within itself the energy that makes transformation and even life possible. It can take solid, liquid, or intangible form. Thus the diversity of the world was simply a matter of varying states of a single stuff. The ancient Greeks used a similar strategy, but their universal matter was dead, and change took place only when form animated it.

Second, Chinese understood natural change on the model of the life cycle, in which things come into being, grow, reach maturity, decline and die. This model applied not only to living things, but to the earth itself, which nurtures them. East Asians thus came to explain most changes as processes, usually cyclic. Each thing and phenomenon had a characteristic *Dao* (literally 'way'), its natural mode of action in the world. What Europeans called Nature, the Chinese from the 3rd century BC onwards saw as the sum of these ways, which they also called *Dao*. The way of the cosmos was integral with the ways of society and the state – which, if they were sound, remained in harmony with it.

Speculations about and observations of Nature appear in writings from about the 8th century BC. A little after 250 BC, philosophers began to make substantial statements about the natural world. From 200 BC onwards, as practitioners and teachers emerged for individual fields, they wrote books devoted to mathematics, astrology and medicine. Scholars began using *yin-yang* and other concepts to analyze every kind of phenomenon.

The full panoply of sciences was in place by about AD 100. Practitioners of each continued to seek deeper and broader understanding and the ability to solve problems until modern science replaced their traditions in the curricula of 20th-century schools.

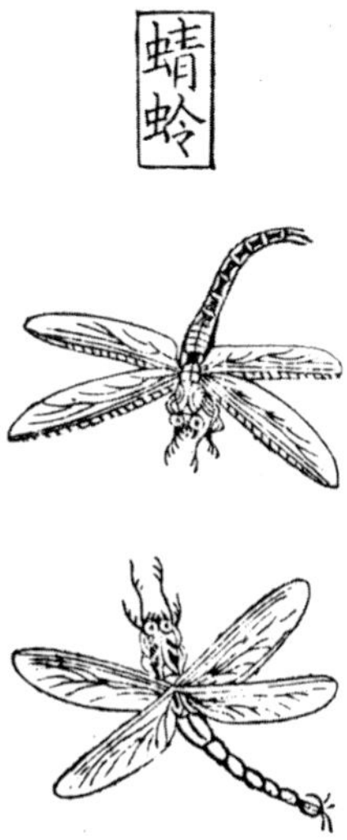

A dragonfly as depicted in a book on drug ingredients printed in 1249. Such books included animal and mineral substances as well as plants, carefully portrayed to aid the choice of authentic materials. Dragonflies were dried and used in a variety of medicines. From a modern photo-reproduction.

The quantitative sciences

The quantitative sciences included not only mathematics but mathematical astronomy and harmonics. Mathematics textbooks took the form of practical problems with solutions, related to tasks of government and commerce. In general, the Chinese chose numerical approaches to problem-solving, in contrast to the Greek and medieval European preference for geometry, but from the 11th century they began developing trigonometrical methods. Chinese mathematicians had the advantage of a decimal system (p. 259) and the ability to deal with very large and very small numbers.

Astronomy from about 100 BC was centred in palace bureaux. Because of the generous support for it and the pressure for more exact calendars, it evolved the most sophisticated applications of mathematics (p. 250). The early discovery that the lengths of pipes and strings were related musically – for instance, one string twice as long as another produces a tone an octave lower – led to the systematic study of mathematical harmonics.

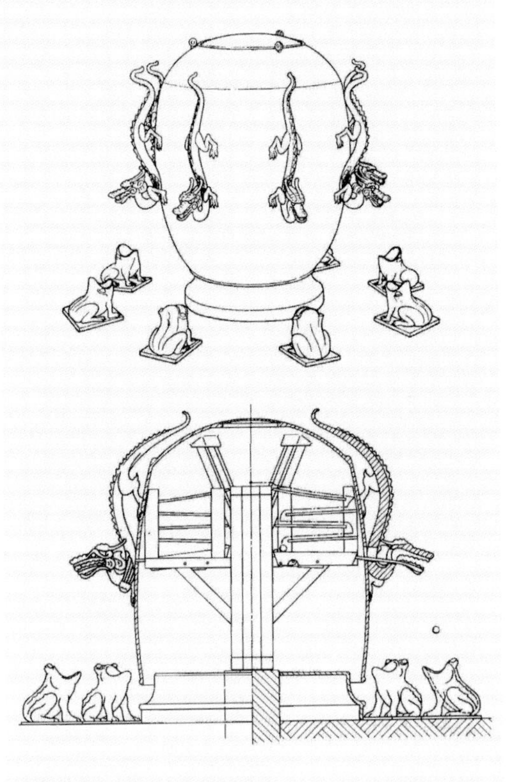

Right *Reconstruction (exterior and interior views) of the world's earliest seismoscope, invented in AD 132 by the scientific polymath Zhang Heng. A tremor too faint to feel rocked a pendulum resting on a slightly rounded, tuned base, releasing one of eight balls that would roll down a track and trigger one of the dragons to drop a ball from its mouth. The toad that caught it signalled the direction of the tremor.*

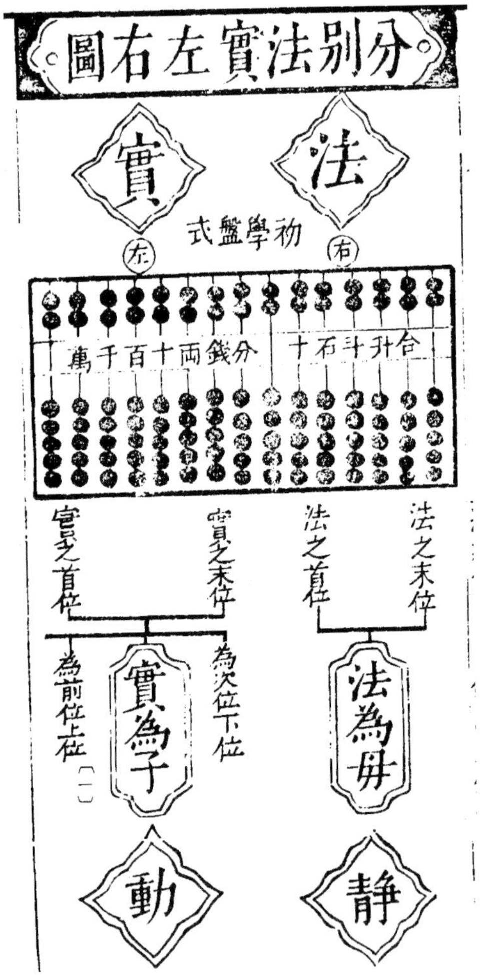

Right *Instructions for recording on an abacus numbers to be divided, from a textbook of 1592.*

The qualitative sciences

Other sciences remained qualitative, but sometimes made use of quantitative relations.

Astrology complemented mathematical astronomy; its practitioners belonged to the same bureaucratic organizations. Celestial events that could not be computed in advance were omens, a warning from heaven of shortcomings in the palace. The astrologers were responsible for observing, recording and reporting omens, using records of previous phenomena to interpret their meaning. The rich data from such archives have been useful to modern scientists reconstructing the sky's past. Chinese researchers have also compiled early records of catastrophic events on earth, leading to by far the most detailed earthquake history anywhere.

Alchemy had useful consequences. Its aim was cultivation of the self to produce eternal life. People everywhere used to believe that metals and minerals slowly grew to perfection in the womb of the earth. For Chinese these processes had two endpoints: gold and cinnabar (blood-red crystals of mercury sulphide). Some alchemists carried out carefully controlled chemical processes with these endpoints. They modelled the attainment of perfection; contemplating these processes made them immortals. Some techniques produced substances that could cure others of diseases, or even of mortality. Alchemical writings preserve much early knowledge of chemical reactions, even quantitative data.

Medicine is not a science, but drew on science. Chinese medicine incorporated systematic knowledge of the human body, normal and abnormal, and of resources for curing illness from dietary regulation to controlled exercise, drugs and techniques for adjusting the circulation of *qi* (p. 256).

Other sciences of pre-modern China were unique. Siting (often called *feng shui*) used knowledge of the circulation of *qi* through the earth – analogous to the human body's circulation system – to find the best places to build houses, public buildings and tombs. Practitioners sought locations with a dynamic balance of high and low places, dry and wet places, and so on. A second characteristically Chinese science was physical studies, diverse genres of reasoning that used *yin-yang* and other technical concepts to cast light on natural processes.

These and other indigenous sciences were rejected by the modern educational systems that replaced traditional learning in the 20th century. Traditional medicine still preserves much ancient knowledge in a quickly changing amalgam with massive borrowings from biomedicine. Today's Chinese scientists wield the same tools as those elsewhere.

A doctor takes the pulse of a female patient in this 19th-century watercolour by Zhou Peiqun.

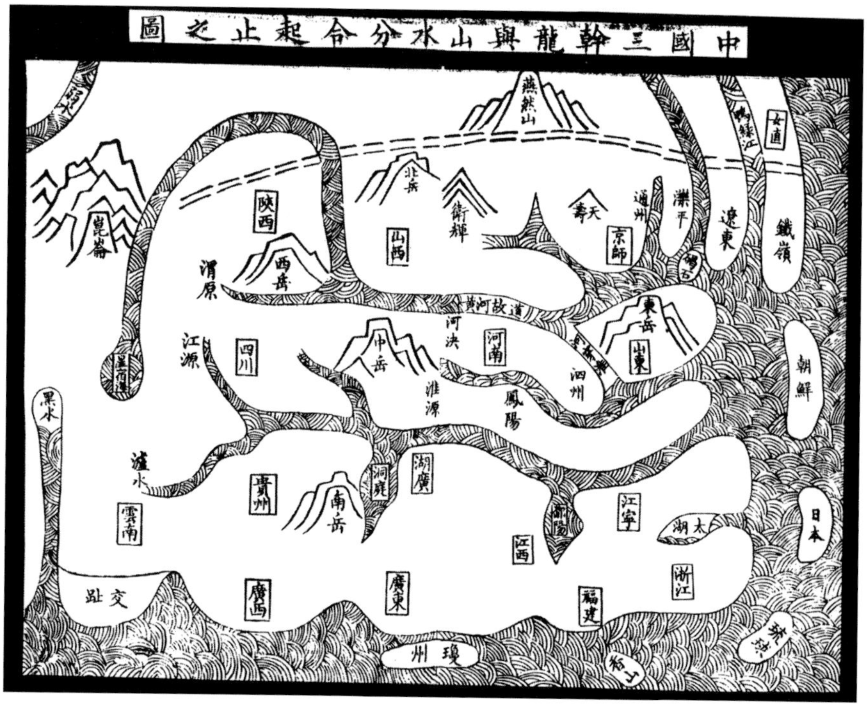

Below left *A diagram of the alchemical process, with cosmic forces focused on the alchemist and the perfected elixir issuing downward from his work.*

Below *Abstract diagram from a general treatise on siting* (feng shui)*, showing China with its balance of water and mountains and flow of* qi *throughout.*

NATHAN SIVIN

58 Astronomy

The Way of Heaven is so subtle, precise measurement so difficult, computational methods so varying in approach, and chronological schemas so lacking in unanimity, that we can never be sure a technique is correct until it has been confirmed in practice.

ANONYMOUS MEMORIAL TO THE THRONE, *C.* AD 179

Cosmology was not a central topic in China. In order to predict celestial phenomena accurately, astronomers there, as in Europe, found the assumption that other bodies revolve round the earth entirely satisfactory. It was not until well after Copernicus (1543) turned the universe inside out for technical reasons that a moving earth became common sense – but modern relativity theory rejected all ideas of a fixed centre.

In China mathematical astronomy *(li* or *lifa,* computing celestial phenomena in advance) and astrology *(tianwen,* observing, recording and interpreting unpredictable phenomena) were complementary.

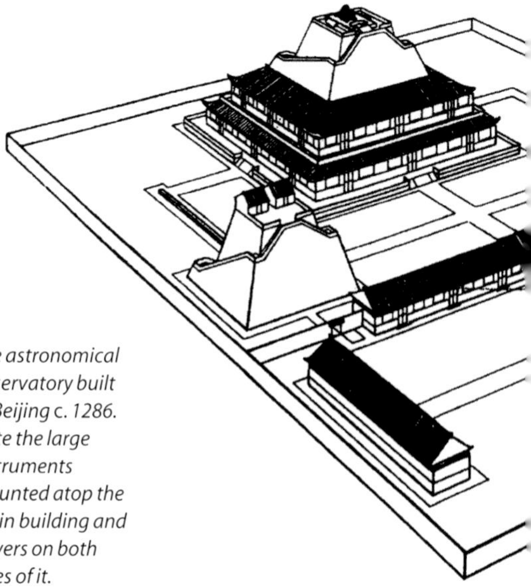

The astronomical observatory built at Beijing c. 1286. Note the large instruments mounted atop the main building and towers on both sides of it.

The literate peoples of antiquity were always attentive to the heavens. Unlike the ever-changing, chaotic phenomena on earth, those in the sky, eternal and regular, seemed the natural abode of the divine. From about 1200 to 1050 BC, among the records of oracles in the royal court, observations of celestial events survive. They can seldom be dated, but from about 720 BC the dates of observations in historic writings are mostly reliable. From AD 434 they include the time of day. In all of the sources, solar eclipses are the most prominent omens.

Guo Shoujing (1231–1316), a peerless astronomer, designer of observational instruments and clocks, and a hydraulic engineer. Chinese postage stamp of 1962.

Bureaucratic character

Astronomy was mostly carried out in state organizations. Imperial governments from the 3rd century BC on claimed that heaven designated the imperial family to rule. Each emperor, by his virtue and the rituals he performed – among them, the granting of an annual calendar – kept the state and the social order in harmony with the natural order. According to this ideology, the ability to predict events in the sky demonstrated his success, and unpredictable ones warned that his governance was flawed. To maximize the accuracy of predictions, dynasties maintained large astronomical bureaux to improve calculations, report all ominous events, and interpret their meaning. It was not exceptional for a bureau to employ more than 100 officials. The government sometimes discouraged private practice, but outsiders occasionally contributed fresh ideas or techniques.

Mathematical astronomy

The product of the astronomers' work was an astronomical system (also called *li*), a sequence of step-by-step instructions for calculating a complete annual calendar (or almanac). They designed it for use by lowly officials with modest mathematical abilities. Unlike modern calendars, those of pre-modern China were based on celestial phenomena. The month began at the new moon. The new year was defined with respect to the winter solstice. The day began at midnight, halfway between two moments at which the sun reached its highest daily point in the sky. Early calendars also included the dates (and later ones the times) of solar and lunar eclipses and certain planetary phenomena. The astrologers also computed what dates were propitious for activities from starting a trip to planting crops.

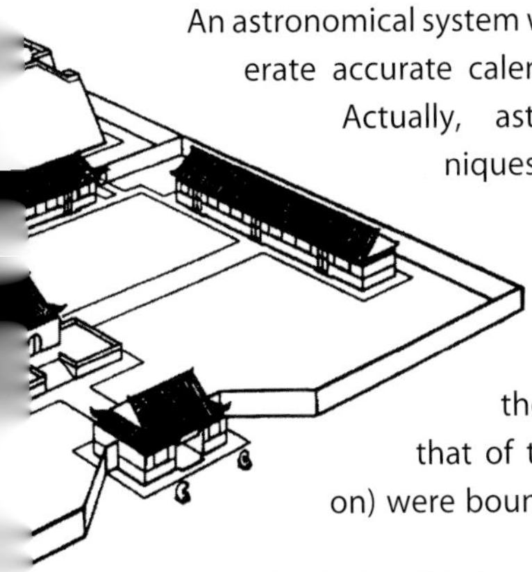

An astronomical system was meant to generate accurate calendars indefinitely. Actually, astronomers' techniques and constants (for the interval between two months, the angle between the sun's path and that of the moon, and so on) were bound to be limited in accuracy. The discrepancies might be unnoticeable for a few years, but eventually they added up to produce noticeably flawed predictions.

Above *A map of stars in the northern hemisphere (1453), from the Longfu Temple, Beijing, restoration.*

If someone knew how to adjust the constants and techniques, the system might again run satisfactorily, but eventually problems would recur. As a result of expert assessment or palace intrigue, or because a new dynasty demanded new rituals, a full revision would be ordered. It was customary not merely to revise parts of the system, but to create a complete new one.

It also happened that a commoner might submit a markedly superior system that, after testing, replaced the official one, its author receiving an official appointment. Historians have details of about 100 systems, roughly 50 of which were official. Though this is an average of about 40 years each, most systems lasted a much shorter time. A few survived much longer; for instance, there were only three (the second a variation on the first) between 1280 and 1911. Since 1911 China has used the Gregorian calendar.

Left *One set of sights and scales from a large bronze instrument, used for measuring the positions of heavenly bodies. (c. 1446 copy of an original made c. 1280.)*

Made of gilt bronze, this fine miniature armillary sphere of 1746 was made to be admired rather than used for astronomical observation. (Height 72 cm / 28 in.)

Advisory astrology

Astrology provided important services to the court, rather like those of economic advisory panels to modern governments. Panelists do not lose their jobs, or even their memberships, if their forecasts turn out to be inaccurate. Their value lies in introducing topics for political figures to discuss that they might otherwise have ignored. The interpretations of astrologers began, rather than ended, discussions.

Astrology has turned out to be equally valuable to modern scientists because of its careful observation and punctilious recording. Rich archives gathered over the 2,000 years of imperial China have enabled modern scientists to determine when supernovas appeared (and their relations to present sources of X-rays in space), how the number of sunspots varied with time, how the periods of comets have changed, and many other important findings.

Instruments

At its best, palace astronomy was a highly expensive activity. Before the invention of the astronomical telescope in the West at the beginning of the 17th century, all observation depended on the naked eye. It was possible to attain considerable precision using massive bronze instruments. An armillary sphere used several pivoting circles (for the celestial equator, the sun's path, and so on), carefully graduated and provided with a sighting tube, to read positions of any celestial body. One cast *c.* 1437, a copy of one produced *c.* 1280, survives at the Purple Mountain Observatory, Nanjing (see picture on p. 245). It could originally read locations to about 1/20 degree. Preparing the new astronomical system of 1280 required the design of about a dozen different instruments for a new observatory, and four portable ones for use in an empire-wide observational survey carried out by teams of astronomers.

The result of fairly steady activity over many centuries was growth in the precision of observations and the accuracy of forecasts. The Chinese tradition was comparable in both respects to those of the other great ancient civilizations – in chronological order of their best work, the ancient Middle East, Greece, India, the Islamic world, and Europe before 1600, when astronomers began using the telescope. Their strengths and weaknesses varied considerably; but one must explore them all in order to understand astronomy as a world effort and to trace the influences that flowed together in the Islamic world, eventually enabling the rise of modern astronomy in Europe.

NANCY NORTON TOMASKO

Paper & Printing

59

Respectfully treasuring paper bearing words is merit without measure.
DECORATIVE PRINTED LABEL ON THE COVER OF A 19TH-CENTURY PAMPHLET

Papermaking and printing are two of the four great inventions long identified as indigenous to China; gunpowder and the compass round out the quartet of world firsts. To date, archaeological finds unquestionably support China's claim to the invention of true paper. The evidence with respect to printing is more complicated. Rival claims to the invention of printing in Japan and Korea often muddy discussion of this crowning glory of the intertwined cultures of East Asia.

Before paper, the world's civilizations left their pictorial images and written scripts on many different kinds of surfaces – the landscape, cliffs and cave walls, stone slabs, bone, clay, metal vessels, hides, tree bark, papyrus, wax, silk, and wooden or bamboo strips. These records are evidence of mankind's ingenuity in seeking out media on which to make its marks. They are, however, to varying degrees clumsy to handle.

Archaeological finds continue to yield up evidence that paper was used in continental East Asia as early as the 3rd century BC. Its subsequent development forever changed record-keeping, writing and pictorial art, opening them up to a new world of flexibility, portability and artistic culture. Chinese historical records credit Cai Lun, a eunuch in charge of manufacture in the court of Emperor He of the Han dynasty, with the discovery of paper in AD 105. Cai Lun refined rudimentary papermaking processes, probably in response to the need at court for a practical writing medium. He made papers using cellulose fibres derived from hemp, the inner bark of trees, rags and old nets.

Production of paper spread throughout China wherever there was a supply of suitable raw plant material. Cotton-boll fibre and fibres from old rags, prominently used in papermaking that developed centuries later in the West, were prized in China for the manufacture of clothing and never became a significant component of Chinese paper. Chinese artisans made papers out of four main kinds of fibres: bast fibres – the strong inner bark fibres of plants and small trees (such as hemp, mulberry, paper mulberry, mitsumata and wingceltis); grass fibres (such as rice straw, reed and alpine rush); rattan; and bamboo, a widely available resource first used for paper in the 4th century AD.

Age-old papermaking equipment and techniques, illustrated in the 17th-century work on technology by Song Yingxing (b. 1587), *Tiangong kaiwu* ('Products Made from Heaven's Creations'), are mirrored by Chinese hand papermaking processes still in use in the 21st century.

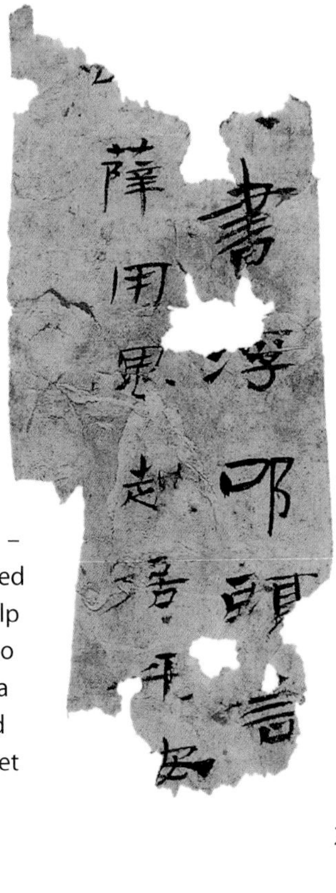

The archaeologist Aurel Stein found this fragment of paper in the Gobi desert. It is dated to the 2nd century AD.

How is traditional Chinese paper made?

True paper is macerated cellulose fibres suspended in water and formed on a porous screen into sheets of matted fibres. Plant fibres are crushed, retted (soaked in water), and cooked in an alkaline solution to break down adhesives. Cooked fibres are rinsed and sun bleached. They are pulverized and mixed in water with formation aid – *zhiyao* – a gelatinous material extracted from plants such as willow branches. Pulp is scooped onto a screen of fine bamboo splints and sloshed around to form a thin layer of wet paper. This is drained and couched onto a 'post' (i.e. pile) of wet

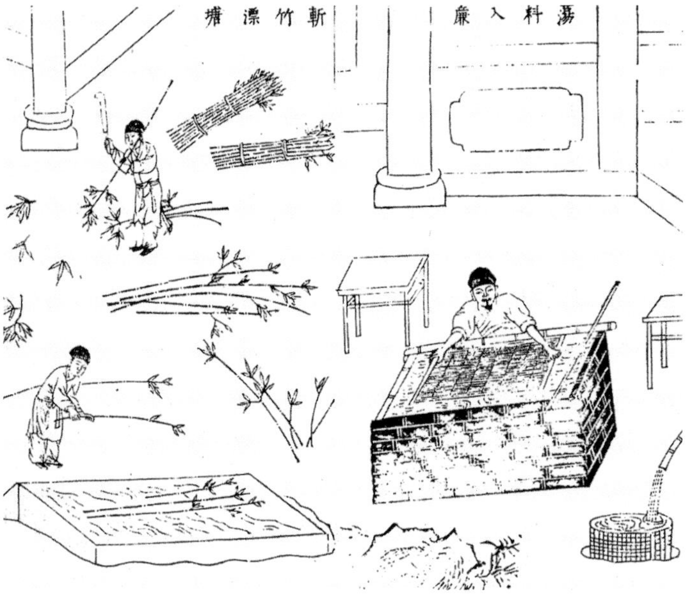

Papermaking in progress: workers cut and soak bamboo and form sheets of paper from bamboo pulp. Ming-dynasty woodcut.

sheets of paper, which is then compressed slowly to remove excess water. Individual sheets of damp paper are peeled off and brushed onto a flat, sometimes heated, drying wall. Dried sheets are trimmed and folded into bolts for storage.

Traditional Chinese paper is large, up to 503 cm wide by 190 cm high (198 x 75 in.), and a sheet commonly used for calligraphy is 138 by 69 cm (54 x 27 in.). Some papers are waterleaf (*sheng*), untreated and unsized. Others are processed (*shu*), made with additions such as alum, starch, calcium carbonate, or pigments mixed into the pulp during production; or given surface treatment such as dying, calendaring, waxing, or coating with alum, mica, paste wash or metallic flecks.

Chinese paper is very thin, lightweight, translucent and not easily damaged by folding, crushing or rolling. It is a malleable and durable material, traditionally put to many household uses – covering windows; making lanterns, kites and folding umbrellas; fabricating clothing (from spun paper strips); insulating; sealing jars; and wrapping foods.

This paper, remarkably responsive in the way it disperses and absorbs ink, made possible China's grand culture of painting (p. 212), calligraphy (p. 198) and printing. Paper, along with writing brushes, ink stones and ink, is treasured as a tool essential for the Chinese scholar's work. Su Yijian's (957–995) 10th-century compilation *Wenfang sipu* ('Four Treatises on the Scholar's Studio') devotes an entire chapter to historic details on the nature and uses of paper.

Printing in China

China's invention of paper led to its invention of printing, perhaps eight centuries before printing

A worker in Jiajiang, Sichuan province, dips the mould into a vat of pulp to form a sheet of paper.

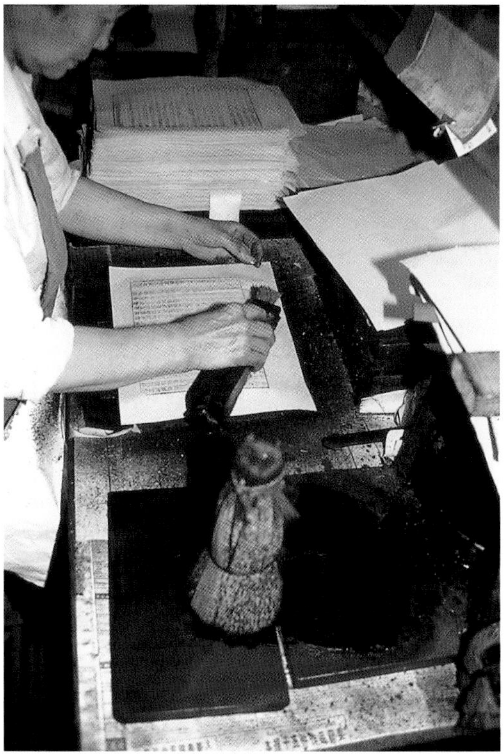

Printing book pages from wooden printing blocks, Nanjing.

was known in the West. Printing-related technologies – seal carving, stamping designs on fabric, wood carving, mould-making, metal casting, and production of ink and pigments – were practised long before they were applied to printing on paper.

Before printing, the only way to obtain a text was to copy it by hand. Discovered in 1900 in Dunhuang on the Silk Road (p. 43), perhaps the earliest extant book on paper is a scroll manuscript of the *Laozi* in the calligraphy hand of Suo Dan (*c.* 250 – *c.* 324) dated 270. However, the earliest relics printed on paper, almost all Buddhist texts, probably date to the 7th century. Future archaeological discoveries undoubtedly will reveal the existence of printed images and texts even older than those currently known.

How is woodblock printing done?

Chinese woodblock printing (xylography) is not mechanized and has changed little since its discovery. Text and images are carved in reverse and in relief on the smooth surface of a plank block of hard wood, such as pear or date wood. The block is placed face-up and inked with the same water-based ink as used for Chinese calligraphy. Paper is laid onto the inked block and rubbed with a baren (*pazi* or *malian*). Chinese paper is usually printed on one side only.

Printing blocks for an entire work can be stored, and the work printed again on demand. Blocks, easily repaired or modified, were often sold or exchanged with other printing houses. Multiple-colour woodblock printing crowned the high-tide of printing towards the end of the Ming dynasty (1368–1644).

Woodblock technology allows the combination of text and image on the same block for printing illustrated books, broadsides, religious devotional images, product labels and art prints. Late in the Tang dynasty (618–907), the Chinese were the first to print and use paper money as a convenient medium of merchant commodity exchange in place of metal coins.

Chinese printers experimented with movable-type printing, first with clay type invented by Bi Sheng (d. 1052) in the Northern Song around 1045. Wooden type was introduced in the Southern Song (1127–1279), and metal type in the Southern Song, Yuan (1279–1368) and Ming dynasties. The difficulty of producing, maintaining and sorting the huge number of type for a font of Chinese characters generally made movable-type printing more cumbersome than woodblock printing.

With the introduction of Western mechanized printing late in the 18th century and the gradual resolution of technological problems with movable type for Chinese characters, woodblock printing faded in importance, though it was still frequently used for printing until the middle of the 20th century.

Today, Chinese artists, designers, print makers, and specialty printing houses show renewed interest in traditional Chinese handmade paper and woodblock printing. And China's modern printing industry is again leading the world with its utilization of new technologies in publishing.

A printed note from the Ming dynasty worth 'one string of cash'.

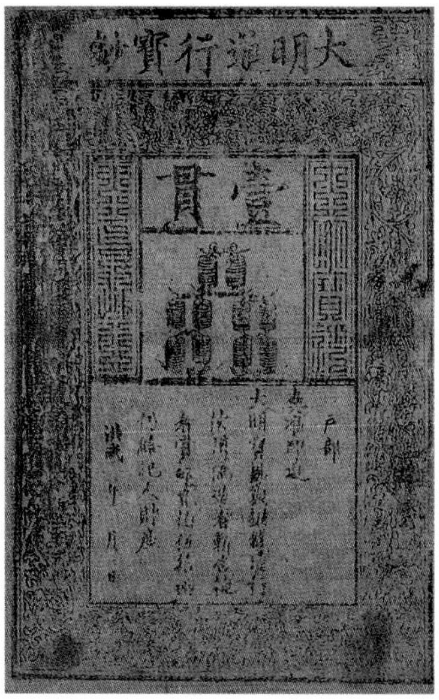

VIVIENNE LO

60 Medicine

Chinese medicine is a great treasure house!
MAO ZEDONG, 1958

From the first medical treatises to the 10,000 extant pre-Communist (to 1949) medical works listed in the 1991 National Chinese Medicine Union Catalogue, we can trace a rich and diverse medical culture in China. From well before the beginning of imperial history (221 BC), there are naturalistic theories of health and disease based upon ideas about man's relationship with the heavens and earth, the weather, and the passing of the seasons. Equally, for most of the past 2,000 years, Chinese scholarly medical traditions have regarded the human body as vulnerable to interference by ancestors, demons and spirits.

Early medicine

Before the 2nd or 3rd centuries, medical works were generally not attributed to individual authors. Our earliest writings on illness are Shang-dynasty (*c.* 1600 – *c.* 1046 BC) inscriptions on cow scapulae, and are a diviners' record of the king's illnesses, determining which spirit ancestor was to be propitiated for a cure. The first complete medical treatises were set down in the late Warring States period (*c.* 476–221 BC) and some survive as mortuary texts excavated from 2nd-century BC tombs.

Much of the central work that describes the classical medical principles of *yin-yang* and the

A Chinese medicine store, 1830s.

wuxing ('five agents' of wood, fire, earth, metal, water) is in the Yellow Emperor corpus, three compilations first assembled in the centuries around the turn of the millennia, and arranged in the form of a dialogue between the Yellow Emperor himself, represented as a patron of natural philosophy, and his ministers, often Qibo, a specialist in acupuncture and other esoteric matters, or Lei Gong the Thunder Duke. Responsible for punishments, law and the calendar, the emperor had a role in divination and dividing the seasons – and it is these skills that linked him with essential medical arts – a knowledge of the body's relationship with the cycles and phases of nature and the accurate prediction of the progress of disease.

It is in *The Yellow Emperor's Inner Canon* that we find the body divided into 12 distinct 'channels' through which *qi* (the all-pervasive stuff that powers the universe) was thought to move rhythmically around the body. The channels surfaced in the form of the pulse at places where ancient Chinese physicians could examine the condition of the body's *qi*, and the organs through which it flowed. A large number of pulse types were distinguished, such as floating, superficial, sunken and hesitant. This form of diagnosis became the pre-eminent method for elite physicians throughout imperial China and remains so today for modern practitioners of traditional Chinese medicine.

The Divine Farmer

A belief in the empirical spirit of Chinese medicine, that knowledge of the virtues of food and drugs comes through trial and error, is enshrined in the Han legend of the Red Emperor, also known as Shennong, the Divine Farmer, who is said to have led humanity out of a state of hunting and savagery, away from eating raw flesh, drinking blood and wearing skins, towards an agrarian utopia.

Stories about the Divine Farmer describe how he thrashed and tasted all plants so that they revealed their essential flavours and smells and so he could know their medical potencies; and how he classified the plants, separating which were fit for consumption and which fit for healing. Calling upon this tradition of empirical testing, his name was evoked in the title of a number of famous *materia medica,* beginning with the *Shennong bencao jing* ('Divine Farmer's *materia medica,*' *c.* 1st century AD). Drug and prescription literature went through a rapid expansion under imperial sponsorship in the Northern Song dynasty (960–1127). By the 16th century Li Shizhen's monumental *Bencao gangmu* ('Systematic *Materia Medica*') recorded 1,898 drugs and 11,096 prescriptions.

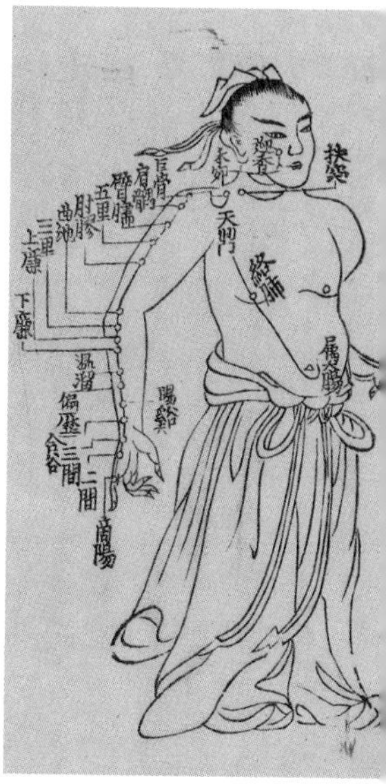

This 19th-century painting of a male figure is labelled with acupuncture points.

Chinese medicine as propaganda

In 1958 Chairman Mao's famous statement with which we open this entry ushered in a new era of national pride in the wonder that is Chinese medicine. This popular slogan encouraged biomedical doctors to value traditional Chinese medicine and to work towards uniting modern and ancient medicine for the greater benefit of mankind. But what did Mao really mean?

Mao's investment in traditional medicine was something of a paradox. Despite his suspicion of religion and folk belief, and a basic faith in the value of modern science, he encouraged traditional healers to support the Chinese Communist Party (CCP), especially during the Long March and the subsequent 'Yenan years', or 'Golden Age' of Communism (1935–1945). After all, there was very little of any kind of medicine available to serve the people at that time.

Mao also expressed a suspicion of the political sympathies of foreign-trained experts, including medical doctors. The Nationalists under Chiang Kai-shek had been keen supporters of modernizing

Ivory statuette of the Divine Farmer, his robe decorated with leaves from medicinal plants.

An early photograph of a street medical man attending to a patient's foot on a Beijing doorstep.

medicine. Mao's defence of indigenous healers was self-consciously patriotic. He initiated a series of successful campaigns to raise the status of traditional medicine. According to World Health Organisation estimates, traditional medicine in 2002 still accounted for about 40 per cent of Chinese health care, excluding the pervasive and enduring Chinese medical culture known as *yangsheng* ('nurturing life'), the sum of those everyday practices aimed at bodily cultivation such as nutrition, exercise, meditation and massage that constitute the preventative aspect of traditional Chinese healing arts.

Mao's eulogy of traditional medicine was probably meant to stimulate modern research and development of traditional medical skills. There was great pride in the international impact of some of the more radical procedures. It did not go unnoticed, for example, that one iconic image of China in the 1970s came from the TV coverage of a brain operation performed with the patient conscious and chatting under local acupuncture anaesthetic, anaesthesia being a relatively modern invention. Deep surgery is not a notable theory of pre-modern Chinese medicine. And if Mao was here today he would also have been impressed by the global distribution of the well-known traditional herb *qinghao* (*Artemisia annua*), reinvented as modern prophylactic and cure for malaria. Traditional medicine, in Mao's view, could be stripped of superstition and pseudoscience, and mined for those elements that would bear up to modern scientific scrutiny.

Modern medicine

In China today most medical practitioners have some training in biomedical and traditional medicine. Varying degrees of integration are evident institutionally in the delivery of health-care at hospitals, in diagnosis, explanatory models of disease, therapeutic paths and drug preparations. Some indigenous traditions, such as pharmacotherapy, acupuncture, moxibustion (technique in which the leaves of the herb mugwort are burned and placed over an inflamed or infected area on the body) and massage, are on offer in modern hospital and clinical settings, and even on emergency wards.

Other traditions are a living part of popular medical knowledge: elderly people gather in the parks to practise *taiji*, the slow, gentle martial art that moves *qi* and strengthens the spirit (p. 76). They pass on assumptions about dietary care and tonic medicines. Far from being subsumed under the high tide of a globally powerful biomedicine, the extremely lucrative trade in prepared Chinese medicines worldwide testifies to a two-way transfer of knowledge. With mass emigration and the globalization of a plurality of medical traditions, Chinese medicine now survives in many different forms, transforming as it comes into contact with different cultures around the world.

Right
Acupuncture is used as an anaesthesia for a patient undergoing a lung operation.

NATHAN SIVIN

The Decimal System & Abacus

61

Now the Season-Granting astronomical system's constants are uniformly based in the sky [that is, on observation]. Ten-thousandth to hundredth, hundredth ... to one day, all of these divisions take 100 as their increment. By comparison with ... other systems, the techniques of which are complicated, artificial, and based on forced reasoning, [the new system] has succeeded in becoming spontaneous.

LI QIAN, ON THE ASTRONOMICAL SYSTEM THAT EXPRESSED ALL NUMERICAL VALUES IN DECIMAL FORM, 1280

The decimal system has the great advantage of expressing numbers in a simple, consistent way, making it easy to understand their relationships. Is a piece of cloth 9 $^{3}/_{16}$ inches long shorter or longer than one $^{1}/_{4}$ yard long? Answering that question is more difficult than comparing 9.19 and 9.00 inches. But the system that permits such uncomplicated comparisons is not simple. It involves:

- a number of any size expressed using only the digits 0 to 9 or their equivalent;
- place value, that is, each digit in a number standing for a power of 10, positive or negative. Thus in the number 342.76, it is obvious that the 3 stands for hundreds (10^2) and the 6 stands for hundredths (10^{-2});
- the use of a symbol to separate positive and negative powers of ten – that is, the whole numbers and the fractional parts.

This system did not exist until the late 16th century. China played an important part in its prehistory.

The Greeks used all the letters of their alphabet to write numbers. The Romans used a few letters to stand for 1, 5, 10, 50, 100, 500, etc. The Chinese, in much older written records from *c.* 1450 BC, were much closer to a decimal system for whole numbers, with separate signs for the digits 1 to 9 and numbers 10, 100, and 10,000. They used other symbols for special purposes (for instance, counting days), but the digits and decimal numbers were standard for recording quantities.

By roughly 2,000 years ago, the Chinese had added a sign for 100,000, and could write much larger numbers by combining the signs they had. They wrote 'a billion' – a number Westerners did not use until early modern times – by putting together symbols for a hundred thousand and ten thousand. This natural move combined a number and a sign for a decimal place, just as 'five hundred' amounts to multiplying 5 and 100.

The Chinese grouped large numbers by fours instead of threes. Thus they wrote a trillion as not 1,000,000,000,000, but 1000,0000,0000 – ten-thousand ten-thousand ten thousands. Then '5,378,240,901' became simply '5 hundred-

Although this Chinese abacus is modern, its design has been used for centuries. The number represented on it is 7,230,189.

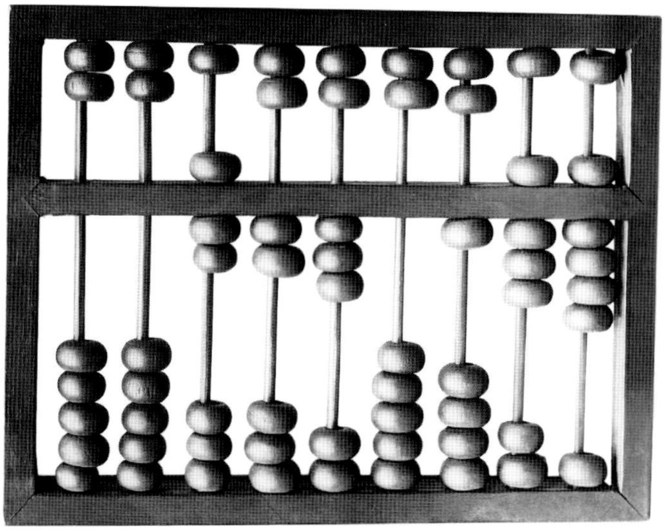

At a government Energy Research Institute in Xining, Qinghai province, a woman uses both an abacus and a calculator to do her sums.

thousands, 3 ten-thousands, 7 thousands, 8 hundreds, 2 tens, 4 ten-thousands, 9 hundreds, 1':

五十三萬七千八百二十四萬九百一

In everyday measuring, details of notation varied, but mathematicians and astronomers (who did the most elaborate mathematics) were on the whole consistent.

The Chinese used a character meaning 'parts' to express numbers less than 1. They wrote $^{43}/_{49}$ as 'of 49 parts, 43'. Up to the 13th century, each of the many early astronomical systems (p. 250) used by the government to generate predictions had its own way of writing fractions. For one, the average interval between new moons was $29\,^{43}/_{81}$ days, for another, $29\,^{499}/_{940}$ days. Both are close approximations to the modern value, 29.53059 days. The high point of the tradition, the astronomical system of 1280, began using decimal fractions for every number. The length of the year was 3 hundreds, 6 tens, 5, 2 tenths, 4 hundredths, 2 thousandths, 5 ten-thousandths – that is, 365.2425 – the same length used for today's calendar:

三百六十五日又萬分之兩千四百二十五

This system, used only for recording, did not need a special symbol for zero. For calculations, mathematicians in China (as elsewhere) used simple computing devices. Through most of history, they depended on sets of little rods laid out in a grid, actual or imagined. They represented the numbers 1 to 5 by laying down that many rods vertically; or a horizontal rod stood for 5, and one with two vertical rods below it for 7. They set out the numbers 10 to 90 in the next square of the grid to the left. To avoid confusing it with the square that contained ones, they used horizontal rods for 1 to 4, a vertical one for 5, and so on. Alternating these arrangements, they arranged rods for hundreds like those for ones, those for thousands like those for tens, and so on.

When setting out the equivalent of 608, it was natural to leave the space for the tens empty. From the 7th century on, when recording computations, mathematicians put a dot in the empty spaces to avoid miscopying, and by the 13th century this sign became a zero-like circle. The zero originated earlier in India or Southeast Asia, and the Chinese move probably resulted from foreign influence.

Of the three characteristics of the decimal system, we can conclude that the Chinese used the equivalent of digits 1 to 9 in writing numbers (and eventually the equivalent of 0 as well). But they relied on words to identify different decimal places. Their number system, combined with those of India and the Muslim world and transmitted to Europe, eased the way towards the mature decimal system of the late 16th century.

Below right *The three numbers (reading downward) in the central column are an equation written as it would be laid out with computing rods. The rods represent the numbers 2, -5 (the diagonal slash makes the number negative) and 0. An ordinary character indicates that the last digit is the constant term. Since the whole always equals zero, the equation is $2x^2 - 5x + 0 = 0$. From a textbook, c. 1250.*

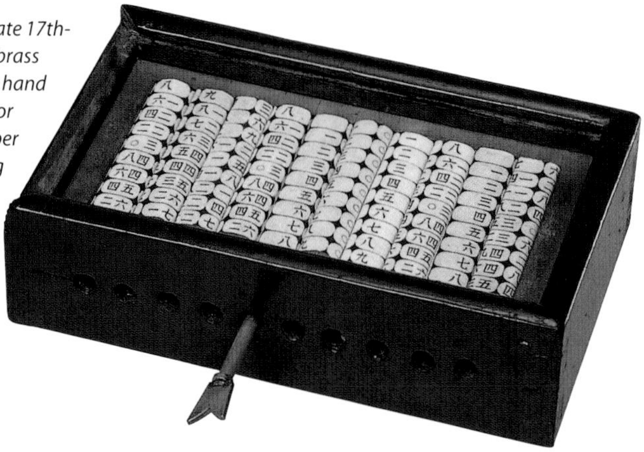

Right *Late 17th-century brass and iron hand calculator with paper counting rods.*

MATHIEU TORCK

The Compass, Navigation & Junks

62

The shipmasters know the configuration of the coasts; at night they steer by the stars and in the daytime by the sun. When the sun is observed they look at the south-pointing needle....

ZHU YU, SON OF A PORT OFFICIAL, WRITING ABOUT THE USE OF THE COMPASS ABOARD OCEANGOING JUNKS IN THE *PINGZHOU KETAN* ('PINGZHOU TABLE TALKS'), 12TH CENTURY

The history of the magnetic compass has its roots in the geomantic lore (prognostication) of ancient times. The pre-modern Chinese geomancy signified the art of *feng shui* ('winds and waters') in which the houses of the living and the tombs of the dead were positioned in harmony with the currents of the so-called 'cosmic breath' (*qi*). 'Winds and waters' not only refer to the physical phenomena but also to that invisible stream of energetic *qi,* thought to circulate in the veins and vessels of the macrocosm as we know it. Magnetism, the underlying principle of the compass, is believed to form part of this complex of ideas.

Early compasses

Already before the Han dynasty (206 BC – AD 220) books appeared in which references were made to the magnetism of certain stones, and by that time a device existed which may be considered the predecessor of the later compass. This diviner's board (*shi*) consisted of two superposed plates. The lower one was square-shaped, symbolized earth, and was engraved with the names of the 28 equatorial divisions or constellations and the 8 chief trigrams. The upper board was round, stood for heaven, and showed the 24 compass points, which would give rise to the later Chinese compass card. In the centre was drawn the Big Dipper (Great Bear), a stable northern constellation. Later on, the upper board appears to have been replaced by a spoon made of the magnetic lodestone. This tool was modelled after the Big Dipper and was placed in the centre whereby its handle indicated the direction.

Needle compasses

The transition from the use of a spoon to that of a needle probably must have happened somewhere around the 4th century AD. The first to make a description of a magnetic needle was the alchemist Ge Hong, and it is generally assumed that by the 9th century the compass had developed into its definitive form. Actual descriptions of the device appeared as early as the 11th century. In the work of the Song-dynasty

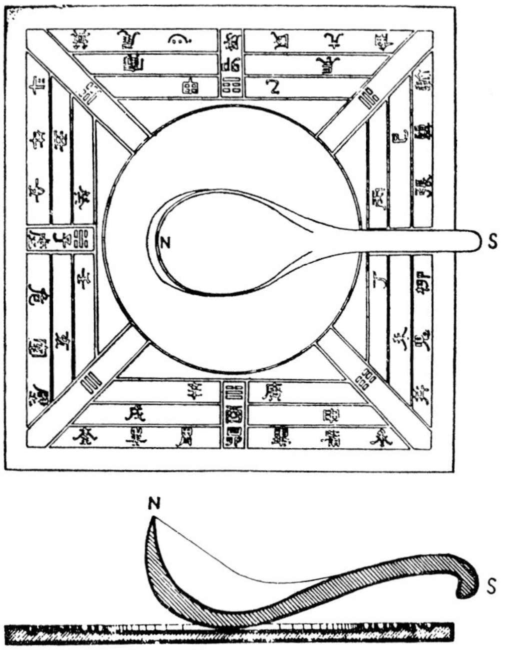

A reconstructional diagram made by Wang Zhenduo in 1948 of the predecessor of the compass, with earth-plate and lodestone spoon.

Far right
A coloured engraving of two different types of Chinese junk, in an early 19th-century book by Giulio Ferrario.

Right
Reconstruction by Wang Zhenduo (1950) of an early form of magnetic compass: the pointer is represented by a floating fish made of wood and filled with lodestone.

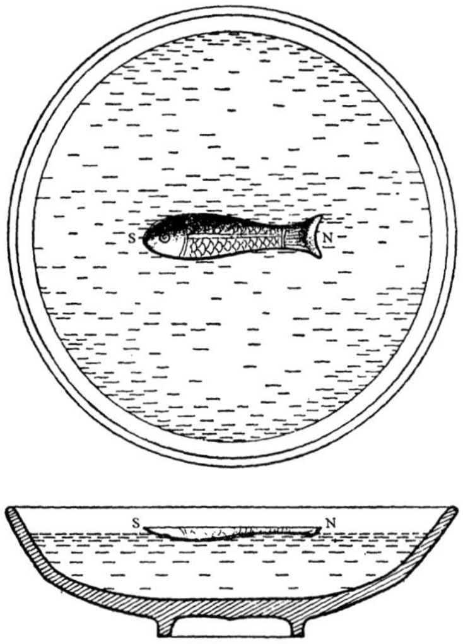

astronomer, engineer and high official Shen Gua, the earliest complete and clear description of the magnetic needle compass can be found. This is roughly 100 years before the first mentions of the compass in European and Arabic sources. Shen Gua's reference to north- and south-pointing needles reflects basic understanding of magnetic polarity.

In the Song dynasty (960–1279) several types of compasses existed. When weather circumstances hindered the use of the celestial bodies for orientation, armies used a basin of water in which a small wooden fish containing a filling of lodestone was set afloat. An attached needle fixed with wax thus indicated the southern direction. A similar 'dry' variant consisted of a little wooden turtle that, equipped with a needle, functioned as the indicator. This object was stuck on a pin which in itself rotated on a board. Later on a needle magnetized with lodestone simply replaced the fish and the turtle. In the wake of these evolutions the Chinese also became aware of the fact that the compass needle did not point to the geographical poles but to the magnetic poles, the so-called 'magnetic declination'.

The compass and the junk

The ultimate evolution of the magnetic compass was the application of the device aboard a ship. It was during the Song, a dynasty characterized by intensive maritime trading, that the son of a port official, Zhu Yu, in his work entitled *Pingzhou Ketan* ('Pingzhou Table Talks') from 1117, gave a detailed description of the use of the needle compass by Chinese mariners. Before this they had to rely on the celestial bodies, landmarks, winds, weather signs and characteristics of the sea; now they could sail in open seas without the danger of losing their way.

Close-up of the construction of a compass by traditional methods.

From the 11th century, Chinese sailors were thought to have possessed some form of cross-staff (an early form of the quadrant) with which the altitude of stars could be measured, important in reckoning position. Measuring latitudes posed few problems, and the same could be said for longitude. While in European seafaring the determination of the longitudinal position of a ship continued to be a major problem until the invention of an accurate timekeeper by John Harrison (1693–1776) in the 18th century, the Chinese managed to solve the problem long before this by means of burning incense sticks for measuring watches.

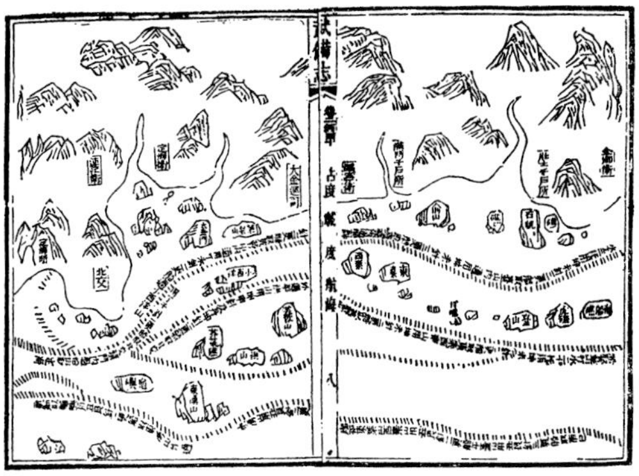

Zheng He's nautical charts as forming part of the military work Wubei zhi *(1628). This fragment shows landmarks of China's southeast coast. The dotted lines represent the sailing routes.*

The great expeditions

The heyday of Chinese oceangoing voyages took place between 1405 and 1433 when the Ming emperors Yongle (r. 1403–1424) and Xuande (r. 1426–1435) launched a total of seven gigantic expeditions of diplomacy. These involved a stunning 27,000 crew and hundreds of ships to all major places around the eastern and western Indian Ocean, stretching as far as the East African shores. During these impressive voyages the Chinese had the best of nautical technology at their disposal. The ships themselves were a product of an age-old development of experience in shipbuilding materialized in huge junks, and sailing equipment including very typical oars, rudders, anchors, the square-shaped lug-sails made of mats and bamboo battens, and formidable inventions such as the division of the hull into watertight compartments in order to prevent shipwreck. Moreover, the Chinese admiral Zheng He's fleet had gunnery and a whole array of incendiary weapons with which enemy ships could be attacked. On board a special cabin was installed for the *huozhang*, or compass watcher.

During Zheng He's expeditions sea charts were drawn of all the regions that were visited by the fleet, showing a detailed picture of coastal landmarks and compass routes. A number of navigation diagrams have also survived, which indicate the stars that had to be followed by the junks. Both charts and diagrams were included in the 1628 military work *Wubei zhi* ('Treatise on Armament Technology') by the encyclopaedist Mao Yuanyi, and are among the most important accomplishments of pre-modern Chinese navigation.

Modern navigation

Nowadays the traditional compass has been replaced by more advanced versions such as the electrically powered gyrocompass, and positioning is mainly reckoned by means of satellite. The age of the wooden vessel has long since gone, but with Shanghai as the largest port in the world, China has become a major player in maritime transportation.

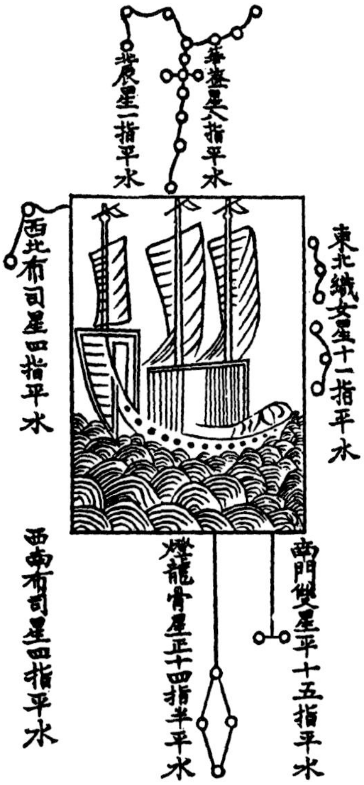

One of the navigational diagrams drawn during Zheng He's expeditions in the early Ming dynasty, and later inserted in the Wubei zhi. *This drawing gives instructions for the track from Sri Lanka to Sumatra.*

RONALD G. KNAPP

63 Bridges

... a new moon rising above the clouds, a long rainbow drinking from a mountain stream ....
MING-DYNASTY DESCRIPTION OF THE ZHAOZHOU BRIDGE, HEBEI PROVINCE

Bridges, the least known of China's architectural wonders, nonetheless represent extraordinary world-class engineering achievements while often expressing aesthetic qualities through combining the lines and textures of their structures. Stitched across the rural and urban landscapes of China, bridges fulfil specific utilitarian requirements while, according to Joseph Needham, expressing 'a subtle combination of the rational with the romantic'. Chinese bridge building includes innovations pre-dating better-known advances in Europe and elsewhere. Indeed, long before engineers applied mathematics and science to bridge design, Chinese craftsmen found solutions to building problems by employing empirical approaches that tested the nature of matter, especially wood and stone.

Chinese legends tell of the Sage emperor Yu, known as a great 'engineer' and the legendary founder of the Xia dynasty (*c.* 2070–1600 BC), who is said to have summoned giant turtles to position themselves as a means for him to cross a river. In some areas of China today, one still crosses shallow streams by utilizing a continuous but broken line of cut stones, placed so that a person on foot need not alter his rhythmic gait as he moves across. These pragmatic efforts were supplanted later by three elemental bridge types – beam, suspension and arch – that differ fundamentally in the ways in which their weight or load is carried. Bridge builders considered utilitarian aspects of each span, that is, whether traffic was pedestrian or wheeled and whether space beneath must allow for boat traffic. Successful bridge building involves experimentation by craftsmen with the inherent properties of materials and engagement with their aesthetics.

Beam bridges

Beams simply rest, with gravity transferring the weight of the horizontal piece of wood or stone to the supports on both ends. There are reasonably predictable limits to the length of beams because beams tend to sag and break, but through cantilevering and the use of intervening piers, deficiencies could be overcome. The characters *qiao* and *liang*, together today meaning 'bridge' and in use since the 12th century BC, include the radical for 'wood'. This suggests that the earliest spans across narrow streams or ditches were probably logs laid side by side, which were limited in extent only by the height of available trees. Piled stones as rudimentary piers and trestles came later, allowing the effective lengthening of a span by utilizing intermediary support.

Perspective view of the Xianju Bridge in Taishun county, Zhejiang province. First built in 1452 during the Ming dynasty with a soaring span of 34.14 m (112 ft), the bridge is described as having a 'woven timber arch-beam' structure.

During the reign of the First Emperor of Qin, the unifier of China in 221 BC, an imposing 18-m (60-ft) wide and 544-m (1785-ft) long multi-span bridge was built across the Wei River near the capital Xianyang in today's Shaanxi province. Here, 8-m (26-ft) long timbers resting on massive cut stone columns traversed each of its 68 spans. Long wooden beam bridges, some of which were supported by rattan cylinders containing rocks and earth, were built during the succeeding Han dynasty and served as critical transit features along the fabled Silk Road (p. 43).

Rainbow bridges

Horizontal log beams have limits to the distances they can span, rarely reaching 10 m (33 ft). Simple cantilevering, using counterbalanced logs that project out from abutments, was first employed in China in the 4th century AD. In time, cantilevering became increasingly sophisticated, as exemplified by sweeping hump-backed 'rainbow' bridges that were given shape by interlocked multi-angular beam-arches made of logs. An arch of piled beams of this type was a feature of Zhang Zeduan's famed 12th-century silk handscroll *Qingming shanghe tu* ('Going Upriver During the Qingming Festival'). While rainbow bridges were believed to have died out, scores of covered wooden spans have been discovered in recent decades in the mountains of Fujian and Zhejiang provinces.

Stone arch bridges

The aesthetic sense and technical originality of Chinese bridge building is epitomized in the modelling of stone arches, the earliest depictions of which can be seen on engraved brick tiles in Han-dynasty tombs. Stone arch bridges, which carry great weight and transfer that load diagonally – rather than vertically – pushing outward on the terminal supports at the ends of the structure, are physically in a state of compression

Above *Not only is daily activity apparent in Zhang Zeduan's well-known ink-and-colour silk handscroll, the underlying structure of the 'rainbow bridge' shows the piled logs that give form to its arches beneath.*

Below *The structure of a single-arch stone bridge.*

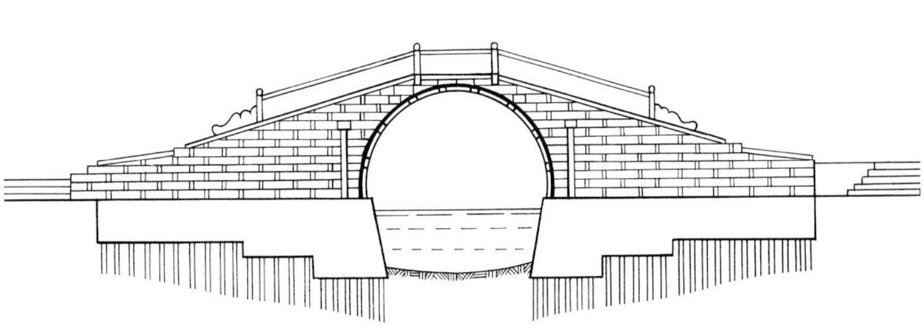

Built between 1751 and 1764 in Beijing's Summer Palace, the symmetrical 150-m (492-ft) long Seventeen Arch Bridge joins the bank of Kunming Lake with an island.

in that the component parts are squeezing together. Usually composed without mortar and sometimes utilizing stone mortises or metal cramps, stone arch bridges express a remarkable elasticity and often tolerate a striking degree of deformation.

Unpretentious workaday semicircular single-arch bridges are ubiquitous in China, especially in the canal-laced Jiangnan coastal region. An outstanding example of single-arch building artistry in north China is the Jade Belt Bridge, whose apparent lightness denies the massive weight of the white marble and granite slabs from which it was constructed. While serving as a functional means to cross an inlet of water along a causeway in Beijing's Summer Palace, the lithe Jade Belt Bridge rises precipitously, yet gracefully, like a wave as a critical element in a landscape panoramic portrait that includes five other bridges.

Multiple-arched bridges include some with precipitous approaches across narrow canals while others span broad streams via a repeated series of low, relatively level, arches. Triple-span bridges, with steep approaches supported by thin piers, utilize a large central span that is approximately 20 per cent broader than the flanking smaller arches. With 53 arches, of which three middle arches were enlarged to accommodate boat traffic, the 317-m (1,040-ft) long 9th-century Baodai or Jewel Belt Bridge was built outside Suzhou in Jiangsu province; the horizontal thrusts of its thin piers tended to balance each other with only slight deformation over time. However, when one of the arches was removed in 1857, 26 adjacent arches fell one after another like a pack of shuffled cards.

Massive piers were employed in the building of the fabled Lugou Bridge, often called the Marco Polo Bridge, described by the Venetian explorer in 1280 to be 'perhaps unequalled by any other in the world'. Said to be countless, but actually numbering 485, the distinctively carved lions that sit atop the balustrade capitals are a notable feature of the Lugou Bridge. With a span of 266.5 m (874 ft) and 11 arches, this bridge crosses the shallow Yongding (formerly Lugou) River, whose massive blocks of ice in winter would have damaged a bridge with lighter piers.

The magnificent Seventeen Arch Bridge, built between 1751 and 1764 in Beijing's Summer Palace, reposes like a symmetrical 150-m (492-ft) long rainbow joining the bank of Kunming Lake with an island. On the east end of the bridge is a large bronze ox, incised with inscriptions by the Qianlong emperor expressing how the Sage emperor Yu calmed floods by controlling water. Hundreds of carved lion figures sit atop the balusters along the edges of the bridge, some say in imitation of those along the celebrated Lugou Bridge.

Segmental arch bridge

The Zhaozhou Bridge, also called Anji Bridge, is considered one of China's principal contributions to engineering design because of its revolutionary structural form. Completed in Hebei province in 605 during the Sui dynasty and credited to an historical craftsman named Li Chun, the bridge is geometrically a segment of a circle rather than a semicircle. Similar structural forms did not appear in Europe for 800 years. The segmental design overcomes the seemingly contradictory demands for both a broad span with gentle approaches for cart traffic, and the need for sufficient height to permit boat traffic. An essential innovation in the building of the Zhaozhou Bridge is the two openings in each of the spandrels (the roughly triangular areas between the roadway above and the underlying arch beneath). Open spandrels did not appear in Western bridges until the 19th century. Indeed, with its structural sophistication and extraordinary elegance, in spite of its age, the Zhaozhou span has the appearance of a contemporary bridge.

As the 21st century begins, the world is beginning to acknowledge China's remarkable achievements in science and technology, including architecture in general. China's bridge-building traditions should be more than a footnote in this narrative. Moreover, many Chinese bridges have a poetic quality in that the crescendo or diminuendo of their form evokes imagery of a moon emerging from the clouds, a turtle back reaching the clouds, or a rainbow lying on the clouds as it reaches into the shadowy distance. While some extraordinary Chinese bridges are now being acclaimed, it is important to recognize that there are still likely to be countless bridges showing ingenuity and skill that remain undocumented throughout China.

Above *The world's first segmental span with symmetrical pairs of open spandrels, the Zhaozhou Bridge in Hebei was completed in 605.*

Below *The wonderfully space-age Nanpu Bridge, Shanghai.*

ROBIN D. S. YATES

64 The Art of War

War is a vital matter of state. It is the field on which life or death is determined and the road that leads to either survival or ruin, and must be examined with the greatest care. Warfare is the art of deceit. To win a hundred victories in a hundred battles is not the highest excellence; the highest excellence is to subdue the enemy's army without fighting at all.

SUNZI (MASTER SUN), *ART OF WARFARE*, 4TH CENTURY BC

China's numerous contributions to the military arts span over 4,000 years of history. Among the most significant from a technological perspective are the crossbow, the cast iron sword, chemical warfare in the form of gas pumps, the 'trebuchet' or lever-catapult, the stirrup, gunpowder (p. 270), cannon and rockets. Military theory was also prominent.

The 'loyal general' in a set of seven royal treasures from the 18th century. These sandalwood stands are decorated with gold, jade and semi-precious stones. (Height 32 cm / 12 in.)

In the Shang and Zhou periods (*c.* 1600–221 BC), the 'great affairs of state were sacrifice and warfare'. Both were central to social and religious life: animal and human offerings to ancestral spirits were to placate and nourish them. Forces were controlled through fluttering multi-coloured flags, and bronze drums and bells. In the army of pottery warriors buried to protect the tomb of the First Emperor of Qin when he died in 210 BC (p. 155), we see officers without weapons – their duty was to command and direct, not to engage in killing.

The weakening of Zhou power in the Spring and Autumn period (770–476 BC) had given rise to increased warfare by aristocratic elites of competing states, mounted on chariots and accompanied by less well-equipped and protected peasant infantry. They fought according to strict rules of etiquette, like chivalrous medieval Western knights. By the early 5th century BC, the beginning of the Warring States period, infantry armies of conscripted peasants were equipped with bronze and metre-long cast iron swords and wore iron or leather armour; they were led by professional officers and accompanied by chariots. Cavalry was adopted by the mid-4th century from steppe peoples in the north.

Crossbows and stirrups

At this time, the Chinese invented the crossbow with its bronze trigger mechanism that required precision engineering. It could fire a bolt more accurately over a longer distance (the arc of flight was flatter than that of a regular bow and arrow), and a soldier could hold the bolt in the stock for longer than with an ordinary bow. Its main disadvantage was that it was slower to load. The crossbow gave the Chinese technological superiority over nomad foes, especially when they developed a much larger and heavier version called the 'arcuballista', which could fire iron-tipped bolts 3-m (10-ft) long.

At the time of the Qin–Han transition (3rd–2nd centuries BC), the Wusun people invented the horse stirrup, but the Chinese realized its potential only much later. First, a single stirrup was suspended on the horse's left side to assist mounting. By the 5th century AD, stirrups were placed on both sides, leading to the development of heavy cavalry, with both man and horse protected by lacquered leather or iron armour. This new mode of fighting travelled rapidly west to Iran and Europe, transforming war and social relations. But China, faced with the threat of highly mobile light Turkish cavalry in the 7th century, abandoned heavy cavalry in favour of light forces.

Sunzi's *Art of Warfare*

Chinese warfare was theorized by Sun Wu (Sunzi, or Master Sun) in his famous *Art of Warfare*, (5th–4th centuries BC). His basic principles for waging war have been influential down to our times. He emphasized that one should fight only on a pre-conceived plan, never in anger, and when a careful evaluation of all aspects provides clear superiority. Any action has strong and weak points; both you and the enemy have advantages and disadvantages: one should turn the enemy's strengths into weaknesses and one's own weaknesses into strengths.

Nothing stays the same, so one should always seek to maximize profit and defeat the enemy without using actual force: force is more effective when held in reserve and not applied; it is far better to capture an enemy whole than to destroy him and, in the process, damage one's own resources. It is especially important to strike where the enemy is unprepared, by indirect means that the enemy cannot anticipate – weaken him, and hit with overwhelming power to force a response. Sunzi emphasized 'strategic advantage' (*shi*), where your position, both spiritual, logistic, physical (in terms of space) and morale in relation to the enemy was the key to victory. The general had to be given complete authority in the field and mould his army into an efficient fighting force that would obey his every order. He was the mind, the army his limbs. A ruler was not to interfere with battlefield decisions.

Above left *Diagram of a multiple-arrow crossbow catapult.*

Above *The Great Wall is here breached by the Manchus as the Chinese general Li Yongfang surrenders.*

ROBIN D. S. YATES

65 Gunpowder

Political power grows out of the barrel of a gun.
MAO ZEDONG, 1938

The Chinese were experts in deploying fire in military action from the 5th century BC, and brilliant engineers in siege warfare, having invented the lever-catapult (trebuchet) and giant multiple-arrow crossbow (arcuballista) by the 3rd century BC. Chinese technicians were put on the road to inventing gunpowder by a group of Central Asian Sogdian Buddhist priests, who identified one of the three key ingredients of gunpowder, saltpetre (potassium nitrate), on top of a patch of soil in north-central China in the mid-7th century AD. Experimentation with this new substance by Daoist alchemists quickly followed and by the end of the Tang dynasty (AD 907), saltpetre had been mixed with sulphur, realgar (arsenic sulphide) and honey, in other words with the other two essential components, sulphur and carbon, with the resulting mixture bursting into flames and burning down the houses where the mixture had been lit.

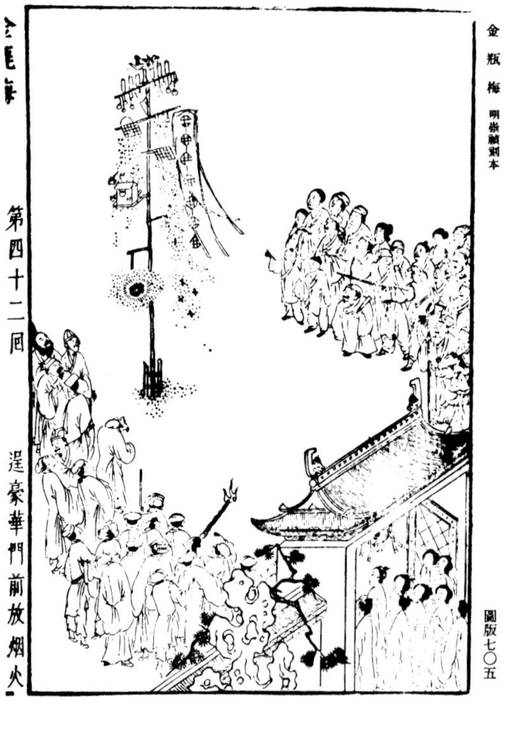

Scene of a fireworks display from a mid-17th-century Ming novel called Jin Ping Mei.

Early gunpowder

In the early 10th century this early form of gunpowder was used to light flame-throwers, as seen in a Buddhist banner painting from Dunhuang, where a devil is attempting to disturb the Buddha's meditations by loosing this new fearsome weapon on him. The component parts of a flame-thrower are illustrated in the Northern Song-dynasty military encyclopaedia, *Wujing zongyao* ('Collection of the Most Important Military Techniques') of 1044. The flame-thrower was a kind of pump that used a petroleum distillate, naptha, a product introduced from the Mediterranean world, as its fuel. This encyclopedia also contains details of the earliest gunpowder formula, which was undoubtedly a state secret at the time.

Pressed on their northern borders by, first, the Khitan Liao dynasty, and then the Jurchen Jin, who captured the whole of north China in 1126, forcing the Song court to decamp to Hangzhou (p. 131), Song Chinese artillerymen sought ways to exploit their discovery of gunpowder on the field of battle. First, they realized that if they increased the amount of nitrate in relation to the other ingredients, they could create an explosion; over the next centuries, this level was increased until gunpowder's true potential as an explosive was realized as a propellant in bronze cannon, with devastating consequences. Next, they developed various delivery systems, such as bombs, land-mines, grenades, rockets and, of course, cannons, not to mention the use of gunpowder as a form of entertainment in fireworks.

Bombs

The earliest type of bomb is described in the *Wujing zongyao*, and was used to defend against enemy sappers digging mines against a city. The bomb was made out of two or three sections of two pieces of split dried bamboo filled with sharp broken shards of pottery. The whole was carefully glued together with a fuse sticking out at one end and about 2 kg (5 lbs) of the gunpowder mixture was daubed all over the outside. The enemy mine was opened up from the top, the fuses of the bombs were lit with a hot iron brand, and the bombs thrown into the hole using trebuchets. They exploded with a rumble like thunder.

Subsequent bombs were developed that were round in shape and made out of either weak or hard casings, often filled with a foul mixture of shrapnel made from bits of old iron and pottery, faeces that could infect wounds caused by the shrapnel, and chemicals that emitted a poisonous smoke. The earliest illustration of a bomb bursting in flight is to be found in a Japanese painting showing the defence of their islands against Kubilai Khan's Mongol invasion fleet in 1274 (see image below).

Cannons

The earliest forms of cannon, using gunpowder as a propulsive force, seem also to have fired mixtures of projectiles like the bombs described above, and it took several centuries to realize that a missile occluding the barrel of the cannon could be fired greater distances with higher accuracy. The former seems to be the type of vase-shaped bombard, with exaggerated explosion chamber, illustrated in a wall sculpture in the Buddhist cave temples at Dazu, Sichuan (p. 120), in approximately 1126, but whether this really represents a contemporary weapon is debated. Still, by the time the Chinese were fighting the Mongol invasions in the late 13th century, they had invented bronze cannons and handguns, as well as rockets and various types of rocket launchers. The world would never be the same.

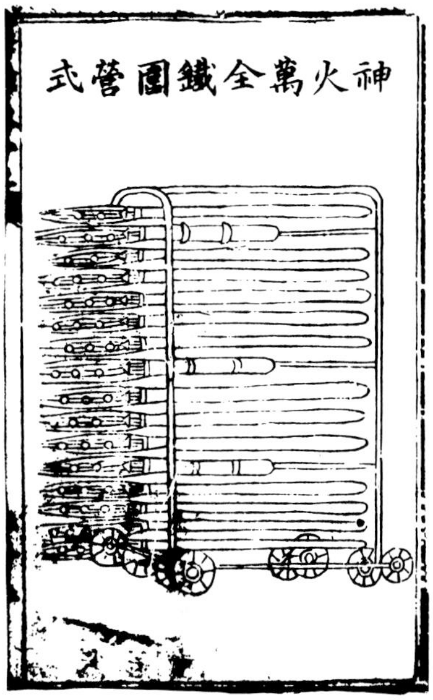

Above *Mobile rack for holding fire-lances, useful for supplying guards on battlements with a steady stream of flame-throwers. Alternatively, all the lances could be lit at once and directed on the enemy like a broadside to protect a retreat.*

Left *The only surviving picture of a bursting bomb-shell, taken from an almost contemporary record of the Mongol invasion of Japan, c. 1274.*

MAREILE FLITSCH

66 Everyday Objects

We are apt to think that anything more or less mechanically complicated is the product of the Western world, and if we look at our fishing reel, nicely finished and nickel-plated, we would scarcely expect to find its prototype in China.
RUDOLF P. HOMMEL, *CHINA AT WORK*, 1937

Everyday artifacts tell of the work, leisure, luxury and passion of the Chinese people, reflecting the fascination of techniques and of finding solutions to the problems of life. Many were known in China long before Europeans thought them up, as Joseph Needham and others have shown – and some everyday artifacts used across the globe originated there.

Chopsticks and fishing rod reels

Let us start with the emblematic eating instrument – chopsticks. The oldest to have been found (made of metal) date from the 2nd century BC, but they are mentioned in earlier sources. To begin with, they probably served as cooking utensils, made of bamboo or wood. At that time, the ancestors of today's Chinese mainly used one hand for eating with fingers, with a spatula and spoon for particular foods and liquids. The elite differentiated themselves from the lower classes by using chopsticks – this implied preliminary preparations like cutting foodstuff into fine pieces and refined techniques of cooking food into a proper texture. The fact that one hand is free while the other is dexterously manipulating chopsticks has contributed to the development of a social and technical orientation at meals that differs significantly from those where the knife and fork are employed.

The fishing apparatus developed in China in the 3rd to 4th centuries AD is commonly regarded as the earliest combination of rod and reel, which

Fisherman on a Winter Lake. *This painting by Ma Yuan, c. 1300, is the earliest illustration of the fishing-rod reel as used by the Chinese.*

did not come into use in Europe until the 18th century. Angling was an activity for women as well as men in early China. The reel was not only an extension of the older fishing rod, but also opened up opportunities for catching particular kinds of fish – or even turtles. It enabled Chinese people to fish from boats or from banks and shores. Thus the reel is a sign of knowledge about different kinds of fish and their behaviour, of skill in luring them. At the beginning of the 20th century, Chinese reels were still simply, as Rudolf Hommel puts it, 'a wooden hub with six wooden spokes stuck into it equidistant from each other with notches at their ends for receiving the fishing line. From the reel the line passed through an eye-bolt fastened on the rod, and along the rod through glass rings tied at intervals to it.'

Enjoying the Landscape of the West Lake. *Children are entertained by the moving imagery of the* laterna magica *in this late 19th-century painting.*

Magic lanterns and umbrellas

The projection of moving pictures on a screen by putting transparent images along a source of light was a technique that may have originated in a form of magician's art, or in the invention of (and experimentation with) toys for everyday amusement. From the 2nd century, Chinese sources tell of moving picture series showing animals, and depicting tales to amuse emperors and their families. By the 12th century, there is mention of *zoumadeng*, the 'lantern of running horses' on which mounted riders were seen jumping and moving. It was this form of *laterna magica* that Jesuit missionaries discovered in China, and brought back to Europe in the 17th century.

Knowledge of the mechanical principle of sliding levers was applied in China to a collapsible umbrella (*san*) possibly as early as the 1st century BC. It was then used as a secret technology for the construction of the baldachins of a ceremonial carriage. Pictorial evidence of bamboo umbrellas covered with paper dates back to about 1270. Umbrellas or parasols became part of elite attire, particularly women, while the lower classes protected their bodies with straw hats or reed capes. Initially, they were carried by 'umbrella holder' servants. The trend towards the 'democratization of fashion' and consumption at the end of the 19th century made umbrellas manufactured in Japan and other foreign countries accessories of modern dress, and thus a symbol of Western-oriented lifestyles. With the rise of a new Chinese national identity after the Republican revolution of 1911, 'patriotic umbrellas' manufactured domestically staged a comeback over foreign-made umbrellas.

Left *A Chinese lady and her son are sheltered by a servant who holds a parasol in this painting, c. 1798.*

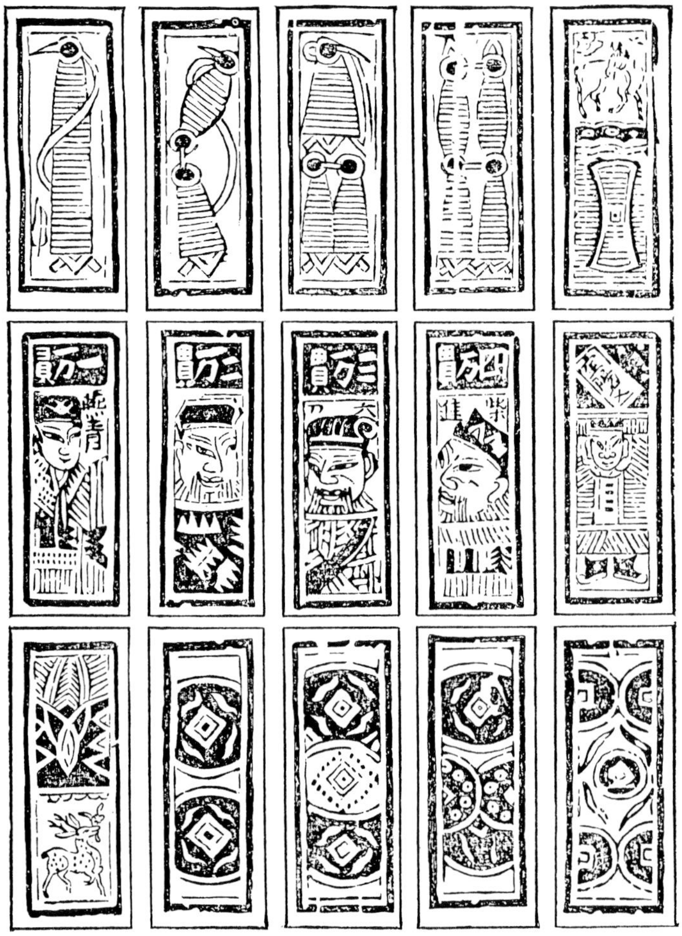

The Chinese have always had a passion for both simple and complex game-playing. Repeatedly, games were invented, rose in popularity and then eventually disappeared. Some scholars hold that playing cards were first used in China in the 9th century AD, became popular during the era of Mongol rule in the late 13th and 14th centuries, and spread to the West hundreds of years later. Other scholars state that the earliest proof of the use of playing cards dates from 1294, less than 100 years before the earliest mention of them in Europe in 1377.

It is thus not exactly clear when playing cards were invented and from which playing tradition they sprang, but it is generally assumed that they were a side effect of the invention of paper and progress in printing technology in China. The earliest-known Chinese cards differed according to the way in which they were manufactured. They were rectangular pieces of card, often hand-coloured and with designs of figures from popular novels. Playing cards and the rules relating to them bear testimony to the projection of rank and suit, of the social convention of ruse, of fate and probability calculations, and of strategic thinking in a given time. The numbers and motifs on cards are symbolic and culturally meaningful.

Above *Chinese playing cards published in an 1876 book on the invention of printing.*

Matches and playing cards

The first use of small sticks of pinewood impregnated with sulphur is generally credited to China from about AD 950 – the earliest appearance in Europe of sulphur sticks is put at around 1530. However, to use this invention, most Chinese had to wait for the beginning of the 20th century, when modern safety matches gradually became available to a larger public, first in the urban centres and later in the countryside. Like umbrellas, they were among commodities that involved competition between national and foreign products during the Republican era. Match boxes were neatly decorated, their covers promoting cultural and political values, new lifestyles, auspicious scenes and symbols and historical personalities. The cover designs have become objects of collections worldwide.

Right *Chinese match box designs from the end of the Qing dynasty.*

ERLING HOH

The History of Tea

67

The first cup kisses the throat softly
The second vanquishes the torpor of solitude
The third uncovers 5,000 scrolls of stories
hidden within my parched soul ....
START OF A POEM BY LU TONG, TANG DYNASTY

The first people known to have cultivated tea were the Ba, who lived in the eastern part of the Sichuan Basin some 3,000 years ago. Records state that the Ba presented the first king of the Western Zhou (1046–771 BC) with a tribute of cinnabar, lacquer, tea and honey. In the Warring States period (476– 221 BC), tea cultivation spread down the Yangtze. A new county, 'Tea Hill', was even named after its main produce in Hunan province (Western Han, 202 BC–AD 8).

At first, tea was chewed raw, cooked as a food and drunk as a medicinal herb, prized for its stimulating properties. The fresh leaves were picked in early spring, steamed, pounded and pressed into cakes. Among the early tea-drinkers were religious practitioners: Daoists, who roamed in search of the elixir of eternal life, and Buddhists, who required tea to keep themselves awake during meditation. According to one legend, tea was discovered by Bodhidharma, the Indian monk who founded Zen Buddhism at the Shaolin Monastery. Weary, he wept, and where his tears fell, tea leaves sprang up.

Standing 10 cm (4 in.) tall, this silver teapot with attached lid dates to the Yongzheng period.

Tax and trade

The opening of the Grand Canal in the Sui dynasty (581–618), which connected the Yangtze and the Yellow Rivers, accelerated China's economic

Early 19th-century Chinese painting showing tea pickers.

Right *A 19th-century Chinese sculpture at Luis de Camoes Museum, Macau, showing a man sipping tea.*

growth, and greatly facilitated the transportation of commodities from the south such as tea. In the late 8th century, at the height of the Tang dynasty, when tea drinking had become a part of daily life in China, the errant scholar Lu Yu composed *The Tea Classic*, the first major work on tea, describing its origins, preparation methods and the tea-growing regions of China, even ranking different sources of water.

In 782, the imperial court imposed China's first tea tax, with stiff penalties, even death, for smugglers. The imperial tea gardens in the region west of Lake Tai, where some 30,000 corvée labourers toiled, produced a tea known as Purple Bamboo Shoot exclusively for the emperor and his court. Having spread to the neighbouring peoples in Tibet, Korea and Japan, tea became a crucial commodity in China's Sisyphean attempts to keep the covetous semi-nomadic tribes on its northern and eastern borders at bay. Through the addiction of these tribes to tea, the Chinese were able to acquire from them the very horses they needed to defend themselves. This was the beginning of the fabled Tea & Horse trade, which, having failed in its purpose in the face of Genghis

Below *Modern-day tea harvesters at work in Yixing.*

Khan's onslaught, was later revived as a cornerstone of Chinese foreign policy in the Ming.

The Song to the Ming

In the Song dynasty (960–1279), the country's tea production centre shifted to the northern parts of Fujian, as the Song court established a monopoly on the trade. The most exclusive tea of this era was the so-called 'wax tea', a green powdered tea produced through an elaborate process, then perfumed, pressed into cakes and sealed in wax. At the same time, the Song saw a gradual move from steamed green brick tea to loose leaf green tea, which was easier to produce. In their mountain retreats, scholars, poets and painters held *dou cha* gatherings, competing to see who could beat the powdered tea into the most perfect froth and make the best-tasting brew. For this purpose, the black-glazed tea bowls from the Jian'an kiln in Fujian were deemed the most appropriate.

After the Mongols conquered all of China, establishing the Yuan dynasty in 1279, the blue-and-white porcelain tea cups from Jingdezhen replaced the black-glazed cups as the most fashionable tea ware. Buddhist and Daoist temples convened large tea gatherings that provided the impetus for what later was to become the most formalized ritual ever conceived by man: the Japanese tea ceremony. The Mongols, for their part, under the influence of the Tibetans, whose Lamaist religion they had adopted, added a new twist by taking their tea with horse milk and salt.

By the Ming dynasty (1368–1644), loose leaf tea was firmly established as the main tea type, while the brick teas were almost exclusively used for the border trade. Pan-frying the leaves replaced steaming as the most common processing method. As well as the traditional green tea, post-fermented black tea, yellow tea and white tea began to appear. Fully fermented black tea was developed in the Wuyi Mountains of Fujian province, and teas flavoured with flowers like jasmine, roses and osmanthus were also popular.

Tea and the West

The first reference to tea in European literature was in 1559 by the Venetian author Gian Battista Ramusio in his *Voyages and Travels*. In 1610, the Dutch East India Company returned to Europe with its first cargo of tea. The British, other European countries and the Americans soon followed suit, and during the 18th and 19th centuries, tea became the pivotal commodity of the China trade, leading to the Opium Wars and the birth of India's tea industry. The Russians, for their part, traded over land, transporting enormous quantities of brick tea back to Moscow with caravans through Central Asia.

During the 19th century, British imports of black tea skyrocketed, creating a gold rush for China's tea farmers, who broke new land and expanded production to keep pace with the ever-increasing demand. But the Indian tea industry, with its industrial-scale plantations and tailor-made blends for the British public, proved a ruthless competitor. By the 1880s, China's tea export to the West had peaked, and was not revived until the Communist revolution in 1949. The country's tea industry has been gaining pace ever since. Since the death of Mao and China's opening to the world, tea has enjoyed a commercial and cultural renaissance in China. In 2005, the country regained its former position by replacing India as the world's largest tea exporter.

A member of the Chinese literati being served tea in south China.

TONESE FOOD
CHIN WAH SPORT ASSOC

Greater China

Beyond the mainland of China stretches a network of societies which extend the Chinese presence in varied ways. Closest are the former European colonies of Hong Kong and Macau. Furthest afield lie the Chinatowns of the United States, Europe and Australia. In Southeast Asia, Chinese emigrants and their descendants play a major economic role, sometimes behind the scenes because of local resentment, but often occupying leading functions in business. The region's main city state, Singapore, has a Chinese majority. Overseas Chinese (p. 288) in different countries and continents interact, forming what has been called the 'Bamboo Network'. In all, they number more than 20 million; their combined wealth that of a medium-sized country.

The Chinese diaspora really got underway in the later 19th century when the empire lifted the official ban on emigration. Chinese sailed to labour in the gold rush and build railways in North America and Australia, and formed growing communities in New York and London's East End. Largely self-contained, they retained their provincial roots at home and, over more than a century, have provided funds and expertise for economic development on the mainland.

Recently, they have been joined abroad by very different groups of emigrants – professionals studying business methods, students, those seeking work in the West, and political and artistic dissidents such as Gao Xingjian, winner of the Nobel Prize for literature in 2000. Some well-known figures, like the musician Yo-Yo Ma or the recent crop of Chinese actors who have starred in

The neon lights in Hong Kong, the most modern city in the People's Republic.

Western-backed films, move easily between the two cultures.

Apart from the Chinese living across the seas, there are three places with strong links to the mainland that find themselves in special situations.

Hong Kong (p. 281) is divided between the rocky island ceded by the Qing empire to London in 1842 and Kowloon and the New Territories across the bay, which were acquired later. It has long served the role of a bridge between the mainland and the world, becoming a haven for Chinese businessmen who found it a more comfortable place in which to operate than in their homeland – whether under the empire, the Nationalist Republic or Communism. Waves of refugees sought shelter over the decades, fuelling its rise into one of the great international business centres.

Recognizing Hong Kong's uniqueness and economic value, Beijing proposed the formula of 'One Country, Two Systems' when it regained sovereignty in 1997. The territory became part of China but kept its way of life, including liberty of speech and movement, and its own currency and legal system. Though the pace of democratization has been slow, Hong Kong is still administered by a civil service whose senior members were trained under the British. Despite its reputation as a 24/7 agglomeration of tower blocks and businesses, it has large country parks, where it is easy to get away from the urban bustle, a dramatic coastline and a string of islands stretching into the Pearl River delta.

Across the delta, the former Portuguese colony of Macau has a similar status. Smaller than Hong Kong, it was traditionally the sleepy sister, with restaurants and architecture that reflected its one-time European masters. But Macau has developed strongly since rejoining China in 1999 as a result of the growth of its casino industry, attracting investors from Las Vegas and punters from all over Asia, including the mainland.

Almost 145 km (90 miles) off the coast of Fujian province, with a beautiful, wild interior and spectacular natural sites, Taiwan (p. 285) is regarded by Beijing as an integral part of China although it became the refuge for Chiang Kai-shek's Nationalist regime at the end of the civil war in 1949. Reaching back further into the history of the island, which was a Japanese colony from 1895 to 1945, autonomists assert that their 'Taiwanese identity' and the island's democratic politics mean they do not belong to China. Still, the heritage of the roots brought by the Nationalists 60 years ago is evident. Taiwanese companies are major investors in the mainland, and some 300,000 Taiwanese live in the Shanghai region. How Beijing and the island work out their relationship is likely to be a continuing theme for the early 21st century.

The National Theatre in Taipei, Taiwan.

JONATHAN FENBY

Hong Kong & Macau

68

The skyscrapers ... jam-packed at the foot of the hill, seemed to vibrate with pride, greed, energy and success, and all among them the traffic swirled, and the crowds milled, and the shops glittered and the money rang.
JAN MORRIS, *AMONG THE CITIES*, 1985

As a British colony for 155 years, Hong Kong became a unique place, a bridge between China and the world, a highly modern, cosmopolitan city enjoying greater average wealth per inhabitant than its imperial master on the other side of the globe. Since it returned to Chinese sovereignty as a Special Administrative Region (SAR) of the People's Republic in 1997, it has been the richest city in China, offering a unique blend of internationalism, financial and commercial services, a strong legal system and a superb infrastructure – from the highly efficient underground railway to the escalator that takes pedestrians up the steep slope in the middle of the island. Its soaring architecture is epitomized by the gleaming skyscrapers along the waterfront and in the Central District where two major late 20th-century buildings – the homes of the Bank of China and the Hong Kong and Shanghai Bank (HSBC) face one another. The Peak towers above the island, with its colonial-era mansions reached by a tramway that runs vertiginously to the top. There lies one of the great walks of any city, a circular path from which the panorama of the densely populated metropolis and its teeming harbour unfold.

Hong Kong and a portion of Victoria Harbour, c. 1880. Industrial smokestacks send a column of smoke into the air.

Unseen by most visitors, the SAR also has extensive country parks where one may encounter water buffalo wandering along paths or, less picturesquely, packs of wild dogs.

Vestiges of the colonial era remain – the Cenotaph to war dead, the cricket club and a few buildings like the Anglican cathedral and the former residence of the colonial governors. But Hong Kong has long been a predominantly Chinese city, its people speaking the Cantonese tongue of the south and treasuring their identity as 'Hong Kong Chinese'. Today, they make up 95 per cent of the population. For all the fine Western restaurants, the SAR probably has the widest variety of Chinese cuisine, and is a major centre for Chinese media, publishing, Cantopop and cinema. For decades before the handover to China in 1997, Chinese businessmen and civil servants had taken a major role in running the commerce and efficient administration that have become the hallmarks of Hong Kong. Despite the last-ditch introduction of democracy by the final British Governor, Christopher Patten, just before the handover, the old colonial pattern of rule was re-established after China assumed sovereignty. Though elections are held on various franchises for the Legislative Council, the introduction of democracy has been slow. Still, the 7 million people of the SAR enjoy a large degree of liberty – freedom of speech, religion and the press, freedom to demonstrate, freedom to move in and out through the spectacular new airport, and freedom to shift their money round the world as they wish.

History

When Britain gained possession of Hong Kong Island in 1842 after the First Opium War against the Qing dynasty (1644–1911), the Foreign Secretary of the time was disappointed that London had gained only a 'barren rock', rather than a concession in a prosperous trading port. By 1860, the benefits that the rocky, waterless island offered as a strategically placed post had become evident, and Britain added territory across the bay in the Kowloon area. In 1898, London made another move by leasing from China for 99 years land known as the New Territories which neighbours

Chinese painting entitled Victoria, Hong Kong, from the Harbour, c. *1850–1859.*

Residential skyscrapers on Tsing Yi Island, Hong Kong.

China's southern province of Guangdong – it was the expiry of that lease which determined the timing of the handover in 1997.

From the start, Hong Kong was both a fast-growing trading centre, and a haven for Chinese wanting to leave the mainland for political or commercial reasons. The British introduced modern methods and governance which impressed Chinese reformers and revolutionaries. Sun Yat-sen, the anti-imperial thinker and agitator who became the first president of Republican China in 1912, studied medicine and converted to Christianity during a spell in Hong Kong. British trading firms prospered greatly by using the harbour to run their commerce with China, while Chinese businessmen saw its potential as an entrepôt between their homeland and the outside world, safe from the upheavals of the late imperial era.

By the 1930s, Hong Kong was a prosperous, if socially somewhat sleepy outpost of empire. Then the Japanese over-ran it at Christmas 1941, and imposed an often brutal occupation for three-and-a-half years. When Japan was defeated in 1945, the British returned, and did not carry through proposed democratic reforms. But, although the governors still came from London and Hong Kong was seen as a jewel of the British empire, the crushing defeat of 1941 had destroyed the myth of European superiority.

The Communist victory in China in 1949 sent a flood of refugees heading south from Shanghai and the east coast, many of them businessmen whose descendants still figure prominently in the SAR's commerce and finance. As the refugees established factories, Hong Kong became the first great exporter of cheap goods from China; but its entrepreneurs rapidly moved up the value chain, adding to their fortunes by property development of the territory's rare and increasingly expensive land. As China turned towards a market economy in the 1980s and movement across the border with Guangdong became easier, most of Hong Kong's manufacturing was transferred to the mainland, leaving the city as a base for management, finance and services. Recently, mainlanders have repaid the compliment by taking advantage of relaxed regulations on cross-border travel to patronize Hong Kong's glitzy retailers and buying property.

Macau

Prosperity has also boosted the former Portuguese colony of Macau, an hour's trip by hydro-foil ferry, across the Pearl River delta, and now another SAR after being handed back to Beijing by Lisbon. Once a somnolent outpost of Europe, complete with Portuguese cuisine, brightly painted houses and the magnificent façade of a Jesuit cathedral, its economy is based firmly on gambling (which is forbidden in Hong Kong except for horse-racing and a lottery). Punters from China and Asia flock to its casino. American promoters from Las Vegas have arrived recently. Tower blocks have sprouted along the waterfront, and Macau has been singled out for praise by the Chinese president. Still, away from the roulette wheels and blackjack tables, Macau and its two outlying islands offer an older way of life, with simple beach restaurants and a less frantic pace than its big brother across the water.

What does the future hold for Hong Kong?

When Hong Kong returned to Chinese rule in 1997, pessimists saw it becoming 'just another Chinese city'. But there has been little sign of that. Beijing has intervened on occasion, for instance in replacing the first Chief Executive of the SAR after his performance was regarded as falling short, or in seeking to stimulate the economy during a property slump at the start of the 21st century. Links with the mainland have been steadily fostered, particularly in the Pearl River delta stretching up into Guangdong. Many more mainlanders are to be found in the SAR these days.

But none of that has done much to cramp Hong Kong's exuberant, self-confident style or to lessen its role in the globalized world. In its new guise as the SAR, it remains a great international centre, home to global companies attracted by its administrative, managerial, legal and infrastructural strengths as the base from which to do business in the mainland. Despite periodic upsets such as the SARS disease outbreak, bird 'flu and short-lived property slumps, Hong Kong appears to have found a formula for success which rests on its people, its geographical position and its sheer usefulness to the rest of the world.

Traders work at the Hong Kong stock exchange on the first trading morning of the Bank of China.

JONATHAN FENBY

Taiwan

69

Isla formosa! Isla formosa! (Beautiful island! Beautiful island!)

CRY OF PORTUGUESE SAILORS AS THEY SAILED PAST TAIWAN IN THE 16TH CENTURY

Long known in the West from that sailor's cry, the island 145 km (90 miles) off the coast of China has had an eventful history, in which its relationship with the mainland has gone through many twists and turns. Taiwan's older history is still shrouded in a good deal of mystery, but, in more modern times, it has seen a European and Japanese presence as well as settlers, pirates and one of China's greatest figures.

The island's rugged beauty, with mountain peaks (the highest reaching 4,000 m or 13,114 ft), deep gorges, fast-running rivers and lakes, have always appealed to Chinese sensibilities, and attract growing numbers of tourists today. Its deep forests of cedar, oak, pine and camphor trees house abundant wild life. The cultural heartland in the south of the island is rich in temples, pagodas and classical pavilions.

In the central mountains lies one of Taiwan's greatest beauty spots, the Sun Moon Lake, surrounded by thick forests and peaks; it gets its name from the way in which it looks like a round sun from some viewpoints and a crescent moon from others. Though it can be clogged with tourists, early morning walks along the forest and shore trails remain an uplifting experience. In the north of the island lie paddy fields, hot springs, beaches, strange geological formations, orchid farms and winding highland roads.

Modern cities

The island's cities are resolutely modern, the capital of Taipei boasting a new skyscraper reaching up 101 floors into the sky. The memorial to the former ruler, Chiang Kai-shek, towers over a huge square flanked by halls for exhibitions and performances with 18 different styles of Chinese windows used in the surrounding walls. The city is full of temples, epitomized by the Dragon Temple in the old section known for its fine carvings, and is also celebrated for its markets, selling everything from gutted snakes to the counterfeit luxury goods which became one of the island's specialities as it began its economic growth.

The National Palace Museum in Taipei is a great wonder, housing a unique collection of Chinese art, brought to the island in 4,800 packing cases when the Nationalist government of Chiang Kai-shek fled across the Strait from the advancing Communists on the mainland in 1949. Among the endless treasures are the finest porcelain and lacquer, intricately carved jade and ivory, ancient bronzes, books and manuscripts – and 79

Evening traffic in Taipei with one of the world's tallest buildings, the 101 Tower, in the background.

The grand entrance to the Chiang Kai-shek Memorial Hall, Taipei.

wooden cups so thin that they can all fit into a single large cup.

Long a predominantly agricultural territory, Taiwan developed into one of the 'tiger economies' of the Far East, becoming a major producer of computer chips and other electronic goods. But its separation from the mainland since 1949 has created a complex political issue, with Beijing insisting it is an integral part of China and the presidency in Taipei following a course that amounts to autonomy, with some politicians calling for independence that the Chinese government and army are committed to preventing.

Covering 36,000 sq. km (13,890 sq. miles), with the small islands of Quemoy and Matsu close to the mainland, Taiwan has a population of about 23 million. Most are descended from aboriginal peoples, only 14 per cent descended from mainland Chinese. Some native Taiwanese have their roots in farming communities which prospered on the rich plains in the centre and southwest of the island. Others are from more warlike people who lived in the mountains and kept their traditional way of life well into the last century.

Immigrants, merchants and pirates

The first explorers probably crossed the 145-km (90-mile) Taiwan Strait from the mainland in the early period of the Han dynasty around 200 BC, when the Chinese called it 'the island of Yangchow'. In AD 239 the Kingdom of Wu sent a 10,000-man force to take the territory, but the occupation was evidently not permanent since, in the 15th century, the eunuch navigator Cheng Ho reported his discovery of the island which then became known as Taiwan, meaning 'terraced bay'.

Immigrants had come from the provinces of Fujian and Guangdong during the 1st millennium, the newcomers settling on the agricultural land and joining in cultivation of sugar, rice and tea. Successive waves from the mainland pushed the original inhabitants of the island further and further inland.

Taiwan administered itself largely independently of the Chinese mainland and, in the 16th century, its geographical position made it a favoured port of call for Western merchants. The Dutch set up a settlement in Taiwan, drove out the Spaniards who tried to colonize the north of the island, and built three forts, the ruins of which can be visited today. They also imported opium from their colony of Java in the East Indies, and taught the island's inhabitants to smoke it with tobacco – a habit which subsequently spread across the Taiwan Strait into China.

failed to defeat the Manchus as they advanced from the northeast, drove the Dutch from the island and turned Taiwan into his personal fiefdom centred on the southern city of Tainan.

At the same time, Taiwan gained notoriety from the pirates who sheltered in the inlets along its rocky coast. One was appointed by the last Ming emperor to command his forces as the dynasty fought against the challenge from the Manchus in the mid-17th century – the pirate's son became one of the most famous Chinese figures, the admiral Koxinga who, after the Ming

Political change

The Japanese had long had designs on Taiwan and, after defeating China in a war in 1895, forced Beijing to cede the island as a colony. Japanese rule was harsh, but also brought some modernization in fields like education and public services. In 1945, however, the defeat of Japan brought the island's return to Chinese rule and, as his Communist enemies advanced, Chiang Kai-shek prepared to evacuate his government and remaining troops across the Strait.

A massacre of native inhabitants in 1947 set the tone for the oppressive Nationalist regime which ruled under martial law after 1949. But, in the last decade, democracy has been introduced. The Kuomintang Party (KMT), which Chiang and his son led, lost two successive presidential elections to the Democratic Progressive Party (DPP), which appealed to 'Taiwanese identity' against the rule of Chinese who had come to the island in 1949. But the island still calls itself the Republic of China, and faces a future as challenging as its past.

The 228 Memorial Peace Park in Taipei is at odds with the modern skyscrapers in the background.

JONATHAN FENBY

70 Overseas Chinese

You can only trust close relatives.
SOCIOLOGIST PETER BERGER SUMMING UP OVERSEAS CHINESE BUSINESS, IN *THE CULTURAL CONTEXT OF ECONOMICS AND POLITICS*, 1994

Emigrant communities stretching from Britain to Australia, from Canada to Indonesia make the Chinese one of the most widely spread peoples on earth. Chinatowns give cities like New York and London part of their character. Chinese have moved in to British Columbia and California in large numbers while, in many Southeast Asian nations, they play a major role in business. But this empire – dubbed the 'Bamboo Network' by two American writers, Murray Weidenbaum and Samuel Hughes, in their book of the same name – is little recognized as a significant global economic force despite numbering an estimated 34 million people.

Musicians like the cellist Yo-Yo Ma or figures like the architect, I. M. Pei, may be internationally famous, alongside Chinese actors making their mark in the film world. But most Overseas Chinese keep a low profile. Traditionally, they concealed their wealth behind the blank walls of their houses. There is a good reason for this. They are the sons and daughters of refugees who fled turbulence and regime change in their homeland, and found it prudent to draw as little attention to themselves as possible as they settled in their new countries.

Like the Jews in Europe, whom they resemble in a number of ways, they have been subject to, at best, discrimination, and, at worst, pogroms. This began at the start of the 20th century; the United States passed legislation to limit the rights of Chinese immigrants who had crossed the Pacific

Chinese parade at Chinatown in Manhattan, New York.

to help build railways or mine gold, and then stayed. More recently, mobs in several Southeast Asian countries have taken Chinese as targets – tens of thousands were killed in Indonesia in 1965, and fresh attacks erupted in the 1990s.

Business success

Such attacks are fuelled largely by the economic success of the Overseas Chinese. As the author Lynn Pan has observed, 'It is … hard to imagine Southeast Asia without Chinese commerce.' In Thailand, Chinese run big banks, and the huge CP agricultural group – and the much-revered King Bhumibol is the son of a Thai-Chinese mother. In the Philippines, they control major companies. In Malaysia, despite a policy of positive discrimination towards the majority Malays, they are still major economic players – companies are sometimes described as 'Ali Baba' businesses, with native 'Ali' front men who ensure that they qualify for subsidies allocated to Malays, and the 'Baba' Chinese behind actually managing the concern.

In Vietnam, the Chinatown of Ho Chi Minh City (formerly Saigon) has revived as the country has moved towards market reforms. In Indonesia, the Chinese-owned Salim Group is estimated to have accounted for 5 per cent of the gross domestic product under the former President Suharto.

Though some American-Chinese have gone into politics, emigrant Chinese rarely seek positions of state power in Asia since this would expose them to further unwelcome attention and jealousy. When Corazon Aquino became President of the Philippines after democratization there, few knew that the maiden name of Corazon which gave her the nickname of 'Cory' came from the name of her immigrant Chinese grandfather. In Thailand, a further disguise of nomenclature was introduced when ethnic Chinese were obliged to take a Thai name.

Throughout the Overseas Chinese world, family networks are of extreme importance, partly as a matter of tradition, partly for protection. Family members are sent to run branches of the central business dispersed across several countries. When the patriarch dies, the elder son is called back from wherever he is working to assume the leadership of the business empire. Relationships between families stretching back for generations and between businessmen from different countries with common provincial or clan roots also play key roles. How that fits with modern requirements of corporate governance and transparency is a sensitive issue for Asian business in the 21st century.

In 1890s California, thousands of Chinese immigrants were employed by the railroads to do the toughest work.

Growth of emigration

Under the Chinese empire, emigration was not encouraged and, at times, positively prohibited. Though great fleets of imperial junks sailed far and wide in the 17th century, links with the rest of the world were tightly controlled by the court in Beijing. Still, Chinese traders settled in Indonesia, Japan and the Philippines. But, before the coming of the Westerners in the middle of the 19th century, the port city of Guangzhou (previously Canton) in southern China was the only one officially allowed to trade with foreign nations by sea. As a result, it became the channel through which Chinese, mainly from the southeast coast, went abroad, and the language spoken today in most

Chinatowns (and most Chinese restaurants in the West) is the Cantonese dialect.

As emigration grew in the 19th century, inhabitants of the east coast province of Fujian (Fukien) and from the island of Hainan made up another big wave of emigrants, many of them moving to the British colony of Singapore where they came to constitute a majority of the population. The imposition on China of treaty ports by the Europeans during the 19th century brought another point of departure for Chinese from their homeland, including labourers who helped build US railways. The spread of Western Christian missionary activity led to bright young converts being sent for further study abroad, such as Charlie Soong from Shanghai who returned home from America to start building a huge fortune by printing Bibles, and became father to a powerful clan.

Canton, now known as Guangzhou in southern China, was the only port officially allowed to trade with foreign nations. Cantonese emigrants made up a big portion of the Overseas Chinese.

Though some travelled to Europe, the main destinations were Southeast Asia and the Pacific Rim, stretching from Australia to Canada and the United States, from where they retained close links with their native regions, regarding themselves as remaining Chinese even if they never returned home.

As the Qing empire stumbled towards its grave in the early 20th century, the Overseas Chinese provided havens and funding for revolutionary movements. The first president of Republican China, Sun Yat-sen, cultivated them assiduously, and was on a fund-raising tour of the United States in October, 1911, when the revolution broke out in China which would overthrow the empire. In the opposite direction, Overseas Chinese moved back across the Pacific from America, Canada and Australia in the early 20th century to apply technologies and lessons they had absorbed abroad, for instance setting up the first Chinese department stores in the booming city of Shanghai.

When China adopted market-orientated economic policies in the 1980s, Overseas Chinese were the natural financial and industrial partners, even if many of their fathers had fled the mainland after the Communist victory of 1949. They operated primarily through Hong Kong which, despite returning to Chinese sovereignty in 1997, retains an equivocal status – half now part of China, half still the hub of the Overseas Chinese. In recent years, an increasing number of Chinese from the diaspora have returned to their mainland, primarily to oversee businesses on the spot or to bring expertise in the law, accounting and other professional services. But the Overseas Chinese remain one of the world's major transnational and trans-continental entities as they go about their business so successfully that, were they to be a single country, they would occupy a significant place among the economies of the world.

Further Reading

Natural Wonders

1 Mountains

Geil, W. E., *The Sacred Five of China* (London,1926)
Naquin, S. & Yu, *Pilgrims and Sacred Sites in China* (Berkeley, 1992)
Songqiao, Z., *The Physical Geography of China* (Beijing, 1986)

2 Guilin

Guilin Tourist Map (Cartographic Publishing House, Beijing, 1982)
Liu, S., *The Hills and Rivers of Guilin* (Beijing, 1987)

3 The Yangtze River

Butler, L., *Yangtze Remembered: The River Beneath the Lake*, (Stanford, 2004)
Dai, Q., *The River Dragon Has Come! The Three Gorges Dam and the Fate of China's Yangtze River and its People* (New York, 1998)
Van Slyke, L. P., *Yangtze: Nature, History and the River* (Reading, 1988)
Winchester, S., *The River at the Center of the World: A Journey Up the Yangtze and Back in Chinese Time* (New York, 2004)

4 The Yellow River

Chengrui, M. & Dregne, H. E., 'Silt and the Future Development of China's Yellow River', *The Geographical Journal* 167-1 (March 2001), 7–22
Greer, C. E., *Water Management in the People's Republic of China* (Austin, 1979)

5 Deserts

Cressey, G. B., *China's Geographic Foundation: A Survey of the Land and its People* (New York, 1934)
Mallory, J. P. & Mair, V., *The Tarim Mummies* (London & New York, 2000)
Stein, Sir M. A., *Ruins of Desert Cathay* (New York [1912], 1987)

6 The Silk Road

Whitfield, R., & Farrer, A., *Caves of the Thousand Buddhas: Chinese Art from the Silk Route* (London, 1990)
Whitfield, S. & Sims-Williams, U., *The Silk Road: Trade, Travel, War, Faith* (London, 2004)
Wood, F., *The Silk Road: Two Thousand Years in the Heart of Asia* (London, 2003)

7 Yunnan

Booz, P. & Booz, P., *Yunnan: Southwest China's Little-Known Land of Eternal Spring* (Columbus, 1987)
Little, A., *Across Yunnan: A Journey of Surprises* (Boston, 2005)
Unger, A. H. & Unger, W., *Yunnan: China's Most Beautiful Province* (Munich, 2002)
Xu, G., Miller, L. & Kun, X., *South of the Clouds: Tales from Yunnan* (Washington, 1994)

8 Northern Grasslands & Pastures

Committee on Scholarly Communication with the People's Republic of China, National Research Council, *Grasslands and Grassland Sciences in Northern China* (Washington, 1992)
Longworth, J. W. & Williamson, G. J., *China's Pastoral Region: Sheep and Wool, Minority Nationalities, Rangeland Degradation and Sustainable Development* (Wallingford, 1994)
Williams, D. M., *Beyond Great Walls: Environment, Identity, and Development on the Chinese Grasslands of Inner Mongolia* (Stanford, 2002)

9 Wildlife

Elvin, M., *The Retreat of the Elephants – An Environmental History* of China (New Haven, 2004)
Li W. & Zhao X., *China's Nature Reserves* (Beijing, 1989)
MacKinnon, J., *Wild China* (Cambridge, 1996)
Schaller, G., Hu, J., Pan, W. & Zhu, J., *The Giant Pandas of Wolong* (Chicago, 1985)
Tang Xiyang, *Living Treasures – An Odyssey Through China's Extraordinary Nature Reserves* (London, 1988)
Websites:
BirdLife International Red Data Book – *Threatened Birds of Asia* http://www.rdb.or.id
The IUCN Red List of Threatened Species http://www.iucnredlist.org

10 Trees & Flowers

Bretschneider, E., *History of European Botanical Discoveries in China* (St Petersburg, 1898)
Fearnley-Whittingstall, J., *Peonies: The Imperial Flower* (London, 1999)
The Flora of China series published jointly by Science Press, Beijing & Missouri Botanical Garden Press, St Louis (newsletter http://www.fna.org/china/mss/ news.htm)
Keswick, M., *The Chinese Garden: History, Art and Architecture* (London, 1986)
Lancaster, R., *Travels in China: A Plantsman's Paradise* (Woodbridge, 1989)
Lauener, L. A. & Ferguson, D. K., *The Introduction of Chinese Plants into Europe* (Amsterdam, 1996)
The 3rd Global Botanical Gardens Congress, held at the Wuhan Botanical Gardens, April 2007 (www.3GBGC.com/index.asp)
Valder, P., *The Garden Plants of China* (London, 1999)

People & Life

11 Han Chinese

Blunden, C. & Elvin, M., *Cultural Atlas of China* (London 1983, 1998)
Buchanan, K., *The Transformation of the Chinese Earth* (London, 1970)
Eberhard, W., *A History of China* (Berkeley & London, 1992)
Ebrey, P., *Cambridge Illustrated History of China* (Cambridge, 1996, 2006)
Elvin, M., *The Retreat of the Elephants – An Environmental History* of China (New Haven, 2004)
Schafer, E., *The Golden Peaches of Samarkand: A Study of T'ang Exotics* (Berkeley 1963, reprint 1985)
Schafer, E., *The Vermilion Bird: T'ang Images of the South* (Berkeley, 1967)

12 The Imperial System & its Downfall

Hsü, I., *The Rise of Modern China* (Oxford, 2000)

Krahl, R., Murck, F., Rawski, E. & Rawson, J., *China: The Three Emperors 1662–1795* (Royal Academy exhibition catalogue, London, 2005)
Paludan, A., *Chronicle of the Chinese Emperors* (London & New York, 1998)
Rawski, E., *The Last Emperors: A Social History of Qing Imperial Institutions* (Berkeley, 1998)
Schurmann, F. & Schell, O., *Imperial China* (London, 1977)
Spence, J., *The Search for Modern China* (New York, 1990)

13 Philosophy
Chan, W., *A Source Book in Chinese Philosophy* (Princeton, 1963)
Cheng, C. & Bunnin, N. (eds), *Contemporary Chinese Philosophy* (Malden & Oxford, 2002)
Confucius, *The Analects*, trans. D. C. Lau (London, 1979)
Graham, A. C., *Disputers of the Tao: Philosophical Argument in Ancient China* (Peru, IL, 1989)
Lao Tzu, *Tao Te Ching*, trans. D. C. Lau (London, 1963)
Mencius, *Mencius*, trans. D. C. Lau (London, 1970)
Yu-lan, F., *A Short History of Chinese Philosophy* (New York, 1948)
Zhuangzi [or Chuang-tzu], *Chuang-tzu, The Inner Chapters*, trans. A. C. Graham (London & Boston, 1981)

14 Religion
Adler, J. A., *Chinese Religious Traditions* (Upper Saddle River, 2002)
de Bary, W. T. & Bloom, I. (eds), *Sources of Chinese Tradition* (2nd ed., Vol. 1, New York, 1999)
Lopez, Jr., D. S. (ed.), *Religions of China in Practice* (Princeton, 1996)

15 Taiji & the Dao
Hua, W., *Grand Dictionary of Zhou Yi* (Zhongshan, 1993)
Jingfang, J. & Shaogang, L. (trans.), *Zhou Yi* ['Book of Changes'] (Jilin City, 1996)
Lao Tzu [Laozi], *Tao Te Ching [or Dao De Jing]*, trans. D. C. Lau (London, 1963)
Sima Qian, *A Historical Record [of the Han dynasty]* (Hong Kong, 1959)

16 Martial Arts
Hong, Y., *Monasteries and Temples* (Beijing, 2004)
The Overseas Chinese Affairs Office, *Common Knowledge about Chinese Culture* (Hong Kong, 2004)

17 Ethnic Minorities
Hansen, M. H., *Frontier People: Han Settlers in Minority Areas of China* (London, 2005)
Mackerras, C., *China's Minority Cultures: Identities and Integration since 1912* (London, 1995)
Mackerras, C., *China's Ethnic Minorities and Globalisation* (London, 2003)

18 The Tarim Mummies
Barber, E. W., *The Mummies of Ürümchi* (New York & London, 1999)
Hadingham, E., 'The Mummies of Xinjiang', *Discover*, 15.4 (April 1994), 68–77
Mair, V. H., 'The Bronze Age and Early Iron Age Peoples of Eastern Central Asia', 2 vols., *Journal of Indo-European Studies Monograph Series*, no. 26 (Washington, DC & Philadelphia, 1998)
Mair, V. H., 'Genes, geography, and glottochronology: the Tarim Basin during late Prehistory and history', in Jones-Bley, K., *et al.* (eds) *Proceedings of the Sixteenth Annual UCLA Indo-European Conference* (Los Angeles, November 5–6, 2004), *Journal of Indo-European Studies Monograph Series*, no. 50 (Washington, DC, 2005), 1–46. (Appendix: 'Proto-Tocharian, Common Tocharian, and Tocharian – on the value of linguistic connections in a reconstructed language' by Carling, G., 47–71)
Mair, V. H., 'Mummies of the Tarim Basin', *Archaeology*, 48.2 (March / April 1995), 28–35
Mallory, J. P. & Mair, V. H., *The Tarim Mummies: Ancient China and the Mystery of the Earliest Peoples from the West* (London & New York, 2000)

19 Circuses & Acrobats
Chen, Y. & Liu, J. (eds), *Zhong guo qu yi. za ji. mu ou xi. pi ying xi* ['Musical drama, acrobatics, puppetry, and puppet silhouette show in China'] (Beijing, 1999)
Fu, Q. & Fu, T., *Zhong guo za ji shi* ['History of acrobatics in China'] (Shanghai, 2004)
Ni, Y., 'Performing Arts', in *China*, ed. Shaughnessy, E. L. (London, 2005)

20 Agriculture
Hsiao-Tung, F., *Peasant Life in China: A Field Study of Country Life in the Yangtze Valley* (New York, 1939)
Kueh, Y. Y. & Ash, R. F. (ed.), *Economic Trends in Chinese Agriculture: The Impact of Post-Mao Reforms* (Oxford, 1993)
King, F.H., *Farmers of Forty Centuries or Permanent Agriculture in China, Korea and Japan* (reprinted Kila, 1911, 2004)
Lardy, N. R., *Agriculture in China's Modern Economic Development* (Cambridge, 1983)
Lossing Buck, J., *Land Utilisation in China* (Chicago, 1937; reprinted New York, 1964)
Perkins, D. H., *Agricultural Development in China, 1368–1968* (Chicago, 1969)

21 Food & Alcoholic Drinks
Anderson, E. N., *The Food of China* (New Haven & London, 1988)
Chang, K. C. (ed.), *Food in Chinese Culture* (New Haven & London, 1977)
Dunlop, F., *Sichuan Cookery* (London, 2003)
Lin, H. J. & Lin, T., *Chinese Gastronomy* (New York, 1996)
Sabban, F., 'China' in Kiple, K. F. & Ornelas, K. C. (eds), *The Cambridge World History of Food*, (Cambridge, 2000)
So, Y., *Classic Food of China* (London, 1992)

Cities & Towns

22 Imperial Beijing
Arlington, L. C. & Lewisohn, W., *In Search of Old Peking* (Peking, 1935, 1991)
Bredon, J., *Peking: A Historical and Intimate Description of its Chief Places of Interest* (Shanghai, 1920)
Bridge, A., *Peking Picnic* (London, 1932)
Naquin, S., *Peking: Temples and City Life 1400–1900* (Berkeley, 2000)
Pan, G., 'The Yuan and Ming dynasties' and Sun, D., 'The Qing dynasty', in Steinhardt, N. S., *Chinese Architecture* (New Haven, 2002)

23 The Forbidden City
Johnston, R., *Twilight in the Forbidden City* (Hong Kong & Oxford, 1934, 1987)
Krahl, R., Murck, F., Rawski, E. & Rawson, J., *China: The Three Emperors 1662–1795* (Royal Academy exhibition catalogue,

London, 2005)
Rawski, E. S., *The Last Emperors: A Social History of Qing Imperial Institutions* (Berkeley, 1998)
Shambaugh Elliott, J., with Shambaugh, D., *The Odyssey of China's Imperial Treasures* (Seattle, 2005)
Wood, F., *Forbidden City* (London, 2005)
Yu, Z. & Hutt, G., *Palaces of the Forbidden City* (Harmondsworth, 1984)

24 The Summer Palace
The Summer Palace (Beijing, 1981)
Ling, Princess D., *Two Years in the Forbidden City* (London, 1912)

25 The Temple of Heaven
Arlington, L. C. & Lewisohn, W., *In Search of Old Peking* (Peking, 1935, 1991)
Naquin, S., *Peking: Temples and City Life 1400–1900* (Berkeley, 2000)

26 Beijing Today
Becker, J., *The Chinese* (London, 2001)
Broudehoux, A.-M., *Beijing: The Making and Selling of Post-Mao Beijing* (London & New York, 2004)
DeWoskin, R., *Foreign Babes in Beijing: Behind the Scenes of a New China* (New York, 2005)
Schell, O., *Mandate of Heaven* (London 1905, 1996)
She, L., *Rickshaw: The Novel Lo-t'o Hsiang Tzu* (Hawaii, 1979)
Spence, J. D., *The Gate of Heavenly Peace: The Chinese and Their Revolution, 1895–1980* (Harmondsworth, 1981)

27 Shanghai – 'Paris of the Orient'
Dong, S., *Shanghai, The Rise and Fall of a Decadent City* (New York, 2000)
Fenby, J., *Generalissimo* (London, 2003)
Pan, L., *Old Shanghai* (Singapore, 1999)
Pan, L., *Shanghai, A Century in Photographs, 1843–1949* (Hong Kong, 1993)
Seagrave, S., *The Soong Dynasty* (New York, 1986)
Sergeant, H., *Shanghai* (London, 1991)

28 Shanghai Today
Denis, E. & Yu Ren, G., *Building of Shanghai* (London, 2006)
Wei Hui, Z., *Shanghai Baby* (London, 2003)
Yatso, P., *New Shanghai* (London, 2000)
See also relevant passages in Kynge, J., *China Shakes the World* (London, 2006) and in Gittings, J., *The Changing Face of China* (Oxford, 2005)

29 Hangzhou
Gernet, J., *Daily Life in China on the Eve of the Mongol Invasion 1250–1276* (Stanford, 1970)
Macartney, G., *An Embassy to China: Being the Journal Kept by Lord Macartney During his Embassy to the Emperor Ch'ien-lung 1793–1794* (reprinted London, 2004), 126–129

30 Suzhou
Brook, T., *The Confusions of Pleasure: Commerce and Culture in Ming China* (Berkeley, 1998)
Keswick, M. (rev. Hardie, A. & Jencks, C.), *The Chinese Garden: History, Art and Architecture* (London, 2002)

31 Xi'an
Bishop, K. (rev.), *Xi'an: China's Ancient Capital for a Thousand Years* (Hong Kong, 1987)
Wu, B., *History of Xian* (Xi'an, 1981)
Wu, F., *Chang'an: The Starting Point of the Silk Road* (Xi'an, 1985)

32 Nanjing
Bowers Museum of Cultural Art, *Symbols of Power: Masterpieces of the Nanjing Museum* (Chicago, 2002)
Chang, I., *The Rape of Nanjing* (London, 1997)
Courtauld, C., *Nanjing, Wuxi, Suzhou and Jiangsu Province: Land of Lakes and Classical Gardens* (London, 1987)
Danielson, E. *Nanjing and the Lower Yangzi: From Past to Present* (New York, 2004)
Ye, Z., *Nanjing 1937: A Love Story* (New York & London, 2004)

33 Shenyang
Shenjing tongzhi ['Record of Shenyang and its Environs'], Qing dynasty
Till, B. & Swart, P., 'Nurhachi and Abahai: their palace and mausolea', *Arts of Asia* (May/June 1988), 149–157
Wang, P. (ed.), *Shenjing sanling* ['Three Tombs in Shenjing'] (Shenyang, 1990)

Monuments & Buildings

34 Domestic & Religious Architecture
Fu, X., *et al.*, *Chinese Architecture* (New Haven, 2002)
Knapp, R., *China's Traditional Rural Architecture* (Hawaii, 1986)
Needham, J., *Science and Civilisation in China*, Vol. 3: 'Civil Engineering and Nautics' (Cambridge, 1954)
Prip-Moller, J., *Chinese Buddhist Monasteries* (Hong Kong, [1937] 1967)

35 The Tomb of the First Emperor
Ciarla, R., The Eternal Army: The Terracotta Army of the First Chinese Emperor (Vercelli, 2005)
Cotterell, A., *The First Emperor of China* (London, 1981)
Hessler, P. & Mazzatenta, O. L., 'Rising to Life, Treasures of Ancient China', *National Geographic* (October, 2001)
Mazzatenta, O. L., 'China's Warriors Rise From the Earth', *National Geographic* (October 1996)
Topping, A., 'China's Incredible Find', *National Geographic* (April 1978)

36 The Great Wall
Geil, W. E., *The Great Wall of China* (London, 1909)
Michau R., *The Great Wall of China*, trans. M. Jan (New York, 2001)
Newton Hayes, L., *The Great Wall of China* (Shanghai, 1929)
Waldron, A., *The Great Wall of China: From History to Myth* (Cambridge, 1990)
Zewen, L., *et al.*, *The Great Wall* (St Louis, 1981)
Zhuantong, W., *Wanli changcheng* ['The Ten-Thousand-*li* Great Wall'] (China, 1987)

37 The Ming Tombs
De Groot, J. J. M., *The Religious System of China*, 6 vols. (Leyden 1892–1920; reprint Taibeh, 1967)
Paludan, A., *The Imperial Ming Tombs* (New Haven, 1981)
Paludan, A., *The Chinese Spirit Road* (New Haven, 1991)
Segalen, V., *The Great Statuary of China*, trans. E. Levieux (Chicago, 1978)

38 Leshan Great Buddha & Caves
Wood, F., *Blue Guide: China* (London, 2001)
World Heritage List: China (Beijing, 2005)

39 Labrang Yellow Hat Monastery

Gruschke, A., 'The Cultural Monuments of Tibet's Outer Provinces', in *The Gansu and Sichuan Parts of Amdo*, Vol. 2 (Bangkok, 2001)

Nietupski, P. K., *Labrang: A Tibetan Buddhist Monastery at the Crossroads of Four Civilizations* (New York, 1998)

40 Great Monuments of Tibet

Guise, A. (ed.), *The Potala Palace of Tibet* (London, 1988)

Larsen, K. & Sinding-Larsen, A., *The Lhasa Atlas: Traditional Tibetan Architecture and Townscape* (London, 2001)

Meyer, F., 'The Potala Palace of the Dalai Lamas in Lhasa', *Orientations* (July 1987)

Ricca, F. & Lo Bue, E., *The Great Stupa of Gyantse: A Complete Tibetan Pantheon of the Fifteenth Century* (London, 1993)

41 The Grand Canal

Needham, J., *Science and Civilisation in China*, Vol. 4: 'Physics and Physical Technology', Part 3: 'Civil Engineering and Nautics' (Cambridge, 1971)

Twitchett, D. & Fairbank, J. K. (eds), *The Cambridge History of China*, Vol. 3: 'Sui and Tang China 589–906', Part 1 (Cambridge, 1979), 135–138, 355–357

42 Buddhist Cliff Carvings at Dazu

Dazu Rock Carvings Museum, *Dazu Rock Carvings of China* (Chongqing, 1991)

Howard, A., *Summit of Treasures: Buddhist Cave Art of Dazu, China* (Weatherhill, 2001)

Paludan, A., *Chinese Sculpture: A Great Tradition* (Chicago, 2006)

43 Modern Buildings & Infrastructure

Becker, J., *The Chinese*, Chap. 5 (London, 2001)

Dai, Q., *The River Dragon Has Come! The Three Gorges Dam and the Fate of China's Yangtze River and its People* (New York, 1998)

Fishman, T., *China Inc: How the Rise of the Next Superpower Challenges America and the World* (New York, 2005)

The Arts

44 Bronze Work

Chang, K., *The Archaeology of Ancient China*, 3rd ed. (New Haven, 1978)

Li, B., *Studies on the Structural System of Chinese Bronze Culture* (Beijing, 1998)

Ma, C., *Chinese Bronze Work* (Beijing, 1992)

The Metropolitan Museum of Art, *Treasures from the Bronze Age of China: An Exhibition from the People's Republic of China* (New York, 1980)

45 Jade

Rawson, J., *Chinese Jade from the Neolithic to the Qing* (London, 2002)

Watt, J., *Chinese Jades from Han to Ch'ing* (New York, 1980)

Wilson, M., *Chinese Jades* (London, 2004)

46 Calligraphy

Fong, W. C. & Watt, J. C. Y., *et al.*, *Possessing the Past: Treasures from the National Palace Museum, Taipei* (2000)

Harrist, Jr, R. E. & Fong, W. C., *The Embodied Image: Chinese Calligraphy from the John B. Elliott Collection* (New York, 1999)

Ledderose, L., *Ten Thousand Things: Module and Mass Production in Chinese Art* (Princeton, 1999)

Sturman, P. C., *Mi Fu: The Style and Art of Calligraphy in Northern Song China* (New Haven, 1997)

Sullivan, M., *The Three Perfections: Chinese Painting, Poetry and Calligraphy* (New York, 1980)

47 The Orchid Pavilion Preface

Ledderose, L., *Mi Fu and the Classical Tradition of Chinese Calligraphy* (Princeton, 1979)

48 Literature

Idema, W. L. & Haft, L., *A Guide to Chinese Literature* (Ann Arbor, 1997)

Lau, J. S. M. & Goldblatt, H. (eds), *The Columbia Anthology of Modern Chinese Literature* (New York, 1995)

Mair, V. H. (ed.), *The Columbia Anthology of Traditional Chinese Literature* (New York, 1994)

Mair, V. H. (ed.), *The Columbia History of Chinese Literature* (New York, 2001)

Nienhauser, W. H., Jr, *et al.* (eds), *The Indiana Companion to Traditional Chinese Literature* (Bloomington, 1986; Vol. 2, 1998)

Owen, S. (ed.), *An Anthology of Chinese Literature: Beginnings to 1911* (New York, 1996)

49 Music & Beijing Opera

Chen, D., Ye, C., *et al.* (eds), *Zhongguo jingju* ['Beijing Opera'] (Shanghai, 1999)

DeWoskin, K., *A Song for One or Two: Music and the Concept of Art in Early China* (Ann Arbor, 1982)

Fei, F. C. (ed. & trans.), *Chinese Theories of Theater and Performance from Confucius to the Present* (Ann Arbor, 1999)

Lai, T. C. & Mok, R., *Jade Flute: The Story of Chinese Music* (Hong Kong, 1981)

Nettl, B., *et al.*, *Excursions in World Music* (Upper Saddle River, 1997)

Shen, S., *China: A journey into its Musical Art* (Chicago, 2000)

Xu, C., *Peking Opera*, trans. C. Gengtao (Beijing, 2003)

50 Painting

Barnhart, R. M, *et al.*, *Three Thousand Years of Chinese Painting* (New Haven, 1997)

Clunas, C., *Art in China* (Oxford History of Art) (Oxford, 1997)

Fong, W. C., *Beyond Representation: Chinese Painting and Calligraphy 8th–14th Century* (Princeton Monographs in Art and Archaeology, No. 48) (Princeton, 1992)

Loehr, M., *The Great Painters of China* (London, 1980)

McCausland, C., *First Masterpiece of Chinese Painting: The Admonitions Scroll* (London, 2003)

Thorp, R. L. & Vinograd, R. E., *Chinese Art and Culture* (New York, 2001)

51 Porcelain

Harrison-Hall, J., *Ming Ceramics in the British Museum* (London, 2001)

Needham, J., *et al.*, *Science and Civilisation in China*, Vol. 5, Part 12: 'Ceramic Technology' ed. R. Kerr (Cambridge, 2004)

Pierson, S. (ed.), *Qingbai Ware: Chinese Porcelain of the Song and Yuan Dynasties* (London, 2002)

Qingzheng, W. (ed.), *Underglaze Blue and Red* (Shanghai, 1993)

Vainker, S., *Chinese Pottery and Porcelain* (London, 1991)

52 Lacquer Work

Clifford, D., *Chinese Carved Lacquer* (London, 1992)

Garner, Sir H., *Chinese Lacquer* (London, 1979)

Hu, S., *et al.*, *2000 Years of Chinese Lacquer* (Hong Kong, 1993)

Scott, R., *et al.*, *Lacquer: An International History and Collector's Guide* (Marlborough, 1984)
Watt, J. C. Y & Brennan Ford, B., *East Asian Lacquer: The Florence and Herbert Irving Collection* (New York, 1991)

53 Sculpture
Howard, A., *et al.*, *Chinese Sculpture* (New Haven, 2006)
Paludan, A., *Chinese Sculpture: A Great Tradition* (Chicago, 2006)
Rawson, J. (ed.), *Chinese Art* (London, 1992)
Sickman, L. & Soper, A., *The Art and Architecture of China* (London, [1956] 1971)
Siren, O., *Chinese Sculpture from the Fifth to the Fourteenth Century*, 2 vols (London, 1925; reprint 1998)

54 Silk Work
Gao, H., *Chinese Textile Designs*, trans. R. Scott & S. Whitfield (London, 1986)
Garrett, V. M. (ed.), *Heaven's Embroidered Cloths: One Thousand Years of Chinese Textiles* (Hong Kong, 1995)
Vainker, S., *Chinese Silk: A Cultural History* (London, 2004)
Watt, J. C. Y. & Wardwell, A., *When Silk Was Gold: Central Asian and Chinese Textiles* (New York, 1997)
Wilson, V., *Chinese Textiles* (London, 2005)
Wilson, V., *Chinese Dress* (London, 1986)

55 Furniture
Berliner, N., *Chinese Furniture of the 16th and 17th Centuries* (Boston, 1996)
Clunas, C., *Chinese Furniture* (London,1988)
Clunas, C., *Superfluous Things: Material Culture and Social Status in Early Modern China* (Cambridge, 1991)
Handler, S., *Austere Luminosity of Chinese Classical Furniture* (Berkeley & Los Angeles, 2001)
Jacobsen, R. & Grindley, N., *Classical Chinese Furniture in the Minneapolis Institute of Arts* (Chicago, 1999)
Wang, S., *Connoisseurship of Chinese Furniture, Ming and Early Qing Dynasties* (Hong Kong, 1990)
Zhu, J., *The Complete Collection of Treasures of the Palace Museum, Furniture of the Ming and Qing Dynasties*, Vols I & II (Hong Kong, 2002)

56 Gardens
Clunas, C., *Fruitful Sites: Garden Culture in Ming Dynasty China* (London, 1996)
Cheng, J., *The Craft of Gardens*, trans. A. Hardie (New Haven & London, 1988)
Dongchu, H., *The Way of the Virtuous: The Influence of Art and Philosophy on Chinese Garden Design* (Peking, 1991)
Keswick, M., *The Chinese Garden: History, Art and Architecture*, 3rd ed. (London, 2003)
Valder, P., *Gardens in China* (Portland, 2002)

Inventions & Achievements

57 Science
Dainian, F. & Cohen, R. S. (eds), 'Chinese Studies in the History and Philosophy of Science and Technology', *Boston Studies in the Philosophy of Science*, 179 (Boston, 1996)
Lloyd, G. E. R. & Sivin, N., *The Way and the Word: Science and Medicine in Early China and Greece* (New Haven, 2002)
Needham, J., *et al.*, *Science and Civilisation in China*, 23 vols to date (Cambridge, 1954–)
Pregadio, F., *Great Clarity: Daoism and Alchemy in Early Medieval China* (Asian Religions and Cultures No. 4) (Stanford, 2006)

58 Astronomy
Cullen, C., *Astronomy and Mathematics in Ancient China: The Zhou bi suan jing* (Needham Research Institute Studies No. 1) (Cambridge, 1996)
Needham, J., *et al.*, *Science and Civilisation in China*, 23 vols to date (Cambridge, 1954–)
Selin, H. & Xiaochun, S. (eds), *Astronomy across Cultures: the History of Non-Western Astronomy* (Dordrecht, 2000)
Xiaochun, S. & Kistemaker, J., *The Chinese Sky during the Han: Constellating Stars & Society* (Leiden, 1997)

59 Paper & Printing
Hand Papermaking, a twice-yearly publication, Washington, DC (http://www.handpapermaking.org)
Hunter, D., *A Papermaking Pilgrimage to Japan, Korea, and China* (New York, 1936)
International Dunhuang Project (http://idp.bl.uk)
Luo, S. (ed.) & Chan S. (trans.), *An Illustrated History of Printing in Ancient China* (Beijing & Hong Kong, 1998)
Polastron, L. X., *Le Papier: 2000 Ans d' Histoire et de Savoir-faire* ['Paper: Two Thousand Years of History and Know-how'] (Paris, 1999)
Tsien, T., 'Paper and Printing', Vol. 5, Part 1 of *Science and Civilisation in China*, ed. Needham, J. (Cambridge, [1985] 1993)
Tsien, T., *Written on Bamboo and Silk: The Beginnings of Chinese Books and Inscriptions* (Chicago & London, [1962] 2004)

60 Medicine
Bray, F., 'The Chinese Experience', in Pickstone, J. V. & Cooter, R. (eds), *Medicine in the Twentieth Century* (Amsterdam, 2000) 719–738
Goldschmidt, A., 'The Song Discontinuity', *Asian Medicine* 1(1) (2005) 53–90
Harper, D., *Early Chinese Medical Literature: The Mawangdui Medical Manuscripts* (London, 1998)
Hsu, E., *The Transmission of Chinese Medicine* (Cambridge, 1999)
Lo, V. & Cullen, C., *Medieval Chinese Medicine* (London, 2005)
Scheid, V., *Chinese Medicine in Contemporary China: Plurality and Synthesis* (Durham, 2002)
Taylor, K., *Medicine in Early Communist China* (London, 2005)
Unschuld, P., *Huang di nei jing su wen* (Berkeley, 2003)

61 The Decimal System & Abacus
Martzloff, J.-C., *A History of Chinese Mathematics*, trans. S. L. Wilson (Berlin, 1997)

62 The Compass, Navigation & Junks
Dreyer, E. L. & Stearns P., *Zheng He: China and the Oceans in the Early Ming, 1405–1433* (London, 2006)
Gang, D., *Chinese Maritime Activities and Socioeconomic Development, c. 2100 BC–1900 AD* (Westport & London, 1999)
Hirth, F. & Rockhill, W. W. (ed. & trans.), *Chau Ju-kua: On the Chinese and Arab Trade in the Twelfth and Thirteenth Centuries* (St-Petersburg, 1911; Amsterdam, 1966).
Mills, J. V. G., *Ma Huan, Ying-yai Sheng-lan* ['The Overall Survey of the Ocean's Shores'] (Cambridge, 1970)
Needham, J. (with Ling, W. & Girwood Robinson, K.), *Science and Civilisation in China*, Vol. 4: 'Physics and Physical Technology' Part 1: 'Physics' (Cambridge, 1962)
Needham, J. (with Ling, W. & Lu, G.), *Science and Civilisation in China*, Vol. 4: 'Physics and Physical Technology', Part 3: 'Civil Engineering and Nautics' (Cambridge, 1971)

63 Bridges
Coyne, P., 'Carpenters of the Rainbow', *Archaeology* 45(2) (1992), 32–36
Knapp, R. G., 'Bridge on the River Xiao', *Archaeology* 41(1) (1988), 48–54
Knapp, R. G., *Chinese Bridges* (Hong Kong & New York, 1993)
Liu, J. & Shen, W., *Lounge Bridges in Taishun* (Shanghai, 2005)

64 The Art of War
Ames, R. T., *Sun-tzu: The Art of Warfare – The First English Translation Incorporating the Recently Discovered Yin-ch'üeh-shan Texts* (New York, 1993)
Graff, D. A., *Medieval Chinese Warfare, 300–900* (London & New York, 2002)
Graff, D. A. & Higham, R., *A Military History of China* (Boulder, 2002)
Needham, J. & Yates, R. D. S., *Science and Civilisation in China*, Vol. 5, Part 6: 'Military Technology: Missiles and Sieges' (Cambridge, 1994)
Sawyer, R. D., *The Seven Military Classics of Ancient China* (Boulder, 1993)
Van de Ven, H. (ed.), *Warfare in Chinese History*. Leiden, Boston & Köln, 2000)

65 Gunpowder
Chase, K., *Firearms: A Global History to 1700* (Cambridge, 2003)
Crosby, A. W., *Throwing Fire: Projectile Technology through History* (Cambridge, 2002)
Liang, J., *Chinese Siege Warfare: Mechanical Artillery and Siege Weapons of Antiquity* (Singapore, 2006)
Needham, J., *Science and Civilisation in China,* Vol. 5, Part 7: 'Chemistry and Chemical Technology: The Gunpowder Epic' (Cambridge, 1986)
Sawyer, R. D., *Fire and Water: The Art of Incendiary and Aquatic Warfare in China* (Boulder, 2004)

66 Everyday Objects
Dabry De Thiersant, P., *La pisciculture et la pêche en Chine* ['Fishing Culture and Fish in China'] (Paris, 1872)
Dikötter, F., *Things Modern: Material Culture and Everyday Life in China* (London, 2006)
Gernet, J., trans. Wright, H. M., *Daily Life in China on the Eve of the Mongol Invasion 1250–1276* (London, 1962)
Gerth, G., 'China Made: Consumer Culture and the Creation of the Nation', *Harvard East Asian Monographs* 224 (Cambridge & London, 2003)
Hommel, R. P., *China at Work: An Illustrated Record of the Primitive Industries of China's Masses, Whose Life is Toil, and Thus an Account of Chinese Civilization* ([1st ed. New York, 1937] Cambridge, 1969)
Needham, J. (ed.), *Science and Civilisation in China*, Vol. 4: 'Physics and Physical Technology', Part 2: 'Mechanical Engineering' (Cambridge, 1965)

67 The History of Tea
Ball, S., *An Account of The Cultivation and Manufacture of Tea in China* (London, 1848)
Blofeld, J., *The Chinese Art of Tea* (London, 1985)
Evans, J. C., *Tea in China* (New York, 1992)
Fortune, R., *A Journey to the Tea Countries of China* (London, 1852)
Yu, L., *The Classic of Tea*, trans. Carpenter, F. R., (Boston, 1974)

Greater China

68 Hong Kong & Macau
Fenby, J., *Dealing with the Dragon: A Year in the New Hong Kong* (London & New York, 2000)
Morris, J., *Hong Kong* (Chicago, 1988)
Snow, P., *The Fall of Hong Kong: Britain, China, and the Japanese Occupation* (New Haven, 2003)
Tsang, S., *A Modern History of Hong Kong: 1841–1997* (London & New York, 2003)
Welsh, F., *A Borrowed Place: The History of Hong Kong* (New York, 1993)

69 Taiwan
Clements, J., *Coxinga* (London, 2005)
Fenby, J., 'Two Chinas One Problem', *Prospect* (March 2004)
MacDonald, P., *Taiwan* (London, 2004)
Manthorpe, J., *Forbidden Nation: A History of Taiwan* (London & New York, 2005)

70 Overseas Chinese
Pan, L., *Sons of the Yellow Emperor* (Boston, 1990)
Seagrave, S., *Lords of the Rim: The Invisible Empire of the Overseas Chinese* (London & New York, 1995)
Weidenbaum, M. & Hughes, S., *The Bamboo Network: How Expatriate Chinese Entrepeneurs are Creating a New Economic Superpower in Asia* (New York, 1996)

Sources of Illustrations

a: above; b: below; c: centre; l: left; r: right

Alamy: A. M. Corporation 146, Tibor Bognar 135, Dan Bachmann 97a, Dennis Cox 142a, Kevin Foy 116–117, franzfoto.com 52l, Eddie Gerald 171, JTB Photo Communications Inc 142b, Yadid Levy 288, Mary Evans Picture Library 274br, Panorama Media (Beijing) Ltd 105, 132, 143, 193r, 241, Keren Su 208, Reven T. C. Wurman 192b,View Stock 106–107;

American Museum of Natural History, New York, N. Y., Courtesy of Department of Library Services 65b;

Ancient Art & Architecture Collection 257b

B. L. Arlington, *The Chinese Drama From The Earliest Times until Today*, Kelly and Walsh Ltd, Shanghai, 1930, p. 25 210;

Art Archive/Private Collection 66;

Ashmolean Museum, Oxford 74b;

Bibliothèque Nationale de France, Paris 72b, 131, 204;

Bodleian Library, Oxford (Sinica 94) 234a;

Ingrid Booz Morejohn 74a;

BPK/Staatsbibliothek zu Berlin 145;

Bridgeman Art Library: Victoria & Albert Museum, London 178, 224, Private Collection 219a, 262a, Peabody Essex Museum, Salem 256;

British Library, London: 47a, 110, 155a, Sir Marc Aurel Stein 85b, 253;

British Museum, London 65ar, 69, 71b, 73, 75a, 213, 243b;

Charis Chan, *China,* Odyssey Passport, Hong Kong, 1998, p. 45 93;

Christie's 64r,

Corbis: Albright-Knox Art Gallery, Buffalo, N. Y., Gift of Northrup R. Knox, 1999 282, Archivo Iconografico, S. A. 68, 72a, Arte & Immagini srl 53a, Asian Art & Archaeology, Inc 222–223, Tiziana & Gianni Baldizzone 173b, Dave Bartruff 144, 276b, Bettmann 38a, 259, 277, Tibor Bognar 22–23, 169, Kazuyoshi Nomachi 207, Bohemian Nomad Picturemakers / Kevin R. Morris 179, Brooklyn Museum, N. Y. 56b, Burstein Collection 70l, Christie's Images 54a, Dean Conger 166, 266 Jerry Cooke 258b, EPA 185, EPALi Yang 62, Wu Hong 70r, Adrian Bradshaw 117r, Michael Reynolds 172b, Diego Azubel 211, Ric Ergenbright 40, Eye Ubiquitous / Julia Waterlow 24, 36, 37, 180–181, 182a, Fine Art Photographic Library 56a, 275b, Free Agents Limited 2–3, 16–17, Dallas and John Heaton 227, 280, Jose Fuste Raga 108, 183, Marc Garanger 6a, Justin Guariglia 58–59, Robert Harding World Imagery 136, 161, Jon Hicks 14, Historical Picture Archive 141, Hulton Archive 61, 81b, J. Thompson 101, Imagemore Co. Ltd 285, Wolfgang Kaehler 41a, 81a, Earl & Nazima Kowall 133a, Daniel Lainé 82a, Yann Layma 49, Liu Liqun 6b, 33b, 50, 100, 192–193a, 230b, Yang Liu 184b, 283, Olivier Martel 276b, Michael Masian Historic Photographs 281, NASA 27, Tom Nebbia 154r, Louie Psihoyos 7a, Ann Purcell 168, Carl & Ann Purcell 75b, Ryan Pyle 148–149, Enzo & Paolo Ragazzini 182b, Reza, Webistan 44–45a, Reuters / China Newsphoto 42, Bazuki Muhammad 79b, Andrew Wong 109, Jim Richardson 47b, Roger Ressmeyer 244–245, Royal Ontario Museum, Toronto 219, 221, Bob Sacha 260a, John Slater 63, 113, 172–173a, Keren Su 39, 46a, 57, 91, 164, 176–177b, 186–187, 228, 262b, Underwood & Underwood 289, Brian A. Vikander 150, Nik Wheeler 51, Xiaoyang Liu 20–21, Xinhua 32, Xinhua Press/Long Hongtao 35a, Zefa / Frank Lukasseck 7b, Liang Zhuoming 38b, 41b;

Cultural Institute of Chun Hua County, Shaanxi Province 94a;

Cultural Relics Bureau, Luoyang City 19;

Cultural Relics Bureau, Xindu County, Sichuan Province 87;

from De Vinne, T. L., *The Invention of Printing*, F. Hart, New York, 1876 274a;

Fuchsia Dunlop 96;

EMPICS: AP Photos / Color China Photo 119b, Vincent Yu 284b;

Eslite Gallery, Taipei, photo Lin Ri-shan, 201b;

from Favier, Alphonse, *Peking: Histoire et Description*, Peking, 1897 153b;

R. B. Fleming 154l;

Eugene Fuller Memorial Collection, Seattle 64l;

Flickr: Eneko Ametzaga 29, Jason Fasi 104, Stuart Forster 21, Jack French 31, Richard Gibbon 119a, Vincent LaConte 118–119, Peter Morgan 34, 35, 82b, 83r, Alexander Moss 94b, Pan Shijun 80, Pedro Szekely 225, Bill Tyne 155b, Neil Yeung 95;

Freer Gallery of Art, New York 214a;

Getty Images: Glen Allison 112, Mike Brinson 5a, Rex Butcher 184a, Angelo Cavalli 175, China Tourism Press 84, Cancan Chu 78b, Gary Cralle 284a, DAJ 287, Dorling Kindersley / Nick Hicks 48, Greg Elms 139, Macduff Everton 111, Robert Everts 30, 102, Grant V. Faint 278–279, Robert Harding World Imagery / Gavin Hellier 114, Gavin Hellier 129a, 156–157, 177a, 177b, Hulton Archive 98–99, Spencer Arnold 258a, Jeff Hunter 55, Sean Justice 127a, Yann Layma 130, 147a, Alex Mares-Manton 286a, Tony Metaxas, 199, National Geographic / Raymond Gehman 92, David Noton 120, Richard Nowitz 167, Panoramic Images 127b, Martin Puddy 26, 138l, 267b, Steve Satushek 25, Keren Su 53b, 54b, 77b, 128–129b, 133b, 140, 163, 181a, Harald Sund 4;

Nicholas Grindley 237l, 238a, 238b, 239r;

Robert Harding World Imagery 115a;

Hebei Provincial Museum 191a;

Henan Provincial Museum, Zhengzhou 88a, 89;

from *Historical Relics Unearthed in New China*, Peking, 1972, ill. 107 203r;

Hong Kong Museum of Art 137, 223br;

From *Honglou meng xiezhen* (facsimile reproduction of a woodblock print) 206;

from Pieter van Hoorn, *Denkwürdige Verrichtung der Niederländischen Ostindischen Gesellschaft in dem Kaiserreich Taising oder Sina, etc.* Amsterdam, 1674 107;

M. Hosokawa Collection, Tokyo 18;

from the Daoist medical work *Hsing-ming-Huei-chih*, illustrated block-print published 1622 76b;

Institute of Archaeology and Cultural Relics Bureau, Sichuan Province 188, 191r;

Institute of Cultural Relics, Hebei Province 190a;

Ronald G. Knapp 264–265, 265r, 267a;

Vivienne Lo 257a;

Martin Lubikowski 10–11, 12, 13a, 13b, 33a, 36r, 44b, 85al, 103a, 106a, 115b, 132b, 139b, 156l, 164b

from *Manzhou shilu*, Volume I, Liaoning, 1930 269r;

Carol Michaelson 195ar, 197;

Musée Guimet, Paris (MG 21449) 90a;

Museum of Famen Temple, Shaanxi Province 229;

Museum of Fine Arts, Boston 200b;

Museum of Nanjing, Jiangsu Province 218;

Museum of Suining, Sichuan Province 217;

NASA/GSFC/METI/ERSDAC/JAROS and U.S./Japan ASTER Science Team 35b;

National Museum of China, Beijing 190b;

National Museum of China, Beijing. Photo © ChinaStock/Sun Kerang 227;

National Museum of Chinese History, Beijing 134, 137, 197al, 230a, 231;

National Palace Museum, Taipei, Taiwan 28b, 215;

The Joseph Needham Research Institute, Cambridge 79a;

Nelson-Atkins Museum, Kansas City 214b;

Nancy Norton Tomasko 254b, 255a;

Office for Metropolitan Architecture, The Netherlands, architects Rem Koolhass & Ole Scheren 118l;

Chester Ong 264;

Palace Museum, Beijing 60, 67, 102b, 103b, 192al, 194, 202–203, 205, 209, 232, 234b, 235, 236, 239al, 252, 260b, 265a, 268, 275a;

Ann Paludan 165;

from Wang Qi, *San cai tu hui*, early 17th century 160, 162l, 162r;

Qin Terra-cotta Museum, Lintong, Shaanxi Province 158l, 158r, 159a;

Reuters: China Daily Information Corp. 5b, China Newsphoto 88b;

Seattle Art Museum 200a;

Shanghai Museum 195al;

Sichuan Provincial Museum, Chengdu 90b;

Nathan Sivin 247, 248a, 248b, 249bl, 249br, 250, 250–251, 251a, 251b;

from *Taohuawu Woodblock New Year Prints*, Jiangsu Ancient Book Publishing House, Suzhou 88c;

Drazen Tomic 189r

Mathieu Torck 261, 262al, 263a, 263b,

Alfred Tozer 43;

Trek Earth: James Chou 242, Alfred Marion Ronduen 243;

Eileen Tweedy 152b;

Shelagh Vainker 235;

V&A Images, London 237r;

Victoria & Albert Museum, London 246;

The Wellcome Trust 249a;

Wikimedia Commons 76a, 78a, Agnieszka Bojczuk 126, Yáo Zǐyuān 45;

Frances Wood 170;

Xinjiang Autonomous Region Museum, Ürümchi 84r, 85a, 85c, 86

Sources of Quotations

p. 36 Translation modified from Waley, A., *Chinese Poems* (London, 1949); p. 39 Marco Polo, *The Travels,* trans. Latham, R. (London, 1958); p. 43 Flecker, J. E., *The Golden Journey to Samarkand* (London, 1913); p. 48 Rock, J., in one of his nine articles as resident photo-journalist for *National Geographic* (1922–1935); pp. 52 & 68 Confucius, *The Analects,* trans. D. C. Lau (London 1979); p. 71 From Watson, B. (trans.), *Chuang Tzu: Basic Writings* (New York, 1964) pp. 41–42; p. 76 From Deng, M., *365 Tao Daily Meditations* (San Francisco, 2006) p. 212; p. 93 From an essay by Knechtges, D. R., *Journal of the American Oriental Society*, Vol. 106, 1986; p. 131 From Gernet, J., *Daily Life in China on the Eve of the Mongol Invasion 1250–1276* (Stanford, 1970); p. 145 From de Tocqueville, A., *Democracy in America* (Paris, 1835); p. 151 From Bredon, J., *Peking: A Historical and Intimate Description of its Chief Places of Interest* (Shanghai, 1920); p. 155 From Topping, A., China's Incredible Find, *National Geographic* (April 1978); p. 160 From Newton Hayes, L., *The Great Wall of China* (Shanghai, 1929); p. 165 From De Groot, J. J. M., *The Religious System of China*, 6 vols (Leyden 1892–1920); p. 171 Adapted from Li, A., History of Tibetan Religion (Beijing, 1994), p. 129; p. 174 From McGovern, W. M., *To Lhasa in Disguise* (London, 1924); p. 178 From Macartney, G., *An Embassy to China: Being the Journal Kept by Lord Macartney During his Embassy to the Emperor Ch'ien-lung 1793–1794* (reprinted London, 2004); p. 189 From Li, B., *Studies on the Structural System of Chinese Bronze Culture* (Beijing, 1998); p. 194 From *Li Chi, Book of Rites: An Encyclopedia of Ancient Ceremonial Usages, Religious Creeds, and Social Institutions* (New York, 1967), Vol. 2, p. 464; p. 198 From *Xizhi lun* (a colophon to calligraphy by the Calligraphic Sage Wang Xizhi), AD 1298, quoted in Ren, D., *Zhao Mengfu xi nian* (Shanghai, 1984), p. 84; p. 202 From Zhao, M., *Thirteen Colophons to the Orchid Pavilion Preface* (collection of Tokyo National Museum), AD 1310; p. 212 From Zhang, Y., *Li dai ming hua ji* ('Record of Famous Paintings Through the Ages'), AD 847, quoted in Wen C. Fong, *Beyond Representation*, pp.4–5; p. 226 From Waley, A., *Chinese Poems* (London, 1971), p. 131; p. 236 From Wen, Z., *Zhang Wu Zhi* ('A Treatise on Superfluous Things'), *c.* 1615–20, on Couches and Tables, p. 225; p. 240 From Tao, C., *Tao the Hermit: Sixty Poems by Tao Chien (365–427)*, trans. Acker, W. (London & New York, 1952); p. 247 From Needham, J., *et al., Science and Civilisation in China*, 23 vols to date (Cambridge, 1954–); p. 268 From Ames, R. T., *Sun-tzu: The Art of Warfare – The First English Translation Incorporating the Recently Discovered Yin-ch'üeh-shan Texts* (New York, 1993); p. 272 From Hommel, R. P., *China at Work: An Illustrated Record of the Primitive Industries of China's Masses, Whose Life is Toil, and Thus an Account of Chinese Civilization* (Cambridge, 1969), p. 129; p. 281 From Morris, J., *Among the Cities* (Oxford, 1985); p. 288 From Quinlivan, T. W. & Boxx, G. M., *The Cultural Context of Economics and Politics* (Lanham, 1994).

Index